Political and Religious Ideas in the Works of Arnold Schoenberg

BORDER CROSSINGS
VOLUME 5
GARLAND REFERENCE LIBRARY OF THE HUMANITIES
VOLUME 2190

A headshot of Schoenberg taken in the 1920s. Used by permission of Belmont Music Publishers, Pacific Palisades, California 90272.

POLITICAL AND RELIGIOUS IDEAS IN THE WORKS OF ARNOLD SCHOENBERG

edited by

CHARLOTTE M. CROSS
AND
RUSSELL A. BERMAN

GARLAND PUBLISHING, INC.
A MEMBER OF THE TAYLOR & FRANCIS GROUP
NEW YORK & LONDON / 2000

Published in 2000 by
Garland Publishing, Inc.
A Member of the Taylor & Francis Group
19 Union Square West
New York, NY 10003

10   9   8   7   6   5   4   3   2   1

Library of Congress Cataloging-in-Publication Data
Political and religious ideas in the works of Arnold Schoenberg / edited by
Charlotte M. Cross and Russell A. Berman.
        p.   cm. — (Border crossings ; v. 5. Garland reference library of the
humanities ; v. 2190)
        Includes bibliographical references (p. ****).
        ISBN 0-8153-2831-1 (alk. paper)
        1. Schoenberg, Arnold, 1874–1951—Criticism and interpretation.
2. Schoenberg, Arnold, 1874–1951—Political and social views.   3. Schoenberg, Arnold, 1874–1951—Religion.   I. Cross, Charlotte Marie.   II. Berman,
Russell A., 1950– . III. Series: Garland reference library of the humanities ; vol.
2190.   IV. Series: Garland reference library of the humanities. Border
crossings ; v. 5.
ML410.S283P65   1999
780'.92—dc21   99-31282
                                                                              CIP

Cover photograph: Schoenberg, seemingly in deep contemplation, in the late
1940s. Used by permission of Belmont Music Publishers, Pacific Palisades,
California 90272.

Printed on acid-free, 250-year-life paper
Manufactured in the United States of America

Contents

Series Editor's Foreword

THE NEED FOR COMPARISON AMONG THE ARTS

To study one artistic medium in isolation from others is to study an inadequacy. The twentieth century, so rich in literature, in music, and in the visual arts, has also been rich in criticism of these arts; but it is possible that some of the uglinesses and distortions in modern criticism have arisen from the consideration of each artistic medium as an autonomous field of development, fenced off from other media. It is hard for us to believe, but when, long ago, Horace said *Ut pictura poesis*—the poem should be like a picture—he meant it.

The twentieth century, perhaps more than any other age, demands a style of criticism in which the arts are considered as a whole. This is partly because the artists themselves insisted again and again upon the inextricability of the arts. Ezra Pound, for one, believed that, in antiquity, "music and poetry had been in alliance . . . that the divorce of the two arts had been to the advantage of neither, and that melodic invention had declined simultaneously and progressively with their divergence. The rhythms of poetry grew stupider." He thought that it was the duty of the poet to learn music, and the duty of the musician to study poetry But we must learn to challenge the boundaries among the arts not only because the artists we study demanded it, but because our philosophy demands it as well. The linguistics of Ferdinand de Saussure, the philosophy of Ludwig Wittgenstein and Jacques Derrida, tend to strip language of denotation, to make language a game of arbitrary signifiers; and as words lose connection to the world of hard objects, they become more and more like musical notes,

Wittgenstein claimed. "To say that a word has meaning does not imply that it *stands for* or *represents* a thing. . . . The sign plus the rules of grammar applying to it is all we need [to make a language]. We need nothing further to make the connection with reality. If we did we should need something to connect that with reality, which would lead to an infinite regress." And, for Wittgenstein, the consequence of this disconnection was clear: "Understanding a sentence is much more akin to understanding a theme in music than one may think." To Horace, reading is like looking at a picture; to Wittgenstein, reading is like listening to music. The arts seem endlessly inter-permeable, a set of fluid systems of construing and reinterpreting, in which the quest for meaning engages all our senses at once. Thinking is itself looking, hearing, touching—even tasting, since such words as *savoir* are forms of the Latin *sapere,* to taste.

THE TERM *MODERNISM*

Modernism—like any unit of critical terminology—is a fiction, but an indispensable fiction. It is possible to argue (as Vladimir Nabokov did) that each work of art in the universe is unique and incommensurable: that there is no such thing as a school of artists: that an idea such as *influence* among artists arises from sheer intellectual laziness. This line of argument, however, contradicts our intuition that certain works of art look like one another; that, among many works of art produced at the same time or in the same place, there are family resemblances. Such terms as modernism need have no great prestige: they're simply critical indications convenient for describing certain family resemblances.

Furthermore, these terms denote not only kinship relations established by critics from outside, but also kinship relations determined by artists from within. The term modernism had tremendous potency for the modernists themselves: when Ezra Pound first read a poem by T. S. Eliot, he was thunderstruck that Eliot had managed to *modernize* his poetry all by himself, without any contact with other poets. Pound regarded modernism itself as a huge group project. To this extent, modernism isn't just a label attached by students of a period, but a kind of tribal affiliation, one of thousands of examples of those arbitrary loyalty groups that bedevil the human race. Nearly every early twentieth-century artist felt the need to define himself or herself as a modernist or otherwise. When Stravinsky at last met Rachmaninov in Hollywood, Stravinsky obviously greeted his colleague not simply as a fraternal fellow in the order of Prussian expatriate composers, but as a (self-sacrificing) modernist condescending to a (rich and successful) romantic. The label *modernist* shaped the interactions of artists themselves—sometimes as a help, sometimes as a hindrance.

Of course, it is the task of criticism at the end of the twentieth century to offer a better account of modernism than the modernists themselves could. Stravinsky's ideas about Rachmaninov were wrong in several ways; not just because Rachmaninov's royalties weren't noticeably greater than Stravinsky's, but also because their music was somewhat more similar than Stravinsky would have liked to admit. For instance, compare the Easter finale from Rachmaninov's Suite for Two Pianos, op. 5, with the carillon evoked by the piano in Stravinsky's song "Spring," op. 6 no. 1: they inhabit the same aesthetic realm.

A theory of the modernist movement that might embrace both Rachmaninov and Stravinsky, or Picasso and Balthus, could be constructed along the following lines: modernism is a *testing of the limits of aesthetic construction.* According to this perspective, the modernists tried to find the ultimate bounds of certain artistic possibilities: volatility of emotion (expressionism); stability and inexpressiveness (the new objectivity); accuracy of representation (hyperrealism); absence of representation (abstractionism); purity of form (neoclassicism); formless energy (neobarbarism); cultivation of the technological present (futurism); cultivation of the prehistoric past (the mythic method). These extremes have, of course, been arranged in pairs because aesthetic heresies, like theological ones, come in binary sets: each limit-point presupposes an opposite limit-point, a counter-extreme toward which the artist can push. Much of the strangeness, the stridency, the exhilaration of modernist art can be explained by this strong thrust toward the verges of the aesthetic experience: after the nineteenth century had established a remarkably safe, intimate center where the artist and the audience could dwell, the twentieth century reaches out to the freakish circumferences of art. The extremes of the aesthetic experience tend to converge; in the modernist movement, the most barbaric art tends to be the most up-to-date and sophisticated. For example, when T. S. Eliot first heard *The Rite of Spring,* he wrote that the music seemed to "transform the rhythm of the steppes into the scream of the motor-horn, the rattle of machinery, the grind of wheels, the beating of iron and steel, the roar of the underground railway, and the other barbaric noises of modern life." *The Waste Land* is itself written to the same recipe: the world of London, with its grime, boredom, and abortifacient drugs, overlays the antique world of primal rites for the rejuvenation of the land through the dismemberment of a god. In the modernist movement, things tend to coexist uncomfortably with their exact opposites.

Wallace Stevens referred to the story we tell ourselves about the world, about our presence in the world, and about how we attempt to configure pleasant lives for ourselves, as a Supreme Fiction; and similarly, critics live by various critical fictions, as they reconfigure the domain of similarities and differences in the arts. Modernism is just such a "high critical fiction."

THE SPAN OF THE MODERNIST AGE

The use of a term such as modernism usually entails a certain restriction to a period of time. Such a restriction is rarely easy and becomes immensely difficult for the interdisciplinary student: the romantic movement, for example, will invariably mean one age for a musicologist, another (perhaps scarcely overlapping) for a student of British poetry. One might say that the modernist age begins around 1907-1909, because in those years Picasso painted *Les Demoiselles d'Avignon,* Schoenberg made his "atonal" breakthrough, and the international careers of Stravinsky, Pound, Stein, and Cocteau were just beginning or were not long to come. And one might choose 1951 for a terminus, since in that year Cage started using the *I Ching* to compose chance-determined music, and Samuel Beckett's trilogy and *Waiting for Godot* were soon to establish an artistic world that would have partly bewildered the early modernists. The modernists did not (as Cage did) abdicate their artistic responsibilities to a pair of dice; the modernists did not (as Beckett did) delight in artistic failure. Modernism was a movement associated with scrupulous choice of artistic materials, and with hard work in arranging them. Sometimes the modernists deflected the domain of artistic selection to unusual states of consciousness (trance, dream, etc.); but, except for a few Dadaist experiments, they didn't abandon artistic selection entirely—and even Tristan Tzara, Kurt Schwitters, and the more radical Dadaists usually attempted a more impudent form of non-sense than aleatory procedures can generate. The modernists *intended* modernism—the movement did not come into existence randomly.

But the version of modernism outlined here—a triumphalist extension of the boundaries of the feasible in art—is only *one* version of modernism. There exist many modernisms, and each version is likely to describe a period with different terminal dates. It isn't hard to construct an argument showing that modernism began, say, around 1886 (the year of the last painting exhibition organized by the Impressionists, at which Seurat made the first important show of his work). Nietzsche had privately published *Also Sprach Zarathustra* in 1885, and Mahler's first symphony would appear in 1889. And it is possible to construct arguments showing that Modernism has only recently ended, since Beckett actualized certain potentialities in Joyce (concerning self-regarding language), and Cage followed closely after Schoenberg and Satie (Cage's *Cheap Imitation,* from 1969, is simply a note-by-note rewriting, with random pitch alterations, of the vocal line of Satie's 1918 *Socrate*).

And it is also possible that modernism hasn't ended at all: the term *postmodernism* may simply be erroneous. Much of the music of Philip Glass is a straightforward recasting of musical surface according to models derived from visual surface, following a formula stated in 1936 by an earlier American composer, George Antheil, who wrote of the "filling out of a certain time canvas with musical abstractions and sound material composed and contrasted against one another with the thought of time values rather than tonal values . . . I used time as Picasso might have used the blank spaces of his canvas. I did not hesitate, for instance, to repeat one measure one hundred times." Most of the attributes we ascribe to postmodernism can easily be found, latently or actually, with the modernist movement: for another example, Brecht in the 1930s made such deconstructionist declarations as "*Realist* means: laying bare society's causal network / showing up the dominant viewpoint as the viewpoint of the dominators." It is arguable that in the 1990s we are still trying to digest the meal that the modernists ate.

If modernism can be said to reach out beyond the present moment, it is also true that modernism can be said to extend backwards almost indefinitely. Wagner, especially the Wagner of *Tristan und Isolde,* has been a continual presence in twentieth-century art: Brecht and Weill continually railed against Wagnerian narcosis and tried to construct a music theater exactly opposed to Wagner's; but Virgil Thomson found much to admire and imitate in Wagner-even though Thomson's operas sound, at first hearing, even less Wagnerian than Kurt Weill's. In some respects, the first modernist experiment in music theater might be said to be the Kotzehue-Beethoven *The Ruins of Athens* (1811), in which the goddess Minerva claps her hands over her ears at hearing the hideous music of the dervishes' chorus (blaring tritones, Turkish percussion): here is the conscious sensory assault, sensory overload, of Schoenberg's first operas. Modernism is partly confined to the first half of the twentieth century, but it tends to spill into earlier and later ages. Modernism created its own precursors; it made the past new, as well as the present.

THE QUESTION OF BOUNDARIES

The revolution of the Information Age began when physicists discovered that silicon could be used either as a resistor or as a conductor of electricity. Modernist art is also a kind of circuit board, a pattern of yieldings and resistances, in which one art sometimes asserts its distinct, inviolable nature and sometimes yields itself, tries to imitate some foreign aesthetic. Sometimes music and poetry coexist in a state of extreme dissonance (as Brecht thought they should, in the operas that he wrote with Weill); but on other occasions music tries to *become* poetry, or poetry tries to *become* music. To change the metaphor, one might say that modernism investigates a kind of transvestism among the arts—what happens when one art stimulates itself by temporarily pretending to be another species of art altogether.

Modernist art has existed in an almost continual state of crisis concerning the boundaries between one art medium and another. Is a painting worth a thousand words, or is it impossible to find a verbal equivalent of an image, even if millions of words were used? Are music and literature two different things, or two aspects of the same thing? This is a question confronted by artists of every age, but the artists of the modernist period found a special urgency here. The literature of the period, with its dehydrated epics and other semantically supercharged texts, certainly resembles, at least to a degree, the music of the period, with its astonishing density of acoustic events. But some artists tried to erase the boundaries among music and literature and the visual arts, while other artists tried to build foot-thick walls.

Some of the modernists felt strongly that the purity of one artistic medium must not be compromised by the encroachment of styles or themes taken from other artistic media. Clement Greenberg, the great modernist critic, defended abstractionism on the grounds that an abstract painting is a pure painting: not subservient to literary themes, not enslaved to representations of the physical world, but a new autonomous object, not a copy of reality but an addition to reality. Such puritans among the modernists stressed the need for fidelity to the medium: the opacity and spectral precision of paint or the scarified, slippery feel of metal; the exact sonority of the highest possible trombone note; the spondaic clumps in a poetic line with few unstressed syllables. As Greenberg wrote in 1940, "The history of avant-garde painting is that of a progressive surrender to the resistance of its medium; which resistance consists chiefly in the flat picture plane's denial of efforts to 'hole through' it for realistic perspectival space." To Greenberg, the medium has a message: canvas and paint have a recalcitrant will of their own, fight against the artists' attempts to pervert their function. He profoundly approved of the modernist art that learned to love paint for paint's sake, not for its capacity to create phantoms of solid objects.

But this puritan hatred of illusions, the appetite for an art that possesses the dignity of reality, is only part of the story of modernism. From another perspective, the hope that art can overcome its illusory character is itself an illusion: just because a sculpture is hacked out of rough granite doesn't mean that it is real in the same way that granite is real. The great musicologist Theodor Adorno was as much a puritan as Greenberg: Adorno hated what he called *pseudomorphism,* the confusion of one artistic medium with another. But Adorno, unlike Greenberg, thought that all art was dependent on illusion, that art couldn't attempt to compete with the real world: as he wrote in 1948, it is futile for composers to try to delete all ornament from music: "Since the work, after all, cannot be reality, the elimination of all illusory features accentuates all the more glaringly the illusory character of its existence."

But, while the puritans tried to isolate each medium from alien encroachment, other, more promiscuous modernists tried to create a kind of art in which the finite medium is almost irrelevant. For them, modernism was *about* the fluidity, the interchangeability, of artistic media themselves. Here we find single artists, each of whom often tried to become a whole artistic colony—we see, for example, a painter who wrote an opera libretto (Kokoschka), a poet who composed music (Pound), and a composer who painted pictures (Schoenberg). It is as if artistic talent were a kind of libido, an electricity that could discharge itself with equal success in a poem, a sonata, or a sculpture. Throughout the modernist movement, the major writers and composers both enforced and transgressed the boundaries among the various arts with unusual energy—almost savage at times.

It is important to respect both the instincts for division and distinction among the arts, and the instincts for cooperation and unity. In the eighteenth century, Gotthold Lessing (in *Laokoon*) divided the arts into two camps, which he called the *nacheinander* (the temporal arts, such as poetry and music) and the *nebeneinander* (the spatial arts, such as painting and sculpture). A modernist *Laocoön* might restate the division of the arts as follows: not as a tension between the temporal arts and the spatial—this distinction is often thoroughly flouted in the twentieth century—but as a tension between arts that try to retain the propriety, the apartness, of their private media, and arts that try to lose themselves in some pan-aesthetic whole. On one hand, *nacheinander* and *nebeneinander* retain their distinctness; on the other hand, they collapse into a single spatiotemporal continuum, in which both duration and extension are arbitrary aspects. Photographs of pupillary movement have traced the patterns that the eye makes as it scans the parts of a picture trying to apprehend the whole—a picture not only may suggest motion, but is constructed by the mind acting over time. Similarly, a piece of music may be heard so thoroughly that the whole thing coexists in the mind in an instant—as Karajan claimed to know Beethoven's fifth symphony.

There are, then, two huge contrary movements in twentieth-century experiments in bringing art media together: consonance among the arts, and dissonance among the arts. Modernism carries each to astonishing extremes. The dissonances are challenging: perhaps the consonances are even more challenging.

In the present series of books, each volume will examine some facet of these intriguing problems in the arts of modernism—the dissemblings and resistings, the smooth cooperations and the prickly challenges when the arts come together.

Daniel Albright
Richard L. Turner Professor in the Humanities
University of Rochester

Editors' Introduction

Since Roman antiquity, the term "modern" has pointed to the present moment in time, understood to stand in contrast with the past. The tension between the present and the past, between the worlds of the moderns and the ancients, is sometimes cast as a narrative of decline from a distant golden age, replaced by the disappointments of today: how has culture fallen from the mighty heights of former glory! More often, however, the reverse is true: it is the modern present that is treated as the location of great accomplishment, while the dusty, tired past is dismissed as hopelessly conventional and trapped in tradition. "*Tradition ist Schlamperei!*" [Tradition is thoughtless disorder!]—Gustav Mahler is reputed to have asserted in front of the recalcitrant musicians of the Viennese orchestra he had arrived to conduct. Their allegiance to old habits and customs, their loyalty to the way things have always been, turns out to be little more than a lazy reluctance ever to try anything new. Here the modern becomes the triumph over the ancient, and modernism the project of expelling from the work of art any vestige of the sloppy past.

Yet such a modernization of the work of art, its emancipation from convention and cliche, is hardly restricted to the narrowly defined era of modernism, the decades around 1900. On the contrary, the well-known history of music, literature, and art in "modernity," the Western world since the Middle Ages, entails the gradual but inexorable removal of strictures and taboos: instead of composition for the church or the state, music begins, especially in the generations after J. S. Bach, to pursue its own internal logic and to become autonomous, free of externally imposed restraints. One can trace similar developments for literature and the visual arts, culminating in the programmatic slogan of *l'art pour l'art*—which should be taken not as an effete flight from a putatively more real world, but as the emancipation proclamation of the artist.

This aesthetics of autonomy has a long and complex history with many distinct nuances in the particular national traditions, and we should surely be aware that external pressures on art—from religious institutions, from political institutions, and, perhaps especially, from the marketplace—never disappear. What distinguishes the modern sensibility regarding art is not that works of art are genuinely free from such pressures but that we recognize the normative ideal of aesthetic autonomy and tend to condemn efforts to restrict artistic freedom.

Given this wider frame of aesthetic modernity and its pursuit of artistic freedom, it is noteworthy that the composer Arnold Schoenberg, whose modernist allegiances are surely beyond doubt, would leave such an extensive legacy of works in which music appears to be a vehicle—a "mere" vehicle?—of religious and political ideas. Was not the history of modern music an extended struggle for emancipation from ecclesiastical tutelage or political manipulation? How is Schoenberg's specifically modernist pursuit of a pure music, a music stripped of romantic sentimentalism or structural conventionalism, compatible with a willingness to put music in the service of nonmusical ideas? Is music free or just a means to some other end?

Part of the answer surely has to do with the dialectical complexity inherent in the legacy of autonomy aesthetics, which resonates in the term "emancipation." Freeing art from political control was, historically, hardly an unpolitical act, but very much part of the profound transformation of Western society associated with modernization. Schoenberg inherits the mantle of the heroic, modern artist, the Byronic warrior challenging the powers that be, in the name of freedom and independence, and not only in art. Genuine art retains an emancipatory potential, an implicit vision of the "good life," even when it is abstract, perhaps even when it is most abstract and therefore most free.

At the same time, however, Schoenberg explores religious dimensions in the autonomous work of art, but in a way that breaks with romantic notions of the artist-priest. The eighteenth and nineteenth centuries dwelled on the problem of creativity, artistic and divine, in ways that contributed to a celebration of the artist himself. In contrast, Schoenberg provides a quite distinct transformation of the relationship between art and religion through his assertion of a metaphoric relationship between aesthetic autonomy and absolute divinity: pure art, subject to no law except its own, is equivalent to the omnipotent deity Moses encounters on Sinai. This is a problematic that drives his articulation of twelve-tone composition, and it is explored and examined in work after work.

Is it odd that the modernist artist turns to religion? No odder than the fact that he turns to politics as well. Schoenberg's religious and political concerns become pronounced in the years during and after the First World War, that is, after the initial explosion of compositional creativity in the prior decade. This move from pure art to a music often tied to other agenda certainly has to do with a response to the enormous carnage of the First World War: a deep-seated mourning spread across Europe and it can be traced through a range of cultural expressions. More specifically, the war upset the sanguine world of Central European Jewry. Political destabilization and economic dislocation magnified an earlier anti-Semitic potential that quickly became a mortal threat. Political and religious ideas merge for Schoenberg in his increasingly urgent engagement with the dangers facing European Jews, and his answers involve both sides: Zionist politics together with an assertion of a return to a religious legacy.

From aesthetic autonomy as the core modernist project to engaged art—be it engagement for religion or politics or both—Schoenberg's trajectory can be traced through a series of crucial works: "Das obligate Rezitativ" ["The Obbligato Recitative"], the fifth piece of the *Five Orchestral Pieces*, op. 16, composed in 1909; the incomplete oratorio *Die Jakobsleiter* [*Jacob's Ladder*], Schoenberg's major artistic achievement from the war years through the early 1920s; the comic opera *Von heute auf morgen* [*From One Day to the Next*], *Six Pieces for Male Chorus*, op. 35, and the sacred opera *Moses und Aron*, three works from the late 1920s and early 1930s whose unique messages address specific audiences; and *A Survivor from Warsaw*, op. 46, "Dreimal tausend Jahre" ["Three Times a Thousand Years"], op. 50a, and "Modern Psalm," op. 50c, composed in 1947, 1949, and 1950-51, respectively, and among Schoenberg's final musical utterances.

Arranged in the order in which these works were composed, the essays in this volume chronicle Schoenberg's career over a span of some forty-two years. His musical development, especially during the period from the end of the first decade of the twentieth century until the early 1930s, was remarkable. Schoenberg made the decisive break with traditional tonality and began writing in the style of "free atonality" only a few years before he composed the orchestral pieces of op. 16. In 1914, he took the first tentative steps that would lead to the discovery of the twelve-tone method in the early 1920s, and by the latter part of that decade he had mastered its essential techniques and was once again able to compose with freedom. At the end of his career, Schoenberg had extended the technical possibilities of the method far beyond its original premises, at times even combining it with styles from earlier periods of music history as well as with styles from earlier stages of his own development.

Schoenberg's career is also shown from the perspective of its three main geographical settings: Austria, the Weimar Republic, and America. In 1909, Schoenberg was living in Vienna. Following a sojourn in Berlin from 1911 to 1915, he returned to Austria where he remained until 1925. From 1926 until 1933, he held a prestigious faculty appointment at the Prussian Academy of the Arts in Berlin. In 1933 he sought sanctuary from the Nazi threat, and, after a brief stay in France, emigrated to America where he spent the remainder of his days (he died in 1951), contributing richly not only to the musical life of his adopted land but also to the world scene as a composer, theorist, teacher, and, to some extent, an activist for the Jewish cause. Each of these vantage points presented Schoenberg with unique challenges. This volume thus divides naturally into three discrete units according to the different sociopolitical settings in which its protagonist worked.

Musical techniques and biographical issues are integral to the subject. Nevertheless, the book's main focus is the specific political and religious material that Schoenberg sought to express in music. With the notable exception of "Das obligate Rezitativ," the works make use of literary material —poems, prayers, libretti—to convey their ideological content. The contrast between the lone instrumental work from 1909 and all of the other works discussed, in which literary material is harnessed to music, highlights the move from aesthetic autonomy to engaged art. It also points out another critical aspect of Schoenberg's aesthetic, one which he expressed particularly in the prewar years and continued to espouse long after: his belief that music can convey its message in purely musical terms for those with the capacity to understand the language. William Benjamin grapples with the issue of comprehending Schoenberg's music on its own purely musical terms in the opening essay. From a careful scrutiny of the opening measures of "Das obligate Rezitativ," Benjamin develops an analytical approach to this piece based upon the rather paradoxical notion of its "incomprehensibility." Although this work is in the "free atonal" style, Benjamin points out the implications of his analytical method for Schoenberg's twelve-tone music. Moreover, even this apparently autonomous music, composed at the behest of intuition, represents a philosophical stance. Benjamin maintains that it reflects the moment in the development of Schoenberg's world view in which he conceived of life and art in Nietzschean terms.

Schoenberg's "antirational" view of art and instinctive approach to composition proved incompatible with the changes his spiritual position underwent during the First World War and the years immediately following. As his external supports—his public, his students, the sociopolitical structure of the Habsburg Monarchy—gradually fell away and were reconfigured during the war and its aftermath, Schoenberg claims to have turned completely inward to a religion that he himself defined. He articulated his ideas fully in the text of *Die Jakobsleiter*. David Schroeder analyzes the text of the oratorio for ways in which Schoenberg fused a variety of related dichotomies—Jewish and Christian beliefs, the literary styles of poetry and prose, the dualities of matter and spirit, male and female, feeling and intellect—into a higher unity which also defined symbolically the immediate course of his aesthetic, religious-philosophical, and musical futures. Jennifer Shaw explores how notions of androgyny, which Schoenberg might have known from as diverse a group of sources as Plato, Indian philosophy, a variety of nineteenth- and early-twentieth century painters and writers, and even contemporary political and social debates, influenced not only the text, but also the music of *Die Jakobsleiter*. Shaw asks to what degree Schoenberg was successful in achieving the androgynous ideal in the music of this work, and suggests that his striving to achieve this ideal may have played a role in shaping the twelve-tone method itself.

Personal experiences with anti-Semitism in the early 1920s awakened Schoenberg to some of the implications of being a Jew in post–World War I Europe. His acknowledgement that he could not escape his Jewish heritage initiated a protracted period of reflection upon Jewish issues from both theological and political points of view culminating in the early 1930s with yet another attempt to give a comprehensive statement of his position by means of words and music—this time in his opera *Moses und Aron*, which presents his personal vision of Judaism. While this great work gestated, Schoenberg used his now mature twelve-tone method to reach out to a broader cross-section of the public, making forays into the popular genre of *Zeitoper* with *Von heute auf morgen* and music for workers' choral societies with his *Six Pieces for Male Chorus*, op. 35. One of the main problems all of these works pose is that of discerning Schoenberg's message. Stephen Davison interprets *Von heute auf morgen* as a critique with multiple targets: the contemporary musical scene, cultural life in general, and modern social life. Robert Falck reads op. 35 as a commentary on conflicts between the individual and society in the Weimar Republic. How does Schoenberg propose that these dilemmas be resolved? Edward Latham draws upon dramatic theories of the Russian dramaturg Constantin Stanislavsky and a method of musical analysis that takes its cues from Carolyn Abbate, Roger Parker, and Milton Babbitt to demonstrate that Schoenberg's ultimate motivation in *Moses und Aron* was to communicate his idea of the incomprehensibility of God. Bluma Goldstein reflects upon why Schoenberg emphasized the metaphysical and spiritual side of Judaism in *Moses und Aron* to the exclusion of any notion of Israel as a real political and social entity.

Schoenberg arrived in America in 1933 with a clearly defined position with respect to Zionism and determined to devote his energies to the Jewish cause, even if it meant giving up his art. He did not in fact abandon his art at that time, but his willingness to do so may point to a conflict—most likely a subconscious one—between his identity as a Jew and the recognition that any musical expression of his Zionist persuasions would use a compositional method developed from and for the furtherance of the German tradition. According to David Lieberman, this conflict was finally resolved with the composition of "A Survivor from Warsaw" in 1947. Recognized as Schoenberg's monument to the horrors that European Jews experienced at the hands of the Nazis, "A Survivor from Warsaw" seems to have been motivated by a variety of sources ranging from experiences of Schoenberg's own family members and friends to a specific commission, all of which are examined by Camille Crittenden. Schoenberg's dream of a safe haven for the Jewish people was finally realized in the late 1940s with the founding of the state of Israel. "Dreimal tausend Jahre," analyzed by Naomi André, was one composition in which Schoenberg recognized this event. In his last work, "Modern Psalm," op. 50c, Schoenberg grappled with some difficult questions about the individual's relationship to God. Knowing that he did not have long to live, Schoenberg made a conscious choice to bring his career to a close in the midst of composing music for a text that he himself had written. Mark Risinger examines the factors that might have caused Schoenberg to cease his activities at a critical juncture.

The astute reader will certainly have noticed that the book does not contain essays on every work by Schoenberg that contains political and/or religious material. The most striking omission is undoubtedly "Ode to Napoleon," op. 41, to a text by Lord Byron. Composed in 1942, at about the time the United Stated entered the Second World War, "Ode

to Napoleon" is a strong expression of Schoenberg's antifascist sentiments. Also not discussed at length is the symphonic fragment that
Schoenberg conceived as early as 1911. He worked on the text, which he
assembled from poems by Richard Dehmel and Rabindranath Tagore,
Bible passages, and a contribution of his own, and also made sketches for
the music between 1912 and 1915. This work was crucial to the religious
position that Schoenberg defined during the First World War. In chronological order, other major works not covered include *Four Pieces for
Mixed Chorus*, op. 27, composed in 1925, which includes the setting of
"Du sollst nicht, du musst," a milestone in Schoenberg's return to Judaism; his play *Der biblische Weg* [*The Biblical Way*] from 1926-27, in
which he hoped to awaken Jews to their situation and to motivate them to
action; *Kol Nidre*, op. 38, a work from 1938 which Schoenberg hoped
might be suitable for use in the synagogue; his Prelude "Genesis," from
1945, an orchestral work in which he tried to portray conditions *before*
the Creation; and the fragment "Israel Exists Again," from 1949, and "De
Profundis," op. 50b, a Hebrew setting of Psalm 130, from 1950, both of
which commemorate the creation of modern Israel.

Comprehensive coverage of all of the relevant works was initially
one of our goals for the book. That we did not achieve it is perhaps a
commentary on the state of Schoenberg research. We simply could not
find scholars to study each work. Still, almost all of the works not covered are mentioned in the various essays, providing the reader with a
sense of their subject matter and significance. Comprehensive coverage
was not our only goal, however. We hope that the book will stimulate
scholars to consider the implications of Schoenberg's enlistment of
music to give voice to his reflections upon political and/or religious
themes for the history of the shifting relationships between art, politics,
and religion.

On an editorial note, we have endeavored to maintain high standards
of scholarship while making the book accessible to nonspecialists. As
often as possible, titles of musical and literary works and excerpts from
poems, libretti, and so forth, that were originally in a foreign language
have been presented in the original language followed by an English
translation. The only exceptions are those titles whose translation would
be obvious (e.g., it seemed unnecessary to translate a title such as *Moses
und Aron*). Each author has supplied his or her own translations. Therefore, there are variations in the translations of some frequently cited
works. Also as an aid to nonmusicians, the authors were asked to explain
any specialized musical terms used. We hope that these explanations

have been incorporated in such a way that they are not disruptive to more knowledgeable readers.

In closing, we wish express our appreciation to all of those who have supported this project in various ways. At the top of the list are Professor Daniel Albright, the general editor of the *Border Crossings* series, who has been enthusiastic about this volume since its inception, and the family of Arnold Schoenberg, which has also maintained a keen interest in our work. We especially thank Mr. Lawrence Schoenberg of Belmont Music Publishers for graciously granting numerous permissions for the use of materials from his father's legacy. Mr. Leo Balk, Vice-President of Garland, Mr. Richard Wallis, and Ms. Soo Mee Kwon, the former and current music editors at Garland, and Ms. Chuck Bartelt, Garland's technical expert, all greatly facilitated the process by cheerfully answering our numerous inquiries. The Arnold Schoenberg Institute, formerly at the University of Southern California, kindly agreed to handle requests from us even after they had officially closed in preparation for the relocation of the archives to Vienna, Austria. Dr. Camille Crittenden, who was then a Research Associate and Assistant Archivist at the Institute, provided us with several wonderful photographs of Schoenberg, from which we selected those for the cover and frontispiece. Finally, our most profuse thanks should perhaps go to the contributors, without whose essays this book would not exist.

Charlotte M. Cross
Russell A. Berman
December 1998

POLITICAL AND RELIGIOUS IDEAS IN THE WORKS OF ARNOLD SCHOENBERG

CHAPTER 1

Abstract Polyphonies
The Music of Schoenberg's Nietzschean Moment

WILLIAM E. BENJAMIN

The development of Arnold Schoenberg's religious thought, in the direction of an uncompromising ethical monotheism, is paralleled by gradual changes in his approach to composition, in the direction of conscious, rational control of the creative process.[1] This parallelism seems straightforward in one sense: as he moved towards an explicit and consciously articulated religious position, one deeply felt and self-generated but philosophically in accord with liberal Judaism, he also adopted a more formal, more deliberately intellectual, and thus more describable way of composing.[2] Both moves, in other words, involved a shift from the emotional and necessarily private to the deliberate and communal, the relevant community having been actual in the case of religion and potential where composition was concerned. Looked at more carefully, however, what looks like the transposition of a process of transformation from one sphere into another conceals a relationship of inversion. For as his music became, in a sense, more knowable and intersubjectively describable, Schoenberg came to understand God as absolutely unknowable and indescribable, as the God of Moses as interpreted by Jewish philosophers since Maimonides.[3]

Schoenberg made his radical break with musical tradition in 1908, full of confidence in his intuitive powers—his ear for unorthodox pitch combinations and his instinct for rhythm and form—and with the conviction that he was genuinely inspired, that he was composing as if under the compulsion of some mysterious (inner) force. In his writings from the years 1908–11, he insists repeatedly, and with the greatest vehemence,

1

that inspiration is the beginning and end of authentic artistry. He writes, for example, that

> the artist's creativity is instinctive. Consciousness has little influence on it. He feels as if what he does were dictated to him. As if he did it only according to the will of some power or other within him, whose laws he does not know.[4]

Moreover, one has only to examine the compositional sources from those years to see that these are not empty proclamations, that the music he penned at that time flowed directly from his musical unconscious. I will justify this statement in what follows, but taking it at face value leads one to conclude that the unprecedented leaps Schoenberg made—in the *Three Piano Pieces*, op. 11 (1909), the song cycle, *Fifteen Poems from the "Book of the Hanging Gardens,"* op. 15 (1908–9), the *Five Pieces for Orchestra*, op. 16 (1909), and the dramatic work for soprano and orchestra, *Erwartung [Expectancy]*, op. 17 (1909)—arose from and were probably made possible by an essentially antirational view of art. In these pages I will try to explain why this attitude, which was compatible with Schoenberg's broader philosophical stance at the time, was unable to survive the ideological turn that he executed between 1912 and the early 1920s. In this way, I hope to show that there is no incongruity between the spiritual and compositional paths that he took as he moved from free atonality to twelve-tone composition, despite their apparent divergence.

The antirational view is clearly expressed in Schoenberg's 1911 treatise, the *Harmonielehre [Theory of Harmony]*, in which he inveighs against the possibility of defining the beautiful by way of rules.[5] He declares that which most people find beautiful in art to be, instead, a nonessential by-product of the artist's exploration of nature, a process that draws only on the artist's integrity as its guide. In his view, true beauty (or true worth) resides in faithfulness to life, in capturing aspects of life's complexity and fullness. And this relationship of art to life can in no ways be expressed as an equation, life form=artistic representation. "Life is not symbolized that way," he writes, "for life is: activity."[6] This conception of musical worth can be linked to that of the philosopher Arthur Schopenhauer, whose idea that "the composer reveals the inmost essence of the world and utters the most profound wisdom in a language which his reason does not understand" is quoted approvingly in Schoenberg's 1912 essay, "The Relationship to the Text."[7] But Schoenberg's understanding of this "inmost essence" in the period under consideration, bespeaks the influence of the young Nietzsche, who tropes it as a primal unity that is also a site of "pain and contradiction."[8] Nietzsche gives this unity the name of Dionysus and sees its experience as the object of ancient Dionysian ritual. In such ritual and symbolically in Dionysian art, as he sees them, individuals merge in a paroxysm of annihilation, in which the pain of being destroyed recedes before the joy of becoming part of a higher creativity, that of the unitary life force. Moreover, the ugly has its rights in his conception of art, because it is part of the truth of life, perhaps more authentically so than the beautiful. As he puts it,

> . . . the ugly and the disharmonic are part of an artistic game that the will in the amplitude of its pleasure plays with itself. But this primordial phenomenon of Dionysian art is difficult to grasp, and there is only one direct way to make it intelligible and grasp it immediately; through the wonderful significance of *musical dissonance*. . . . The joy aroused by the tragic myth has the same origin as the joyous sensation of dissonance in music.[9]

One may dispute my association of Schoenberg's conception of music (in 1908–11) with Dionysian art as characterized by Nietzsche,[10] because the two are not entirely congruent. Schoenberg, after all, spends many pages of his *Harmonielehre* arguing that there is no such thing as a nonharmonic tone (a tone that is foreign to the prevailing chord). "Disharmony," then, might seem to be foreign to him as a musical concept. Yet it is hard not to see in Schoenberg's views a reflection of the Nietzschean dictum that "nothing is more conditional—or, let us say, narrower—than our feeling for beauty."[11] Moreover, Nietzsche's striking image in the quoted passage, of musical dissonance as standing for Dionysian joy, seems to cry out for appropriation by the composer who was, after all, dissonance's emancipator.

Other important aspects of Schoenberg's overall artistic outlook in 1908–11 are specifically Nietzschean. One is the idea that artistic activity is a striving toward the future, the basic theme of *Also sprach Zarathustra* [*Thus Spake Zarathustra*].[12] A second is the condemnation of traditional aesthetics as a means by which the artistically weak attempt to subdue the artistically strong, which parallels Nietzsche's view of traditional morality.[13] And a third manifests itself in a correspondence between Schoenberg's description, in the summer of 1909, of what he was trying to accomplish with his new music (to be discussed below), and Nietzsche's discussion of "frenzy"—a physiological state in which the excitability of the artist's nervous system has been maximally enhanced—as an indispensable condition for the creation of significant art in the era he was heralding.[14]

I shall assume that these relationships speak for themselves in the first and second cases. Of the third I shall have more to say in what follows. And the idea behind all of these, that Schoenberg's early atonal music instantiates Nietzsche's conception of Dionysian art—by reflecting a vision of life (nature) as essentially multiplex and conflicted—will be taken up as the basis of the musical analysis that is the principal contribution of this paper.

If there is anything categorically true of Nietzsche's philosophy, despite his rabid opposition to final truths, it is his rejection of the traditional dichotomies of mind and body, of spirit and matter, and of the world beyond and this world. One may summarize this rejection as deicide, and Nietzsche would have been happy to have it so regarded. It is clear that, in his aesthetic vision of reality, there is no place for God. Indeed, there is no place for ideal, unchanging entities of any sort. Although Schoenberg left us little indication of his metaphysical commitments in the years 1908–11, it seems to me significant that the idealist dichotomy between *idea* (the essence of a work, which has an ideal, ahistorical existence) and *style* (the work's historical garb or manner) has no important place in the *Harmonielehre*. This opposition, in which "idea" is of course the platonically privileged term, is basic to Schoenberg's later thought. Whereas it is doubtless an overstatement to equate Schoenberg's religious views at the time he broke with normal tonality with Nietzsche's, it is not wrong to say that, in the former's world view at this time, God has no existence apart from human creativity, and manifests himself only in works of genius.

The libretto for the short stage work, *Die glückliche Hand* [*The Fortunate Hand*], op.18 (1910–13), which Schoenberg wrote in 1910, shows some change in this regard. It identifies humans as formed in God's image, and bemoans their degradation by materialism. It cannot be described, however, as a religious text, one concerned with articulating the nature of divinity or of our relationship to it. But it may be significant that Schoenberg could not advance very far with the composition of the music for this text in 1910, and was able to complete it only in 1912–13. It is as if he felt that his purely intuitive approach to composition was unsuited to the expression of openly spiritual concerns and needed to wait until he was ready to work in a more intellectual and systematic manner. This manner evolved in 1912–13, during which he became openly preoccupied with mystical concepts, and especially with the radical affirmation of the reality of spirit in such literary sources as Balzac's short novel, *Seraphita*. This strange, fable-like story, based on the writings of the eighteenth-century mystic, Emanuel Swedenborg, discourses on such matters as reincarnation, the relationship between humans and angels, and the geography of heaven. It is inconceivable that Schoenberg would have contemplated basing a work on a text such as this in 1909, but in 1912 he began to conceive a large choral symphony that would use the final scene of *Seraphita*, in which a seventeen-year-old hermaphrodite, who is half human, half angel, is assumed into heaven. In the end, this project came to naught, but it turned into *Die Jakobsleiter* [*Jacob's Ladder*], for which a libretto was completed in 1915. Here, elements of Balzac's novella are grafted on to the story from the Hebrew Bible, marking a further stage in Schoenberg's religious odyssey back to Judaism, or rather towards a full engagement with it. Although he never completed the music for this work—he began it in 1917 and resumed it many years later, after World War II—by 1916 he had completed four songs on texts of an explicitly spiritual nature, published as op. 22.[15] Precisely in these years (1912–17) we see a gradual change in his attitude as an artist. In the first place he writes much less, and more uncertainly, finishing few of the projects he contemplates. In terms of approach and technique, there is a progressive return to sketching and other kinds of planning, a partial reversion to more traditional formal and textural procedures, and, with his incomplete setting of his own text to *Die Jakobsleiter*, the beginnings of the twelve-tone system.[16]

Of course, Swedenborgian theosophy is a long way from ethical monotheism. The latter posits God as radically other, as pure idea, while the former sees God and man as a unity, obscured for man by the error of materialism, by the impediment of his body.[17] Theosophy, therefore, could allow the artist to see his or her art as a manifestation of godliness, which in no wise would imply abandonment of an instinctual approach. For Schoenberg, though, engagement with God implied new modes of *acting*, a sense of service, even learning how to pray.[18] It involved taking a step back from total faith in oneself, or, in Schoenberg's case, in the power of his musical ear.

The dynamic seems clear. As the visionary who can see through to the heart of nature, the expressionist artist (Schoenberg in 1908–11), through untrammeled reliance upon instinct, produces works that spring forth as godlike acts, that look to the future and defy explanation in terms of accepted disciplinary theorizing. But as soon as this artist begins to think about what the divine might actually be, he or she begins to sense a distance from this entity, and thus to doubt the infallibility of instinct. With the arrival at monotheism, the artist recognizes God as totally other, and reevaluates the Nietzschean conception of creativity as a form of idolatry. No longer an "Overman," or a materially encumbered emanation of divine spirit, the artist becomes a simple person, and the artist's works take on a dimension of ethical responsibility, a requirement of a kind of truthfulness. In Schoenberg's case, the identification with God is replaced by one with Moses, the lawgiver.[19] No longer is the act of composition beyond reason, because ultimately at one with the world. Now only the law is truth, and its pursuit demands the partial renunciation of instinctual attunement and the compensatory embrace of intellect.

If the account I have given of the music of 1908–11 is valid, it should be expected to pose intractable problems for those who attempt to read the music formalistically. The contemporary discipline of music theory, practiced mainly in North America and with its roots in the 1950s, has been (until recently) as resolutely formalist as any in the academic world. It has focused on analysis, the task of describing musical works with reference to specific ideas about ways of interrelating musical objects. These ideas are the theories of the discipline, and the usual aim of analysis has been to show coherence in terms of a theory, that is, to show how the events of a piece might be seen as connected in terms of the theory in such a way as to explain or justify our interest in that piece. But if, as I have claimed, the comprehensibility of Schoenberg's music increases only as he progressively dissociates his own activity from God's, it would follow that the music of the breakthrough years, of 1908–11, should be expected to resist the coherence-making activity of theory. I believe that it has, and this in spite of the considerable effort directed, since the 1950s, to analyzing this music.[20] More radical, though, is the implication that, for this music, theory and analysis might well aim at showing why the surface of the music is ultimately impenetrable, in spite of the many planes of coherence it does exhibit; might demonstrate its incomprehensibility, in other words, not as something negative, but as the source of its meaning. This is the position I will take, and much of this essay is in fact just such a demonstration. But first I must dismiss the claim that modern theory has in fact already succeeded in implementing its normal strategies with respect to this music.

MODERN ANALYTICAL APPROACHES, COMPREHENSIBILITY, AND PLAUSIBILITY

By modern analytical approaches I mean those that apply ideas and tools from what is known in the discipline as set theory. While this has something to do with the mathematical theory of the same name, more important is the fact that it refines the traditional approach known as motivic analysis. In the latter, very small segments of music are described and related to one another with a view to showing their observable similarities and to characterizing the ordered progression—in Schoenberg's terms, the path of developing variation—that they trace. Set theory deals with segments mainly in terms of their pitches, which are usually translated into integers (C=0, C#=1, D=2, etc.) before an attempt is made to describe the relationships among the segments, or sets. Relationships are then arrived at by operating on the resulting sets of numbers. This is where the theory first runs into trouble, and irremediably so.

The usual objections to set theory analyses, and they are widespread, are of two kinds.[21] Those of the first kind complain that the results are disorderly, and might well be posited of random, or at least obviously inartistic, pitch data. Those of the second, more frequently encountered kind, claim that neither the entities (sets or groups of sets) nor the transformational relationships among them can be heard. Sufficient as these objections may be to limit the influence of set theory among musicians in general, they are not in themselves convincing. The best set-theoretical analyses, like those by David Lewin, reveal an order scarcely attributable to jumbles of notes or, for that matter, to the music of this or that composer in general. They are carefully engineered, in fact, to capture striking properties of particular passages, and often only those.[22] As for hearability, the obvious rejoinder is that some music is not for everyone, that some can hear what most cannot. One might pursue the first kind of objection by insisting that a coherent view of four or five bars does little for one's understanding of an entire piece, and the second kind by asking the alleged experts to take a test, but neither pursuit is likely to lead anywhere, and neither has.

My view is that analysis of this type is bound to seem unconvincing to disinterested parties because it turns *so quickly* in the direction of abstraction, by forgetting the tones that the numbers on which it operates represent. In the case of Schoenberg's so-called atonal music, the headlong dash to abstraction fatally avoids the issue he called "comprehensibility" (sometimes "perceptibility").[23] Repeatedly, when writing about the music he composed in and after 1908, as well as his later twelve-tone music, Schoenberg refers to the difficulty of comprehending (or perceiving) its chords because of their level of internal dissonance, often a function of the number of distinct tones (pitch classes) they contain.[24] This seems a strange usage, until we understand that by "comprehending" chords and dissonant tones within chords, Schoenberg meant relating them to acoustic fundamentals or, more generally, relating tones to one another in terms of their inherent potentials to so relate, by virtue of their nature as compound (overtone bearing) entities, and of the rhythmic contexts in which they function.[25] This explains his vehement rejection of the term "atonal," his saying that

> Everything implied by a series of tones constitutes tonality, whether it be brought together by means of direct reference to a single fundamental or by more complicated connections. . . . A piece of music will always have to be tonal in so far as a relation has to exist from tone to tone by virtue of which the tones, placed next to or above one another, yield a perceptible continuity. The tonality may then be neither perceptible nor provable; these relations may be obscure and difficult to comprehend, even incomprehensible.[26]

It is obvious that what Schoenberg called "comprehensible," most people speaking informally today would call "hearable," and obvious, for that reason, why most of the results of set theoretic analysis are, in this sense, unhearable. The rush to abstraction, to numbers, means that set theory overlooks the properties of tones as actualized in musical circumstances, the ways in which tones group together and subordinate themselves to one another because of what they are and where they happen. Of all these properties, the theory salvages only two, those of octave equivalence (the similarity and partial syntactic equivalence of octave-related pitches) and interval identity under transposition (the fact that we can recognize two different pairs of pitches as being the same distance apart if they are in the same frequency ratio). Strong properties to be sure, but scarcely sufficient to characterize the depth and complexity of the perceptual and cognitive grid we bring to the apprehension of tonal relationships—relationships among tones—in musical contexts. Therefore, whether or not a particular result of the theory can be heard by the optimal listener under optimal conditions, the theory is powerless to capture most of what anyone with a cultivated ear could hardly avoid hearing.

Another good reason for rejecting set theoretical analyses of the music Schoenberg composed in 1908–11 has to do with their implausibility with respect to his creative process at this time. There is a sizeable amount of extant sketch material for his "tonal" compositions written between 1904 and 1908; some for the later parts of *Die glückliche Hand* (1910–13), the *Vier Lieder* [Four Songs], op. 22 (1913–16) and various incomplete works from the 'teen years; and a great deal for just about everything he composed after 1920. For the works composed between 1908 and 1912, however, there is almost nothing in the way of sketches.[27] For a work like op. 16, no. 5 (1909), the orchestral piece that Schoenberg somewhat reluctantly (in 1912) entitled "Das obligate Rezitativ" [The Obbligato Recitative],[28] there is only a short-score draft, on both sides of a single sheet of manuscript paper, of the entire work.[29] The music appears hastily written out in pencil, with instrumental indications inked in afterwards. This work, in which a texture of almost unprecedented complexity (between five and seven independent lines) is carried on unremittingly for one hundred thirty-seven measures at a fast tempo, was evidently set down, almost without revision, in a matter of days in late July and early August of 1909.[30] That such music could spring forth fully formed, except for orchestrational details, is evidence enough that Schoenberg, just as he claimed, was taking dictation from a mysterious source. This can only have been the rich storehouse of his unconscious musical memory, to which he had an immediacy of access that is so outside the ordinary, so seemingly miraculous, that it is not hard to see why, a few years later, he would have resorted to a religious image in describing the result. For in a diary entry of early 1912, in reference to a lecture in which he had spoken about this piece, Schoenberg says

> . . . I managed to present and substantiate my ideas on the "obligatory recitative" . . . rather clearly. [But] not completely. The idea goes deeper: the *unutterable* is said in free form (=recitative). In this it comes close to nature, which likewise cannot be completely grasped, but is effective nonetheless.[31]

The word with religious overtones is "unutterable." However, I do not think we can interpret this as the name of God, utterable by the High Priest only once during the year in the Temple's Holy of Holies. The reference is there, but whereas it could legitimately have had this sense many years later with respect to the music of *Moses und Aron*, here it merely designates that which cannot be said using language, including the artificial languages of science. What cannot be grasped through calculated combinations of symbols, through intellect, this music *can* convey. It does so by being of a piece with nature, and thus quite beyond human attempts to account for it, in terms of a set of rules of formation. As was noted earlier, Schoenberg expressed the same idea in terms borrowed from Schopenhauer in his 1912 essay, "The Relationship to the Text." There he writes that the attempt to translate music's content into language is a betrayal, because music is "the essential, the language of the world, which ought perhaps to remain incomprehensible and only perceptible."[32] A letter to the painter Wassily Kandinsky, of 19 August 1912, goes further in an explicitly religious direction.[33] Here Schoenberg declares the artist's duty to be the creation of puzzles analogous to the puzzles presented by reality. The artist's goal is only to decipher (meaning, presumably, to find a way to notate or otherwise encode) these puzzles, not to explain them. In this way one learns that God, the "ungraspable," is possible without being understood.

It is not because Schoenberg lacked the ability to think in its terms that set theory is implausible when applied to this music. Who are we to say this of a person of such unparalleled gifts? It is simply that he tells us, as the evidence cited above amply confirms, that he could not work in a self-conscious, logical, or calculating manner at that time. This is revealed with the greatest eloquence in a letter to Ferruccio Busoni, written two weeks after the completion of op. 16, no. 5, in which he pens these powerful words:

> And thus I come to answer your other question: how much is intentional and how much is instinctive.
> My only intention is
> To have *no* intentions!
> No formal, architectural or other artistic intentions (except perhaps capturing the mood of a poem), no aesthetic intentions—none of any kind; at most this:
> To place nothing inhibiting in the stream of my unconscious sensations. But [not] to allow anything to infiltrate which may be invoked by intelligence or consciousness.[34]

The theorist might argue that the source of the music makes no difference, that whatever the process from which it arises, what matters is what is on the page. In my view, though, this is exactly where the implausibility comes in. We cannot know precisely what was in Schoenberg's unconscious, but for its musical substance it can only have drawn upon stored images of the music he knew deeply, including especially his own works;

images in which the literal content of that music had been chemically acted upon, as it were, by a fiery imagination of unparalleled recombinative and transformative power. The sets and set networks of atonal theory can have had no place in this storehouse, and thus no plausible relevance to the act of composition as Schoenberg described it. Of course, a total separation of act and results is possible, but as a critical stance it is not likely, in my view, to yield insights that will seem humanly and culturally compelling.

WHY AND HOW INCOMPREHENSIBLE?

A number of commentators have addressed the question as to why Schoenberg's music is so difficult to understand, among them Alban Berg, in an eponymous article dealing with the opening of the First String Quartet,[35] and Schoenberg himself, in a talk for the Frankfurt Radio, given in 1931.[36] But Berg deals with the First String Quartet, op. 7, and Schoenberg with the *Variations for Orchestra*, op. 31 (1928). In both of these works, there is a lot that can be explained and understood—pertaining to the presence of traditional harmonies in the first and to twelve-tone structure and phrase construction in the second—and neither commentator engages what this leaves out. In a work such as op. 16, no. 5, what this leaves out appears to have been coextensive with the musical data as a whole, to judge by the literature. This is not to say that nothing illuminating has been written about it, but that what has been written has not much advanced the cause of comprehension when the latter is understood in Schoenberg's terms, as the grouping of pitches, on various levels, in terms of their inherent, multifarious, overlapping, and often conflicting interrelationships, as perceived in rhythmic circumstances by a cultivated listener.[37]

To advance incomprehensibility as a serious theoretical claim seems preposterous, as it is easy to confuse it with throwing up one's hands. But it is not that. As something *theoretically* claimed, incomprehensibility is not a response to something registered as musical gibberish. Rather, it is the result of a condition in which the things that are individually comprehended are presented to us in mutually interfering ways, so that the comprehension of one makes the simultaneous comprehension of the other a psychological problem, if not an impossibility. Incomprehensibility might well be described as a kind of psychological indeterminacy. Viewed in this way, it is not a categorical state, but a matter of degree. States of affairs are not incomprehensible, pure and simple. They resist comprehension and may be said, in particular cases, to lie close to or at some limit of our potential to comprehend, or even beyond it.[38] A simple example, drawn from traditional music, would be that of a four-voiced fugue. A richly melodic four-voiced composition, such as one by J. S. Bach, resists comprehension as such, that is, as four melodic voices simultaneously comprehended. In listening to such a piece, the usual response is to simplify, by taking it in as one or two voices harmonized by the others, as something essentially homophonic rather than polyphonic. And, indeed, virtually all theoretical writing about the structure of such pieces rests on this kind of simplification.[39] But comprehension of a four-voiced fugue as a fully polyphonic entity may be a legitimate goal to strive for, particularly for the performer, and may even be attained in rare cases.

My point with reference to the music Schoenberg composed in 1908–11 is not that it makes little sense to the ear, just the reverse. It makes too much sense. There are too many things drawn up all at once from the musical storehouse of his unconscious and taken over into the music, by his editor-intellect, as such—as coexisting and mutually interfering things. There are several references in his *Harmonielehre* to such mutual interference,[40] and to a related matter, the requirements of progressive music for speed in perception.[41] The two are obviously related, because the ear's adaptive strategy, when faced with mutually interfering phenomena, is to shift back and forth between them at the fastest possible speed, just as in the example of the four-voiced fugue. Referring to the simultaneous deployment, or rapid alternation among the four potential roots of a diminished-seventh chord in music by Strauss, he says, "Naturally, that is not for fastidious ears, rather only for good ones! For those with quick perception!"[42] This acceptance of, and more, this pleasure in cultivating simultaneously interfering phenomena is explained by way of analogy in another section of the treatise, where Schoenberg writes,

> Just as it is hardly inevitable that a conqueror will endure as dictator, so it is no more inevitable that tonality must take its direction from the fundamental tone, even if it is derived from that tone. Quite the contrary. The struggle between two such fundamentals for sovereignty has something indeed very attractive about it, as numerous examples of modern harmony show.[43]

The underlying aesthetic aim, and thus the justification, for this indulgence in complexity does not emerge, however, in the *Harmonielehre*,

which is more concerned with technical means than with ultimate meanings. It comes out forcefully, however, in another letter to Busoni, this
one undated but probably written, on the basis of its content and what is
known about the dates of completion of pieces it refers to, shortly after
11 August 1909.[44] The following sentences are justly famous.

> I strive for: complete liberation from all forms
> from all symbols
> of cohesion and
> of logic.
>> Thus:
> Away with "motivic working out."
> Away with harmony as cement or bricks of a building.
>> Harmony is *expression*
>> and nothing else.
>> . . .
>>> My music must be
>>> *brief.*
>> Concise! In two notes: not built, but *'expressed'*!!
>>> And the results I wish for:
>>> no stylized and sterile protracted emotion.
>>> People are not like that:
>>> It is *impossible* for a person to have only one sensation at a
>>> time.
>>>> One has *thousands* simultaneously. And these thou-
>>> sands can no more readily be added together than an apple and
>>> a pear. They go their own ways.
>>>> And this variegation, this multifariousness, this illogi-
>>> cality which our senses demonstrate, the *illogicality* presented
>>> by their interactions, set forth by some mounting rush of
>>> blood, by some reaction of the senses or the nerves, this I
>>> should like to have in my music.[45]

Significantly, this beautiful and telling passage is formatted for the
most part as a kind of poem, whereas most of the letter in which it occurs
has the usual prose format. The purpose is clearly to highlight the passage,
it being in essence the composer's credo. I have perhaps quoted more of it
than is necessary to make the immediate point, which is that the justification for the multifarious, mutually interfering phenomena in the music is
expressive: a desire to capture the reality of life as experienced by the
human organism. What the music expresses, in consequence, is exactly

akin to what Nietzsche calls frenzy, a state of maximal nervous excitation and the heightened awareness it betokens. This statement also reiterates the aim of liberation from the constraints of logical procedure and constructive method. And it introduces another point, which I will mention here only in passing: the rejection of idealism in its late-Romantic musical incarnation. Many large post-Wagnerian works conclude with the resolution of massively prolonged conflict—of opposed tonics, opposed modal systems, and harmonic dualisms—in great all-absorbing triadic endings that symbolize an end to alienation and an achievement of integration, the attainment of some ideal state. Mahler's First Symphony provides a good example of this approach, as does Bruckner's Eighth.[46] This is what Schoenberg calls "stylized and sterile protracted emotion," and rejects in favor of conciseness, but it is the conciseness of one overflowing with things to communicate, not of the laconic. Banishing idealism, it replaces it with immersion in nature, or rather a supplement to nature, the musical surface attended to in all its phenomenological richness. Curiously, though, in respect to Schoenberg's music, the intended cancellation of idealism results instead in a kind of displacement. The musical object is so dense that it cannot be fully grasped by the active auditory imagination, but so filled with graspable content that it compels us to regard its totality as a limit towards which that mental organ aspires, and in that sense as an ideal. I will pursue this displacement and its implications for the listener in the final section of this essay. Now it is time to turn to a concrete example.

POLYPHONIES OF MELODY, METER, PHRASE STRUCTURE, AND TONALITY IN *"DAS OBLIGATE REZITATIV"*

Perhaps the first question that merits attention, as one confronts this labyrinthine piece, the fifth and last of the *Fünf Orchesterstücke* [*Five Pieces for Orchestra*], op. 16, has to do with its title. Schoenberg settled on "obbligato" after considering "fully developed" and "endless."[47] Carl Dahlhaus, in a short paper,[48] takes "obbligato" to refer to strictness of structure, and tries to make sense of the apparent contradiction between this term and "recitative," which Schoenberg's diary paraphrases as "free form." Committed as he is, however, to the uncritical conception of this music as atonal, asymmetrical, and athematic, he is at pains to say what about it is strictly conceived. He therefore interprets "obbligato" as referring not to the music's structure, but to its aesthetic quality as music that is endlessly melodious in Wagner's sense, that is, always significant and without padding. This interpretation seems to me farfetched. Would

Schoenberg not have used "obbligo" rather than "obbligato" if he meant "strictness" of some kind?[49] And if "endless" in Wagner's sense is what he had in mind, why did he reject it in favor of "obbligato?" In my view there is a simpler interpretation of "obbligato," as referring to an essential accompanying part, like the featured solo instrumental parts that accompany the singer in arias from the Bach Cantatas (these are called "obbligato parts"). And, indeed, the music does feature a continuous melody, almost always the highest voice and always the dominant one, the *Hauptstimme*.[50]

From this standpoint, however, the designation "recitative" becomes puzzling. A recitative is a kind of singing in which the singer imitates the rhythm and intonation patterns of speech. It is used in sections of works that are dramatic or rhetorical in nature (operas, oratorios, cantatas) to develop plot or, more generally, to narrate. Normally, recitative is sparsely accompanied, by chords that punctuate the melodic line, and function also to modulate between the musical numbers (arias, choruses) that surround it. Turning now to Figure 1-1, which presents the first seventeen bars of the music in short score format, we see that the principal voice (the "obbligato") is notated on the topmost staff throughout, with upward pointing stems for all of its notes. It is a full-blooded melody, full of repeated patterns, heavily accented, wide-rangingly energetic, and decisive in its metric and phrase-structural implications. Where then is the "recitative?" Schoenberg's diary entry, quoted above, tells us that recitative has something to do with "free form," but this is not much help. Nor is reference to the remaining voices, which are as far from the typical chordal accompaniment of a sung recitative as anything one could imagine. Not really accompanying voices at all, these others are fully independent, and constantly compete with the principal voice for our attention, equalling it in intensity if not in overall persistence and continuity.

It is known, of course, that the title of this piece was an afterthought, and that Schoenberg did not attach much importance to it.[51] Still, it is part of his commentary on the piece, so little of which has survived that it forces us to cling to what does. Recitative is "free," in terms of rhythm and tonal direction, but more importantly it is a kind of speech rather than a species of melody, speech accommodated to a surrounding context of true (expressive) melody. The identity of the expressive (aria-like) context is clear here: it is the polyphony of instrumental parts around the obbligato as principal part. The speech (recitative-like) component of this music is clearly not interspersed among its expressive limbs, as in opera. In my view it is, rather, the very same context viewed in a different way, that is, as a totality that "speaks." By this I mean that rather than

Figure 1-1. Op. 16, no. 5, mm. 1–17: short score, after Schoenberg's draft of early August 1909. Used by kind permission of C. F. Peters Corporation, New York.

Figure 1-1. (*continued*)

coming together by virtue of implying a single underlying stream of harmony, the way the voices of a Bach fugue do, the polyphonic voices of
this music come together in mutual contradiction, or in spite of it. If the
secondary parts can all be understood in relation to the obbligato, that is,
as relating to it harmonically, it is by virtue of their responding to diverse
harmonic implications, simultaneously inherent in particular segments
of the melody yet contradicting one another.[52] The speaking here is, accordingly, a metaphorical speech, a resultant of voices (melodies) res-
onating with one another (harmonically) in ways that are mutually
contradictory, or disharmonic. It is, in symbolic terms, the voice of
Schopenhauer's "will," or "innermost essence of the world," addressing
us with Nietzschean content, as a voice of anguish and contradiction, but
as a *single* voice nonetheless. According to Nietzsche, as I indicated
above, this univocality lies at the heart of the Dionysian. It is a characteristic of the Dionysian ritual that "in song and dance man expresses himself as a member of a higher community,"[53] but not in the sense of
contributing an individual voice to a harmonious whole. Rather,
"through the spirit of music we can understand the joy involved in the annihilation of the individual."[54] As a Dionysian expression, then, this
music of Schoenberg speaks with one voice, as recitative, by *annihilat-
ing* the contradictory voices of its melodic parts, including the obbligato,
a process that we experience as anguished yet profoundly joyful.

Figure 1-1 is closely based on the short score draft of the work referred to above. It is not a diplomatic transcription: I have incorporated
the very few revisions of the notes from the final score, omitted indications of instruments, added measure numbers, and annotated the bass
line (lowest part) with some dynamics and articulation marks, again

from the final score. Otherwise, though, the draft is faithfully transcribed, down to the details of staff placement, beaming of notes, even
accidentals (which I think are telling).[55] The visual appearance of Figure
1-1 is suggestive in very subtle ways. For example, the placement of
notes on separate staves could indicate their belonging to separate, mutually contradictory strands. But pursuing this leads quickly to nothing, as
these indications are sporadic and inconsistent. Clearly, one needs more
powerful methods.

A better approach, it might seem, would be to consider the melody *per
se*, as a source of potential harmonizations, and to see if some of these are
not in fact simultaneously present in the other voices. For example, the line
that descends chromatically (by half steps, the half step being the smallest
interval in our tuning system) in mm. (bars) 7–10—B, B-flat, A, G-sharp,
G—can be heard as moving within the scale of E minor, from the fifth
scale degree to the third; or it can be heard as moving within the scale of E-
flat major, from a lowered form of the sixth scale degree to the third. For
each of these motions there are a number of standard harmonizations. In
fact, suggestions of appropriate harmonizations of the melody segment in
question, under both of these interpretations, are present in the other
voices, and almost inextricably interwoven. For the melody as a whole,
however, this inviting prospect turns out to be a chimera: the melody,
viewed in broader ways, suggests too many harmonic possibilities, and
none of them with enough certainty. It is too elusive, too fluctuant, for the
project at hand, carrying no "certificate of domicile and passport . . . indicating country of origin and destination."[56] But help may be at hand if the
project is looked at from another angle. Instead of listening to the melody
as a repository of harmony, one could listen to it as implicative of meter,
determined by patterning and accentuation of various kinds. Then, the
other voices could be evaluated either as supporting these implications or
as contradicting them, and grouped accordingly. This revised project offers
much promise, first because meters are in general much simpler things
than harmonic continuities, and second (and especially) because so much
of Schoenberg's music is consistently polymetric, that is, it projects two or
more meters (beats and/or beat patterns) at once.[57] The possibility then exists that, having performed a segmentation of the music with respect to
conflicting meters, the results would point to a convincing way of seg-
menting it tonally, on the assumption that the two segmentations, if both
exist, are partially reinforcing of each other.

Figure 1-2 teases apart two metric strands in the music, labeled "W"
and "X." All the data of Figure 1-1 is contained in these strands, a certain
amount of it twice, since *the two strands overlap in note content*, reflect-

Figure 1-2. Op. 16, no. 5, mm. 1–17: strands of metrical and phrase-structural polyphony. Used by kind permission of C. F. Peters Corporation, New York.

Figure 1-2. (*continued*)

ing my perception that many melodic figures, or parts of figures, contribute to more than one metric continuity. The W strand is in a sense primary, because it contains the primary voice (the melody) in its entirety,
and is in fact metrically determined by it. In other words, all linear con-

tent in W is judged to reinforce the metric interpretation that I have given
to the melody. The latter seems to me uncontroversial, based as it is on
very clear accentuation. The melody (in W) begins with two 7/8 bars
(2+2+3 eighths), created by motivic repetition and the contour and
length accents on G#5 and A#5[58] in mm. 3 and 5 of the score, respectively (see Figure 1-1). These two 7/8 measures are then exactly balanced
by a further two measures, which add up to seven quarter notes, divided
after the first three, hence 3/4 followed by 4/4. The division is made here
by the long B4 in mm. 7–8 of the score. Linking activity during the last
three beats of the 4/4 measure forms an extended upbeat to the next measure, which begins with the G#4 on the downbeat of m. 10 in the score.
In strand W, this downbeat is only the fifth, and it is understood to begin
a new phrase, also of four measures, which answers the first phrase, the
two forming a period, or balanced pair of phrases. (In the absence of harmonic criteria, "phrase" will have to remain an intuitive term, signifying
a continuity of several measures that exhibits a degree of closure due to
melodic shape and internal motivic balance.) The "antecedent" ends with
B4, on the downbeat of the fourth (4/4) measure (in W), and the "consequent" begins with the immediately following Bb4. While the G#4 that I
have called the first downbeat of this consequent may not seem to be
contextually accented (see Figure 1-1, m. 10), it is, significantly, marked
with an accent in Schoenberg's draft, the *only* note so marked! Like the
first phrase, the consequent has four measures, articulated by clear
melodic accents, and it, too, falls into balanced segments of two measures each, (7/8 + 5/8) followed by (6/8 +5/8).

Besides the melody, W includes everything in the music that rein-
forces the metric and phrase structure just described. Included, for example, are all relatively long, and thus "agogically" accented, bass notes
that coincide with the melody's downbeats or its important secondary
beats; accented bass notes that do not so coincide are not included. It
would have been possible, perhaps, to further thicken W at points of accent with a few discreet additions, but this would not change its overall
effect or its linear substance. To put it another way, all melodic activity
not included in W clearly contradicts the rhythmic structures I have just
described. This activity forms the substance of strand X. This strand begins a sixteenth note in advance of strand W, but its first downbeat, the
C#4 of m. 1 in the score, comes an eighth after that of W. Strand X is in
6/8 time and is at first metrically more stable than its counterpart. It begins with a four-measure phrase, which ends with the sixteenth-note A-
flat major triad that occurs in the score (Figure 1-1) on the downbeat of
m. 7. In Figure 1-2, this triad is on the downbeat of the fourth bar, a 3/8

bar. Fragments of the principal melody are heard in X, but on the whole it is melodically self-contained and independent of W. As for metric coordination with W, X's second downbeat coincides with the second of W, but its third and fourth come an eighth before the corresponding downbeats of W.

Having heard an antecedent phrase in X, we might expect a consequent to follow, but that is not what happens. Instead, the motives of X contract and its accents come more quickly, making for shorter measures. As a result, the rest of X sounds like eight measures in 3/8 time. Interestingly, X retains its complex, out-of-phase relationship to W through all of this, but it comes into exact alignment with the notated score. Of course it has been so aligned since the start, if we understand its first three (6/8) measures as the measures of the score taken in pairs. In its eight concluding bars, beginning with a second "antecedent" indication, X is determined by the lowest part in the music, just as W is determined throughout by the melody. These eight bars fall into two phrases of four bars each, and are so labeled. The first, labeled "antecedent," begins with the bass's swinging motive that spans m. 7, beat 2 to the end of m. 9 (in Figure 1-1). It cadences definitively with the quarter-note chord on the downbeat of score-measure 11. It is then followed by the consequent, in which a melodic figure in the first two bars (in an inner voice in the full score, beginning on the third eighth of m. 11) is imitated by a bass figure in the next two. At the start of the last bar of strand X, the cadence of the consequent is overridden by a new figure in the bass, that beginning on the G2 of m. 15 in the score (Figure 1-1). This is a link to the next period of the music. It is four quarter notes long, and with its ongoing movement subverts the cadential effect of the final chord in strand W.

An interesting result has emerged thus far. The meter notated in the score corresponds roughly to strand X, with its complex phrase structure, but in perceiving the music we might well be drawn to follow strand W, determined as it is by the leading melody, and having a simpler phrase structure. Such complexities are not unprecedented in polyphonic music, but whereas earlier examples (for example, in Renaissance polyphony) normally involve a single voice opposing another single voice, or deviating from a group of voices, here we have *two polyphonic strands that interact in a higher-order, more abstract polyphony*, one of meters and phrase structures. This brings me to consider yet another kind of abstract polyphony, one of lines of harmonic roots.

Playing over and listening to the strands in Figure 1-2, one can hardly help noticing harmonic phenomena: clear points of tonal emphasis at rhythmic cadences, roots and root progressions in the lowest voice, and tonally implicative voice leading. Examples are, in strand W, the fleeting dominant to tonic motion in the key of C that leads into the third beat of the second measure; and, in mm. 5–7 (1-3 of the consequent), the sense that the melody is trying to enter E major, in which effort it is supported by a V/V (dominant of the dominant), on the third beat of m. 5 (the 7/8 bar), and a V (dominant) on the first beat of m. 7. In strand X, there is a clear sense of an F-sharp minor sonority serving as a fleeting tonic in the second beat of m. 2; and an implication that the A-flat major triad arrived at so decisively on the downbeat of m. 4 is, in fact, introduced by the augmented triad on the downbeat of m. 3, acting as a dominant; while in mm. 5–10 we move quickly through A minor (mm. 5 through 7, beat 2), and, by way of a fleeting E tonic on the downbeat of m. 8, to the V of E-flat major, arrived at on the downbeat of m. 10. But the strands of Figure 1-2 are merely suggestive, and one would not describe either of them as tonally clear throughout. Neither strand expresses a single, connected line of harmonic roots, in which there are no lacunae—patches without apparent roots—and in both strands there are places where melodic connections (voice-leading) are not convincingly coordinated with apparent roots. In W, for example, the root progression D, (C), B-flat, A, G, C can be plausibly inferred from the first two measures, but a clear sense of root progression is lost thereafter, at least until the bass E3 of m. 3, if not for longer. In X, likewise, the first two measures contain a clear root progression, C-sharp, B-flat, A, F-sharp, B . . . A-flat, in its first phrase (mm. 1-4 in X), but the voice leading in the third measure, indicated by the ellipsis between B and A-flat, is unclear.

I will not belabor this point. Instead of trying to square the circle by hearing harmonic clarity where there is none, it makes sense to use the numerous harmonic hints given to us by the segmentation in Figure 1-2 to construct a different segmentation of the data, in which these implications are realized with the fullest possible clarity. This is the intention behind Figure 1-3. Here we have two strands, labeled "Y" and "Z," the content of which once again adds up to everything in the score. Once again, too, there is overlap of content between strands—significantly, somewhat more than in Figure 1-2. This indicates that harmonic ambiguity in this music is more extensive than metric ambiguity, which is perhaps not surprising in view of the composer's love of "vagrant" harmonies, dissonant chords that can be interpreted in any one of a large number of keys. The reader will notice that many of the same tonal phenomena that emerged in W and X are here, too, but that they are not

Figure 1-3. Op. 16, no. 5, mm. 1–17: strands of tonal (root-line) polyphony. Used by kind permission of C. F. Peters Corporation, New York.

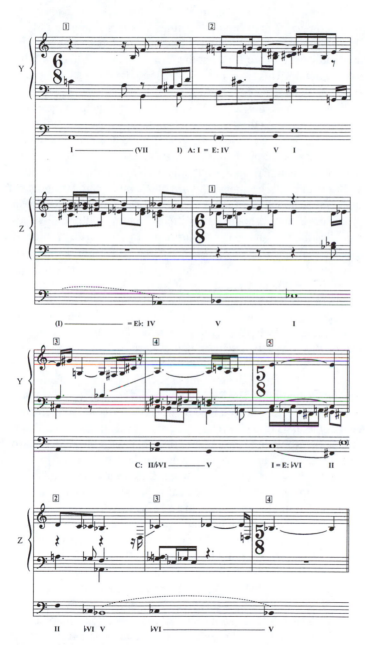

Figure 1-3. (*continued*)

linked in the same way. Y may resemble W at the start, and Z resemble X, but they soon go off in different directions. Another important difference between Figure 1-3 and Figure 1-2 is that the latter preserves the notation of the score (Figure 1-1), but the former changes it to clearly indicate tonal function. This gives many of the melodic figures in W and X a very different appearance in Y and Z.

The reader will also notice that Y and Z are organized into measures and phrases. The same symbols are used to indicate phrase structure as in Figure 1-2. Here, however, the organization is quite distinct from that in W and X. For example Y, in Figure 1-3, starts out rather like W in Figure 1-2, but begins to diverge from it, rhythmically, by the third measure. Beginning in its fifth bar, Y becomes a hybrid of W and X. Similar observations can be made about Z in Figure 1-3, when it is compared with X in Figure 1-2. That Y and Z should have different metric and phrase-structural properties than W and X is not surprising in view of the profound influence that harmonic rhythm has on meter. Once a clear harmonic progression is sensed, it implies a rhythm that is, in conventional tonal music, the most powerful determinant of meter. One would not expect the harmony of this music to be without metric consequences, and it is not. Moreover, where the melodic content is organized into bars, phrases emerge, and these too will necessarily be distinct from those in a metric segmentation that is largely undetermined by harmonic phenomena.

Figure 1-3 contains some additional information. Below each of its strands is a staff containing the root progressions implied by the music. These are further interpreted by Roman numerals that signify tonal function, according to a scale-degree model (whereby roots are numerically designated as the first (I), second (II) . . . seventh (VII) tones of particular scales) in relation to various keys that the music passes through. (I have used the scale-degree model because it is standard in North America. Also, Schoenberg used it. In fact, however, a Riemann-type functional model would do as well—perhaps better, as it would not bias the analysis in a diatonic direction.) In most cases, these keys are extremely transitory, often consisting only of a pair of harmonies; but in other cases a key is developed at some length, by means of longer scale-degree successions.

Strand Y begins with the root progression D, B-flat, A, G, (C), interpreted as a modulation from the key of D to that of C, the latter only implied. The root G is also interpreted as bVI in B, leading to B: I in the third measure (of strand Y). In this interpretation, which overlaps the first, the C3 on beat 3 of m. 2 is not heard as a root, but this kind of ambiguity of function is basic to chromatic music (tonal music in which all twelve tones are freely used). The B root in m. 3 (of strand Y) progresses to E and thence to A, entering the key of A minor, which is developed in mm. 5–6, whereupon a speeding up of root progression takes us to the key of E. The last three measures of strand Y are based on the root progression A (m. 7), A-flat leading to G (m. 8), C giving way to F-sharp (m. 9). The A-flat is represented as cofunctioning with D, its tritone equivalent (substitute). Tonally, this represents a modulation to C, which is subverted by the implication, at the very end of the strand, of a return to E.

Space prevents me from reviewing the harmonic analysis of strand Z. I hope the reader can use the information provided thus far to decipher it. This strand uses different intervals of root progression from those seen in the other strand (more thirds, for example). But as I shall demonstrate, its overall tonal structure closely mirrors, indeed shadows, that of strand Y. It gives an impression of tonal instability and jerkiness in its first four bars, but the last four bars are the most tonally stable of any in either strand, as they remain entirely in the key of Eb, expressed in terms of the simplest progressions.

My final example juxtaposes the root progressions of strand Y with

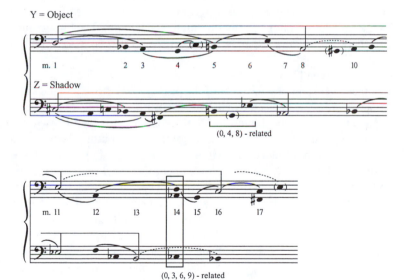

Figure 1-4. Op. 16, no. 5, mm. 1–17: root-line polyphony interpreted. Used by kind permission of C. F. Peters Corporation, New York.

those of strand Z, showing the polyphony that they make. This is once again an abstract polyphony, not of actual notes, but of theoretical constructs implied by the actual notes. It corresponds to the polyphony of metric and phrase structures discussed above, in that both are abstract theoretical constructs. In Figure 1-4, the analytical information provided by the Roman numeral analysis is absorbed into a notation similar to that often used in analysis of tonal music[59] to show relative degrees of hierarchical importance. We have here, then, an attempt to hierarchize the roots of each strand. Those of strand Y are said to begin with D, which moves through B and E to reach A, the root at the start of strand Y's second phrase. A then continues to E, which is retained through the terminal motion to C.

Strand Z begins on C-sharp, a semitone below the first root of strand Y. Where the other strand reaches A as its first major goal, this one reaches A-flat (via F-sharp and a {B, G, E-flat} augmented-triad root complex), reproducing the lower-semitone relationship. Strand Z then moves to E-flat, through B-flat, reaching it just exactly where strand Y reaches E. Once again a semitone separates the goals. At this juncture, Z moves by another rising fifth to B-flat, which it reaches via F and C-flat. This means that, with Y on its way to C, the fading out of the period brings with it a softening of tonal-contrapuntal conflict. The biting semitone between strands expands and resolves to a whole tone (B-flat against C).

The relation I have just shown between strands, in which Z shadows Y at the lower semitone for most of the passage—as if one and the same tonality were being projected in double exposure—is hardly coincidental or a matter of mere local interest. On the contrary, it is well known that Schoenberg was fascinated by the possibilities of putting two keys a semitone apart in the closest proximity. All the songs of op. 6 (1903–05) feature this kind of interlock in a prominent way, as do passages in the first and second string quartets. Moreover, he writes about such procedures both in the *Harmonielehre* and in *Structural Functions of Harmony*, where he refers to them in analyses of two of the op. 6 songs.[60] In the music he composed after 1908, he radicalized this procedure, using one line of tonics (or prominent roots) to shadow another, slightly more prominent line (as strand Z here shadows strand Y), so as to interfere with it in the most harmonically aggressive manner imaginable. My research has indicated that this abstract polyphonic technique, which results in an intense, even tortured mode of expression, is found everywhere in the music of this period, in the piano pieces of op. 11, in all the pieces of op. 16, and in the monodrama *Erwartung*, op. 17. The technique causes the most complex harmonic effects and presents the listener with the greatest challenges to comprehension. It is an essential Schoenbergian technique, and a basic source of the sound of his expressionist period. At the same time it is, in my interpretation, the key signifier for everything that is Dionysian in Schoenberg's music of this period. The conflicting strands of meter shown in Figure 1-2 and the polyphony of tonal strata revealed in Figures 1-3 and 1-4 are the individuals that, in Nietzsche's terms, suffer annihilation as they come together in something higher. Full of content and coherence, these "obbligati" merge in a single, anguished outpouring, the "recitative," in which they are no longer heard and, therefore, as musical individuals, have ceased to exist. Through this act of creative destruction, however, a musical entity arises that expresses life, "the unutterable," in which pain and joy are enigmatically fused.

IDEOLOGIES OF COMPOSERS AND LISTENERS

The problem of the listener has been with Schoenberg's music since the beginning, and continues to dog it today. It is not just that there are so few willing listeners, but also that those who are receptive receive such limited guidance in what to listen for from the literature and training available to them. While Schoenberg, referring to his twelve-tone music, insisted that one listen to what it is, and not to how it was made,[61] he said nothing very specific about this "being," and probably too much about its manufacture. And there is no question that, whatever there is to listen for in twelve-tone music, the influence of academic theory and composition has made the twelve-tone system an obstacle to hearing it. As I have pointed out, it has also made it difficult to talk about what there is to hear in so-called free atonality.

Why Schoenberg retreated from his position of 1908–11, with its total faith in intuition, is not absolutely clear. Not surprisingly, he did not see it as a retreat, steadfastly maintaining that he could not write large works using the ad hoc procedures of his early atonal works; that he needed the twelve-tone method, as a substitute for tonality, whereby meaningful relationships could be struck between the new harmonies he had begun to use in 1908 and large-scale forms. But this does not ring true. In what sense is *Erwartung*, op. 17 (1909), not a large work? That it has a text should not make any difference, in view of Schoenberg's insistence that his vocal music should be understood as essentially text-independent.[62] "Das obligate Rezitativ" itself is large in concept: very few Classical or Romantic works sustain a single texture at a fast tempo for as long.

The post-Nietzschean explosion, in art and philosophy, called for creators and recipients who would eschew oversimplification, reduction, and especially the search for ultimate unity. It involved rejecting systems and theories as models of reality, and embracing the fullness of life as total attunement to phenomena. It meant cultivating one's awareness in depth and extent at the same time. Schoenberg had proved himself the very personification of the Nietzschean "ideal" (a contradiction in terms, of course), and yet he clearly felt that it was wanting. He began to sketch compositions once again, to employ more and more explainable devices, and ultimately embraced some of the most acutely self-conscious and communicable methods of composing in all of music history. Moreover, once he had the twelve-tone method well in hand (by the late 1920s), he would indulge himself from time to time by composing tonal works.[63] As an approach to understanding what happened, I have suggested a correlation with his evolving conception of the Deity. As he began to conceptualize God as something infinitely greater than life itself, and apart from it, this argument would have it, he also began to take a different view of his responsibilities as an artist. The artist's indulgence in full awareness, the striving to become the total register of all sensation, became for him a form of idol worship, the artist's freedom a path to sin. His adoption, after 1920, of a conscious and extremely rigorous compositional technique was, accordingly, an act of self-abasement, and ultimately of worship.

Other interpretations, perhaps supplementary ones, are possible. Schoenberg's turn was also a turn from Europe, and perhaps he saw in post-Nietzschean thought a final incarnation of Europe's overweening pride, saw its rejection of metaphysical hierarchies as an excuse to wreak havoc, as had happened in 1914–18. He may have even foreseen its rejection of law-determined solutions as leading (paradoxically) to a different kind of (final) solution. And there is no doubt that personal experiences of anti-Semitism in the years immediately following the Great War played a role, though they seem only to have accelerated developments already taking place in his psyche.

However altered his attitudes toward society and his place in it as a Jew and an artist may have become, it is an open question whether the music itself changed in a profound way. Did the adoption of the row technique change Schoenberg's ear? Did it subdue his music's inner conflicts, mitigate its self-contradiction, negate its indeterminacy? Did it, in a word, make the music truly comprehensible? Or, was the row merely another way of getting the same kinds of results he had achieved earlier on through intuition? The answers to these questions await further research, which is now possible on the basis of descriptions of his early "atonal" music such as that provided here. And the time seems ripe for such research because formalism has lost its hold on the academic mind, making it possible to see the row as a device both heuristic and ideological, and not only as a determinant of what the music actually is.

This is not to say that ideology could not itself be an important determinant of what some music is. Everything I have said about Schoenberg's development implies that it could be. It is hard to imagine that an important change in a composer's way of thinking about the world would not change the music that he or she writes, and in some basic way. The same, I believe, goes for the listener. We are accustomed to dividing listeners in terms of alleged competence, based on acculturation, training, and talent. But listener ideology also plays an important part in what the listener will be willing to attend to, and what form that attention will take. Failure to recognize this is probably the greatest mistake made by those who lament the difficulty of programming new music and blame it on listeners' lack of exposure, when it is just as much listener's views of the meaning and purpose of listening that are at issue.

It seems to me crucial that the person listening to a piece like op. 16, no. 5 be prepared ideologically as well as with respect to musical background and training, important as the latter are. This does not mean the usual cynical ploy of telling the listener that the music is merely ahead of its time, that he or she should not expect to understand it, but must on that account revere it. (This is so obviously an absurd tack to take with music composed almost a century ago that it would not bear mention were it not still resorted to, perhaps cleverly disguised, on many occasions.) Rather it involves letting the listener know what is expected of him or her, and what he or she should expect to get from the experience. Not that the listener is totally constrained in this respect. There are always choices. With respect to Schoenberg's earlier atonal music, the basic choice is between an attitude of contemplation and one of struggle, between being an observer and being a participant. Both choices are possible, and neither is to be dismissed, nor is either entirely false to the music.

Schoenberg described op. 16, no. 5 as being like an object in nature. As such, it is possible to take a contemplative stance toward it, to attend to it without struggle, that is, without the attempt to comprehend it in the sense described in this essay. This approach might take various concrete forms, none of which should be confused with listening to the piece as background music, or treating it as a warm sonic bath (that threatens perpetually to turn into a cold shower). It has, as a basic feature, a positive but relaxed attitude that, despite the multifacetedness of the music, aims at hearing it as one thing. This might be achieved by attending to textural, registral, and dynamic development, to patterns of growth and decay, in respect of which the music is relatively clear. In effect, one would be hearing the music as "recitative," without much sense of the polyphonic elements, concrete and abstract, that have been "sacrificed," as it were, to produce this unitary effect. The alternative is the one I have tried to provide a basis for in this essay. It demands comprehension of the music's detail, recognizing that this may necessitate the music's division into irreducibly separate strands, this division taking effect in more than one dimension. It will struggle with these strands, not in an effort to reduce them to something unitary, not asking by what rules they "fit together," but in the effort to perceive them all at once. In other words, the person who listens in this active way struggles to experience the music as a polyphony of "obbligati." (This is not to say that the music's polyphonic strands do not, in fact, fit together in some sense. In my last example (Figure 1-4) I demonstrated one basic way in which they do fit together, and other principles of their coordination may also be discovered, probably in the nature of negative attributes.)

It might be objected that such an approach contradicts the spirit of the music: if the polyphonic elements have been "annihilated," why attempt to recover them? Several answers suggest themselves. First, there is a difference between a music that is unitary in origin and one that achieves its univocality though the fusion of contradictory elements. Univocality of the second kind can only be grasped imperfectly and in a fragmentary way, but its apprehension as such is to be preferred to the pretence that the music is purely "gestural," that is, without meaningful tonal substance. It recommends itself, in other words, as an approximation to the music's truth. Second, from the listener's point of view, it is more deeply absorbing than listening only for gestural shape, and leads further in the direction of musical self-development. Philosophical considerations provide a third response. That the object of comprehension is probably unattainable in some instance does not invalidate the attempt to grasp it; it only makes the object an ideal, a limit to which we aspire, as I wrote above. Maybe, too, this kind of listening provides a kind of postmodern religious experience, in that the full appreciation of coexisting, mutually opposing strands is sought as a kind of epiphany, and on rare occasions, perhaps, achieved. In the end, though, the most persuasive answer may be that Arnold Schoenberg appears to have been listening to himself in this way at the time he composed this music. On that ground alone, the approach taken in this essay recommends itself to us.

NOTES

1. A useful survey of the development of Schoenberg's religious thought is found in Pamela C. White, *Schoenberg and the God-Idea: The Opera "Moses und Aron,"* Studies in Musicology, No. 83 (Ann Arbor: UMI Research Press, 1985), 49–89. A penetrating study of Schoenberg's path to monotheism is Alexander Ringer, *Arnold Schoenberg: The Composer as Jew* (Oxford: Clarendon Press, 1990).

2. Schoenberg explicitly articulated his position first in 1928, in initial work on the text for his opera *Moses und Aron*, but one can only assume that his identification with a classically Jewish perspective antedates this mature statement by some years. He declared himself "no longer a European" but a Jew, in a letter to the painter Wassily Kandinsky written in 1923, but this declaration may be understood as more political than religious, that is, as a reaction to manifestations of anti-Semitism in the early 1920s. In my view, as he struggled towards the twelve-tone method in the years 1920–24, Schoenberg realized that Judaism provided a historical model for what he was attempting as an artist. He came to see that the Jewish concept of law—as mediation between an unknowable God and the task of constructing a meaningful social existence—offered a parallel, on a grand scale, for his efforts to devise a method of pitch organization that could mediate between the idea of a piece—an intricate web of tonal relationships that appeared to him instantaneously and as a unit—and the listener's need to follow a musical argument over time. Schoenberg does not draw this parallel himself, but it is suggested in the opening paragraphs of the famous essay "Composition with Twelve Tones" (1941), published in *Style and Idea: Selected Writings of Arnold Schoenberg*, ed. Leonard Stein (Berkeley and Los Angeles: University of California Press, 1984), 214–45.

3. Moses Maimonides (1135–1204), the most influential codifier of Jewish law in the post-Talmudic period, formulated the thirteen essential principles of Judaism, which figure in Jewish liturgies as a sort of credo. Implicit in these is the notion that God is infinite in time and space but, apart from that, can only be said to have negative attributes (to be not this and not that). This concept of God is of course basic to the libretto for *Moses und Aron*.

4. Arnold Schoenberg, *Harmonielehre*, original ed. (Vienna: Universal Edition, 1911); 3rd rev. ed. (1922), trans. Roy E. Carter (London: Faber and Faber, 1978), 416. (Subsequent notes refer to this translation.)

5. *Theory of Harmony*, 325–26.

6. Ibid., 326.

7. Schoenberg, *Style and Idea*, 141–45. The translation of the Schopenhauer passage is taken from the essay. White, *Schoenberg and the God-Idea*, 67–76, contains a substantial discussion of the importance of Schopenhauer for Schoenberg.

8. Friedrich Nietzsche, *The Birth of Tragedy*, trans. Walter Kaufmann (New York: Random House, 1967), 49. Nietzsche's view of music that I see as relevant to Schoenberg is set forth in this, his first book, where he declares (p. 52) that "it is only as an *aesthetic phenomenon* that existence and the world are eternally *justified*." Nietzsche's views on music changed in his later years, but he continued to advocate the interpretation of science and reality from the standpoint of art.

9. Ibid., 141.

10. At all events, one cannot argue that Schoenberg did not know Nietzsche. His library included four volumes by the philosopher, published respectively in 1901, 1903, 1904, and 1906. Whatever he did not read of Nietzsche he would have certainly encountered through intellectual contacts, given this author's enormous impact on the German-speaking world in the first decade of this century. Schoenberg set one text by Nietzsche, the poem "Der Wanderer," as the last song of his op. 6 (1905).

11. From Section 19 of *Twilight of the Idols*, in *The Portable Nietzsche*, trans. Walter Kaufmann (New York: Viking, 1954), 525.

12. See Schoenberg, *Theory of Harmony*, 239 and 325.

13. Ibid., 415.

14. See Nietzsche, *Twilight of the Idols*, section 8, in Kaufmann, *The Portable Nietzsche*, 518.

15. The texts are Ernest Dowson's "Seraphita," (after Balzac) translated by Stefan George, and three poems by Rainer Maria Rilke.

16. In several articles, Joseph Auner describes Schoenberg's move away from total dependence on instinct in the later, and most important, stages of composition of *Die glückliche Hand*, in 1912–13. See, for example, his "In Schoenberg's Workshop: Aggregates and Referential Collections in *Die glückliche Hand*," *Music Theory Spectrum* 18/1 (1996): 77–105.

17. This, at any rate, is Balzac's précis of Swedenborg's theology. I cannot claim first-hand acquaintance.

18. Ringer, *Arnold Schoenberg: The Composer as Jew*, 177.

19. Ibid., 67–82.

20. Three seminal figures in this effort are the composer George Perle and the theorists David Lewin and Allen Forte. All three base their analyses on small collections of tones (cells, or sets) and their transformations. Perle's principal work is *Serial Composition and Atonality: An Introduction to the Music of Schoenberg, Berg, and Webern*, 6th ed. (Berkeley: University of California Press, 1991). Lewin has written numerous papers on Schoenberg. His work is characterized by extreme sensitivity to the context of a specific piece and concern for its

continuity. See, for example, "Toward the Analysis of a Schoenberg Song (op. 15, no. XI)," *Perspectives of New Music* 12/1–2 (1973–74): 43–86. His important book, *Generalized Musical Intervals and Transformations* (New Haven: Yale University Press, 1987) contains brief analyses of two of Schoenberg's atonal compositions, the piano piece op. 19, no. 6 and "Die Kreuze," ["Crosses"] no. 14 from *Pierrot Lunaire*, op. 21. Allen Forte has developed the idea of a set of pitches in very abstract directions, coming up with analytical tools of great generality. He has applied these, with arguable success, to Schoenberg's pre-twelve-tone music in a number of articles as well as in the seminal book, *The Structure of Atonal Music* (New Haven: Yale University Press, 1973). His way of labeling sets of pitches has become standard in the field.

21. See my review of *The Structure of Atonal Music* by Allen Forte, *Perspectives of New Music* 13/1 (1974): 170–90; and my "Ideas of Order in Motivic Music," *Music Theory Spectrum* 1 (1979): 23–24.

22. See, for example, David Lewin, "A Tutorial on Klumpenhouwer Networks, Using the Chorale in Schoenberg's Op. 11, No. 2," *Journal of Music Theory* 38/1 (1994): 79–101.

23. Schoenberg wrote extensively about comprehensibility in the general sense of following a musical argument, principally in relationship to its motivic development. It is in this sense that he regarded Brahms's music as posing special challenges and saw himself as Brahms's heir. Here I am talking about comprehensibility in a narrower sense, as a predicate referring to intervals and chords. Schoenberg also used it in this narrower sense. Documentation is provided in the following note.

24. Schoenberg, *Style and Idea*, 101 (in "New Music: My Music"); 216–17 (in "Composition with Twelve Tones (I)"); and 282–83 (in "Problems of Harmony").

25. Schoenberg, *Theory of Harmony*, 316 and 319.

26. Ibid., 432.

27. Extant sketch material for Schoenberg's completed and incomplete works is documented in Jan Maegaard, *Studien zur Entwicklung des dodekaphonen Satzes bei Arnold Schönberg,* I (Copenhagen: Wilhelm Hansen, 1972), 20–24 and *passim*. Most of Schoenberg's sketches are found in his several sketchbooks. The third of these (chronologically) contains entries made between April 1906 and December 1916. The only entries dating from the years 1908–12 are for the tonal works, the *Second String Quartet* (27 July 1908) and the *Second Chamber Symphony* (23 November 1911). Apart from that, there remain a few loose sketch pages pertaining to these years. These contain very fragmentary sketches for a couple of the op. 15 songs (1908) and a few sketches for the beginning of op. 18, *Die glückliche Hand*. Other sketches for the last-named work date from 1912–13.

28. This reluctance is expressed in the so-called Berlin Diary (1912), with reference to a request by the publisher, Peters, for names for the five pieces. See Arnold Schoenberg, "Attempt at a Diary," trans. Anita Luginbühl, *Journal of the Arnold Schoenberg Institute* 9 (1986): 14.

29. The Schoenberg archive, now in Vienna, contains drafts of all the op. 16 pieces in short-score format. That for no. 5 is on both sides of a single oblong sheet of music paper (29 by 37 cm.). It is undated. The two sides of this page are sketch numbers 1484–85, as catalogued at the former Institute in Los Angeles. No. 1484 is immediately identifiable by the presence of an elaborately drawn hat in the lower right corner.

30. The short-score drafts for all five op. 16 pieces (see preceding note) are contained on eleven loose manuscript sheets. Dates on two of these drafts (for nos. 1 and 4), and on the fair copies of the full scores of all the pieces, suggest that the pieces were drafted in the order in which they appear in the work. The dates on the fair copies indicate that, for nos. 1–4, Schoenberg wrote out the full score of each piece after composing its draft and before drafting the next piece. The full score of no. 3, for example, is dated July 1 (1909), the draft for no. 4, July 17, and the full score of no. 4, July 18. It is therefore very likely that Schoenberg began to draft no. 5 after July 18 and that the draft was completed a few days before the (lengthy) full score, which is dated August 11. Since he also completed the piano piece op. 11, no. 3 on August 7 (date on draft), it is probable that op. 16, no. 5 was fully drafted by very early in August.

31. Schoenberg, "Attempt at a Diary," 10.

32. Schoenberg, *Style and Idea*, 142.

33. In *Arnold Schoenberg—Wassily Kandinsky: Letters, Pictures, Documents*, ed. Jelena Hahl-Koch, trans. John C. Crawford (London: Faber and Faber, 1984), 53–55.

34. Ferruccio Busoni, *Selected Letters*, trans. and ed. Antony Beaumont (London: Faber and Faber, 1987), 396. I have added "not" to the final sentence, on the assumption that its omission was an oversight. As it stands, the sentence makes no sense. I have not seen the German original, but another English translation, by Daniel M. Raessler (*Journal of the Arnold Schoenberg Institute* 7 (1983): 16) has "not" here, as does a French translation that I consulted. Charlotte Cross was kind enough to direct me to the Raessler translation.

35. Alban Berg, "Warum ist Schönbergs musik so schwer verständlich? [Why is Schoenberg's Music So Difficult to Understand?]," *Musikblätter des Anbruch* (a Universal Edition publication) 6 (August-September, 1924), trans. A. Swarowsky and J. H. Lederer, *The Music Review* 13 (1952): 187–96.

36. Schoenberg gave the talk on the Südwestdeutscher Rundfunk on 22 March 1931, in preparation for a radio performance of the Variations, op. 31,

under Hans Rosbaud. A translation of the lecture text appeared in *The Score* 27 (July 1960): 27–40.

37. The literature on op. 16 as a whole is surprisingly small. The third of the five pieces has received the most attention, probably because it is highly schematic. Paul Lansky, in "Pitch-Class Consciousness," *Perspectives of New Music* 13/2 (1975): 30–56, makes strenuous efforts to explain away tonal phenomena in the second piece. Theodor W. Adorno, "Fünf Orchesterstücke, op. 16," written in 1927 but reprinted in Rudolf Stephan, ed., *Die Wiener Schule* (Darmstadt: Wissenschaftliche Buchgesellschaft, 1989), 23–34, includes some analysis of the first piece, which he regards as prefiguring twelve-tone technique. Alan Street, "The Obbligato Recitative: Narrative and Schoenberg's Five Orchestral Pieces, Op. 16," in Anthony Pople, ed., *Theory, Analysis, and Meaning in Music* (Cambridge: Cambridge University Press, 1994), 164–83, is an attempt to find an autobiographical narrative in the five pieces. It mixes post-Freudian and other critical-theory ideas with isolated examples of pitch sets, the note names of which are said to encode the names of Schoenberg, his first wife, Mathilde, and the latter's lover (in 1908), Richard Gerstl. The results are not very happy. The musical note names in "Mathilde," (A, H, D, E) with H the German equivalent of B in English, are likely to appear in close proximity in any work that uses the C major scale. Finally, there is Carl Dahlhaus, "'The Obbligato Recitative,'" in *Schoenberg and the New Music*, a collection of essays by the author, trans. Derrick Puffet and Alfred Clayton (Cambridge: Cambridge University Press, 1987), 144–48. This is discussed in the main text.

38. See Arnold Schoenberg, *Coherence, Counterpoint, Instrumentation, Instruction in Form*, ed. Severine Neff, trans. Charlotte M. Cross and Severine Neff (Lincoln: University of Nebraska Press, 1984), 9, where Schoenberg writes, "the limits of comprehensibility are not the limits of coherence, which can be present even where comprehensibility has ceased. For there are connections inaccessible to consciousness." Also see Schoenberg, *Theory of Harmony*, 30, where he writes, "Comprehensibility and clarity are not conditions that the artist is obliged to impose on his work."

39. Analysis in the Schenkerian tradition treats Bach's fugues like other conventionally tonal music, as having only one structural voice above the bass, with which it forms a two-part skeletal framework.

40. Schoenberg, *Theory of Harmony*, 28, 128, 366, and 418.

41. Ibid., 323 and 367.

42. Ibid., 366–67.

43. Ibid., 128.

44. The third of the op. 11 piano pieces was completed on 7 August 1909. The letter refers to its completion. The letter also refers to several orchestral

pieces recently completed. The full-score manuscript of op. 16, no. 5 is dated 11 August 1909.

45. Busoni, *Selected Letters*, 389

46. See my "Tonal Dualism in Bruckner's Eighth Symphony," in *The Second Practice of Nineteenth Century Tonality*, ed. William Kinderman and Harald Krebs (Lincoln: University of Nebraska Press, 1996), 237–58.

47. The three terms appear together in the diary entry mentioned in note 28.

48. Carl Dahlhaus, " 'The Obbligato Recitative.' " See note 37.

49. *The New Harvard Dictionary of Music* defines "obbligato" as "an accompanying part that is nevertheless of considerable importance and not to be omitted." "Obbligo" is defined as "a technical requirement or constraint on which a composition is based."

50. This was the first work in which Schoenberg used the symbol "H" (for *Hauptstimme*), to designate a principal voice. After this he used it routinely, along with "N" (for *Nebenstimme*, or secondary voice), in his larger scores.

51. This is also clear from the diary entry referred to in note 28.

52. Any fragment of the melody of Figure 1-1 (the obbligato) can be harmonized, in post-Wagnerian style, the style of Schoenberg's own earlier music, in a number of mutually contradictory ways.

53. Nietzsche, *The Birth of Tragedy*, 37.

54. Ibid., 104.

55. Contrary to his later practice of putting accidentals (including naturals) in front of all notes, Schoenberg's practice is partly traditional at this stage. In other words, he usually notates the seven "white" notes without accidentals except where the intention is to cancel preceding sharps or flats (as if the music were in C major). Sometimes, however, there are extra natural signs. Precisely for this reason, however, the notation is revealing. The absence of an accidental indicates a degree of stability for the white note in question, that is, some kind of tonal-functional status. This serves as a useful guide to tonal interpretation, particularly where reinforced by diatonically meaningful choices of sharps vs. flats. All this is not to say, however, that Schoenberg was thinking diatonically. He was thinking tonally, and instinctively represented important tonal relationships in diatonic terms.

56. Schoenberg, *Theory of Harmony*, 129.

57. In this connection see John Roeder, "Interacting Pulse Streams in Schoenberg's Atonal Polyphony," *Music Theory Spectrum* 16 (1994): 231–49.

58. I am using one of the standard ways of differentiating the members of an octave class of pitches, for example, the various C's or D's. According to this convention, the lowest C on the piano is C1, the next is C2, and so on. This gives middle C the name "C4." Other pitches are named relative to C's, that is, the D

above middle C is D4. G#5, accordingly, is the G-sharp above the C which is one octave higher than middle C.

59. This notation derives from that developed by the Austrian theorist Heinrich Schenker (1868–1935), but I have adapted it to purposes which are not Schenkerian.

60. Arnold Schoenberg, *Theory of Harmony*, 384; and *Structural Functions of Harmony*, ed. Leonard Stein (New York: Norton, 1969), 110–13.

61. In a letter to the violinist Rudolf Kolisch, written in 1932, Schoenberg warns against analyses that consist mainly in pointing out the rows in his twelve-tone music. He claims that he has always tried to help people see what the music *is* rather that how it was *done*. See Arnold Schoenberg, *Letters*, ed. Erwin Stein, trans. Eithne Wilkins and Ernst Kaiser (London: Faber and Faber, 1964), 164.

62. See Schoenberg, "The Relationship to the Text," in *Style and Idea*, 141–45.

63. These include a concerto for cello and one for string quartet, both from 1933, and both based on pre-existent (Baroque) compositions; the *Suite for String Orchestra* (1934); the *Second Chamber Symphony* (1939); the *Variations on a Recitative for Organ*, op. 40 (1941); the *Theme and Variations for Band*, op. 43A (1943); folksong arrangements (1928, 1929, and 1948); and arrangements of compositions by Bach (1928) and Brahms (1937).

CHAPTER 2

Arnold Schoenberg as Poet and Librettist
Dualism, Epiphany, and *Die Jakobsleiter*

DAVID SCHROEDER

Arnold Schoenberg could have chosen a career from any one of a number of fields, and his extraordinary achievements as a composer, painter,
essayist, theorist, and teacher have long been recognized. His work as
poet and librettist has attracted less attention, even though he wrote many
of the texts for his major vocal compositions. His own expressions of
self-deprecation in this area may have contributed to the apparent notion
that these efforts should be taken less seriously than his others. In writing
to Richard Dehmel in 1912 requesting a text for what would ultimately
become *Die Jakobsleiter* [*Jacob's Ladder*], he remarked, "originally I intended to write the words myself. But I no longer think myself equal to
it."[1] This disclaimer should not be taken literally. When the appropriate
text was not forthcoming he did not hesitate to provide his own, and in
fact was more than equal to it. The exceedingly complex text of *Die
Jakobsleiter* draws on a vast array of literary, religious, and biblical
sources, and weaves an intricate pattern of images which define his aesthetic, philosophical, and, to some extent, his musical future. Such a text
deserves a closer look, a probing beyond the sources, associations, and
images that present themselves most readily. This essay focuses on the
words rather than the music, but this will open some new possibilities for
an interpretation of the music as well.

GENESIS OF *JAKOBSLEITER*

A year after Gustav Mahler's death in 1911, Schoenberg had planned to
write an enormous symphonic work in the tradition of Mahler. It was to

have had four movements, each one based on a literary or philosophical text, using vocal soloists and chorus. The projected third movement, "Totentanz der Prinzipien" ["Death Dance of Principles"], with a pessimistic text written by Schoenberg, was to be followed by a finale with the solution to his philosophical and spiritual quandary entitled "Die Jakobsleiter." The symphony never materialized, as it became increasingly clear to Schoenberg that he was not Mahler's musical heir, but completion of the fourth movement as an independent oratorio remained a high priority. Work on the text was under way as early as January 1915, and composition of the music commenced in mid-1917.[2] Schoenberg completed only half of the musical score in the next few years, although he came back to the work at various points in his life, including near the end, reaffirming its importance to him.

Die Jakobsleiter, the text of which was completed and published in 1917, stands as a watershed for Schoenberg, in spite of the fact that he never completed the musical part of the work. Here he defined his spiritual objectives in composition in a new way, and at the same time he took a large step in charting his future musical course and revealing the linkage between musical and spiritual matters. He wrote the text as a libretto rather than an independent dramatic-poetic work, but that did not prevent a richness of literary style, language, and imagery. In attempting to write a modern epiphany, Schoenberg strove for a type of religious universality which he was in a unique position to realize because of his Jewish background and Christian persuasion.

The years 1908–1922 stand as a particularly trying time for Schoenberg in his artistic and spiritual quest, flagged by Alan Lessem as the "critical years," or even more pressingly as the years of crisis.[3] The crisis revealed itself in his struggle with musical technique, as the works from this time show various facets of his use of atonality but not in most cases the solutions for a future direction. In expressive terms, the struggle can be seen in his exploration of a wide range of possibilities, including large expressionist works such as *Erwartung* [Expectation] on the one extreme, and relatively austere miniatures such as the *Six Little Piano Pieces*, op. 19, on the other. The problems were compounded by his endeavor to bring the different components of his quest together, a welding of technique, expression, and spirituality. The results of the crisis reveal themselves most vividly in his lack of accomplishments during these years; in the decade after the completion of *Pierrot lunaire* in 1912, Schoenberg managed to complete only one major new work, the Four Orchestral Songs, op. 22, finished in 1916. His striking operatic accomplishments with *Erwartung* in

1909 and *Die glückliche Hand* [*The Magic Touch*], which he composed during 1910–13, pointed, along with *Pierrot lunaire*, to the musical, expressive, and dramatic amalgamation he sought, but the idiosyncratic nature of each prevented a new musical language from emerging.[4]

Schoenberg himself most articulately stated the problem and its apparent solution in a letter written in 1922 to his friend Wassily Kandinsky:

> When one's been used, where one's own work was concerned, to clearing away all obstacles often by means of one immense intellectual effort and in those 8 years found oneself constantly faced with new obstacles against which all thinking, all power of invention, all energy, all ideas, proved helpless, for a man for whom ideas have been everything it means nothing less than the total collapse of things, unless he has come to find support, in ever increasing measure, in belief in something higher, beyond. You would, I think, see what I mean best from my libretto "Jacob's Ladder" (an oratorio): what I mean is—even though without any organisational fetters—religion. This was my one and only support during those years—here let this be said for the first time.[5]

Inevitably for Schoenberg this crisis would come to be defined in spiritual terms, and the solution, involving a grand fusion of the technical, the personal, and the creative, would ultimately be expressed as a spiritual solution. This was realized at a new level in *Die Jakobsleiter*, and the text itself prompted the possibilities; one of those included his conception of the music.

RELIGIOUS DUALITY

In some studies of this work in recent years, a certain amount of denominationalism has crept in, with both Christian and Jewish commentators claiming the work for their side.[6] When Schoenberg joined the Lutheran church in 1898, it is unlikely that he took that step with a sense of revulsion to Judaism, which typified the attitudes of certain fellow Jewish-born writers such as Karl Kraus, Otto Weininger, or Franz Werfel.[7] His own explanation of his conversion in 1935 put the matter in the context of the all too common outlook held by persons such as Houston Chamberlain, who claimed that (as Schoenberg himself phrased it),

> not only is the Jewish race an inferior race and one to be detested, but, we had also to realize, the Jewish race possessed no creative capacity. . . .

> You have to understand the effect of such statements on young artists.
> An artist cannot create without being convinced of his creative capac-
> ity—at least an artist of higher art needs confidence in the necessity
> and originality of his doings.[8]

His embracing of Christianity at the turn of the century was a genuine
step, but it did not remove Jewishness from his consciousness: far from
it. In 1933, Schoenberg made it very clear that his road of return to Judaism was an exceedingly long one.[9] It appears that Schoenberg's spiritual outlook well before the years leading up to 1933 was a combination
of Jewish and Christian elements, a particularly difficult feat during the
second decade of the twentieth century because of the rising tide of anti-
Semitism. The forces in question are in opposition, certainly within society, and also, it appears, to an extent within Schoenberg himself. It was
within his capacity to bring these polar forces together, and in the act to
find a higher level of spiritual attainment; this he realized brilliantly in
Die Jakobsleiter.

Dualism permeates this work at various levels, and the temptation is
great to see one side favored over the other. The spiritual and the material
interact, and some may choose to see the work as a triumph of the former
over the latter. Similarly, with the two media in question, music and literary text, an argument for the superiority of music has been advanced.
One prominent study of this work reduces the text to a type of programmatic prompting: "And for the composer that same superior reality was
present also in the music, as the text could only represent the surface of
what he wanted to say. For him it was essential that the definitive truth
had to be explained ultimately not with words, but with music."[10] If
music reaches higher on Jacob's ladder than literature, we then run the
risk of music also falling short of some other yet to be devised medium.
That line of thinking might explain why he never completed *Die Jakobsleiter*, but we can, one suspects, rest fairly sure that this was not the
essence of Schoenberg's crisis before 1922. He solved the crisis, and the
solution was not the abandonment of musical composition.

One of the most striking features of the images in *Die Jakobsleiter* is
the way they set up primary dualities. The text itself unfolds in both
prose and verse. Schoenberg draws material from both Hebraic and
Christian scriptures, distinguishes between the material and the spiritual,
humans and angels (or gods), male and female, and appears to draw a
further distinction between birth and apocalypse. Schoenberg's favorite
"heart and brain" contrast also emerges, and this could be paralleled with

other terms such as love and knowledge.[11] While conflict seems to be embodied in these dualities, Schoenberg bridges the differences in a way that allows a synthesis of the opposites into some type of higher unity.

At the center of the bridging function stands Schoenberg's central character, the archangel Gabriel. Gabriel, the first speaker in the work, can comment on the statements of the other main characters, and he gives a grand soliloquy near the end. In the soliloquy, Gabriel delineates the nature of the dualism arising from the conflict of spirit and matter. The material was created by the spirit and stood inferior to the spirit. The new creation overtook the previous essence, and in asserting itself became "will." A conflict remains inherent, as a dim consciousness of the material's origin—the spirit—lingers:

> Dunkler als der Irrtum, ist es diesem verwandt, wie dem Stoff und dem Geist, hat Züge dieses und jenes, weist vieldeutig wahr und falsch zugleich, erinnert dadurch auch im Falschen ans Wahre: ein Lichtstrahl davon ist immer darin, ist immer in Luft und Leid, in Sehnsucht und Ahnen, in Hoffen und Bangen, in Genuß und Entbehren, in Liebe und Haß, in Gunst und Neid, in Reinheit und Schuld.[12]
>
> [More vague than the delusion, but related to it as to matter and to spirit, it has characteristics of both the one and the other, behaves ambiguously, true and false at the same time, whereby it reflects the truth even in the false; a ray of light from it is always in the false, is always in joy and suffering, in longing and foreboding, in hope and worry, in pleasure and deprivation, in love and hate, in favor and envy, in purity and guilt.][13]

The choice of Gabriel for the role of providing understanding was by no means coincidental, as that corresponds with his primary biblical function. In the book of Daniel (9:22), Gabriel informs Daniel that he has now come "to enlighten your understanding," and similarly, he is called on (8:16) to "explain the vision to this man."[14] Schoenberg's vision of Jacob's ladder stands very much in need of interpretation, and the author therefore provides the appropriate biblical character to offer it. But Gabriel himself needs to be interpreted, as he appears in both the Old and New Testaments and has different roles in each. In the Hebrew scriptures he interprets an apocalytic vision (Dan. 8:17): "for at the time of the end shall be the vision"; and (8:19) "Understand, O man: the vision points to the time of the end." In the New Testament he brings good news, appearing to Zacharias to inform him that his aged wife Elizabeth would bear a son, John the Baptist (Luke 1:11–20), as well as to Joseph to announce the immaculate conception (Luke 1:26–38). Here the subject is birth, not of ordinary mortals, but of a holy man and the Son of God who should transform humanity.

LITERARY MODELS

Schoenberg's use of an angel with an apocalytic association once again should not be taken as coincidental. *Die Jakobsleiter* was Schoenberg's main work during World War I. According to Jean Christensen, its inception corresponded with his "Kriegswolkentagebuch" [the "War-clouds Diary"], in which he attempted to document parallels between the events of the war and weather or cloud formations.[15] Schoenberg was by no means the only artist to find himself in a state of crisis at this time. Karl Kraus, to whom Schoenberg had said "I have perhaps learned more from you than one is permitted to learn if one wishes to remain independent,"[16] had written about the war in the darkest possible terms in his gigantic drama *Die letzten Tage der Menschheit* [*The Last Days of Mankind*]. Schoenberg had a copy of this work in his library, and there are some notable similarities with the text of *Die Jakobsleiter*.

Kraus also uses prose and verse, although he appears to draw a qualitative distinction between the two. Kraus uses prose as the means for expressing dark satire, the language of those who are hastening the destruction of the planet. He reserves verse for the conclusion, when prose can no longer address the gravity of the situation, and with it he introduces an element of hope. Even though destruction comes, the voice of God expresses regret, and a god who speaks in verse and has regrets appears also to have some regard for humanity.[17] The range of speech, from the heights of the voice of God to the lowness of newspaper parlance, bears a similarity to Schoenberg's. Kraus's most enduring target was the press, its distortion of truth, its trivialization of language, its cynical role in the shaping of events such as the war, and its pandering to the ignorant masses. One finds this type of satire of newspaper language near the beginning of Schoenberg's work in the choir of *die Gleichgültigen* and *die Sanftergebenen* [the Indifferent and the Submissive Ones], and later there are exchanges among *Faule, Skeptiker, Zyniker, Schlaue, Tagschreiber*, and *Unreine* [lazy ones, sceptics, cynics, cunning ones, journalists, and impure ones], all of whom are painted with the same brush. At the other extreme stands the *Chor aus der Höhe* [chorus from on high], as well as persons who have attained spiritual heights, angels and gods.

Unlike Kraus's qualitative difference between prose and verse, Schoenberg makes no such distinctions. Near the beginning of the work the *Sanftergebenen* inanely chatter in verse, while Gabriel normally replies in prose. *Ein Berufener* [a Called One], an esthete, speaks in prose, while *ein Aufrührerischer* [a Protestor] rants in verse. Gabriel chastises the *Aufrührerischer* in prose for not being able to see through contradiction, for insisting on "either/or." A gap exists between polarities that must be bridged, and Schoenberg in part achieves the link with a democratization of prose and verse. Most notably, Gabriel's large soliloquy achieves the height of understanding through prose. For Schoenberg, a level of optimism emerges by way of synthesis, an approach to which Kraus could not subscribe. But both appear to reach their respective positions through the addressing of the issues of war and destruction and the durability of spiritual values in the face of these. Schoenberg makes this less explicit, but the presentation of Gabriel as a bridge between the Hebrew and Christian scriptures presupposes his role as the interpreter of visions that are understandable only in an apocalyptic context.

Gabriel's New Testament role, as bearer of the news of the Advent, invokes other literary associations. One of the writers most commonly linked with *Die Jakobsleiter* is August Strindberg, most notably his incomplete prose work *Jacob Wrestling*.[18] The image of Jacob wrestling with God was crucial to Schoenberg, going back to his earliest contemplation of this compositional project, and Strindberg's treatment of the idea had an obvious appeal. In the request to Dehmel in 1912, he inserted a parenthetical note to the poet to consider Strindberg's work as a prime example of the portrayal of the struggle of modern man with God.[19] When Schoenberg himself wrote the text, however, he did not follow this recommendation, as the similarity between these two works can at best be described as vague. Strindberg continued to have a role in Schoenberg's conception, but not through *Jacob Wrestling*.

The seldom performed play *Advent* has a more direct bearing, a work much loved by Schoenberg's pupil Alban Berg. His other notable pupil, Anton Webern, had written to Berg on 27 July 1912 to tell him of Schoenberg's gigantic symphony project after Balzac's *Seraphita*, and Berg wrote back on the 29th to share his enthusiasm. Berg informed Webern that Schoenberg had told him in the spring of 1911 of "his idea of possibly using *Jacob Wrestling* for a musical setting. He wanted at that time to write to Strindberg." In the same paragraph, Berg informed Webern that he had just read two Strindberg plays, one of which was *Advent*, and he then provides a description of Strindberg's use of music in this play:

> In the conciliatory conclusion of *Advent* (in a valley surrounded by
> high mountains near the end) "The scene is filled with shadows, which
> all look up to the mountain in the background." Singing from behind
> the background by 2 sopranos, and one alto, with accompaniment of
> only string instruments and harp. Now a Latin text. Out of this a chorus
> of sopranos, altos, tenors and basses. Again a text. Now Christ appears
> in the crib, with 3 kings and shepherds praying again. Chorus (trio) of
> 2 sopranos and 1 alto: Gloria in excelsis Deo, Et in terre pax, Ho-
> minibus bonae voluntatis. Isn't that fabulous: 2 sopranos and 1 alto,
> string instruments and harp![20]

In *Advent* a hypocritical judge and his mean-spirited wife come to
understand the magnitude of their sins through the help of the Other One
(the devil) and various processions of ghost-like characters. Prayer turns
up as a recurring theme, as it becomes evident that this guilty, aging man
and woman are unable to pray and thus find the conditions for atonement. In the end the Other One succeeds in showing them the way, and
they can then celebrate Christmas. Their lives are now able to end peace-
fully because they have found the meaningful beginning, as the Other
One explains: "There is an end, you see, if there is a beginning."[21] In the
concluding celebration of prayer, as Berg started to describe, there are
three choruses: Chorus I consisting of two sopranos, one alto, string instruments, and harp, singing "Puer natus est nobis" (Isa. 9:6); Chorus II,
with soprano, alto, tenor, and bass, singing "Cantate Domino Canticum
novum" (Ps. 149:1); and Chorus III, two sopranos and two altos, singing
"Gloria in excelsis Deo" (Luke 2:14). Schoenberg certainly knew this
play, and undoubtedly shared Berg's enthusiasm for it. One cannot help
but note that the section before the great symphonic interlude of *Die
Jakobsleiter* concludes with a chorus of women's voices (two soprano
parts and alto), a speaking chorus of women and men, and a grouping of
Gabriel and *die Seele* [the Soul]—the same voice as *der Sterbende* [the
Dying One]. At the beginning of this musical section in Schoenberg's
score (m. 563), the instrumentation is harp, strings in divisi, and percussion (with winds added later). The second half of the text, not set to
music, again concludes with three choruses: the *Chor aus der Tiefe*, the
Hauptchor, and the *Chor aus der Höhe* [chorus from the depths, the
main chorus, and the chorus from on high].

    In the associations with Kraus and Strindberg, the Old and New Tes-
tament aspects of Gabriel are reinforced. Not only are the Hebraic and

Christian scriptures embraced, but the synthesis of birth and death or advent and apocalypse also receives emphasis.

As we know from Schoenberg's letter to Dehmel and discussion with Berg and Webern, the primary literary source for *Die Jakobsleiter* was Balzac's *Seraphita*, especially the last chapter entitled "The Assumption." Much has already been made of this literary connection,[22] particularly the prayer theme, and the discussion here will pursue other possibilities. Love is an exceedingly important theme in Schoenberg's work, emphasized by the final line of text: "Schenkt euch ewige Liebe und Seligkeit" [Send us eternal love and blessedness]. Schoenberg was not interested in exploring the love which happens between a woman and a man, and this he already could specify to Dehmel in 1912 ("least of all through any love of woman").[23] He focuses, as the text makes clear, on eternal love, and here Seraphita provides the ideal model. The two young people in the novel, Minna and Wilfrid, both fall in love with Seraphitus/Seraphita, a possibility that exists because of his/her androgyny. As the novel unfolds they develop an awareness that they have misunderstood Seraphita's love and that he/she offers them spiritual love, a realization paralleled by the decline of Seraphita's material existence.

Love and understanding are fused together in this work, and it is no coincidence that in his own discussion of "heart and brain," Schoenberg begins with a passage from Balzac's *Seraphita*. His "Heart and Brain in Music" essay of 1946 starts with the following lines:

> Balzac in his philosophical story *Seraphita* describes one of his characters as follows: "Wilfred was a man thirty years of age. Though strongly built, his proportions did not lack harmony. He was of medium height as is the case with almost all men who tower above the rest. His chest and his shoulders were broad and his neck was short, like that of men whose heart must be within the domain of the head."[24]

Balzac's use of physiognomy in this passage (heavily marked by Schoenberg in his own copy)[25] embraces the material and the spiritual in that it brings together the body and the soul. Wilfrid's appearance may be somewhat crude, but he has a harmonious form. The heart and brain image is taken further a few pages earlier in the novel when the pastor says, "you, Minna, call yourself a spirit of love; and you, Wilfrid, make yourself out to be a spirit of wisdom." Schoenberg not only underlined this phrase in the German translation he owned but also wrote in the margin "einstige hier die Erklärung" [here the former explanation].[26] The two forces are now represented by female and male, but in Seraphita/ Seraphitus they fuse into one.

The name Seraphita derives directly from the biblical seraphims, the highest order of angels who are the spirits of love (paralleled by cherubims who bring understanding).[27] Seraphita's inability to maintain a material existence and, of course, the final ascendence, confirm the progression to an angelic state. Angels pervade *Die Jakobsleiter* at various levels, including the dominance of Gabriel and the image of Jacob's ladder, which in Genesis (28:12) has angels of God ascending and descending between earth and heaven. The androgynous Seraphita bears resemblance both sexually and spiritually to Schoenberg's dual character *der Sterbende* and *die Seele*, the latter singing melodies but not words. *Der Sterbende* is male, while *die Seele* is female, and both are sung or spoken by the same female voice. In this highest level of achievement, the release of the spirit or soul from the material through death, Schoenberg uses an androgynous character who is beyond sexual orientation.

Sexual issues were of course of critical interest to writers early in the century, including Strindberg, Weininger, Arthur Schnitzler, and Frank Wedekind. On the one hand, there appeared to be a struggle between the sexes, most notable in Strindberg's destructive married couples, such as those in *The Father* and *The Dance of Death*, or Weininger's blatant misogyny in *Geschlecht und Charakter* [*Sex and Character*]. But in the struggle a recognition emerged that both sexes had features of the other. For Strindberg the blending stood as an ideal, that neither male nor female were complete, but the highest level lay in a fusion of the two.

Once again a bridging of polarities is central, and Balzac and Schoenberg are most interested in this bridge. Laurence M. Porter ably describes the tradition from which Balzac came:

> Visionary Romantic authors were male; they use a female to symbolize Otherness, to serve as the vehicle for revelation as she had done in Dante, Petrarch, and Novalis. She must be killed to divest her of her material aspects and to reorient the attention of the protagonists toward the spiritual order to which she has preceded them.[28]

Curiously, the thrust of this thinking is Protestant, since neither a member of the Trinity nor the Virgin Mary facilitates revelation. No priests interfere, nor can Christ be found anywhere.[29] The woman involved does not resemble the Virgin Mary; she is sexually attractive and must be vigilant to deflect sexual attention. She can accommodate dualism and fusion, able, as Porter suggests, to "reorient our understanding by deconstructing the ordinary polar opposites of human perception. They become living metaphors combining two contrasting terms so as to suggest a third that transcends them both."[30]

The process demands death, or the sense of an ending, as Seraphita must go through a deathbed Assumption for her spiritual love to be grasped. There is also a temporal transcendence here, beyond *chronos* or passing time to *kairos* or the significant season, which Frank Kermode describes as the "point in time filled with significance, charged with a meaning derived from its relation to the end."[31] The fused voice of Schoenberg's *der Sterbende* and *die Seele* confirms this, saying "Seligste Hoffnung! Wie liebe ich dich, o du meine Last!" [Most blessed hope! How I love you, oh my burden], and, *ein Engel* [an Angel] proclaims: "Juble: ein Gleicher bist du uns bald!"[32] [Rejoice: you will soon be like us].[33]

The biblical seraphim, the angels of love, embody another apparently important image for Schoenberg. Associated with them is the number six because of their six wings (Isa. 6:2), and here one runs the risk of getting very carried away with number symbolism in music. Schoenberg's song *Seraphita*, op. 22, no. 1, begins with an ensemble of six clarinets in unison and a chorus of six cellos. At measure 9, six violins enter, followed by groupings of three trombones and three cellos.

In *Die Jakobsleiter* he goes even further. The text begins with six directions: "Ob rechts, ob links, vorwärts oder rückwärts, bergauf oder bergab" [right, left, forward or backward, uphill or downhill], and he follows this with two choruses of six parts each, equally divided between male and female voices. Aside from the respondent Gabriel and *die Seele* (who does not have a text), there are six characters at various points on the ladder. Schoenberg's music begins with a six-note motive which repeats six times (until m. 6), and this balances a six-note chord completed at measure six, which provides the other six notes of the chromatic scale. The linking of seraphitic angels and musical hexachords is of course immensely appealing, especially if we can go to the next step (in twelve-tone music) of the often used division by the tritone, the *diabolus in musica* [devil in music]. In the late Middle Ages, this nickname was given to the tritone, and various theorists prohibited its use. Strindberg, it should be noted, felt a particular revulsion to diminished sevenths, tritone chords, and occasionally used music in his plays at appropriate points which featured these.[34] Schoenberg himself does not exclude *Dämonen* [demons] from this work, although they may have more to do with the contemplation of evil than evil itself, combining them with *Genien, Sterne, Götter,* and *ein Engel* [genii, stars, gods, and an angel], presenting yet another fusion of opposites.

FUSION OF DUALITIES

Some of the dualities in the work can now be looked at in greater detail. The text is neither Judaic nor Christian, but reveals an attempted fusion of the two. Gabriel bridges both scriptures and there are various quotations from both. Gabriel's last words are "Klopfet an, so wird euch aufgetan"[35] [knock and the door will be opened],[36] a direct quotation of Christ (Mat. 7:7), and this is immediately followed by the prayer of a chorus with "viele einzelne Stimmen und Gruppen in heftiger Bewegung und stetem Wechsel"[37] [many individual voices and groups in vigorous motion and constant alternation],[38] as one finds in a synagogue rather than a church.

The concluding prayer of the three choruses bears striking resemblance both to the Lord's Prayer given by Christ in the Sermon on the Mount, and, as Dika Newlin notes, "an old Hebrew text paraphrasing two prayers of the Day of Atonement which can be traced back to well before the tenth century."[39] For Schoenberg, Jewish by birth and Christian by choice at this time, there was no conflict here; he himself was the fusion of the two. Christ does not show the way; Gabriel does. Schoenberg avoids denominationalism, including the Swedenborgian theosophy that appealed to Balzac. Strindberg, too, had been interested in Swedenborg, but dropped that quickly when he discovered how mean-spirited this messianic figure had been. Schoenberg had the advantage of Strindberg's response before him.

In the apparent conflict between matter and spirit, one must return to the title of the work: *Die Jakobsleiter*. In Jacob's dream the angels were not moving from earth to heaven only, but were both ascending and descending. The motion is fluid here, a moving back and forth, as the text begins: "Ob rechts, ob links, vorwärts oder rückwärts, bergauf oder bergab." Schoenberg presents not a flow from matter to spirit but an understanding of how the two can be fused. For *ein Ringender* [a Struggling One] at the middle level, Gabriel has a special empathy, and introduces *der Auserwählte* [the Chosen One] to address him. *Der Auserwählte* fears being pulled down by the middle, but observes, "Aber ich muß, so scheint es, mitten hinein, obgleich mein Wort dann unverstanden bleibt"[40] [I have to get into the middle, it seems, even though what I have to say then will not be understood].[41]

After the great symphonic interlude, Gabriel exhorts all to transform themselves:

> Steigt hinab, zieht ein in eure Kerker und werdet, je nach eurer Stufe, wieder solche, die lieben und sich freuen, die leiden und dulden, die treten und getreten werden . . . Nicht besser und nicht schlechter werdet ihr sein, als alle vor euch.[42]
>
> [Climb down, proceed into your dungeons and become again, according to your levels, such ones who love and enjoy, suffer and endure, who tread and are tread upon . . . you will be no better and no worse than all others before you.][43]

When *Die fünfte Stimme* [the Fifth Voice] asks, "Bin ich überhaupt hoh oder niedrig?" [Am I at all high or low?], *ein Gott* [a God] answers,

> Weder eins, noch das andere: du bist die unvollendete Vollkommenheit und oft auch: die vollendete Unvollkommenheit. Du bist zusammengesetzt, aber genötigt, dich für einfach zu geben. Auf unteren Stufen nützte Scheidung. Du mußt homogen werden.[44]
>
> [Neither one nor the other: you are the imperfect perfection, and other also: the perfected imperfection. You are pieced together, but you need to pass yourself off as one piece. On the lower steps division was useful. You must become homogeneous.][45]

In his final speech Gabriel explains the nature of the division between spirit and matter, the former creating the latter which, of course, remains inferior. All those in search of answers experience a struggle of the two forces and position themselves accordingly on the ladder. Again, Gabriel feels most sympathetic to those in the middle: "die mittleren jedoch, die dem Stoff gleich fern, wie dem Geist, sie steigen am schwersten"—[46] [those on the middle levels, however, who are equally distant from matter and spirit, have the most difficult ascent].[47]

Other opposites have already been noted. Male and female are seen to aspire toward androgyny, while a new beginning can only be grasped in relation to the sense of an ending, thus fusing birth and death. As for the artist's language, poetry is not superior to prose, and neither is music to a verbal text. The satirical writing of Kraus does not necessarily inhabit a lower level, and neither does the pedagogical writing of Schoenberg.[48] It should come as no surprise, then, that many of Schoenberg's works during the critical period of 1908 to 1922 combine music and text. Music

can, of course, say something which a text cannot: *die Seele* sings without
a text and the final choruses of the first half are superseded by an instrumental interlude. But that does not make music superior. One can, in fact,
find some peculiar balances or imbalances between music and text, such
as the scene involving *die Sanftergebenen*. Here the use of language is at
its most banal, as "ja, ja" repeats over and over, and he concludes with the
indulgent remark "O wie schön lebt sich's doch im Dreck"[49] [Oh, how
beautiful it is to live in the muck].[50] To accompany the "ja, ja" repetition,
Schoenberg uses close harmony in the full chorus, and the music convey-
ing "O wie schön lebt sich's doch im Dreck" stands as perhaps the most
exquisite of the entire work. The treatment can only be ironic, and a vestige of that irony may be the equality of text and music.

Der Auserwählte, who states, "Mein Wort laß ich hier . . . Meine
Form nehm ich mit"[51] [my word I leave here . . . my form I take with
me],[52] places the issue in focus. Gabriel attempts to explain: while the
word can be had, the form is remote, but later it will become you. Here
again are matter and spirit, and the projection of various opposites which
are fused. The "word" clearly invokes the opening of the gospel according
to John: "When all things began, the Word already was. The Word dwelt
with God, and what God was, the Word was." This New Testament beginning also recalls Genesis: "In the beginning of creation, when God made
heaven and earth [spirit and matter], the earth was without form and void
[spirit formed matter]." John continues, "The light shines on in the dark,
and the darkness has never mastered it," while *Genesis* proceeds: "with
darkness over the face of the abyss, and a mighty wind that swept over the
surface of the waters. God said, 'Let there be light.'" For John to see a beginning, there must also be a sense of an ending, and the final scriptural
vision of apocalypse appears to him in the book of Revelation.

The opposites finally coalesce for Schoenberg (as they do for Balzac,
Strindberg, and perhaps even Kraus) in prayer: "Lernet beten: 'Wer betet,
ist mit Gott eins worden' "[53] [Learn to pray: Whoever prays has become
one with God],[54] Gabriel tells us by quoting Balzac's Seraphita. The
Strindbergian Hauptchor brings the final set of opposites together:

> Vieltausend Stimmen, tausendfach verschieden,
> in Wunsch und Klage, in Bangen und Hoffen,
> in Freud und Leid, in Wut und Angst
> streben zu Gott, dringen zu ihm,
> der sie alle hört, sie einzeln aufnimmt,
> wie sie gefühlt, gedacht und gesagt.[55]

> [Many thousand voices, thousand-fold different, in wish and com-
> plaint, in worry and hope, in joy and suffering, in rage and fear, strive
> toward God, press toward him, who hears all, receives them individu-
> ally, as they felt, thought and said.][56]

Der Chor aus der Höhe assures us that "vor ihm sind alle Wünsche gleich"[57] [before him all desires are equal],[58] presumably whether they
come from low, middle, or high, and a final equity ensues as the
Hauptchor, the *Chor aus der Tiefe* and the *Chor aus der Höhe* all sing together in a Judaic/Christian prayer.

POINTING TO THE FUTURE

In reflecting in 1948 on the breakthrough he had made as a composer—
the discovery of musical principles which ultimately allowed his twelve-
tone music to emerge—Schoenberg gave full credit to *Die Jakobsleiter*:

> Ever since 1906–08, when I had started writing compositions which
> led to the abandonment of tonality, I had been busy finding methods to
> replace the structural functions of harmony. Nevertheless, my first dis-
> tinct step toward this goal occurred only in 1915. I had made plans for
> a great symphony of which *Die Jakobsleiter* should be the last move-
> ment. I had sketched many themes, among them one for a scherzo
> which consisted of all the twelve tones. An historian will probably
> some day find in the exchange of letters between Webern and me how
> enthusiastic we were about this.
>
> My next step in this direction—in the meantime I had been in the
> Austrian army—occurred in 1917, when I started to compose *Die
> Jakobsleiter*. I had contrived the plan to provide for unity—which was
> always my main motive: to build all the main themes of the whole ora-
> torio from a row of six tones.[59]

As Ethan Haimo points out, Schoenberg correctly recalled the main
stages in the development of the serial idea, which the manuscripts and
sketches confirm.[60] Here stood the work, more than any other written
during the crisis years, which pointed most clearly to his future musical
development, prompting through its defining of a six-note figure the arrival of the twelve-tone principle.

The treatment of dualism and integration in this seminal work offers
a variety of marvelous implications for Schoenberg's musical philosophy,

his *Gedanke* [idea], and for the music itself.[61] One of the possibilities may involve the capacity of music to elucidate much more than the words. In the text we have Gabriel to provide interpretations of the other characters and offer a sense-making process for the work itself. At the same time there are literary images that allow a deeper understanding of Gabriel and contribute to the larger purpose of the work. Similarly, the music, in its derivation of themes and motives from a six-tone figure, its use of harmony or counterpoint, or its use in ironic, humorous, or serious ways, may be providing a commentary for music itself, a type of musical instruction that parallels the moral or spiritual didacticism of the text.

NOTES

1. *Arnold Schoenberg Letters*, ed. Erwin Stein, trans. Eithne Wilkins and Ernst Kaiser (London: Faber, 1964), 36.

2. See Alan Lessem, *Music and Text in the Works of Arnold Schoenberg* (Ann Arbor: UMI Research Press, 1979), 180.

3. The subtitle to Lessem's *Music and Text* is *The Critical Years, 1908–1922*.

4. Lessem, *Music and Text*, 165.

5. *Arnold Schoenberg Letters*, 70–71.

6. Alexander Ringer steers the discussion in the direction that his title suggests in *Arnold Schoenberg: The Composer as Jew* (Oxford: Clarendon Press, 1990), 177–78, while Jean Christensen, in "Arnold Schoenberg's Oratorio *Die Jakobsleiter*" (Ph.D. diss., University of California, Los Angeles, 1979), vol. 1, 60–62, especially with the Sermon on the Mount discussion, appears to support the Christian position.

7. For more on these writers and their disparaging views of Judaism, see Edward Timms, *Karl Kraus: Apocalyptic Satirist* (New Haven: Yale University Press, 1986), 237–49; on Weininger, David Abrahamsen, *The Mind and Death of a Genius* (New York: Columbia University Press, 1946), 183–88; and Peter Stephan Jungk, *Franz Werfel: A Life in Prague, Vienna, and Hollywood*, trans. Anselm Hollo (New York: Grove Weidenfeld, 1987), 48–50.

8. Arnold Schoenberg, "Two Speeches on the Jewish Situation," in *Style and Idea: Selected Writings of Arnold Schoenberg*, ed. Leonard Stein, trans. Leo Black (Berkeley: University of California Press, 1984), 503.

9. See Schoenberg to Alban Berg, Paris, 16 October 1933, in *The Berg-Schoenberg Correspondence: Selected Letters*, ed. Juliane Brand, Christopher Hailey, and Donald Harris (New York: W. W. Norton, 1987), 446.

10. Christensen, "Arnold Schoenberg's Oratorio *Die Jakobsleiter*," vol. 1, 66.

11. See Arnold Schoenberg, "Heart and Brain in Music" (1949), in *Style and Idea*, 53–76.

12. Arnold Schönberg, *Die Jakobsleiter: Oratorium* (Vienna: Universal, 1917), 27. Copyright 1974 by Belmont Music Publishers. Revised edition Copyright 1980 by Belmont Music Publishers. Reproduced by permission of Alfred A. Kalmus, Ltd.

13. Christensen, "Arnold Schoenberg's Oratorio *Die Jakobs leiter*," vol. 2, 33–50.

14. All biblical quotations are taken from *The New English Bible* (New York: Cambridge University Press, 1972).

15. Christensen, "Arnold Schoenberg's Oratorio *Die Jakobsleiter*," vol. 1, 44–47.

16. Alexander Goehr, "Schoenberg and Karl Kraus: The Idea Behind the Music," *Music Analysis* 4 (1985): 64.

17. See Timms, *Karl Kraus: Apocalyptic Satirist*, 379, and Harry Zohn, *Karl Kraus* (New York: Twayne, 1971), 83.

18. An English translation appears in August Strindberg, *Legends: Autobiographical Sketches* (London: Andrew Melrose, 1912), 150–245. Schoenberg knew the work as *Jakob ringt*, a German translation of the original Swedish.

19. *Arnold Schoenberg Letters*, 35.

20. Alben Berg to Anton Webern, 29 July 1912, unpublished letter, Wiener Stadt- und Landesbibliothek, Handschriftensammlung, I.N.185.570. My translation.

21. August Strindberg, "Advent," in *Plays*, 3rd series, trans. Edwin Björkman (London: Duckworth, 1913), 177.

22. See Karl H. Wörner, "Schönbergs Oratorium 'Die Jakobsleiter'; Musik zwischen Theology und Weltanschauung," *Schweizerische Musikzeitung* 105 (1965): 250–57, 333–40; Gustave Kars, "Arnold Schoenberg et ses sources littèraires," *Revue Musicale* 298–99 (1975): 129–30; H. H. Stuckenschmidt, *Arnold Schoenberg: His Life, World and Work*, trans. Humphrey Searle (London: Calder, 1977), 234–36; Alan Lessem, *Music and Text in the Works of Arnold Schoenberg*, 181–84; and Christensen, "Arnold Schoenberg's Oratorio *Die Jakobsleiter*," vol. 1, 35–36.

23. *Arnold Schoenberg Letters*, 35.

24. Schoenberg, "Heart and Brain in Music," 53.

25. I would like to thank the former Arnold Schoenberg Institute in Los Angeles for placing the items from Schoenberg's personal library at my disposal.

26. Honoré de Balzac, *Philosophische Erzählungen: Seraphita, Louis Lambert* (Leipzig: Insel, 1910), 85.

27. Northrop Frye, *The Great Code: The Bible and Literature* (Toronto: Academic Press, 1981, 1982), 161.

28. Laurence M. Porter, "Writing Romantic Epiphany: *Atala, Séraphîta, Aurélia, Dieu,*" *Romantic Quarterly* 34 (1987): 437.

29. Ibid., 437–38.

30. Ibid., 438.

31. Frank Kermode, *The Sense of an Ending* (London: Oxford University Press, 1976), 47.

32. Schönberg, *Die Jakobsleiter: Oratorium*, 17.

33. Christensen, "Arnold Schoenberg's Oratorio *Die Jakobsleiter,*" vol. 2, 41.

34. This happens for example in *Crimes and Crimes*, where measures 96–107 from the second movement of Beethoven's Sonata op. 31, no. 2 can be heard being practiced in an adjoining room. See my "Berg's *Wozzeck* and Strindberg's Musical Models," *The Opera Journal* 21/1 (1988): 6–7.

35. Schönberg, *Die Jakobsleiter: Oratorium*, 29.

36. Christensen, "Arnold Schoenberg's Oratorio *Die Jakobsleiter,*" vol. 2, 48.

37. Schönberg, *Die Jakobsleiter: Oratorium*, 29.

38. Christensen, "Arnold Schoenberg's Oratorio *Die Jakobsleiter,*" vol. 2, 48.

39. Dika Newlin, "Self-Revelation and the Law: Arnold Schoenberg in his Religious Works," *Yuval: Studies of the Jewish Music Research Center* 1 (1968): 210.

40. Schönberg, *Die Jakobsleiter: Oratorium*, 11.

41. Christensen, "Arnold Schoenberg's Oratorio *Die Jakobsleiter,*" vol. 2, 37.

42. Schönberg, *Die Jakobsleiter: Oratorium*, 16.

43. Christensen, "Arnold Schoenberg's Oratorio *Die Jakobsleiter,*" vol. 2, 40.

44. Schönberg, *Die Jakobsleiter: Oratorium*, 21.

45. Christensen, "Arnold Schoenberg's Oratorio *Die Jakobsleiter,*" vol. 2, 43–44.

46. Schönberg, *Die Jakobsleiter: Oratorium*, 27.

47. Christensen, "Arnold Schoenberg's Oratorio *Die Jakobsleiter,*" vol. 2, 47.

48. Milton A. Cohen, "Subversive Pedagogies: Schoenberg's *Theory of Harmony* and Pound's 'A Few Don'ts by an Imagiste,'" *Mosaic* 21 (1988): 49–65.

49. Schönberg, *Die Jakobsleiter: Oratorium*, 7.

50. Christensen, "Arnold Schoenberg's Oratorio *Die Jakobsleiter,*" vol. 2, 35.

51. Schönberg, *Die Jakobsleiter: Oratorium*, 12.

52. Christensen, "Arnold Schoenberg's Oratorio *Die Jakobsleiter,*" vol. 2, 38.

53. Schönberg, *Die Jakobsleiter: Oratorium*, 29.

54. Christensen, "Arnold Schoenberg's Oratorio *Die Jakobsleiter,*" vol. 2, 48.

55. Schönberg, *Die Jakobsleiter: Oratorium*, 31.

56. Christensen, "Arnold Schoenberg's Oratorio *Die Jakobsleiter,*" vol. 2, 49.

57. Schönberg, *Die Jakobsleiter: Oratorium*, 32.

58. Christensen, "Arnold Schoenberg's Oratorio *Die Jakobsleiter*," vol. 2, 50.

59. Arnold Schoenberg, "Composition with Twelve Tones" (2) [c. 1948], in *Style and Idea*, 247.

60. Ethan Haimo, *Schoenberg's Serial Odyssey: The Evolution of His Twelve-Tone Method, 1914–1928* (Oxford: Clarendon Press, 1990), 42.

61. For an excellent study on dualism see Robert Fleischer, "Dualism in the Music of Arnold Schoenberg," *Journal of the Arnold Schoenberg Institute* 12 (1989): 22–42.

CHAPTER 3

Androgyny and the Eternal Feminine in Schoenberg's Oratorio *Die Jakobsleiter*

JENNIFER SHAW

In the years immediately following the First World War, Arnold Schoenberg began to revise his 1911 textbook, the *Harmonielehre* [*Theory of Harmony*], for its second printing. In a chapter devoted to a discussion of the minor mode Schoenberg added the following curious passage:

> [I]t is true that the dualism represented by major and minor has the power of a symbol suggesting higher forms of order: it reminds us of male and female and delimits the spheres of expression according to attraction and repulsion. These circumstances could of course be cited to support the false doctrine that these two modes are the only truly natural, the ultimate, the enduring. The will of nature is supposedly fulfilled in them. For me the implications are different: *we have come closer to the will of nature*. But we are still far enough from it; the angels, our higher nature, are asexual; and the spirit does not know repulsion.[1]

In this particular passage from the 1922 edition Schoenberg seems to advocate an androgynous "music of the future"; one without oppositions such as major and minor and one that would aspire to the neutrality of the human spirit and to an angelic asexuality. Perhaps Schoenberg thought that the free-atonal style he had nurtured for over a decade was destined to become the asexual norm in musical composition: yet he could only allude to this radical premise in a textbook that he hoped would appeal to conservative university professors.

But does Schoenberg's atonal music actually realize this ideal? His unfinished oratorio *Die Jakobsleiter* [*Jacob's Ladder*] would seem to be

the musical work most likely to attain the expression of such an androgynous vision. Schoenberg wrote both the libretto and a substantial portion
of the music for his oratorio during the First World War, at the same time
as he began to consider the revisions of his harmony textbook.[2]

Thanks, in part, to recently published studies by Jeffrey Kallberg and
Robert Walser, many of us could name certain composer-performers—
ranging from Chopin to various heavy-metal artists—who have been labelled androgynous.[3] But what constitutes an androgynous music? Aside
from Nattiez's ambitious study of Wagner, few attempts have been made
to identify possible representations of androgyny in music itself.[4] Yet an
examination of the diverse formulations of androgyny that Schoenberg
would have encountered in the literature and in the visual arts of his time
suggests that androgyny may indeed have been at the forefront of Schoenberg's thinking during the war years. In striving to create an androgynous
music, Schoenberg joined a long and fairly conservative tradition of writers and artists who have sought to express the androgynous ideal in religious tracts, philosophical writings, and fictional works. Yet, I would
suggest that, by resisting the ideal's accepted associations, Schoenberg
also attempted to overcome the social and political obstacles which he encountered in prewar Vienna by more transgressive and confrontational
means. Moreover, Schoenberg's efforts to develop a musical language
equal to the androgynous ideal of his harmony textbook may have shaped
both his search for alternatives to the tonal system and his development,
after the war, of the twelve-tone method of composition.

SCHOENBERG AND THE ANDROGYNOUS IDEAL

Schoenberg would have known of various manifestations of the androgynous ideal. Yet, as A. J. L. Busst cautions in his classic survey of androgynous representations in European literature and the visual arts of the
Romantic era, the meaning of the androgynous image must be assessed
individually for each work of art.[5] Nebulously defined, the symbol of the
androgyne in the nineteenth century could incorporate aspects of masculine and feminine gender, male and female sex, or it might be asexual—
that is, in some sense, before or beyond the division of the sexes.[6] In
Plato's *Symposium*, for example, Aristophanes recounts how the original
three sexes of man-man, woman-woman, and woman-man were divided
into separate halves by the jealous gods, so that each half now possesses
only one sex—either male or female—which searches for its missing
partner.[7] While such images abound in the earliest literature and mythol-

ogy of Western Europe, this particular story was revived at the beginning
of the twentieth century in the context of the psychological investigation
of human bisexuality.[8]

Schoenberg may have been familiar with androgyny as a symbol of
asexuality and purity in paintings by the Pre-Raphaelites Edward Burne-
Jones and Dante Gabriel Rossetti.[9] He would have known, at least by
reputation, of androgyny's association with decadence in the prints of
Aubrey Beardsley, including Beardsley's published illustrations for
Oscar Wilde's *Salome*.[10] Schoenberg also would have been aware of androgyny's affiliation with sexual ambiguity in a number of celebrated
works, well-known in Berlin and Vienna before the war, by Edvard
Munch and by Gustav Klimt.[11]

Schoenberg was certainly aware of androgyny's importance in nine-
teenth-century fiction, especially in the stories of Honoré de Balzac. Ambiguous sexuality and bisexuality are prominent themes in several of
Balzac's tales, particularly in *La fille aux yeux d'or* [*The Girl with the
Golden Eyes*]—a tale of bisexual eroticism and lesbian love—and in
Sarrasine, best known through Roland Barthes's deconstruction of its
castrato hero/heroine Zambinella.[12] Schoenberg especially admired
Balzac's *Séraphîta*, the tale of an asexual angel who appears as a man to
women and as a woman to men.[13] In fact, in a letter that Schoenberg sent
in August 1912 to the painter Wassily Kandinsky, Schoenberg wrote that
he believed that his *Pierrot lunaire*, which he had recently completed,
would serve as:

> a preparatory study for another work, which I now wish to begin:
> Balzac's *Seraphita*. Do you know it? Perhaps the most glorious work
> in existence.[14]

Between August and December of 1912 Schoenberg sketched a stage
plan, a plot outline, and a single page of music for an oratorio setting of
Balzac's *Seraphita*, designed to be performed over three consecutive
evenings. This particular project was never completed.[15]

Schoenberg would have encountered androgyny in literary sources
by authors other than Balzac. Both Schoenberg and his student Alban
Berg read Otto Weininger's infamous study *Geschlecht und Charakter*
[*Sex and Character*] and they were aware of androgyny's role in the new
psychological science of Wilhelm Fliess and Sigmund Freud, not only
through Weininger's theories but from Fliess's and Freud's own writings.[16] Fliess first proposed in the 1890s that the psyche was inherently

bisexual—a theory that Weininger and Freud appropriated in their extremely popular publications of the early twentieth century. Schoenberg may have read Fliess's main work, the book *Vom Leben und Tod*, which Berg lent him in 1915.[17] Berg himself was strongly influenced by Fliess's description of female and male biorhythms; a twenty-eight day cycle for women and a twenty-three day cycle for men, which Berg worked into the phrase structure of many of his own musical compositions.[18] Schoenberg was less familiar with Freud's work, but he knew of Freud's writings on bisexuality through his membership in Karl Kraus's intellectual circle in Vienna. A number of Schoenberg's close friends were involved in Freud's weekly meetings and Schoenberg read reviews of Freud's ideas, as well as several essays on transvestism and bisexuality in general, in Kraus's journal, *Die Fackel* [*The Torch*].[19]

Schoenberg was cognizant of the very public intellectual property quarrel between Freud and Fliess over inherent bisexuality. Kraus supported Freud's authorship of the idea and published a scathing attack on Fliess in the October 1906 issue of *Die Fackel*, which Schoenberg owned and read.[20] Kraus reported that, at a recent meeting in Berlin, the Scientific Humanitarian Committee had determined that the idea of an inherent double sexuality had first been expressed by Plato: thus Fliess's claim of authorship did not hold up against his ignorance of the literature nor against Freud's (and Kraus's) support for Weininger.[21]

In addition, Schoenberg may have read one of many works written between 1910 and 1914 that describe androgynous deities of non-Western cultures. The most famous of these texts, *Wandlungen und Symbole der Libido* by Carl Jung (translated as *The Psychology of the Unconscious* in the English language editions), was published in Leipzig and Vienna in 1912.[22] Jung touches on the androgyny of Christ, Dionysus, and of several Babylonian and Indian gods. The English writer Edward Carpenter also examined the meaning of the androgyny of various gods in the Babylonian, Hindu, Jewish, and Christian belief systems in his 1914 study of *Intermediate Types Among Primitive Folk*.[23]

Schoenberg explored various formulations of divine androgyny just before the war when he became interested in the works of the Hindu poet Rabindranath Tagore. Tagore had been awarded the Nobel Prize for literature in 1913 and his poetry was widely translated and disseminated in 1913 and 1914.[24] Schoenberg planned to set a number of Tagore's poems in the context of a large choral symphony, along with Biblical passages and texts by the German poet Richard Dehmel.[25] Dehmel's poems describe the erotic union of a father-spirit and a mother-soul. In his symphony, Schoenberg casts Dehmel's dual-sexed god as *der bürgerliche Gott* [the bourgeois God] and rejects it in favor of Tagore's god; a neutral deity, synonymous with death and with nothingness.[26]

The ideal of the divine androgyne in mystic Jewish and Christian traditions also must have been familiar to Schoenberg.[27] Schoenberg's own libretto for his oratorio *Die Jakobsleiter* borrows overtly from many mystical sources. He combines, for instance, ideas from the Jewish Kabbala, the Old and New Testaments, and contemporary theosophy with the beliefs of the seventeenth-century Protestant visionary Jacob Boehme and the eighteenth-century mystic Emanuel Swedenborg.[28] Swedenborg's teachings were most familiar to Schoenberg from August Strindberg's writings and from Balzac's novel *Seraphita*. According to Swedenborg, men and women must pass through three steps on a ladder—love of self, love of humanity, and love of God—before their souls can become asexual angels which are then androgynously reintegrated with God.[29]

In the volume of Jacob Boehme's writings that Schoenberg acquired in 1916, Boehme describes the androgyny of God, of Christ, and of Adam before the division of the sexes.[30] Boehme describes Adam, for example, in the following terms:

> He had the *limbus* [seed] and also the matrix [womb] in himself; he was no male or man, nor female or woman; as we in the resurrection shall be [neither]. Though indeed the knowledge of the marks [of distinction will] remain in the figure, but the *limbus* and the matrix not separated, as now [they are].[31]

Although this particular passage does not occur in Schoenberg's abridged version of Boehme's text, Schoenberg was well aware of Boehme's conception of original and future divine androgyny and admired his ideas.[32]

Thus Schoenberg would have recognized that the symbol of the androgyne could represent nostalgia for a state of primordial divine unity—as in Plato's myth—or it might reflect a desire for future reintegration with a divine being—as in Boehme's and Swedenborg's writings. At the other extreme, however, Schoenberg must have known that the androgyne often symbolized a deviant or decadent sexual orientation.

COMPOSING ANDROGYNY

In Schoenberg's oratorio *Die Jakobsleiter*, various characters—a monk, a protester, one who is called, one who struggles, one who is chosen, and one who is dying—have come to the ends of their lives and seek to be re-united with God. One by one they tell the Archangel Gabriel how they have sought God. But Gabriel criticizes all of their chosen paths—not one of them is ready to be united with God; all must be reincarnated in human form. At the end of the oratorio Gabriel reveals that reintegration with God is only attained through faith and prayer.[33]

Schoenberg defines his characters either as *Sprechstimme* parts, in which he requires each character to produce a voice halfway between speech and song, or as purely sung roles.[34] Gabriel, as mediator between the souls on the second step of the ladder and God on the highest step, has the ability to move from *Sprechstimme* to baritone singing voice. On the lowest step, the chorus of men and women, who represent humanity, mostly perform in *Sprechstimme*, but they occasionally lapse into song as they recall earthly loves and desires.

Tenor and baritone soloists perform all the solo roles except two: a high soprano soloist performs both the *Sprechstimme* role of *der Ster-bende* [the Dying One] and the virtuosic sung part of *die Seele* [the Soul]. At the moment of death the Dying One is transformed into the Soul, who sings a powerful, expressive melody without words.

In this drama dominated by solo male singing and speaking voices, the high soprano characters of the Dying One and the Soul are particularly enigmatic. Schoenberg consciously modelled both on Balzac's androgy-nous Seraphita, whose soul ascends to heaven and is transformed into an asexual angel.[35] Early text drafts of *Die Jakobsleiter* reveal Schoenberg's unconventional attempts to embody a Seraphita-like gender ambiguity in the roles of the Dying One and the Soul through linguistic means.[36] In these drafts, *der Sterbende* [the dying *man*] alternates with *die Sterbende* [the dying *woman*].[37] *Die Seele* [the Soul]—a feminine noun in Ger-man—is written incorrectly, but deliberately, as a masculine or neutral noun, *ein Seele*. In the published libretto Schoenberg employs "*Seele*" without any article that would indicate the Soul's gender.[38]

Schoenberg also attempted to render the androgyny of these roles by musical means. In the final version of the libretto, the roles of both the Dying One and the Soul are given to the same soprano soloist. The great-est gender ambiguity is retained in the role of the Dying One. Schoen-berg writes in the score that, in this role, the high soprano soloist is to speak in a low register: moreover, when singing softly, she is to use chest voice.[39] In this manner the Dying One falls to E at the bottom of the tenor range, then rises through the alto and treble registers to F-sharp at the top of the mezzo range, before she/he plunges into a *glissando* death cry.

By combining *Sprechstimme* with the soprano's deep chest register Schoenberg attempts to achieve a gender ambiguity or angelic asexuality in the role of the Dying One. Michel Poizat might characterize this voice as "transsexual" or beyond sexual; that is, as a voice suggesting that both gender and sexuality, as we have constructed them, may be transferable.[40] Yet I would argue that Schoenberg's efforts to depict androgyny through vocal means are not entirely successful. I still hear the Dying One's cry as the cry of a *woman*, sung, as Schoenberg indicates in the libretto, "halb schmerzlich, halb freudig erstaunt" [half painfully, half happily surprised].[41] Indeed, the Dying One's death cry resonates with the cries of numerous suffering women in opera, especially those of Wagner's Kundry (in *Parsifal*) and Schoenberg's own tormented protagonist in *Erwartung* [*Expectation*].[42]

At the moment of death, the soprano Dying One in Schoenberg's oratorio is transformed into the Soul.[43] Schoenberg attempts to depict the Soul's asexual androgyny by pushing its voice outside the normal soprano range and beyond the boundaries of language. As the Soul, the soprano sings a demanding coloratura vocalise, replete with agile vocal ornamentation and virtuosic leaps and runs. Her ecstatic, wordless melody soars high above the orchestra, the *Sprechstimme* chorus, the baritone singing voice of Gabriel, and an offstage women's chorus of angels. These other groups simultaneously sing three different texts.[44]

Although Gabriel and the other angels address the Soul in familiar, neutral terms as "*du*," the Soul's suggested androgyny is undermined by the language of the *Sprechstimme* chorus. The women in the chorus notice "ein Regenbogen auf ihrem Kleid" [a rainbow on *her* dress]. While the women see the Soul as female, the men in the chorus then interpret the rainbow as "Zeichen der Schuld" [(a) sign of sin], reinforcing the image of the Soul as sinful female. The men also hear the Soul's voice not as transcendent but as "Erdenjammer!" [earthly wail!].[45] With the plunging death cry of the Dying One still in our ears, the men's identification of the Soul as sinner and their perception of her vocalise as "earthly wail" brands the Soul as kindred in spirit to Kundry.

While it would seem that Schoenberg wished us to understand the roles of the Dying One and the Soul as androgynous, both his libretto and the voice qualities of his singers make this problematic. Ultimately, Schoenberg forces the listener to interpret both of these roles not as truly androgynous, but as representations of women, and, in particular, of the Eternal Feminine; that is, as aspects of a feminine soul enclosed within the psyche of the male artist-hero.[46]

In Goethe's classic formulation of the Eternal Feminine at the end of *Faust*, Gretchen—executed for the murder of her baby—is transformed into the feminine soul that leads Faust to heaven.[47] Schoenberg was familiar with this manifestation of the Eternal Feminine in Goethe's play itself and in the *Faust* settings of both Liszt and Mahler. The language of Schoenberg's 1912 Mahler memorial lecture actually exploits the allegory of the Eternal Feminine. Schoenberg, quoting Mahler's paraphrase of Goethe, writes:

> [']The Eternal Feminine has drawn us upward—we are there—we are at rest—we possess what we on earth could only long for, strive for . . .'
>
> That is one way to reach the goal! Not just with the understanding, but with the feeling that one already lives there *oneself*. He who looks on the earth thus no longer lives upon it. He has already been drawn upwards.[48]

In Schoenberg's oratorio, the Soul's voice, moving beyond the realm of words as it soars above the instrumental accompaniment and choruses, certainly may be interpreted as the power of the Eternal Feminine to mediate between humanity and heaven. But her power is confined: controlled by Gabriel's decision to return the Soul to earth—to be reincarnated as *man*—the Soul's vocalise is framed by Gabriel's cadence.[49] As he intones, "Dann ist dein Ich gelöscht" [Now is your ego dissolved], Gabriel's is the last—and only—voice heard.

THE POLITICS OF ANDROGYNY

Schoenberg's musical representation of the Soul as the Eternal Feminine would seem, by the time of the First World War, to label him as conservative, bourgeois, and decidedly old-fashioned—despite the radical "music of the future" to which he alludes in his *Harmonielehre*. Indeed, in the oratorio we may perhaps read Schoenberg's acceptance of the gender ideologies of his age: the sinful female must be rendered speechless; the feminine soul separated from real women (sopranos) and appropriated as an aspect of the male psyche. Such a conservative, even misogynistic stance certainly reflected the modes of thought and expression of many of Schoenberg's contemporaries, including writers Schoenberg particularly admired such as Karl Kraus, August Strindberg, and Otto Weininger.[50] In the visual arts of the time, too, there are numerous extreme examples in which women's individuality and power were portrayed as deadly threats to men. Munch's *Vampire* print (1893) of a woman devouring her male partner and Klimt's grotesque female figures labelled as *The Hostile Powers* in his Beethoven frieze (1902) are just two such works of art with which Schoenberg probably was familiar.[51]

Schoenberg himself was not immune to such fears. In a letter that he sent to Richard Dehmel in December 1912, Schoenberg wrote that he wanted to compose an oratorio on modern man's struggle to find God. Requesting such a text from Dehmel, Schoenberg explained:

> It is *not* through any action, any blows of fate, least of all through any love of woman, that this change of heart is to come about. Or at least these should be no more than hints in the background, giving the initial impulse. And above all: the mode of thought, the mode of expression should be that of modern man: the problems treated should be those that harass us.[52]

By 1915, when Schoenberg began to write the libretto of his oratorio, one problem that harassed modern man was the war; another was the "woman question"—the issue of women's emancipation. National emancipation movements began to organize in Germany and in Austria only in the mid-1890s: by the war they had made little progress in the legal arena.[53] Nevertheless, small changes had started to occur. The following passage from Otto Weininger's book reveals the inroads that women had made in Vienna by 1903 and the threat that they appeared to pose to men:

> By the term emancipation of a woman I imply neither her mastery at home nor her subjection of her husband. I have not in mind the courage which enables her to go freely by night or by day unaccompanied in public places, or the disregard of social rules which prohibit bachelor women from receiving visits from men, or discussing or listening to discussions of sexual matters. I exclude from my view the desire for economic independence, the becoming fit for positions in technical schools, universities and conservatoires or teachers' institutes. And there may be many other similar movements associated with the word emancipation which I do not intend to deal with. Emancipation, as I mean to discuss it, is not the wish for an outward equality with man, but what is of real importance in the woman question, the deep-seated craving to acquire man's character, to attain his mental and moral freedom, to reach his real interests and his creative power.[54]

Anti-feminist—and anti-female—publications such as Weininger's gained immense popularity in the prewar years as gender, class, religion, and nationality became increasingly more contentious issues in the volatile Hapsburg Empire. During the years immediately preceding the war, especially in Vienna, Weininger's sexual science functioned as a buffer against nascent social change.[55]

In fact, Weininger, at the conclusion of his book, also advances an androgyny of the future; but Weininger's androgyny, unlike Schoenberg's, is a pessimistic, futile symbol. Weininger prophesies:

> Death will last so long as women bring forth, and truth will not prevail until the two become one, until from man and woman a third self, neither man nor woman, is evolved.[56]

In Weininger's androgyny men and women, rather than becoming equals, are replaced. But other studies from the early years of this century suggest that androgyny was associated in some circles with social equality. Fritz Giese's study of early Romantic androgyny, *Der romantische Charakter: Die Entwicklung des Androgynenproblems in der Frühromantik* (1919), specifically links the question of women's emancipation with resurgent interest in androgyny in the era leading up to and including the First World War.[57] Similarly, Edward Carpenter, in the 1918 edition of his book *The Intermediate Sex*, associated the arrival of the "New Woman" with the emergence of "androgynous types" and with a growing sense of equality in behavior and in the workplace.[58]

I suspect that Schoenberg was also aware of the views of the well-known Viennese intellectual and feminist Rosa Mayreder. Her 1905 book, *Zur Kritik der Weiblichkeit*, was criticized by Schoenberg's intellectual associate Karl Kraus but highly praised by his friend and postwar employer, Dr. Eugenie Schwarzwald.[59] Mayreder devotes the entire final chapter of her study to a discussion of the history of the androgynous ideal.[60] She looks at its origins in Plato's *Symposium*, in Jewish mysticism, in Christian thought, and in Buddhism.[61] She then lists its traces in the nineteenth-century writings of Goethe, Balzac, Friedrich Schlegel, Schopenhauer, and Richard Wagner, and notes its reemergence in the latest psychological theories.[62] Androgynous images, she argues:

> represent the most fervent longings of mankind, longings which, in an infinite variety of forms, strive to express themselves, and which have become clearly articulate in the writings of great dreamers, religious

> and profane. . . . They are the natural yearnings for a higher state of ex-
> istence, for more perfect conditions, in which an imperfect humanity
> may advance towards enlightenment and a higher life.[63]

Mayreder suggests that the current "extraordinary interest" taken in androgyny:

> declares itself as a symptom of discordant conditions from which a
> new order can only be evolved by recognition of the new elements.[64]

Perhaps the war itself prompted a shift from the nihilistic, futile androgyny of Weininger's imagination to an androgynous ideal such as
Mayreder's. The war in Europe forced issues of gender and class to be
rethought to such an extent that, by 1918, women in Austria and Germany were given the vote.[65] Even Schoenberg was distanced by the war
from the insular artistic circles of Vienna and Berlin and, after a period of
military training, he found himself working for the Austrian army for
twelve hours a day, sleeping in cheap, noisy boarding houses in Vienna,
and rubbing shoulders with men—and women—from walks of life previously unknown to him.[66] It was just at this time that Schoenberg began
to plan the revisions of his *Harmonielehre* for its second printing. One
wonders whether wartime experiences played into his newly acquired
perception of the tonal system as a tonal battlefield.

A MUSIC OF THE FUTURE

It was also just at this time that Schoenberg tried to complete the musical
setting of *Die Jakobsleiter*. The war directly interrupted Schoenberg's
composition of his oratorio music when, in September 1917, he was
called up for a second period of military service.[67] Discharged in December 1917, Schoenberg seems to have rethought his conception of the oratorio. Most strikingly, he now decided to convey the main *ideas* of the
remaining libretto text, without setting any of the words.

In the music composed after Schoenberg's war service, an orchestral
interlude immediately following the Soul's vocalise replaces a long
monologue in the published libretto in which the Angel Gabriel calls
upon the souls to transform themselves once again into human forms.
Schoenberg then departed from his libretto entirely and ended the oratorio with a wordless, ethereal duet for soprano souls. Schoenberg's own
diagrams and notes map out the staging of this section.[68] While tenor and

bass soloists remain onstage, female soloists are removed. *Die Seele* (the original soul) now sings offstage in an orchestra Schoenberg marks as "*Fernorchester*" [distant orchestra]. A new soprano soul sings onstage, but she is placed behind the main orchestra.[69] She thus functions as an angelic timbre rather than as a soprano soloist. The souls are accompanied by female voices which are placed in an offstage chorus and which—like both souls—sing without words. Gabriel's voice is silenced. At first, the voices of the two souls merge with the orchestra and with the chorus, but their duet then extends beyond the boundaries of the instrumental music.[70]

The music that Schoenberg composed for his oratorio ends with an ecstatic, transcendent high C sung by the original soul, offstage.[71] While the unseen, sirenic voices retain their power as symbols of the mysterious unknown, the brevity of the souls's disembodied duet makes the audience aware of its existence as an impossible ideal—one that Schoenberg was not able to sustain.

In effect, their brief duet replaces the entire second half of Schoenberg's libretto.[72] Yet it is in this substantial section of the text not set to music that Schoenberg explicitly presents an androgynous ideal, which is explained by a character Schoenberg designates as *ein Gott* [a God]. In his typed copy of the libretto Schoenberg describes the god as "*Apollo, Athene*"; as a god that combines aspects of the male god of poetry and music with the warrior goddess of wisdom.[73] Gustav Klimt's famous depiction of Athena, the guardian of Vienna, is possibly the image that Schoenberg had in mind for the god of his oratorio.[74] As Carl Schorske discusses, Athena is a complex figure who featured in turn-of-the-century art as a symbol of ambiguous asexuality. Klimt's famous *Pallas Athene* (1898), dressed for battle in golden chainmail, gazes enigmatically at the viewer; an amalgamation of Joan of Arc, ancient warrior hero, and the "new woman."[75]

In keeping with his androgynous archetype of an "Apollo-Athene" deity, Schoenberg's god, in the brief passages that he sketched for it, is sung by a female alto (see Figure 3-1). To the character of *der Auserwählte* [the Chosen One] who has thought himself superior to others, Schoenberg's Apollo-Athene god promotes a vision of equality. In this passage the god sings:

> Blick um dich: Allen stehst du gleich nah!
> Weilt dein Blick auf Höchstem und Niedrigstem,
> glaubst du immer näher ihm zu kommen.

> Wendest du dich ab, erkennst du
> wie fern du beiden bist:
> Allen gleich nah und fern,
> umschliessen sie dich wie Mauern,
> denen du nur entrinnst,
> wenn dein entrückter Blick sie verliert.
> [Look around you: you stand equally close to all!
> While you look at the highest one or the lowest
> You always think that you are becoming more like that one.
> If you turn aside, you perceive
> How distant you are from both;
> All, equally near and far,
> Surround you like walls,
> From which you can only escape
> If your entranced gaze loses them.][76]

The god then advocates a future ideal where androgyny starts within the psyche. To the Chosen One, the god explains:

> Auf unteren Stufen nützte Scheidung. Du musst homogen werden.
> [On the lower steps division was useful. (But) you must become homo-
> geneous.][77]

In his final prayer the Angel Gabriel rephrases this desired homogeneity of the human spirit as mankind's desire for reintegration with God. Gabriel asks:

> Lass uns wieder ein ganzes werden, mit jenem Ganzen, dessen Teil
> wir jetzt sind!
> [Let us again become a whole, with that whole whose parts we now
> are!][78]

Yet Schoenberg never achieved a musical setting of the androgynous ideal expressed by Gabriel and by the god in his libretto. Indeed, as I have argued, Schoenberg's music for the first half of his libretto is limited by an inherited language of musical tropes and symbols: despite his efforts to express an asexual ideal I suspect that most listeners familiar with some of the Western art-music tradition—and with contemporary popular vocal styles too—would still associate the voices of the Dying One and the Soul with the female sex and interpret them as essentialist expressions of feminine gender—that is, as the Eternal Feminine.

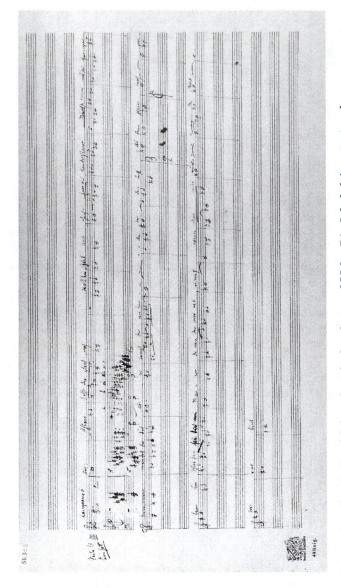

Figure 3–1. Facsimile of Schoenberg's sketch page 355 for *Die Jakobsleiter*: text and music for *ein Gott* [a God]. Reproduced by permission of the Arnold Schönberg Center, Vienna, and Belmont Music Publishers, Pacific Palisades, California 90272.

But there is a twist: while modern audiences can listen to recordings or even to the occasional live performance of *Die Jakobsleiter*, Schoenberg's oratorio was only *read* by his pupils and colleagues; strangely enough, none of them actually *heard* its music. In fact, while the oratorio music remained unfinished, unpublished, and unknown during Schoenberg's lifetime, both parts of his libretto were first published in 1917—and both were republished in 1926.[79] In addition, the complete libretto—without music—was recited at two concerts of the Society for Private Musical Performances in Vienna and Prague in the early 1920s. At these concerts all the parts—including those of the Dying One and the Soul—were spoken by a solo male reciter, Wilhelm Klitsch, who was a well-known Austrian actor. Schoenberg, who coached Klitsch for the performances, was very pleased with the result.[80] Perhaps this style of performance—a recitation of the entire libretto—deserves to be revived.

Moreover, while the music of the oratorio fragment fails in its attempt to express Schoenberg's androgynous vision, I would suggest that it triumphs in one important respect; that is, it succeeds in highlighting the predominant ideologies of prewar Viennese culture as insurmountable obstacles to such an ideal. At the same time, however, Schoenberg realized how those obstacles might be overcome: the crucial text that Schoenberg gives to Gabriel and to the god indicates that, by reconciling the divided aspects of one's own psyche, Schoenberg believed that one might then be able to challenge conventional attitudes to sex and to gender—even if he was not yet able to realize this reconciliation in musical terms. Indeed, Schoenberg hints at these changes in a passage following his discussion of the asexuality of angels in the *Harmonielehre*:

> And even if our tonality is dissolving, it already contains within it the germ of the next artistic phenomenon. Nothing is definitive in culture; everything is only preparation for a higher stage of development, for a future which at the moment can only be imagined, conjectured.[81]

Many years later Schoenberg resurrected the androgynous language of his oratorio's libretto to validate his twelve-tone compositional method. *Die Jakobsleiter* begins with the Angel Gabriel's description of heaven:

> Ob rechts, ob links, vorwärts oder rückwärts, bergauf oder bergab— man hat weiterzugehen, ohne zu fragen, was vor oder hinter einem liegt. Es soll verborgen sein. . . .

[Right or left, forward or backward, uphill or downhill—you must go on. Do not ask what lies in front or behind. It must be hidden. . . .][82]

In a 1941 lecture, "Composition with Twelve Tones," Schoenberg describes twelve-tone thinking in the same terms:

The unity of musical space demands an absolute and unitary perception. In this space, as in Swedenborg's heaven (described in Balzac's Seraphita) there is no absolute down, no right or left, forward or backward.[83]

In Schoenberg's utopian formulation—in contrast to the polarity of the tonal system—his twelve-tone method operates in a neutrally-charged space in which all tones relate to one another, equally. With this powerful image, Schoenberg perhaps once again hoped to invoke an asexual musical language; one capable of overcoming the prejudices of his musical heritage. Yet theorists now concede that this formulation, too, was an impossible ideal.[84] Schoenberg, in fact, was never able to find a musical language appropriate for his oratorio's completion. Perhaps today, eighty years after Schoenberg's first efforts to develop a musical androgyny, composers of our own time should consider taking up the challenge.

NOTES

1. Arnold Schoenberg, *Theory of Harmony*, trans. Roy E. Carter (Berkeley and Los Angeles: University of California Press, 1978), 96. For the equivalent passage from the first edition of his harmony textbook, in which Schoenberg makes no reference to gender dualism or to *die Zweigeschlechtlichkeit* [double-sexuality or bisexuality], see Arnold Schönberg, *Harmonielehre* (Leipzig and Vienna: Universal Edition, 1911), 112–13. I would like to thank Joseph Auner for bringing these passages to my attention.

2. Most of the text and music sources for the oratorio are described in Jean Christensen's comprehensive study, "Arnold Schoenberg's Oratorio *Die Jakobsleiter*," 2 vols. (Ph.D. diss., University of California, Los Angeles, 1979); hereafter cited as Christensen, "*Die Jakobsleiter*."

3. Jeffrey Kallberg, *Chopin at the Boundaries: Sex, History and Musical Genre* (Cambridge, Mass., and London: Harvard University Press, 1996), 62–86; Robert Walser, *Running with the Devil: Power, Gender, and Madness in Heavy Metal Music* (Hanover and London: Wesleyan University Press, 1993), 124–36.

4. Jean-Jacques Nattiez, *Wagner Androgyne: A Study in Interpretation*, trans. Stewart Spencer (Princeton: Princeton University Press, 1993); reviewed by Brian Hyer, *Journal of the American Musicological Society* 47 (1994): 531–40.

5. A. J. L. Busst, "The Image of the Androgyne in the Nineteenth Century," in *Romantic Mythologies*, ed. Ian Fletcher (London: Routledge and Kegan Paul, 1967), 8–12.

6. There are several outstanding contributions in the vast literature on androgynous images: Busst, "The Image of the Androgyne," 1–95; Albert Béguin, "L'Androgyne," *Minotaure* 11 (1938): 10–13; and Diane Long Hoeveler, *Romantic Androgyny: The Women Within* (Philadelphia and London: Pennsylvania State University Press, 1990).

7. Plato, *Symposium*, ed. Louise Ropes Loomis, trans. B. Jowett (New York: Walter J. Black, 1942), 178–83.

8. Kari Weil discusses Freud's reinterpretation of Plato's myth: *Androgyny and the Denial of Difference* (Charlottesville and London: University Press of Virginia, 1992), 2–3.

9. See, for example, Rossetti's masculinized *Joan of Arc* (1864) in *Dante Gabriel Rossetti*, ed. Alicia Craig Faxon (New York: Abbeville Press Publishers, 1989), 154. On the androgyny of Joan of Arc see Marjorie Garber, *Vested Interests: Cross-Dressing and Cultural Anxiety* (New York: Routledge, Chapman and Hall, 1992), 215–17.

10. Pairs of sexually ambiguous androgynes feature in the title page, contents page, and frontispiece designed by Beardsley for Wilde's *Salome* (1894); see Linda Gertner Zatlin, *Aubrey Beardsley and Victorian Sexual Politics* (Oxford: Clarendon Press, 1990), 68–69.

11. On Klimt's popularity and artistic style see Carl Schorske, "Gustav Klimt and the Crisis of the Liberal Ego," in *Fin-de-Siècle Vienna: Politics and Culture* (New York: Vintage Books, 1981), 208–78. Munch's prints were also exhibited many times in Berlin between 1893 and 1913 as part of his "Frieze of Life" collection: *Munch: The Frieze of Life*, ed. Marie-Helen Wood (London: National Gallery Publications, 1992), 70–72.

12. On androgyny in Balzac's tales, see Busst, "The Image of the Androgyne," 76–85; and Weil, *Androgyny and the Denial of Difference*, 79–112.

13. Schoenberg owned copies of Balzac's *Séraphîta* in French and in German: both volumes, especially the German translation, are heavily annotated in Schoenberg's handwriting. In this essay I have rendered *Seraphita* without accents—the guise in which it occurs both in the German translation and in Schoenberg's own writings.

14. Schoenberg to Kandinsky, 19 August 1912, *Arnold Schoenberg, Wassily Kandinsky: Letters, Pictures and Documents*, ed. Jelena Hahl-Koch, trans. John

C. Crawford (London and Boston: Faber and Faber, 1984), 54. Schoenberg expressed the same opinion in a letter to Alma Mahler of 11 November 1913: see *Arnold Schönberg: Lebensgeschichte in Begegnungen*, ed. Nuria Nono-Schoenberg (Klagenfurt, Austria: Ritter, 1992), 125.

15. Schoenberg's *Seraphita* plans and music have been transcribed by Christensen, *"Die Jakobsleiter,"* 2: 3–5.

16. Weininger's 1903 treatise was widely read: by 1906 it had been reprinted six times and had been translated into English. Several reviews and substantial excerpts from it also appeared in issues of Karl Kraus's journal *Die Fackel* just after the initial printing of the book and Weininger's suicide.

17. Wilhelm Fliess, *Vom Leben und Tod: Biologische Vorträge* [*Of Life and Death: Biological Essays*] (Jena: Diederichs, 1909). In a letter to Schoenberg dated 20 June 1915, Berg praises Fliess's book and mentions that he will show it to Schoenberg: see *The Berg-Schoenberg Correspondence*, ed. Juliane Brand, Christopher Hailey, and Donald Harris (New York: W. W. Norton, 1987), 248–49.

18. Douglas Jarman discusses Fliess's influence on Berg's music in "Alban Berg, Wilhelm Fliess and the Secret Programme of the Violin Concerto," *International Alban Berg Society Newsletter* 12 (1982): 5–6.

19. Lewis Wicks, "Schoenberg's *Erwartung* and the Reception of Psychoanalysis in Musical Circles in Vienna until 1910/1911," *Studies in Music* 23 (1989): 88–106. Schoenberg subscribed to *Die Fackel* in most years between 1906–19: his annotations in selected issues, particularly those of 1906–1909, indicate that he read Kraus's aphorisms and articles carefully.

20. Kraus, *Die Fackel* 8, no. 210 (October 1906): 26–27.

21. Ibid., paraphrase mine. The Freud-Fliess debate is discussed by Marjorie Garber, *Vice Versa: Bisexuality and the Eroticism of Everyday Life* (New York: Touchstone, 1995), 169–206; see also Peter Heller, "A Quarrel over Bisexuality," in *The Turn of the Century: German Literature and Art, 1890–1915*, ed. Gerald Chapple and Hans H. Schulte (Bonn: Bouvier Verlag, 1981), 87–115.

22. C. G. Jung, *The Psychology of the Unconscious: A Study of the Transformations and Symbolism of the Libido*, trans. Beatrice M. Hinkle (1917; reprint, Princeton: Princeton University Press, 1991).

23. Edward Carpenter, *Intermediate Types Among Primitive Folk: A Study in Social Evolution* (London: George Allen and Co., 1914), 71–83.

24. Schoenberg owned three volumes of Tagore's poetry in German translation: *Der Gartner* (German translation published in 1914), *Gitanjali* (trans. 1914), and *Fruchtlese* (trans. 1916).

25. The texts by Tagore and Dehmel that Schoenberg intended to use in his symphony are translated by Walter B. Bailey, *Programmatic Elements in the Works of Schoenberg* (Ann Arbor: UMI Research Press, 1984), 88–97.

26. Charlotte M. Cross discusses Tagore's philosophy of death in "Schoenberg's *Weltanschauung* and His Views of Music: 1874–1915" (Ph.D. diss., Columbia University, 1992), 225–31.

27. See Sara Friedrichsmeyer, *The Androgyne in Early German Romanticism: Schlegel, Novalis and the Metaphysics of Love* (Berne, Frankfurt, and New York: Peter Lang, 1983), 15–22.

28. These influences are outlined by Karl H. Wörner, *Die Musik in der Geistesgeschichte: Studien zur Situation der Jahre um 1910* (Bonn: H. Bouvier and Co., 1970), 171–200.

29. Balzac's adaptation of Swedenborg's philosophy is discussed by Busst, "The Image of the Androgyne," 78–83.

30. In December 1916 Schoenberg received abridged versions of Boehme's *Morgenrote im Aufgang, Von den drei Prinzipien*, and *Vom dreifachen Leben*, ed. Joseph Grabisch (Munich and Leipzig: R. Piper, 1912).

31. Jacob Boehme, *The Three Principles of the Divine Essence*, trans. John Sparrow (London: John Watkins, 1910), 160–61.

32. At the outbreak of war, in a series of notes that he later labelled as "Meine Kriegspsychose (1914)" ["My War Psychosis (1914)"], Schoenberg hailed Boehme as a great German mystic: Arnold Schoenberg Institute Archive, unpublished text manuscript T23.1.

33. Schoenberg finished his oratorio's libretto in 1917, but he only completed the first half of his oratorio's music. A 1977 recording of this half of the oratorio, conducted by Pierre Boulez, was rereleased in 1993 on compact disk as Schoenberg, *Die Jakobsleiter, Chamber Symphony No. 1, Begleitmusik zu einer Lichtspielszene*, Ensemble InterContemporain, the BBC Singers and the BBC Symphony Orchestra (Sony Classical SMK 48462). The 1993 reissue includes an English translation by Lionel Salter of the first half of the libretto. Schoenberg's full libretto manuscript (in German) and its complete English translation by Christensen are given in her study, "*Die Jakobsleiter*," 2: 6–50.

34. Schoenberg's own table, dividing the solo roles into G[*esang*] and S[*prechstimme*], may be found on a leaf inserted in the main sketchbook that Schoenberg used for his oratorio's composition (currently labelled as Sketchbook IV, page 30b, Sk 347).

35. Alan Lessem briefly examines some associations between characters in Balzac's *Seraphita* and the various roles in Schoenberg's oratorio: Lessem, *Music and Text in the Works of Arnold Schoenberg: The Critical Years, 1908–1922* (Ann Arbor: UMI Research Press, 1979), 180–84.

36. Christensen labels and transcribes these drafts as *Die Jakobsleiter* Text Sources A and B (JTS A, JTS B1, and JTS B2): "*Die Jakobsleiter*," 2:51–116.

The original manuscripts are currently housed in the Arnold Schoenberg Institute Archive.

37. For example, on page 10v of JTS B1, Schoenberg crossed out *"der"* before *"Sterbende"* and replaced it with *"die,"* which he underlined three times for emphasis: transcribed by Christensen, *"Die Jakobsleiter,"* 2:78.

38. *"Ein Seele"* appears, for example, on page 7r of JTS A: Christensen, *"Die Jakobsleiter,"* 2:63. *"Seele"* appears without gender on page 8r of JTS A (ibid., 2:65) and in the published libretto: Schönberg, *Die Jakobsleiter Oratorium* (Vienna: Universal Edition, 1917), 14 and 17.

39. These references occur on pages 29–30 of Schoenberg's short score for his oratorio. These have been reproduced in the published version, which was completed after Schoenberg's death by his pupil Winfried Zillig: Arnold Schönberg, *Die Jakobsleiter Oratorium (1917–1922) (Fragment)*, scored by Winfried Zillig, ed. Rudolf Stephan (Mainz: B. Schott's Söhne; Vienna: Universal Edition, 1985).

40. Michel Poizat, *The Angel's Cry: Beyond the Pleasure Principle in Opera*, trans. Arthur Denner (Ithaca and London: Cornell University Press, 1992), 105. Elizabeth Wood uses the term "transferable" to describe the disruptive and erotic power of the transsexual voice in "Sapphonics" in *Queering the Pitch: The New Gay and Lesbian Musicology*, ed. Philip Brett, Elizabeth Wood, and Gary C. Thomas (New York and London: Routledge, 1994), 32.

41. Schönberg, *Die Jakobsleiter Oratorium* (1917), 14.

42. On the transcendent female voice in other Schoenberg compositions see David Lewin, "Women's Voices and the Fundamental Bass," *The Journal of Musicology* 10 (1992): 464–82.

43. Although Schoenberg clearly indicates that the Dying One and the Soul are to be sung by the same soprano, Boulez employs two soloists: Ortrun Wenkel (*der Sterbende*), and Mady Mesplé (*die Seele*).

44. Unfortunately, in the commercial recording of *Die Jakobsleiter* most widely available, Boulez either chose to omit the entire *Sprechstimme* chorus or the recording levels were set so that the chorus parts are rendered completely inaudible. These texts are, however, all included in Zillig's completion of Schoenberg's musical score.

45. Translated by Christensen, *"Die Jakobsleiter,"* 2:39–40.

46. On the convergence of the Eternal Feminine and the androgynous ideal in constructions of the Romantic artist see Hoeveler, *Romantic Androgyny*, 7–17.

47. For a detailed history of the "Eternal Feminine" see Marilyn Chapin Massey, *Feminine Soul: The Fate of an Ideal* (Boston: Beacon Press, 1985).

48. Schoenberg, "Gustav Mahler" (memorial lecture, 1912; revised 1948), reprinted in *Style and Idea: Selected Writings of Arnold Schoenberg*, ed. Leonard

Stein, trans. Leo Black (Berkeley and Los Angeles: University of California Press, 1975), 470.

49. The last words of the *Sprechstimme* chorus are: "Er muss noch lange wandern!" [*He* still has far to go!].

50. Schoenberg praises both Strindberg and Weininger in the preface to the first edition of the *Harmonielehre*: Schoenberg, *Theory of Harmony*, 2.

51. Klimt's Beethoven frieze is reproduced and discussed by Schorske, *Fin-de-Siècle Vienna*, 254–63. Munch's *Vampire* lithograph was exhibited many times in Berlin before the war and, like Klimt's frieze, was included in the Berlin Secession of 1902.

52. *Arnold Schoenberg Letters*, ed. Erwin Stein, trans. Eithne Wilkins and Ernst Kaiser (London: Faber and Faber, 1964), 35. The original text of Schoenberg's letter is given by Joachim Birke, "Richard Dehmel und Arnold Schönberg: Ein Briefwechsel," *Die Musikforschung* 11 (1958): 282.

53. See Harriet Anderson, *Utopian Feminism: Women's Movements in Fin-de-Siècle Vienna* (New Haven and London: Yale University Press, 1992).

54. Weininger, *Sex and Character*, trans. from the 6th German edition (London: William Heinemann; New York: G. P. Putnam's Sons, 1906), 65.

55. Elaine Showalter discusses this point in *Sexual Anarchy: Gender and Culture at the Fin de Siècle* (New York: Viking Press, 1990), 8–9.

56. Weininger, *Sex and Character*, 345.

57. Fritz Giese, *Der romantische Charakter: Die Entwicklung des Androgynenproblems in der Frühromantik* (Langensalza: Wendt und Klauwell, 1919), 7. I am grateful to Jeffrey Kallberg for bringing Giese's study to my attention.

58. Edward Carpenter, *The Intermediate Sex: A Study of Some Transitional Types of Men and Women*, 5th ed. (London: Allen and Unwin, 1918), 16.

59. Rosa Mayreder, *Zur Kritik der Weiblichkeit*, 2d ed. (Jena: Diederichs, 1907); translated by Herman Scheffauer as *A Survey of the Woman Problem* (New York: George H. Doran, 1913). Schwarzwald's associations with Mayreder and with Schoenberg are mentioned by Anderson, *Utopian Feminism*, 104–10.

60. Mayreder, *Zur Kritik der Weiblichkeit*, 2d. ed., 261–98; *A Survey of the Woman Problem*, 242–75. All subsequent references are to the 1907 German edition and the 1913 English translation.

61. Ibid., German ed. 265–67; English trans. 246–47.

62. Ibid., German ed. 272–78; English trans. 252–58.

63. Ibid., German ed. 261; English trans. 242.

64. Ibid., German ed. 262–63; English trans. 243.

65. Renate Bridenthal, "Something Old, Something New: Women between the Two World Wars," in *Becoming Visible: Women in European History*, ed. Renate Bridenthal and Claudia Koonz (Boston: Houghton and Mifflin, 1977), 424.

66. Information concerning Schoenberg's military service is included in *Arnold Schönberg: Lebensgeschichte*, ed. Nuria Nono-Schoenberg, 146–52; Willi Reich, *Schoenberg: A Critical Biography*, trans. Leo Black (New York and Washington: Praeger, 1971); and in letters sent by Schoenberg during the war to his brother-in-law, Alexander Zemlinsky, some of which have been published in *Alexander Zemlinsky: Briefwechsel mit Arnold Schoenberg, Anton Webern, Alban Berg und Franz Schreker*, ed. Horst Weber (Darmstadt: Wiss. Buchgesellschaft, 1995).

67. Schoenberg wrote the date 19 September 1917 and the comment "*einrücken zum Militär!*" [report for military service!] on page 96 of his oratorio draft score (Sketchbook IV, Sk 418).

68. See, for instance, Sketchbook IV, page 30f (Sk 350) and Sk 454, transcribed by Christensen, "*Die Jakobsleiter*," 2:131 and 2:162.

69. The soprano soul is placed in an orchestra designated by Schoenberg as the "*Orchester in der Höhe*" [orchestra in the heights]: Sketchbook IV, pages 106–08 (Sk 428–30).

70. Schoenberg's draft score ends at this point in his sketchbook: this is also the oratorio "ending" in Boulez's commercial recording.

71. Schoenberg, Sketchbook IV, page 134 (Sk 452). Alexander Ringer transcribes the final measures of the souls's duet and discusses their extraordinary nature as "completion" in *Arnold Schoenberg: The Composer as Jew* (Oxford: Clarendon Press, 1990), 178–79.

72. Schoenberg sketched only brief, disjunct passages of music for the second half of his oratorio.

73. Transcribed by Christensen, "*Die Jakobsleiter*," 2:22, from Schoenberg's manuscript libretto, DICH[tung] 14, page 19.

74. Ubiquitous color reproductions of Klimt's *Pallas Athene* are reprinted in many *fin-de-siècle* monographs and commercial art-house calendars: see, for instance, Schorske, *Fin-de-Siècle Vienna*, 223.

75. See Schorske's excellent discussion of Klimt's transformation of Athena; *Fin-de-Siècle Vienna*, 212–23.

76. Schönberg, *Die Jakobsleiter Oratorium* (Vienna, 1917), 20–21, translation mine. Schoenberg's musical setting of this passage is found in Sketchbook IV, page 35 (Sk 355); transcribed by Christensen, "*Die Jakobsleiter*," 2:285–86.

77. Schönberg, *Die Jakobsleiter Oratorium*, 21; trans. Christensen, "*Die Jakobsleiter*," 2:44.

78. Schönberg, *Die Jakobsleiter Oratorium*, 27; trans. Christensen, "*Die Jakobsleiter*," 2:47.

79. The 1917 libretto was reprinted in Schoenberg, *Texte* (Vienna: Universal Edition, 1926).

80. Christensen, *"Die Jakobsleiter,"* 1:29. See also Schoenberg's letter to Thor Johnson, 24 July 1950 in *Arnold Schoenberg Letters*, 282.

81. Schoenberg, *Theory of Harmony*, 97. In a footnote to the 1922 edition Schoenberg relates this passage to his country's defeat in the war.

82. Schönberg, *Die Jakobsleiter Oratorium*, 3; trans. Christensen, *"Die Jakobsleiter,"* 2:33.

83. Schoenberg, *Style and Idea*, 223: this passage was written by Schoenberg in English.

84. Despite Schoenberg's comparison of his twelve-tone universe to a neutral Swedenborgian heaven, tonal system tropes permeate his twelve-tone sketches and compositions; see, for instance, Ethan Haimo, *Schoenberg's Serial Odyssey* (Oxford and London: Oxford University Press, 1990), 85; and Anne C. Schreffler, "'Mein Weg geht jetzt vorüber': The Vocal Origins of Webern's Twelve-Tone Composition," *Journal of the American Musicological Society* 47 (1994): 294–98.

CHAPTER 4

Von heute auf morgen
Schoenberg as Social Critic

STEPHEN DAVISON

Von heute auf morgen [*From One Day to the Next*] was Arnold Schoenberg's response to *Zeitoper*, the extraordinarily popular operatic genre of
the later 1920s.[1] Why did Schoenberg write *Von heute auf morgen*, his
only compositional foray into light-hearted comedy? Was he truly attracted to *Zeitoper*, a genre that attempted to capture the spirit of the time
through the use of contemporary themes and characters; or was he in fact
rejecting it, intending his opera as an alternative and a critique? What
does the opera tell us about Schoenberg's attitude toward popular culture, specifically the cultural life in Berlin of the period? The relationship
of Schoenberg's opera to *Zeitoper* is not a simple one. This essay explores some of these issues through an examination of both the libretto
and music of the opera, in the context of the political, social, and cultural
climate of the time.

AMERICAN INFLUENCES ON GERMAN CULTURAL LIFE IN THE LATE 1920s

Schoenberg composed *Von heute auf morgen* in 1928, near the end of a
period of political and economic stability in Germany; a period that had
begun in 1924 with the stabilization of the currency. The Wall Street stock
market crash, with its devastating effect on the German economy and subsequent rise in the power of the Nazis, was yet one year in the future. At
this time the country was enjoying a veritable explosion in artistic activity. German governments of the day tended to be middle-of-the-road—
right-of-center at the federal level, and left-of-center in its most important

province, Prussia.[2] The arts, and opera in particular, were thriving during this period, enjoying the benefits of increased spending as a result of generous subsidies from all levels of government, and increased revenues from a newly enriched public.[3] Nowhere was this more evident than in Berlin, which became the most important cultural center in Europe during these years. When Otto Klemperer became musical director at the newly independent Kroll Opera in 1926, the city boasted three State-subsidized opera houses, in addition to the numerous private theaters in which musical dramatic works were produced.

During this period there were very significant American economic and cultural influences in Germany. Under the Dawes plan, 800 million gold marks, mostly from American banks and finance houses, were loaned to revive Germany's finances; agreements were established between the German and American film industries, providing distribution opportunities for American films;[4] and American performers, especially jazz musicians, were finding enthusiastic audiences. As the critic and Schoenberg biographer, H. H. Stuckenschmidt, reported:

> America, in many respects, was a great model, and we were eager to know all American art, American jazz, American dance, and so on. . . . Everything that came from America, except the business, interested us deeply.[5]

Writers, artists, and composers included American themes and influences in their works: for instance, Lion Feuchtwanger parodied American efficiency and attention to detail in the poem "Music," and Bertolt Brecht placed his city of Mahagonny somewhere between Florida and Alaska. American influence in Berlin was so great that the Soviet novelist Ilya Ehrenburg, returning after an absence of five years in 1927, called the city "an apostle of Americanism." He found a smoothly functioning municipality full of practical new inventions; a model of American efficiency.

American entertainment, particularly cinema, jazz, and sport, became increasingly prominent in Germany—in Berlin in particular—and these themes, along with technology and urban life, became key elements in the work of a wide range of artists in Europe and Russia in the 1920s.[6] Jazz had increased steadily in popularity in Germany since the end of the World War, and was propagated principally by the public's interest in jazz-related dances. The fox-trot and the tango were popular in 1918, followed by the one-step and the Boston (1919), the shimmy (1921), and the two-step (1922).[7] In 1925 Sam Wooding and his band

were the first of many American bands to visit Germany, with Paul
Whiteman following in 1926. Both these bands played initially in Berlin,
the most important center for jazz performances of all types, including
those by the increasing number of native German jazz ensembles. The
black dancer Josephine Baker visited Berlin in 1925, introducing the
Charleston for the first time. More than any other single figure Baker represented a freedom and lack of inhibition that many associated with
America, and with jazz in particular.

A GENRE FOR THE TIMES

In opera, the passion for jazz was reflected most obviously in the short-
lived genre of *Zeitoper*. It began with the extraordinary success of Ernst
Krenek's *Jonny spielt auf* [*Jonny Strikes Up* (the Band)], premiered in
1926, and continued with works such as Kurt Weill's *Der Zar lässt sich
photographieren* [*The Czar Has His Photograph Taken* (1927)] and Paul
Hindemith's *Neues vom Tage* [*New of the Day* (1928)].[8] This genre, which
dominated the operatic stage of the period between 1926 and 1931, reflected the spirit of the age often referred to as *die Neue Sachlichkeit* [the
new objectivity]. In all of the arts there was a movement to capture everyday subject matter with detachment, with a deemphasis—even renunciation—of the artistic individuality that had characterized the preceding
expressionist movement. In art, the subject of everyday life came to dominate, and on the stage the attributes of modern life became common
through documentary techniques. One that was incorporated into *Zeitoper*
was popular music, and most importantly, dance music and jazz.

Ernst Krenek's *Jonny spielt auf* is generally considered to be the pro-
totype of the genre, and the rise and fall of its popularity generally parallels that of *Zeitopern*.[9] It contains all the elements we associate with the
genre: stage settings and characters drawn from real life, and a libretto
that mixes comedy with social observations. Elements of modern technology—trains, automobiles, loudspeakers, and radio—are prominent features, and the musical score incorporates features of jazz harmony and
rhythm, at least as much as Krenek understood them. The two principal
characters are a black jazz musician, Jonny, and an intellectual composer,
Max. These two characters clearly represent the old and the new; the received, stable culture of the Old World versus the vitality of the New
World; the inwardly focused, brooding romantic artist versus the uninhib-
ited, confident, and brash jazz musician. At the opening of the opera Max
is to be found at the edge of a glacier attempting to conquer the moun-

tains, an unambiguous symbol of his artistic struggle. Away from the mountain, in the company of ordinary folk, he lacks confidence. Jonny, on the other hand, is confident in the modern world. He follows opportunities as they arise, attempting to seduce the chambermaid and then stealing a valuable violin when the seduction fails. At the end of the opera Max realizes that he, too, must overcome his inaction, that he must take control of his own destiny and "catch the train that leads to life."[10] He leaps onto the train after his love, the singer Anita, to follow her to America. In the words of the final chorus, "the glittering New World comes across the sea and conquers old Europe through dance."[11]

Krenek's relatively simple musical language is a step back from his previous atonal works. He incorporates jazz idioms to illustrate the character of Jonny while maintaining a straightforward lyrical style for Max and Anita. In addition he incorporates jazz and popular dance numbers at appropriate dramatic moments, including a "Shimmy," "Blues,"—both so marked in the score—and a tango. In 1931 Krenek published an article giving his reasons for choosing to incorporate jazz idioms into the music: the pursuit of relevancy, and as a foil to atonality.

> Firstly I thought that by using the jazz elements I might hit on an atmosphere that would fit the collective feeling of the age. As jazz music in practice enjoyed undisputed mastery and general validity, it seemed conceivable that from it one might derive an artistic means that after all belonged to the sphere of music, and so was capable of the most serious and intellectual development, while at the same time having a natural place in the life of modern man. This, I felt, might give me the possibility of saying something generally valid.
>
> The second consideration was an internal musical one. As must be fairly well known, there has been a complete disruption of musical systems [i.e. the advent of atonal music]. . . . At first atonality . . . extended the range of musical means to infinity, theoretically at least, so that today there is really nothing that is musically impossible. Every conceivable harmonic combination can be produced at any time, without special preparation, and a new organization from this quarter is not to be hoped for. So far atonality has not proved particularly suitable for versatile dramatic presentation and in the circumstances jazz, with its stereotyped harmonic and rhythmic elements, seemed an effective protection against the ineffectual ubiquity of all musical possibilities, because it offered a sort of new convention. . . . In my attempt, as in all the others I know of, jazz was only alluded to at the points demanded

by the action; apart from this the harmony was colored by its elements, thus guaranteeing the homogeneity of the whole and justifying the way I had deliberately limited the means—a protection against atonality.[12]

This is a retrospective statement: by the time Krenek wrote it jazz was already fading as a source of inspiration for composers.[13]

SCHOENBERG AND HIS PUBLIC

During the 1920s Schoenberg felt increasingly divorced from contemporary developments in musical composition and out of touch with composers of the younger generation such as Krenek and Hindemith. He was among the very few significant composers not to incorporate popular musical styles into his works. His aim, however, was in some respects parallel to that expressed by Krenek: to guarantee "the homogeneity of the whole." Schoenberg rejected the use of jazz and other popular idioms to do this, and instead worked to develop a coherent atonal system of composition: the "method of composing with twelve tones."[14] In the 1937 lecture, "How One Becomes Lonely," he writes:

Though the reasons my opponents gave for their opposition to my music were ridiculous, though their arguments were as confused as possible, since I could not be at one time myself and my own opposite, and though I could laugh about such nonsense, nevertheless, on the other hand, the unanimity of the rebuke was frightening. It was frightening to such an extent that even among some of my pupils an uncertainty appeared and some of them turned to the new fashions of composing which were promoted by the different composers of the so-called New Music. It was the first time in my career that I lost, for a short time, my influence on youth. This took place between 1922 and 1930, and during this time almost every year a new kind of music was created and that of the preceding year collapsed. It started with the European musicians imitating American jazz. Then followed "Machine Music" and "New Objectivity" (*Neue Sachlichkeit*) and "Music for Every Day Use" (*Gebrauchsmusik*) and "Play Music" or "Game Music" (*Spielmusik*) and finally "Neo-classicism." While all this happened and so many styles developed and passed away, I did not enjoy my splendid isolation very cheerfully. . . . I saw with regret that many a great talent would perish through a corrupt attitude towards the arts,

which aimed only for a sensational but futile success, instead of fulfill-
ing the real task of every artist.[15]

During this period Schoenberg was composing his first twelve-tone
works. Far from Krenek's claim that "a new organization from this quarter [i.e., atonality] is not to be hoped for," Schoenberg was demonstrating
the extraordinary flexibility of his "method of composing with twelve
tones" with an outpouring of works for piano, chamber and choral ensembles, orchestra, and the stage.[16] These years were a time of great personal
achievement, but also of increasing alienation from other contemporary
trends in European music. While Schoenberg was demonstrating the validity of developing and extending an atonal musical language, his contemporaries looked to other styles, both historical and contemporary, for
inspiration: Igor Stravinsky was adopting mannerisms of eighteenth-century music in his "neoclassic" works; Kurt Weill was simplifying his harmonic language, utilizing elements of popular styles, and, in works such
as the *Mahagonny Songspiel* and *Die Dreigroschenoper* [*Threepenny
Opera*], developing a new song style that reached intellectual and general
audiences alike; and Paul Hindemith was tempering his earlier expressionistic style by turning to Baroque models.

In "How One Becomes Lonely" Schoenberg continues with a statement that clearly sets him apart from the majority of the significant composers of the period:

> One of the accusations directed at me maintained that I composed only
> for my private satisfaction. And this was to become true, but in a differ-
> ent manner from that which was meant. While composing for me had
> been a pleasure, now [between 1922 and 1930] it became a duty. I
> knew I had to fulfill a task: I had to express what was necessary to be
> expressed and I knew I had the duty of developing my ideas for the
> sake of progress in music, whether I liked it or not; but I also had to re-
> alize that the great majority of the public did not like it.[17]

Schoenberg's ideal of progress in music was based on continuing the
great German tradition in music, extending it through the development of
the twelve-tone technique, rather than reaching out to other musics—
popular and otherwise—or back into musical history for inspiration.
Schoenberg was never one to compromise in order to gain an audience.

Schoenberg's criticisms of his contemporaries—especially promising younger composers such as Hindemith and Krenek—are often

couched in moral terms. In the essay "Linear Counterpoint" of 1931 he acknowledges that both Hindemith and Krenek are capable of writing "good and beautiful music," but that he finds them lacking in conscience: "Their unconcern [for the correct use of traditional musical forms] strikes me as a lack of conscience and bears witness to a disturbing lack of responsibility." He goes on to admit that his criticism is influenced "by their mania for success, their publicity, and their skill in using their elbows."[18] In Schoenberg's critique of Krenek's first full-length opera, *Sprung über den Schatten* [*Leaping Over the Shadow* (1923)], he finds "a lack of real faith in what is uncertain, untested, problematic, dangerous: the essence of composition with twelve tones." In this work Krenek incorporates jazz-inspired elements into his early dissonant musical style, but Schoenberg finds the atonal musical elements "accepted merely as a matter of taste, a fashionable commodity," with the tonal elements derived from a "superstitious belief in the need for tonality, in the eternal laws of art, handed down but quite un-felt." Schoenberg could not countenance the random mixture of musical style in this way: "I heard from the very first moment that these [dissonant] chords will not, for the time being, mix with those used earlier."[19]

VON HEUTE AUF MORGEN AS SOCIAL AND CULTURAL CRITIQUE

Schoenberg had always felt that when properly introduced to well-prepared and open-minded audiences his music could be successful. In the case of his twelve-tone comic opera, *Von heute auf morgen*, he was particularly hopeful. His confidence was such that he turned down an offer of 30,000 marks for publication rights from the firm of Bote und Bock— about 1½ times his annual salary—in order to publish the work himself. In Schoenberg's view, his stature as a composer and the commercial potential of the score were both such that he should receive a better offer. He subsequently lost money on the publishing venture.[20]

Max Blonda, the librettist, is a pseudonym for Schoenberg's second wife, Gertrud (née Kolisch), and this work is probably as much in honor of their love as anything else. It is possible they chose the name "Max" as a reference to the character of the composer in *Jonny spielt auf*, the brooding, internalized intellectual. Indeed, the opening sentence in *Jonny*, "Du schöner Berg!" [Lovely mountain!], sung by Max, must have been intended as a reference to the more senior composer; and it is possible that the Schoenbergs' opening line, "Schön, war es dort!" [How wonderful it

was there!] is a reference back to *Jonny*.[21] However despite these corre-
spondences *Jonny spielt auf* is not a model for *Von heute auf morgen*.
Schoenberg's opera has a much more serious intent, both musically and
dramatically. It displays the mature twelve-tone technique, using the technique simultaneously to demonstrate its musical and dramatic effective-
ness and to critique both social and cultural attitudes of the period. At the
surface level it is also a direct criticism of Krenek's opera.

The libretto has much in common with other *Zeitopern*; the musical
score, on the other hand, is an example of Schoenberg's complex twelve-
tone technique, and bears little resemblance to those of Krenek, Weill, and
Hindemith. The comedy relies on parody, social satire, and burlesque as
dramatic tools, and it incorporates many aspects of contemporary life—a
studio apartment setting, a telephone call, a radio—with ordinary, recognizable characters engaged in an everyday activity, a domestic squabble. It
also features ideas much discussed at the time, especially the rôle of
women in modern society and in a modern family. The discussion between
the husband and wife, who are unnamed characters in the expressionist
manner, revolves to a large extent around what it means to be modern, and
their disagreement concerning the rôle of women in society. It is certain
that Gertrud Schoenberg would have been familiar with views expressed in
the following contemporary extract concerning contemporary women:

> To all appearances, the distinction between women in our day and
> those of previous times is to be sought only in formal terms because
> the modern woman refuses to lead the life of a lady and a housewife,
> preferring to depart from the ordained path and go her own way. . . .
>
> The woman of yesterday lived exclusively for and geared her ac-
> tions toward the future. . . .
>
> In stark contrast, the woman of today is oriented exclusively toward
> the present. That which is decisive for her, not that which should be or
> should have been according to tradition.[22]

In order to demonstrate her "modernity," the wife in *Von heute auf morgen* announces her intention to live for the present, to reject the traditional ties and duties of marriage and parenthood: "Man will doch
schliesslich auch sein eignes Leben" [After all, one should be free to lead
one's own life].[23]

Sexual freedom is also used as a sign of liberation. In the Wife's major
aria, in mm. 283–305 and its musical recapitulation at mm. 483–505, the
Wife announces her plan to take numerous lovers. She will start that

evening, adopting lovers as easily as friends, but forgetting them again when she tires of their company. She will take them as they are, even two at a time, whether old and rich, or young and poor, whether a well-dressed avaricious athlete, or a badly dressed spiritual philosopher. She will live her life without plan, as caprice dictates, and as time allows. Only when she has completely forgotten her husband can he hope to win her back.

In the following contemporary view of the sexual revolution, the poet and journalist Lola Landau links many of the same ideas found in *Von heute auf morgen*: marital crisis, new definitions of morality, and the suggestion that men need to come to terms with the "new woman":[24]

> Unnoticed, a mighty revolution in ways of life had already been com-
> pleted in reality when people first began to discuss openly the crisis in
> marriage.
>
> At the center of these fermenting forces is the woman of our day. As
> an autonomous person economically and intellectually independent
> from the man, the new woman shattered the old morality. The compul-
> sory celibacy of the young woman and the indissolubility of marriage
> were invalidated by the straightforward reality of life. The independent
> woman of today, just as much as the man, assumes for herself the right
> to a love life before marriage. . . .
>
> [If] the man of today continues to seek the woman of yesterday, his
> creature, the pliant helpmate, he will be bitterly disappointed not to
> find her anymore.
>
> Marriage and its value as the cell of community is threatened with
> crisis. For new ideas of marriage have not yet caught on. What is per-
> mitted today? Nearly everything. But what is truly good? What is bad?
> The warning signals of inhibition no longer function.[25]

DRAMATIC AND MUSICAL STRUCTURE

Von heute auf morgen premiered in Frankfurt on 1 February 1930, re-
ceiving only four performances. Although the performances were generally considered to be successful, the opera was not performed again until
the 1950s, and has never entered the general opera repertory. Despite
their transient success, this is also true of *Jonny* and the other *Zeitopern*
of the period.[26]

Although neither the libretto nor the music have labelled divisions,
the opera falls naturally into a number of well-defined sections. The
twenty sections listed below should be interpreted as *ad hoc* to a certain

extent, imposed on the music to provide points of reference. Some sections reflect obvious large-scale recapitulations of the music, while others reflect significant dramatic and musical transitions.

Setting: A modern living room/bedroom.

A. 1. (m. 1) Upon arrival home from a party the Husband expresses his admiration for an old friend of his wife's, who was present in the company of a singer, a tenor. He expresses his dissatisfaction with the cares of ordinary life. His wife expresses her surprise at his dissatisfaction.

    2. (m. 97) They exchange impressions of the Wife's friend.

    3. (m. 168) They exchange impressions of the Singer.

    4. (m. 254) In a duet in which they sing the same text, each vows to show the other that they can live differently, without chains, underestimation, or sacrifice.

    5. (m. 283) The Wife sings an aria in which she outlines her plan: she will dye her hair, paint her face, and take admirers by the dozen.

    6. (m. 314) "Glaubst du wirklich, du kannst mich erschrecken . . . ?" [Do you really think you can scare me . . . ?], he replies. He will turn instead to his wife's friend.

B. 7. (m. 330) The Wife changes into a "stunning negligee"; her husband is astounded. He sings a passionate song in her praise.

    8. (m. 418) "Glaubst du wirklich, du kannst mich erwärmen . . . ?" [Do you really think you can thrill me . . . ?], she replies. She will turn instead to the Singer.

    9. (m. 436) The man mocks the Singer, imitating him. He appeals to his wife again; she rebuffs him.

    10. (m. 483) The woman continues to describe her new life of freedom: she will take lovers of every imaginable type.

    11. (m. 516) She starts to tease her husband, ordering him around and encouraging his jealousy. She dances, singing to herself. The child enters, and is also rebuffed by the woman.

    12. (m. 582) The doorbell rings; it is the gasman, to collect monies owed. To her husband's annoyance she refuses to take this seriously, continuing her mock self-infatuation.

    13. (m. 663) The telephone rings; it is the Singer, who explains that he and his friend would like the couple to join them at the bar. They hang up.

14. (m. 759) The Husband pleads with her not to go out as she is
    currently dressed; he admits his unhappiness and his jealousy.
15. (m. 830) He expresses his misery in a passionate outburst.
C. 16. (m. 851) "Soll ich wieder ich sein?" [Shall I be myself
    again?], she asks. They make up; she reveals that the dress
    belongs to her sister.
D. 17. (m. 940) The Singer and his companion arrive. They mock
    the married couple; they have been waiting for them in vain.
    They ask how the married couple can be so happy: "Ich
    dachte, Sie sind ein Mann / eine Frau von heute" [I thought
    that you were a modern man/woman].
18. (m. 1073) The Singer and Friend give up: "Die sind veraltet,
    leben in vergangenen Idealen und Wünschen" [They are old-
    fashioned, believe in old ideals and desires].
19. (m. 1112) The Singer and the Friend take their leave, saying,
    "Ihr aber seid verblasste Theaterfiguren!" [But you're simply
    faded theater characters!]
E. 20. (m. 1116) The married couple comment: "Regie führt bei
    Ihnen die Mode. . . . Und dabei finde ich sie heute schon
    nicht einmal mehr ganz modern. Das ändert sich eben von
    heute auf morgen." [Their play is directed by fashion. . . .
    And yet I don't find them all that very modern today. But that
    changes from one day to the next.] As the curtain falls the
    child asks, "Mama, was sind das: moderne Menschen?"
    [Mama, what are modern people?]

The following musical recapitulations occur: (1) Section 10 repeats
the music of section 5, and is the "second verse" of the Wife's aria; (2)
Section 8, in which the Wife mocks her husband, is an inversion of section 6, in which the Husband mocks his wife. The Wife has turned the ta-
bles on her husband in the intervening section 7. Although these are the
only "repetitions" in the score, and the score is essentially through-composed, that is, without frequent pauses or repetitions to delineate traditional musical forms, there are numerous well-defined arias, ariettas, and
recitatives. These set pieces are generally short, and the listener's ability
to find structure in the work is aided greatly by the extraordinarily close
relationship between the music and the text.

The letters A-E in the outline of the libretto above mark a broader
dramatic motion. In part A the Wife becomes increasingly distraught as
her husband reminisces about the evening. In part B she takes the upper

hand and her husband becomes increasingly upset. Their reconciliation occurs in part C. In part D the "modern" couple arrives and the attitudes of the two couples are contrasted. In part E the married couple encapsulate the evening's activities with their final comments.

MUSICAL TECHNIQUES AND CHARACTERISTICS

Although over seventy years have passed since Schoenberg first developed his twelve-tone method of composition, there is still much about it that is misunderstood, by both musicians and nonmusicians alike. *Von heute auf morgen* was the first major work by Schoenberg to utilize all of the major features of the twelve-tone method, and before proceeding with a discussion of music and text relationships in the opera it seems prudent to outline the most important features of the technique.[27]

The following list of features is not ordered according to importance, but rather to facilitate an understanding of the techniques used by Schoenberg in composing his music to the opera.

1. The music is based on an ordered set of all twelve pitch classes, commonly referred to as the "row."[28] The row upon which *Von heute auf morgen* is based is often used in two discrete halves of six notes each—referred to as the two "hexachords" of the row. There is an important variant of the row used throughout the work, in which the notes of the second hexachord are arranged to form a simple—though nontonal—scale pattern. (This variant appears predominantly as a melody rather than as a harmony; i.e., the pitches appear in succession within the same octave, rather than simultaneously in one or more octaves. It appears in Figure 4-2, discussed below.)

2. There are forty-eight different possible forms in which the row can appear: the twelve possible chromatic transpositions of: (i) the original row, (ii) its retrograde (i.e., sounding backwards), (iii) its inversion (i.e., upside down), and (iv) its retrograde inversion (i.e., backwards and upside down).[29]

3. Not all row forms are of equal importance. The original row form (i.e., without any transposition) and its *inversion transposed up five chromatic steps* appear at the most important points in the opera: the beginning and end, and at important dramatic moments.[30] In addition, the relationship of *inversion transposed up five chromatic steps* between any two rows is the most important way in which harmonies are created throughout the opera. This is

because pairs of rows related this way have complementary hexachord pitch content, that is, the pitches in the first hexachord of row 1 are the same as the pitches in the second hexachord of row 2, and vice versa. This property allows Schoenberg to present all twelve pitches using two different row forms rather than one, and also to create harmonic motion from row form to row form.

4. Not all pitches are equally represented. Individual pitches do receive emphasis for compositional and dramatic reasons. The twelve-tone technique, however, does ensure that all twelve pitch classes appear on a regular basis.

5. The pitches of the rows are regrouped into smaller subsets (i.e., the rows are partitioned) for compositional and dramatic reasons.

These characteristics of the musical system are exhibited in the musical examples below. Figure 4-1 consists of the final three measures of the opera (mm. 1129–31). The upper staff—labelled "Prime Form"—is based on the principal form of the row: 1st hexachord = D, E-flat, A, D-flat, C-flat, F; 2nd hexachord = A-flat, G, E, C, B-flat, F-sharp. The notes are numbered 1 to 12 to indicate the order in which they appear in the Prime Form. The lower staff—labelled "Inversion"—is based on the inversion transposed up four half steps: 1st hexachord = G, F-sharp, C, A-flat, B-flat, E; 2nd hexachord = C-sharp (D-flat), D, F, A, B (C-flat), D-sharp (E-flat). Again, the notes are numbered to indicate the order in which they appear in the inverted form of the row. The relationship between these rows is that described in no. 3 above: the first hexachord (six notes) of the Prime Form and the second hexachord (six notes) of the Inversion contain the same notes, reordered. It follows also that the second hexachord (six notes) of

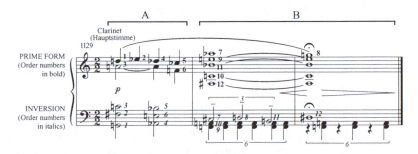

Figure 4-1. *Von heute auf morgen*, mm. 1129–31. Used by permission of Belmont Music Publishers, Pacific Palisades, California 90272.

the Prime Form and the first hexachord (six notes) of the Inversion also have the same pitch content. For this reason, not only does the "harmony" in the final three measures contains all twelve chromatic pitches twice— once in each staff—but all twelve pitches also appear first in m. 1129 (bracket A), and then again in m. 1130–31 (bracket B). The tonal spectrum is saturated in both the vertical and horizontal directions. This is typical of Schoenberg's twelve-tone practice.

It is equally important to note, however, that theme, melody, and order are also all present. The melody in these measures, in the clarinet, marked "*Hauptstimme*" [principal part] in the score, is the most important theme of the work, representing the reconciliation of the husband and wife. This theme, consisting of notes 1, 2, 4, 5, 7, and 8 of the row, although an ordered subset of the row, is not a segment of the row. The essential character of this theme is stability and closure (i.e., cadential), created both by the rising of the bass combined with the falling in the treble register, and the turning in on itself of the melody in m. 1129.

Another important feature to note is the step-wise motion in the melody. Many of the melodies and thematic fragments in the opera feature motion by half- and whole-steps. This motion is a fundamental feature of the alternate form of the second hexachord of the row, as shown in Figure 4-2 (mm. 201–06). Here the Wife is describing her conversation with the Singer—imitating him—to her husband. She uses the alternative, step-wise version of the second half of the row, associated with the shallow-minded Singer and, by extension, his companion, their views, and "modern" views in general. Again we find a tendency to contrary motion between the outer parts, leading naturally to a cadence in m. 205.[31] The rapid changes in emotion—*schmelzend* [sweet], *pathetisch* [emotional], *schwungvoll* [spirited], *kläglich* [miserable]—and in dynamics—ranging from pianissimo to fortissimo—are quite typical of the score.

Figure 4-3 (mm. 547–55) will serve as the basis for discussion of popular dance and associated rhythmic attributes. Here the Wife vocalizes as she dances a few measures of a modern dance. Although Schoenberg considered actually inserting a current number, he composed his own, twelve-tone one, and the "popular" nature of the "song" is reinforced by the doubling of the voice part by the saxophone.[32] For clarity the musical example produced here gives only the vocal/saxophone part and the accompanying rhythmic patterns.[33]

The most striking feature of the rhythmic accompaniment is the figure marked "X," a rhythm that J. Bradford Robinson has associated with Weimar Germany's obsession with jazz.[34] Robinson traces this figure

Figure 4-2. *Von heute auf morgen*, **mm. 201–6 (voice and principal accompaniment melody only). Used by permission of Belmont Music Publishers, Pacific Palisades, California 90272.**

through many works of the period, by Karol Rathaus, Wilhelm Grosz, Kurt Weill and Alban Berg. He argues convincingly that German musicians developed their own brand of jazz, combining techniques derived from their frequently inaccurate perceptions of the American genre with European genres of popular music. This rhythmic figure featured prominently in work after work, and appears as the first "variant of the basic rhythm" in the most prominent German jazz manual of the day, *Das neue Jazz-Buch* by Alfred Baresel. In *Jonny spielt auf* it is associated with the title character, who is a jazz musician. Music from *Jonny* was so often played that for many people the music was synonymous with their understanding of jazz,

Figure 4-3. *Von heute auf morgen*, mm. 547–55 (voice, saxophone, and rhythm of accompaniment only). Used by permission of Belmont Music Publishers, Pacific Palisades, California 90272.

and it is therefore not surprising that this rhythmic figure should be used by Schoenberg to indicate a popular dance.

Schoenberg's other references to dance and jazz are subtle, however. They are embedded in a structure of complex rhythms and counterpoint that assumes a major commitment from the audience. None of his contemporaries expected as much; composers such as Weill, Hindemith, and Krenek deliberately simplified their style to maintain avenues of communication.[35]

Many traditional operatic devices are to be found in *Von heute auf morgen*, supporting the word/music relationships. There are numerous leitmotives, a number of them full-fledged melodies, many others simply short musical figures. The thematic density of the musical material is quite extraordinary, with rapid changes in mood and musical material with every turn of the text. A brief look at the opening 33 measures will be enough to illustrate the point.

The Husband's lyrical opening phrase, "Schön war es dort!" [How wonderful it was there!], is provided with a melodic counterpoint by a solo cello (Figure 4-4). This phrase, based on the row, recurs a number of times in association with his passionate outbursts. His melodic line breaks into a strong triplet rhythm as he mentions the Friend's "glorious teeth," becoming a lilting waltz as he describes her "supple figure." His wife's responses are in recitative; they are brief and matter-of-fact. When she does break into song, in m. 33 ("Träumst du noch immer?" [Are you still dreaming?] it is with a variant of the Husband's opening melody, and the accompaniment of a distorted version of his "passion" motive. The characters of the two protagonists are thus well-defined early and emphatically.

To illustrate the leitmotive technique, consider the following examples from this same section. In each case the melody shown in Figure 4-4 appears in the orchestral accompaniment: as the husband says that he can't stop thinking about the woman (mm. 20–22); as he sings of her beauty (mm. 105–07); as his wife states that she knows he is thinking of the other woman (mm. 216–21); and as he implies that his wife's friend is among "those who charm everyone." This leitmotive is clearly associated with the Husband's daydreams about his wife's friend. It appears in full at points in the drama where the text refers explicitly to the Husband's opinion or thoughts about the Friend. The motive also appears fleetingly, or in modified forms at other points where the text touches on the husband's infatuation. For example, it appears in m. 330 in the violins, at the point where the Wife transforms herself into the type of woman her husband has been lusting after. The object of his passion now shifts to his wife.

In what is perhaps an explicit acknowledgement of this Wagnerian technique, there are two references to the music of Wagner in the opera. In section 13, the telephone conversation, the Singer sings of seeing the light from the wife's "glowing eyes" (m. 693–694). The Husband shouts

Figure 4-4. *Von heute auf morgen*, mm. 6–10 (cello only). Used by permission of Belmont Music Publishers, Pacific Palisades, California 90272.

"Siehe Rheingold," referring to the final scene of *Rheingold* where Fasolt, unwilling to let Freia go, can see the gleam of her eye through the stack of gold. In section 17 (m. 999), the Singer quotes both text and music from the first act of *Die Walküre*, "Schmecktest du mir ihn zu?" [Will you taste it for me?], incorporating the quotation seamlessly into the twelve-tone structure.[36] In *Walküre*, an exhausted Siegmund has been offered a drink of "creamy rich mead" by Sieglinde; but he wishes to spare her his misfortune. In *Von heute auf morgen* all seriousness and chivalry are absent; the Singer is simply trying to impress: "schmeckt ein Milchkaffee sicher wie Gin" [café au lait would surely taste like gin]. It is a commentary on the shallowness of the Singer that his talk is always exaggerated, with grand gestures—and quotations of great works—even as he talks about everyday concerns.

The references to Wagner are symbolic of a heritage of which Schoenberg was well aware, and which is clearly evident in the opera. In common with both Wagner's music dramas and subsequent musico-dramatic works by other composers, including Schoenberg's own earlier operas *Erwartung* [*Expectation*] and *Die glückliche Hand* [*The Lucky Hand*], the music is through-composed, and the musical texture is embedded with themes that are associated with characters and ideas, although not often as obviously as in Wagner's music dramas. In addition, as in Wagner's music, it is possible to identify relationships between various motives and melodies. This last characteristic is partly a result of the way in which Schoenberg uses the twelve-tone system, but also partly despite his use of the system.

SCHOENBERG ON *VON HEUTE AUF MORGEN*

Schoenberg's own comments on *Von heute auf morgen* are limited in scope. The principal documents are an April 1930 draft for a publicity flier that he sent to Benno Balan, the young man who assisted in Schoenberg's self-publication of the score, and a letter of 4 October 1929 to Wilhelm Steinberg, conductor of the Frankfurt premiere.[37] He intended the work to be light entertainment; "only those who care to do so need accept the deeper meaning."

> [The opera] is a portrait of how dangerous it is to rock foundations for the sake of fashion.
>
> It is a portrait of people who are silly enough to convert principles—with which fashion of course merely tries to show off—into practice;

people who risk their marital happiness without suspecting that fashion content, with superficialities may in its turn again glorify that very marital happiness.

Those who consider not just this obvious meaning but the double meaning of the many puns will easily perceive the other themes that may certainly be considered alongside.[38]

In his letter to Steinberg, Schoenberg provides notes on characterization, and instructions on how to rehearse the opera:[39]

The girlfriend should pretend to be very witty, without being so in the least. She should be rather insipid, affected, superior, "sophisticated," false. . . .

The comic effect of the Singer is based on his self-satisfaction. . . . He is very witty, knows that he has all kinds of success and uses what he has without forcing it at all. . . .

The man is also comical up to a point. Especially because of his wavering attitudes, his easy irascibility and his self-importance. . . .

On the other hand, the most prominent characteristics of the Wife, who is not supposed to be funny in any way, and who, therefore, cannot and should not have a comic success, are intelligence, naturalness and tenderness. Without ever being sentimental, she should always show warmth. However, the temperament which she must display in the "disguise" scenes will be most convincing when it is seen to conceal anger, stubbornness, and a desire for revenge. Nevertheless she is quite uncomplicated (while the other three characters are all more or less "pseudo-complex" in the modern manner) and transparent.

Schoenberg warns against some common practices of the time and urges that his music be trusted:

[The singers] must not (as is all too customary in Berlin and elsewhere in Germany) do nothing but scream the text all evening, so that the stage-directors are quite right when, in opera too, they take the whole responsibility on themselves instead of allowing music and song to have their full effect. My opera is vocally conceived from A to Z—in fact, to such an extent that there are hardly any longer instrumental interludes. . . .

The singing and acting must always remain dignified. The singers must never "characterize" at the expense of vocal beauty, must never exaggerate. Better colorless than crude—better no humour than this disgusting slapstick which is rampant in Berlin. They do not need to worry—it is not necessary to "help out" my music; in itself it is so characteristic that, when it is performed correctly, all the characterization is automatically present.

In summary, Schoenberg writes:

The tone of the whole should actually be very light. But one ought to feel, or sense, that behind these simple events something else is hidden; that these everyday characters and happenings are being used to show how, above and beyond this simple story of a marriage, the so-called modern, the merely modish exists only "from today till tomorrow," from a shaky hand to a greedy mouth—not only in marriage, but no less in art, in politics and in attitudes towards life.

SCHOENBERG'S COMMITMENT TO PRINCIPLE

In *Von heute auf morgen* Schoenberg attacks the contemporary view of "modernity." He rejects superficial "fashion" and "elegance." In the opera the Husband is captivated by his wife's friend, who with the Singer represents the "people of today." They set the modern trends, are the talk of the town, are new and exciting. As the Wife reveals in discussing her friend, the Friend "has not known pain" and she has not born children. She does however have a beautiful figure and no shortage of admirers. In contrast the Wife represents solidity and tradition. She is quite capable of playing the role of the modern lover, but this only shows how easy it is to do so. It is clear that she has known pain, and that she has born children. For her, life is a lot more serious.

The Singer also has physical attributes to sway his audiences: his beautiful voice. During the telephone conversation it is clear that his conversation is fatuous and his praise empty, with emotional reactions that are grossly exaggerated and theatrical.

The Husband is the common man. He is easily swayed by current fashions, and after the transformation of his wife into a "modern" woman, he praises her in exactly the same way that he had formerly praised her friend. Clearly the positive attributes that he perceives are superficial for they can be transferred from one person to another as easily as changing a dress. Ultimately he recognizes the superficiality of the "modern" life and recommits himself to his marriage.

As they take their leave, the Singer and the Friend dismiss the married couple's "old ideals and desires." The married couple respond:

Mann:	"Und dabei finde ich sie heute schon nicht einmal mehr ganz modern." [And yet I don't find them all that very modern today.]
Frau:	"Das ändert sich eben von heute auf morgen." [But that changes from one day to the next.]

If we interpret *Von heute auf morgen* as a critique of *Zeitoper* it is clear that Schoenberg was correct: it was a short-lived genre, here one day and gone the next, with musical scores and plots that now seem dated rather than modern. Schoenberg's score suffers less from this problem than others of the period as a result of his refusal to adopt musical symbols so closely tied to the time and place; his use of the twelve-tone technique places the work firmly within the context of his compositional output. To Schoenberg the twelve-tone system represented an artistic advance. It was "modern" in the positive sense: building on the past but providing an avenue for development. Similarly, he did not advocate throwing away old social and political values, but preferred building on them to find a way forward. Schoenberg was never quite the revolutionary he was made out to be; for him the twelve-tone system was a way of preserving the past, not overthrowing it. Gertrud Schoenberg's libretto, however, is clearly of its time, and although it may lack the depth of other texts Schoenberg set—his own included—it still places integrity and faithfulness to a commitment above the temptations that modern life has to offer.

Schoenberg saw about him a culture that was interpreting fad as art, the merely theatrical as drama, and empty phrases as true debate. Society was losing contact with past strengths, and "in art, in politics, and in attitudes towards life" was succumbing to simple pleasures and amusements. This was easy and entertaining, but anathema to Schoenberg.

Von heute auf morgen is best viewed as both critical of and participating in *Zeitoper*. It is Schoenberg's attempt to show that commercial success and adherence to high moral standards are not necessarily opposites, and that an artist can lead and challenge audiences while entertaining them. His references to female sexuality, the rôle of women in society, and their relationship to men are evidence of his familiarity with the subjects of public discourse at the time, and he would therefore expect the subject of the opera to be of interest to his potential audience.

But the most important element of the work is the adherence to principle, both between individual members of society—including husbands and wives—and between the artist and his public. Just as an artist must maintain his integrity as an artist and not succumb to the temptation of easy success, so individuals must behave with integrity toward each other. Just as the man in *Von heute auf morgen* is ready to abandon his marriage for the latest in fashionable women, so Schoenberg saw other composers abandoning their principles for fashionable success. The wife represents Schoenberg's ideal: she knows that her commitment is important and worth fighting for; she rejects the attention-seeking and hedonistic behavior she sees in society around her; but in order to make her point she can mimic this behavior perfectly. To mimic is easy; to really play the artist is difficult. As Schoenberg discovered, to find commercial success simultaneously is the most difficult of all.

NOTES

1. The term *Zeitoper* was coined in the 1920s, along with related terms such at *Zeitstück* and *Zeittheater*. As there is no precise English translation I will follow common practice and use the German term exclusively in this essay.

2. At the expense of both the Communists and the political right, voters in Prussia tended to support Socialist governments that increasingly abandoned their socialist aims "in favor of trying to make capitalism work more justly." John Willett, *Art and Politics in the Weimar Period: The New Sobriety, 1917–1933* (New York: Pantheon, 1978), 95.

3. Spending on both social and cultural projects had grown dramatically, especially in socialist-dominated centers such as Berlin and Frankfurt, where housing and town planning projects were socially and architecturally outstanding, and by 1927 unemployment had fallen sufficiently for an unemployment insurance scheme to be established. John Willett, *The Theatre of the Weimar Republic* (New York: Holmes and Meier, 1988), 96.

4. Ibid., 97.

5. Personal interview quoted in Susan C. Cook, *Opera for a New Republic: The* Zeitopern *of Krenek, Weill, and Hindemith*, Studies in Musicology 96 (Ann Arbor, Michigan: UMI Research Press, 1988), 42.

6. Musical examples include Arthur Honegger's *Pacific 231* (1923) and *Rugby* (1928), George Antheil's music for Fernand Léger's film *Ballet mécanique* [*Mechanical Ballet* (1926)], and his *Jazz Symphony* (1924), and Paul Hindemith's jazz-inspired *Suite "1922"* for piano (1922). Ernst Krenek's opera *Schwergewicht, oder Die Ehre der Nation* [*Heavyweight, or the Nation's Honor*],

is a satire on the hero worship of sports champions. Modern urban life was a key feature of *Zeitopern*, including *Von heute auf morgen*.

7. Michael H. Kater, *Different Drummers: Jazz in the Culture of Nazi Germany* (New York: Oxford University Press, 1992), 5.

8. Other works in the genre include Eugen d'Albert's *Die schwarze Orchidee* [*The Black Orchid*], Ernst Toch's *Prinzessin auf der Erbse* [*Princess upon the Pea*], Wilhelm Grosz's *Achtung! Aufnahme!* [*Attention! Shoot!*] and George Antheil's *Transatlantic*. For a discussion of these works, and of *Zeitoper* in general, see Cook, *Opera for a New Republic*.

9. In its premiere season *Jonny* was seen 26 times on four stages; the next season the opera was seen 421 times on 45 stages. Thereafter its popularity tapered off: 24 performances on eight stages in the 1928–29 season; 18 performances on four stages in 1929–30; and only four performances in Leipzig and Vienna during the 1930–31 season, after which it dropped out of sight. See Appendix D, "Statistics on Opera Performances," in Cook, *Opera for a New Republic*, 217–19. Cook's statistics are drawn from contemporary "Opernstatistik" articles in *Allgemeine Musikzeitung, Anbruch*, and elsewhere.

10. Ernst Krenek, *Jonny spielt auf*, Scene 10, Max.

11. Ibid., Scene 11, Chorus.

12. Ernst Krenek, "New Humanity and Old Objectivity," in *The Weimar Republic Sourcebook*, ed. Anton Kaes, Martin Jay, and Edward Dimendberg (Berkeley: University of California Press, 1994), 586–87. Originally published as "Neue Humanität und alte Sachlichkeit," *Neue Schweizer Rundschau* 24 (April 1931): 244–58.

13. As economic conditions deteriorated bands were reduced in size, and in Germany, traditional dances returned to favor in place of the American imports. See Gunther Schuller, *The History of Jazz,* vol. 1 of *Early Jazz: Its Roots and Musical Development* (New York: Oxford University Press, 1968), 356–57, and Kater, *Different Drummers*, 28, for brief discussions of this decline in the United States and Europe respectively.

14. Schoenberg described the method in a lecture at Princeton University on 6 March 1934. This lecture was repeated at the University of Southern California (Summer, 1935), and presented in its final form at the University of California at Los Angeles (26 March 1941). The lecture appears as "Composition with Twelve Tones" in *Style and Idea: Selected Writings of Arnold Schoenberg*, ed. Leonard Stein, trans. Leo Black (Berkeley: University of California Press, 1984), 214–45.

15. Arnold Schoenberg, "How One Becomes Lonely," in *Style and Idea*, 52.

16. Piano Suite, op. 25 (1923); Wind Quintet, op. 26 (1924); Four Pieces for Mixed Chorus, op. 27 (1925); Three Satires, op. 28 (1925); Suite for Seven Instruments, op. 29 (1926); String Quartet No. 3, op. 30 (1927); Variations for Orchestra,

op. 31 (1928); *Von heute auf morgen*, op. 32 (1929); Piano Pieces, op. 33a (1929) and 33b (1931); *Begleitmusik zu einer Lichtspielszene* [*Accompaniment to a Film Scene*], op. 34 (1930); and *Six Pieces for Male Chorus*, op. 35 (1930).

17. Schoenberg, "How One Becomes Lonely," in *Style and Idea*, 53.

18. Schoenberg, "Linear Counterpoint," in *Style and Idea*, 294.

19. Schoenberg, "Krenek's *Sprung über den Schatten*," in *Style and Idea*, 479.

20. For a description of Schoenberg's publication venture see Juliane Brand, "A Short History of *Von heute auf morgen* with Letters and Documents," *Journal of the Arnold Schoenberg Institute* 14, no. 2 (November 1991): 241–70.

21. Krenek also refers to Schoenberg obliquely at the beginning of Part Two of the opera, described as "Max in Erwartung." In this scene Max is waiting anxiously for his absent lover, as is the woman in Schoenberg's *Erwartung* [*Expectation*].

22. Elsa Herrmann, "This is the New Woman," in *The Weimar Republic Sourcebook*, 206–08. Originally published as *So ist die neue Frau* (Hellerau: Avalon Verlag, 1929), 32–43.

23. Schoenberg, *Von heute auf morgen,* mm. 294–300.

24. The original title of the opera, in an early draft of the libretto, was *Das Eheproblem* [*The Marital Problem*]. For an account of the creation of the libretto see Juliane Brand, "Of Authorship and Partnership: The Libretto of *Von heute auf morgen*," *Journal of the Arnold Schoenberg Institute* 14, no. 2 (November 1991): 153–239.

25. Lola Landau, "The Companionate Marriage," in *The Weimar Republic Sourcebook*, 702– 03. Originally published as "Kameradschaftsehe," in *Die Tat* 20, no. 11 (February 1929): 831–35.

26. The works of this period that we do remember, Kurt Weill and Bertolt Brecht's *Die Dreigroschenoper* (1928) and *Aufstieg und Fall der Stadt Mahagonny* [*Rise and Fall of the City of Mahagonny* (1930)], take the cabaret as their source for more meaningful social commentary than is generally found in *Zeitoper*. Kurt Weill's *Der Zar lässt sich photographieren* may be considered Weill's one true *Zeitoper*.

27. For a technical description of Schoenberg's mature twelve-tone technique see Ethan Haimo, *Schoenberg's Serial Odyssey: The Evolution of His Twelve-Tone Method, 1914–1928* (Oxford: Clarendon Press, 1990), Chapter 2, "Schoenberg's Mature Twelve-Tone Style." For a discussion of the musical language in *Von heute auf morgen* see my "Of its Time or Out of Step? Schoenberg's *Zeitoper*, 'Von heute auf morgen,'" *Journal of the Arnold Schoenberg Institute* 14, no. 2 (November 1991): 271–98.

28. In atonal music theory a "pitch class" contains all pitches that are regarded as equivalent, regardless of how they are notated and irrespective of oc-

tave placement. For instance, all the E-flats and D-sharps in all octaves belong to the same pitch class set.

29. Given that octave equivalency is assumed, there are only twelve different transpositions possible before returning to the starting point. The four orientations—left to right, right to left, upside up and upside down—are self-evident.

30. These row forms—and all pairs of rows that are related this way—are said to display "hexachordal inversional combinatoriality," because when the row is combined with its inversion five steps higher the pitch content of the two hexachords is reversed.

31. In m. 204, the C-natural in the lower part is an anomaly. If Schoenberg was following the row structure strictly, this pitch should be an F. (It is clearly a C in all the scores and manuscripts held by the Arnold Schönberg Center in Vienna.) This is actually very uncommon; deviations from row structure are quite rare in *Von heute auf morgen*, and in most cases, given that there seems to be no musical or dramatic reason for them, they are probably slips of the pen on the composer's part.

32. At this point in the first draft of the manuscript (Arnold Schönberg Center, ms. 2594) Schoenberg writes a note: "Instead of mm. 534–40, some other popular dance can also be played; however, probably better not. This one (consciously or unconsciously) is too firmly integrated into the whole from a motivic point of view!" The reference is to mm. 547–53; the measures were renumbered after the note was written.

33. In the manuscript of the first draft (Arnold Schönberg Center, ms. 2594) Schoenberg clearly separates the melody, the accompaniment, and counter-melodic elements.

34. J. Bradford Robinson, "Jazz Reception in Weimar Germany: In Search of a Shimmy Figure," in *Music and Performance During the Weimar Republic*, Cambridge Studies in Performance Practice, no. 3 (Cambridge, England: Cambridge University Press, 1994), 107–34.

35. This complexity aside, however, there are other attributes that align *Von heute auf morgen* with the *Zeitoper* movement, principally the use of orchestral effects to refer to modern life: the door bell (flexatone/piccolo, m. 581), the telephone ring (flute, piano, xylophone, m. 663), and the sound of static on the radio (tremolo and flute flutter tonguing, m. 543). These are simply coloristic effects however, and they are used in the same way composers have used them for centuries.

36. The melody and accompanying harmony come from Scene One, mm. 285–86. With the added G natural in the bass the pitches are identical to the second hexachord of the row.

37. Copies of both documents are in the correspondence collections of The Arnold Schönberg Center, Vienna. See also Brand, "A Short History," 241–70.

38. Schoenberg, draft of a flier, translated and quoted in Brand, "A Short History," 256–57. Used by permission of Mr. Lawrence Schoenberg, Belmont Music Publishers, Pacific Palisades, California 90272.

39. Schoenberg to Wilhelm Steinberg, 4 October 1929. Carbon copy in the correspondence collections of the Arnold Schönberg Center, Vienna. Translation in Josef Rufer, *The Works of Arnold Schoenberg: A Catalog of His Compositions, Writings and Paintings*, trans. Dika Newlin (New York: Free Press of Glencoe, 1963), 55–57.

CHAPTER 5

Schoenberg in Shirtsleeves
The Male Choruses, Op. 35

ROBERT FALCK

There is perhaps no institution as thoroughly German in its musical, social, and political dimensions as the *Männergesangsverein* [male choral society]. It is a "boys night out," an expression of class and political solidarity, and, often, an occasion for serious music making as well. The institution was about a hundred years old when Schoenberg composed his main contribution to its repertory, and organized workers' societies had been in existence for about forty years. Before op. 35 can be set against the larger historical and political backdrop of this movement, it must first be studied in light of Schoenberg's other musical works, both choral and instrumental. Only when we understand the pieces both individually and collectively will we be able read their political, or moral and ethical message.[1]

The bourgeois choral movement in Germany may be traced back as far as 1832, and workers' choral societies began informally in the 1860s. This double tradition is reflected by the separate national associations for each group: the *Deutscher Sängerbund* [German Singers' Federation, henceforth *DSB*], founded in 1862, for the former, and the *Deutscher Arbeiter-Sängerbund* [German Workers' Singers' Federation, henceforth *DASB*], founded in 1908, for the latter.[2] It was within the context of the workers' societies in the 1890s that Schoenberg had his first professional job as a musician.[3]

By the time of the Weimar Republic, the *DSB* consisted entirely of male choral societies, while the *DASB* had all-male, all-female and mixed societies. Although male societies dominated both national organizations, they were actually on the decline in the *DASB* relative to the more musically ambitious and politically correct mixed societies. With an increased emphasis on high-level performance of quality repertory came a *Verbürgerlichung* and depoliticization of the movement, which was not looked upon approvingly by the extreme left, but is the context in which op. 35 was composed.[4]

Franz Schubert must be considered the founder of the modern male chorus genre, and his forty-six pieces for male voices, both with and without instrumental accompaniment, still form the core of the repertory. Felix Mendelssohn, Robert Schumann, and Anton Bruckner are the best-known of the nineteenth-century composers who were major contributors to the repertory, though it is clear that the bourgeois societies were the consumers at whom their products were aimed. Among Schoenberg's older and immediate contemporaries, Max Reger contributed two substantial collections, all dedicated to individual bourgeois societies, and Richard Strauss composed many more such pieces, both unaccompanied and accompanied.[5] Both Strauss and Reger were thoroughly bourgeois in orientation, of course, and neither had any connection to the *DASB*.

Among his younger contemporaries, Paul Hindemith composed one collection exactly contemporary with Schoenberg's op. 35, to texts by Bertolt Brecht, Gottfried Benn, and Walt Whitman, and a single setting two years later of a poem by Friedrich Hölderlin. Two other collections, one in German and one in English, are from his American years.[6] Hanns Eisler, perhaps surprisingly, contributed only eleven works in five separate collections to the male chorus repertory between 1926 and 1933. The earliest of these is *Tendenz*, to a text adapted from Heinrich Heine, which anticipates the name *Tendenzlied* for the whole genre of politically militant songs. Pieces for mixed chorus and/or female or children's chorus far outnumber the male choruses.[7] I can find no evidence that any of this twentieth-century repertory was ever performed by any of the workers' societies.[8]

It is noteworthy that of those composers usually grouped together as the "second Viennese school," only Schoenberg himself and his erstwhile pupil Eisler composed any music for male chorus. As noted above, it was fast becoming an old-fashioned genre in the Weimar Republic, both for the politically left and for the aesthetically progressive. This explains why it was avoided by Alban Berg, Anton Webern, Alexander Zemlinsky, and relatively neglected in favor of more modern, mixed chorus pieces even by Eisler.

It is against this background that we must judge the *Sechs Stücke für Männerchor*, op. 35 [*Six Pieces for Male Chorus*], which were composed in two stages in 1929–30. Four date from February and March 1930, and the other two from about a year earlier. As the result of a direct commission from Albert Guttmann of the central committee of the *DASB* in Berlin, both "Glück" ["Happiness," no. 4] and "Verbundenheit" ["Bond," no. 6], the earliest of the set, were published in their *Männerchorsammlung* for 1929 and 1930.⁹ The *DASB* was actively seeking out composers of a slightly more modern bent in the late 1920s in order to modernize what had become a rather moribund repertory for the male chorus, so it is not surprising that they would approach the most famous modernist composer in Berlin and in Germany for a contribution to their collection.¹⁰

We must not imagine that only those pieces published by the *DASB* were accorded their approval. When the complete set was given its first performance by an amateur workers' choral society in Hanau near Frankfurt, the central committee in Berlin sent no less a figure than Walter Hänel, the leading proponent of musical modernism in their ranks, to present an introductory lecture on the pieces. This first performance, sung from memory, took place on October 27, 1931. The choral society that undertook this momentous task was the male contingent of the *Arbeitergesangsverein Vorwärts* [Workers' Choral Society "Forward"].¹¹

Three things are important about this performance. First is the fact that it took place at all. In spite of their aim, the pieces are still difficult to perform and hardly the usual fare for *Männergesangsvereine*. Second, the group undertaking this performance was not a traditional *Männergesangsverein*, but the male component (the *"13er Quartett"*) of an otherwise mixed chorus. As noted above, these were the more progressive both socially and musically in the Weimar Republic, and it is doubtful that a purely male society would have been up to the task. Third, the *DASB*'s leading musical expert was dispatched to distant Hanau to prepare the audience for the experience of the pieces. Judging by what is said both about Hänel's remarks and about the performance itself in a contemporary review, the pieces' political or ideological content was not their focus.¹²

The complete op. 35 treats a number of very general topics, as expressed by their titles: (1) "Hemmung" ["Inhibition"], (2) "Das Gesetz" ["The Law"], (3) "Ausdrucksweise" ["Manner of Expression"], (4) "Glück" ["Happiness"], (5) "Landsknechte" ["Yeomen"], (6) "Verbundenheit" ["Bond"].¹³ They are didactic in content: Schoenberg the moralizing pedagogue raising an admonitory index finger. Until now they have been treated as a collection of individual pieces, with little effort having been made to see them as a cycle of movements meant to be performed as a whole.¹⁴

Schoenberg's texts are neither rhymed nor metric, and their language is colloquial without always being transparent in meaning. The ideas and sentiments expressed range from the virtually self-evident to the interestingly original. The only literary genre that offers itself as a model would seem to be the aphorism.[15] All but "Landsknechte" ["Yeomen," no. 5], which is a dramatic narrative in dialogue form, may best be understood in the context of that tradition, especially as represented by Karl Kraus and Peter Altenberg. The aphorism was a favorite literary genre in turn-of-the-century Vienna, and one writer has even proposed a Viennese school of aphorists for the period 1880–1930, which nicely coincides with the period of Schoenberg's life under consideration here. Collections of aphorisms were published by all of the major Austrian writers of the period, including Robert Musil, Elias Canetti, Franz Kafka, and Hugo von Hofmannsthal in addition to Kraus and Altenberg.[16] Schoenberg himself wrote aphorisms and published 32 of them just about twenty years before he wrote the texts for op. 35.[17] The aphorism has at all times been a favored medium of expression for artistic and social outsiders, a category which includes Kraus, Altenberg, and Schoenberg, as well as the eighteenth-century founder of the German aphoristic school, Georg Christoph Lichtenberg.

Of the writers mentioned above, Kraus and Altenberg were the ones closest to Schoenberg. Kraus, whose influence Schoenberg openly acknowledged, is the undisputed king of the aphorists. His collected aphorisms total 2,159, and vary in length from a single sentence to three or four pages.[18] Peter Altenberg cultivated the aphorism, or aphoristic poetry such as the picture postcard texts set by Alban Berg, almost exclusively.[19] Aphorisms, including both Kraus's and Schoenberg's, are fundamentally didactic. This, together with the genre's normally journalistic medium of dissemination, makes it an essentially popular medium.

Viewed as aphorisms, Schoenberg's texts—no. 5 always excepted—display at least one more characteristic typical of the genre: no fewer than four are based wholly on paradox. In "Hemmung," the paradox is that "they" can speak more fluently when "they" are not inhibited by a thought. In "Das Gesetz," it is that it is not the exceptional but rather the predictability of everyday events that is miraculous. In "Ausdrucksweise," "sind wir beisamen, fühlt jeder nur jeden, nicht mehr sich" [together, each feels only the other, and not himself], but "getrennt, handelt jeder wie der andere und dennoch wie er selbst" [separated, each behaves like the other, and still like himself]. In "Glück," happiness is either its anticipation, its undeserved presence, or its unfathomability. In other words, it is anything, or everything, but a describable and knowable state.

"Verbundenheit" is not so much paradoxical as it is a series of parallels that are presented as mirror images of one another. Its aphoristic nature lies more in its economy of expression than in clever paradox per se.

In the context of Schoenberg's musical oeuvre, the pieces to which op. 35 is most directly comparable are the *Four Pieces for Mixed Chorus*, op. 27, and the *Three Satires for Mixed Chorus*, op. 28, both composed in 1925. The three sets are different in many respects, but are alike in that each of the twelve-tone pieces in the three sets uses a different row, rather than a single row as in the multimovement instrumental pieces from the same period: the *Wind Quintet,* op. 26, the *Suite*, op. 29 and the *Third String Quartet*, op. 30. It was a fundamental principle of Schoenberg's serial practice that a multimovement work would be unified by the use of a single twelve-tone row throughout. All of the multimovement instrumental pieces beginning with op. 26, as well as the two operas *Von heute auf morgen [From One Day to the Next]* and *Moses und Aron* adhere to this principle.[20] The fact that opp. 27 and 28 use different rows for the individual movements is a clear signal that they are not to be regarded as unified cycles, but as collections of individual pieces, which need not be performed together or in any particular order. For the same reasons, op. 35 appears, on the surface, to be a collection of the same kind as opp. 27 and 28. As such, it is even more diverse than those works in that it accommodates twelve-tone serial, atonal, and tonal pieces within its confines.

In spite of the diversity of musical treatment in op. 35, it may not be regarded as a mere collection. Among the usual instructions in the published score there is the admonition that, if the whole set is to be performed, it must be performed in the order given. There is no such instruction for either op. 27 or 28, and of course it would be unnecessary for opp. 26, 29, and 30. The point is, this collection of "Stücke" is, in fact, a cycle. If the set is approached as a cycle, both the texts and their musical treatment appear in an altered light. The most important consideration in a cycle is obviously the ordering of the movements and the rationale that determines that ordering in the absence of any conventional plan such as that of the four-movement symphony or the three-movement sonata.

In a typescript of the texts that predates the complete composition, they are presented as follows, with the published order numbers in brackets: (1) "Hemmung," (3) "Ausdrucksweise," (5) "Landsknechte," (2) "Das Gesetz," (4) "Glück," (6) "Verbundenheit."[21] Apparently the ordering of the six texts was important enough for the composer to adopt at least two different approaches to it. The ultimate decision to intercalate the two series to the present ordering, then, leads us to ask both about the reason for the original order and for the revised one. In other words, what characteristics do 1, 3, and 5 share, and which are shared by 2, 4, and 6?

As a beginning, we may note that the pronouns in 1, 3, and 5 are pre-dominantly plural, whereas those in 2, 4, and 6 singular. "Hemmung" speaks of, but does not directly address, *sie* [they or them], though the poet is introduced as *man* [one] in the final line. "Ausdrucksweise" speaks of *uns* and *wir* [us and we], but also of *jeder* and *jeder einzelne* [each one, each individual]. "Landsknechte" is not as clear in this re-spect, as its quasi-dramatic content means that the point of view shifts. The personal pronoun in the first strophe is *man* [one], in the second *ich* [I] and *euch* [you, plural, familiar form]. In the third, we find *mein* [my] and *ich*, and in the fourth, finally, *wir* [we]. The decision about number in this case must, I think, be decided by the title, which is emphatically plural, and which is represented by the *wir* in the final strophe. In "Das Gesetz" and "Glück," the only pronoun is *man*, and in "Verbundenheit," *du* in all of its inflections. There is even a progressive conjugation of per-sonal pronouns over the cycle: the impersonal *sie* (objective case) in no. 1 gives way to *wir* (subjective case) in nos. 3 and 5, while the impersonal *man* (subjective case) of nos. 2 and 4 gives way to *du* (subjective and ob-jective cases, familiar form) in no. 6.

The emphasis in the odd-numbered cycle is thus on the collective, and in the even-numbered one the individual, and in the original order-ing, the collective preceded the individual. "Verbundenheit," composed almost a year before the complete cycle, set the limits for it in some obvi-ous ways. The idea of the "one versus the many" is embodied in it most clearly by its bitexuality: statements in one voice are answered by the re-maining three voices (see Figure 5-1, below). This thematic polarity, as well as the binary musical form in which it is expressed, engendered the multilayered binary structure of the whole opus. It gave the cycle both a goal and a set of parameters in which it could operate.

To begin with the odd-numbered cycle, "Hemmung" asks a number of rhetorical questions about "them," and the difficulty of expressing a thought. "Ausdrucksweise" speaks of two views of the human condition, both of which spring from a "mass instinct." It also speaks about the dif-ficulty of knowing what and who "we" are, and how individual behavior varies when we are alone or in a group. It would be an understatement to say that the persona of this text is not optimistic about the behavior of hu-mankind: "Aber wenn wir schlagen, dann schlagen alle, wie Einer" [When we strike, then we all strike as one]. Although the main emphasis is on "we," the confrontation of "alle und jeden einzelnen" [all and each one] makes this text one key to the whole. The composer's own uncertainty about the message of this difficult text is reflected by the three titles which were attached to it at various stages. On a page with sketches for its tone row, it is called "Masseninstinkt" [Mass Instinct], and in a musical sketch of the first measures that differs from the final version it is called "Aus uns . . ." [From us . . .].[22] It may be seen as a turning point of sorts in the cycle: one is forced to choose between the mass and the individual. "Landsknechte" is about dying, and about human competition for *Lebensraum*, pasture, women: the common fate of the dispossessed.[23]

In the even-numbered cycle "Das Gesetz" speculates about what "one" can and/or should understand, and the thoroughly mundane quality of the miraculous. "Glück" tries to apply this insight to the idea of happiness by positing the difficulty of even grasping the concept, or the quality, of happiness. "Verbundenheit" is about the consolation of mutual obligations in human society, and, like "Ausdrucksweise," confronts the individual and society. Like the odd-numbered cycle, this cycle also leads to death, but to a death that is not a violent one.

In the original order, there is clear movement from pessimism to optimism, but in the intercalated order, each negative, odd-numbered, text is answered, in effect, by a more optimistic even-numbered one. Rather than the somewhat crude cumulative effect of the original ordering, the intercalated one produces a kind of dialogue, which goes something like this: "Hemmung" says "the masses are unable to formulate a thought, and often speak thoughtlessly." "Das Gesetz" replies "the miracle is that things never change"—including, presumably, the condition described in no. 1—and this is as it should be. Even the fact that some will try to resist this inevitability is "eine banale Selbstverständlichkeit" [a foregone conclusion]. "Ausdrucksweise" says "whichever view you take of the human condition, we—as human beings, and/or as members of one group or another—will be dissatisfied." "Glück" replies "without even realizing it, you are happy." "Landsknechte" says "life is cheap, and our best efforts will gain us nothing in the end." "Verbundenheit" replies "you *will* be looked after, just as you look after your fellow man; everything will be all right."

The "one versus the many" of the two cycles has musical parallels as well. This is clearest in the even-numbered cycle. In "Das Gesetz," there is always a complete statement of the tone row presented in one voice, with the other voices cast in an accompanying role. For the first thirty-three of the piece's forty measures, it is the tenor 1 part that carries the tune, and in the final phrase the bass 2 part takes this role. This is the line about the "one who rebels," and the shift of voice may possibly mean that here it is the composer himself who is speaking. (He sometimes represents himself in instrumental pieces in his persona as a cellist in the same pitch range.) "Verbundenheit" is even clearer in this respect. In the first half of the piece, the bass 1 part is the solo, and the other three voices respond with their own text and music. In the second half, the entire musical texture is literally mirrored from top to bottom, and tenor 1 carries the tune. The reversal in the direction of the melodic line in the excerpts from the beginning of each half of "Verbundenheit" shown in Figures 5-1a and 5-1b will be obvious enough by comparing the bottom line of Figure 5-1a with the top line of Figure 5-1b. What will not be so obvious is that the chords that result when the responding voices enter in the second measure of each also represent a kind of inversion. In this kind of inversion, it is the intervals in the chord that are taken in inversion, and not the direction of the melodic line. In Figure 5-1a, all of the chords are major:

Figure 5-1. "Verbundenheit," (a) mm. 1–3; (b) mm. 19–21. Copyright by Bote & Bock, a Boosey & Hawkes company. Reprinted by permission of Boosey & Hawkes, Inc.

G-flat, C, and D-flat respectively. The chords in Figure 5-1b are A-sharp minor, E-minor, and D-sharp minor respectively. In a major chord, the first interval above the root is a major third, to which a minor third is added to make a full triad. When the order of these intervals is reversed, the minor third comes first, and the triad is completed by a major third, producing a minor chord.[24]

"Glück" does not respond as readily to this grammatical interpretation, but most of the time a single voice carries the main thematic material (mm. 1–5, 9–11, 17–28), or a duet is accompanied by the other voices (mm. 6–9, 11–13). In the central section of the piece, however, the voices are treated as quite equal in a dauntingly complex contrapuntal web featuring imitative counterpoint in four and eight parts (mm. 11–17). It would probably be best to simply admit that this does not conform to the solo/response pattern postulated for the even-numbered cycle. The solution to this problem, if that is what it is, lies in the relationship of "Glück" to "Ausdrucksweise" and to the cyclic conception of the whole opus.

Figures 5-2a and 5-2b. "Hemmung," mm. 1–5. Copyright by Bote & Bock, a Boosey & Hawkes company. Reprinted by permission of Boosey & Hawkes, Inc.

On the odd-numbered side, no. 1 is clearly two duets (mm. 1–15, 19–22, 25–30), alternating with passages in which the voices are absolutely equal in prominence and thematic significance (mm. 16–18, 23–25). That is, no single voice ever emerges as the dominant one as it did in the even-numbered cycle. This, of course, is a twelve-tone piece, but one which uses only one form of the row and its retrograde. It is presented as two-note motives which together make a cadence in the key of C (Figure 5-2a), and two four-note motives that are related by transposition at the fourth (Figure 5-2b). In other words, while the texture emphasizes "the many," its musical manifestation is much simpler even than the nonserial "Glück."

"Ausdrucksweise" is likewise serial, but much more complex than no. 1. It not only uses more transpositions of the row, it sometimes presents them simultaneously. What is more, we do not hear an explicit melodic statement of a complete row until the second verse of the text, beginning in m. 13. Even there, it is presented canonically, with two forms of the row unfolding simultaneously. The beginning of the third major musical section on "Lob oder Tadel" [praise or blame, m. 29 ff] is marked by a full presentation of the original row form in the highest voice, but this is the only moment in the piece where one voice is the sole focus of melodic interest. The ambiguity of the "one versus the many" in this piece, in other words, reflects its own musical wrestling with that very same dichotomy. In "Landsknechte" this tendency toward greater complexity is even clearer, and is further underlined by the fragmentary character of the text. It is as if we were hearing fragments of a dialogue, or perhaps an argument, and none of the eight voices ever gains the upper hand for more than a couple of measures. In every respect, it is the most extreme. With its fragmented diction and vocal sound effects, it is the only one of the texts which could be considered expressionistic in both language and content. It comes in the penultimate position, to be balanced off by the conciliatory "Verbundenheit."

The "one versus the many" opposition is clearest in musical terms in the pairs 1/2 and 5/6, and much less clear in the middle pair 3/4. "Ausdrucksweise," no. 3, has been identified as the turning point of the cycle because of the opposition there between the one and the many, and the same opposition is felt in "Glück," no. 4, at least in its musical dimension. This pair is thus the crux of the whole opus, where the two cycles meet headed in opposite directions.

Although certainly conciliatory, "Verbundenheit" sends a complex message. In the first half, it is the subject "du" who is helped in all of life's difficult moments, and ends, in D major, with the line "Hilfe naht, du bist nicht allein!" [Help is at hand, you are not alone!]. The inevitable consequence of strict inversion, as explained above, is that the second half of the piece, and thus the cycle, must end on a minor chord. The final line begins "leugne doch, daß du dazu gehörst!" [deny (i.e., you cannot deny) that you belong!], and the response is "bleibst nicht allein" [you will not remain alone]. Thus the end of the second strophe echoes the end of the first, and both echo the "one versus the many" theme of the cycle, and especially of "Ausdrucksweise," no 3. This rounds the cycle off in an aesthetically satisfying way, but the D-minor chord certainly qualifies the otherwise "happy ending." It might also be said that the two halves, with their major and minor colorings, echo not only the dual thematicism of the cycle, but also its division into two parts.

But the cycle is both an alternating series and a binary structure. Nos. 1–3 are more about abstract "intellectual" concepts: thought, law, and God, and nos. 4–6 are about down-to-earth, "human" themes: happiness, exploitation of the many, and the mutual obligations of individuals in society. By intercalating the two series, Schoenberg also put no. 3, "Ausdrucksweise," approximately in the middle, so that the "rounding off" effect of no. 6 may refer both to the beginning of the cycle and to its midpoint. There is also a cumulative effect from no. 1 to no. 6, expressed in both the texts and in their musical treatment. The more generalized emotions of the first three pieces give way to increasingly personal utterances in the last three. The progression from simple to complex and back again is equally clear in the musical settings. The twelve-tone set of the first piece does not even produce Schoenberg's usual combinatoriality, and in any case the composer uses only one form of it along with its retrograde.[25] In other words, it is a "primitive" serialism of a sort which Schoenberg had certainly outgrown by 1930. In the row sketches for the second piece, "Das Gesetz," Schoenberg provides for two transpositions of the row a fifth apart, and their combinatorial inversions at the usual I5 and in fact he uses all of these forms. For no. 3, Schoenberg lays out three transpositions at the interval of a fifth, plus their I5 counterparts, but uses only two of these. For "Landsknechte," no. 5, the longest piece by far, there are five such pairs, all of which are used. In sum, the two cycles seem to be going in opposite directions from the grand music-historical evolutionary point of view which Schoenberg emphatically endorsed: nos. 1, 3, 5 "progress" through ever greater degrees of serial sophistication and complexity, while 2, 4, 6 "regress" from serialism back through free atonality to tonality. This is precisely the opposite of Schoenberg's own evolution from ca. 1899–1907 (tonality), through the free atonal phase of ca. 1908–21, to the arrival at serialism in the period ca. 1922 to the "present," that is, 1930. In the years after 1930, Schoenberg would revert with increasing frequency to tonality in larger and smaller works. Opus 35 is the first hint that "evolution" may have gotten somewhat sidetracked.

The only texts that are in the same positions in each ordering are nos. 1 and 6. In either ordering they are thus the anchors of the form, and the chronological priority of "Verbundenheit" further underlines their status. If we look again at musical Figures 5-1 and 5-2, another feature of the two pieces that both links and separates them emerges. In Figure 5-1, the content of each of the two passages quoted in Figure 5-1a and b is presented with nothing left out. All of the harmonic intervals in Figure 5-1 are consonant according to traditional harmony: the intervals are thirds, fourths, fifths, and sixths, without a single simultaneous dissonance. In Figure 5-2, on the other hand, the two components of mm. 1–5 are separated into (a) and (b) for the purposes of illustration. Viewed separately, 5-2a and 5-2b are likewise consonant: thirds and fourths only for Figure 5-2a, and thirds, fourths, fifths and sixths in the case of Figure 5-2b. Further, Figure 5-2a represents a cadence from the dominant to the tonic in the key of C, whereas Figure 5-2b begins roughly in F-sharp minor and ends on the key of A-flat. When we combine the two, as they are combined in the actual music, extreme dissonances occur in every measure but the first. This pairing of consonant duets and the incipient bitonality that it represents continues to the end of the first of its three strophes, at m. 15. Thereafter dissonance prevails, even in the sections that again feature paired duets (mm. 19–22, 25–30). This divides "Hemmung" exactly into two halves: (1) mm. 1–15, with its characteristic combination of consonance and bitonality, and (2) mm. 16–30 with its more egalitarian musical texture and more stridently dissonant sound. "Verbundenheit" is cast even more clearly into two halves, each eighteen measures long. The inversional parallelism between the two halves of "Verbundenheit" is clear and obvious, whereas the two-part division of "Hemmung" is less so, and the musical content is cumulative rather than parallel. Still, the pieces are comparable in pace and tempo, and are the only two that may be divided into equal halves.

Just as the extreme conflict of nos. 3 and 4 represents the dramatic crux of the set, the relationship between nos. 1 and 6, especially in its musical dimension, measures the journey that is travelled in the course of the cycle. Both the bitonality and primitive serialism of "Hemmung" allows for a progression from the relative consonance of its first half to an increasingly aggressive dissonance in the second. The twelve-tone row guarantees that both halves will be fashioned from the same materials, so that the "thought" of which it speaks is constant, while the poet's consternation at the disparity between the fluency and the content of most speech can grow in intensity: the final line is "wie oft muß man da staunen!" [how often is one astonished (by that)!]. Social harmony is inhibited [gehemmt] in no. 1 by the dichotomy between thought and expression. "Verbundenheit" almost had to be tonal, or at least triadic, in order to make both its major-minor inversional point, and its point about social harmony. The dialogue between the "one," represented by one voice, and the "many," represented by the remaining three voices, is harmonious in both the musical and the social sense.

Schoenberg was only openly political after 1935 when he pursued the Jewish cause, more by word than by deed. He summarizes his political history in a brief article written in the United States in 1950 roughly as follows: exposure to Marxist thought as a young man, conversion to monarchism after World War I, and a studied distance from politics since. He ends this brief piece by saying that he had never been a Communist, an important qualification in McCarthyist America.[26] Although we must take at face value his statement there that he continued to be a "quiet believer" in the monarchy, the difference in his attitude toward politics in the pre– and post–World War I periods is nowhere better demonstrated than by the difference between op. 35 and the alarmingly chauvinist nationalism of his only other contribution to the male chorus repertory: a setting of "Der deutsche Michel" ["The German Michael"], dating from 1914–15. This 1901 poem by Ottokar Kernstock, a Viennese priest and poet, is just the sort of nationalistic and militaristic stuff [*Deutschtümelei*] that was at the core of the traditional bourgeois male chorus repertory.[27] St. Michael is portrayed as the patron saint of German nationalism, and a brief quote from the refrain will suffice to suggest its character: "Tu' um dein Schwert und zäum' den Roß und zeuch voran dem Heere; es gilt der deutschen Ehre! Sankt Michel, salva nos!" [Gird thy sword and rein thy steed and lead the troops into battle; for German honor is at stake! St. Michael, save us!]. The first two-and-a-half strophes are set in D minor as German honor is under attack by its enemies. With victory in sight in the third strophe, however, the music shifts dramatically to D major for a triumphant and affirmative conclusion. The final refrain is repeated for a rousing conclusion: "Laß uns nicht eh'r vergehen, bis wir den Sieg gesehen, Sankt Michel, salva nos!" [Do not let us perish before we have seen victory, St. Michael, save us!]. Of course, the rather hysterical nationalism of the war years is partly to blame for this rather embarrassing musical document. This would have perhaps been excusable for a young man, but when he wrote it Schoenberg would have been forty years old. Even in extreme old age in 1950, he admits to having been an enthusiastic supporter of the war effort.[28]

This forms an interesting and informative contrast to the opposite modulation in "Verbundenheit." In fact, virtually all of Schoenberg's large tonal compositions make the journey travelled in "Der deutsche Michel." *Verklärte Nacht [Transfigured Night]*, op. 4, the *String Quartet no.1*, op. 7, *Gurrelieder*, and the *String Quartet no. 2*, op. 10 all begin in minor and end affirmatively, and conventionally, in major, following the tradition best represented by Beethoven's *Symphony No. 5*. Of the early tonal works, only the tone poem *Pelleas und Melisande*, op. 5 is an exception to this rule, but a minor ending is demanded in this case by the tragic ending of the story on which it is based. This makes the opposite journey in "Verbundenheit" all the more interesting and significant.

If Schoenberg was a monarchist in 1915, the texts of op. 35 show no such tendencies, and clearly Schoenberg knew by 1930 where his political interests lay. Whatever his intent may have been, it seems to have gone largely unnoticed by contemporary commentators and audiences. As noted above, when he introduced the pieces to the Hanau public in 1931, Walter Hänel of the *DASB* apparently did not emphasize their political message. Except for Reich's reference to the "pessimistic" character of the texts, none of the reviews I have seen of the published score even mention this aspect, or relate them in any way to the workers' choral movement.[29] In other words, both from the point of view of the professional critics and from the leadership in the *DASB*, artistic and aesthetic considerations seem to have held the upper hand. If we compare them to the usual *Tendenzlieder* of the period, we can find mostly negative points of comparison.[30] Like them, Schoenberg's texts avoid nationalism, militarism, and religion, at least in their conventional forms. "Landsknechte" could be read as an antiwar text, and even in the apparently religious "Ausdrucksweise," belief in God is more a cause of divisiveness than of harmony. The social contract suggested by "Verbundenheit" is certainly in the spirit of the *Tendenzlied*, though the rather facile optimism of "Glück," one of the pieces commissioned by the *DASB*, would seem to contradict the idea of struggle, as does the fatalism of "Das Gesetz." Although both their music and their message were evidently acceptable to the *DASB* in 1931, they clearly would not have been to the more radical wing of the workers' musical movement, as represented by Eisler. According to Eisler, it was ". . . no longer enough for a piece to have an effect on an audience because it was well sung," but ways had to be found to "revolutionize the singers" and "not to regard them simply as interpreters."[31] This was obviously not a position compatible either with Schoenberg's politics or his aesthetics, and events that lay only two years in the future when op. 35 was first performed and Eisler's little article written would mean that there was no place in Germany either for op. 35 or for its composer. Or, for that matter, for Eisler himself, who, like Schoenberg, was forced into exile after 1933.

If it is not already clear that it was his intent to reach out to a public usually closed to modernist music, a little article written at the same time as op. 35 dispels all doubt. In "My Public," Schoenberg begins by saying that he probably does not have a "public." He then rehearses his familiar argument that it has been the musical entrepreneurs, ignorant critics, and corrupt conductors who have stood between him and public recognition. Toward the end of the article, he relates four anecdotes about chance encounters with ordinary people—all of them men—who spontaneously recalled for him positive impressions of his music. One was a corporal in the Austrian army who had been a cutter in civilian life, and who was proud to make the acquaintance of the famous composer whose works he admired. In the second case, he was recognized by the night porter at a hotel and by the taxi driver who drove him there, and who both remembered having heard *Gurrelieder*. In the third case, he was recognized by a servant at a hotel in Amsterdam, who had actually sung in the chorus at a performance of *Gurrelieder* conducted by Schoenberg himself in Leipzig some years earlier. Finally, he recalls a recent encounter in Berlin in which the elevator operator in yet another hotel asks him if he was the composer of *Pierrot lunaire*, the first performance of which he attended in 1912. This modest but highly interesting article is dated March 17, 1930, just about a week after the completion of the last of the choruses, and was published in April of 1930 shortly before the publication of the *Six Pieces*. Although op. 35 is not mentioned in Schoenberg's article, it is not difficult to make a connection between both attempts to reach a larger public over the heads of the musical establishment.[32]

The composition of op. 35 was preceded by the "comic" opera *Von heute auf morgen*, and followed almost immediately by *Moses und Aron*, Schoenberg's last and arguably greatest work for the stage. The former is more or less popular, and addresses the problem of modern marriage, coming down more or less on the side of "family values." The more timeless themes of op. 35 anticipate some features of *Moses und Aron*, the conception of which goes back to at least 1928, or possibly even 1926.

Pamela White refers to both "Ausdrucksweise" and "Das Gesetz" in her discussion of the "God-Idea" in *Moses und Aron*, the musical composition of which was begun only three months after the completion of op. 35.[33] The difference is that the context in op. 35 is thoroughly secular. Even the God of "Das Gesetz" represents nothing more than the existing order of things, rather than a divine presence in human affairs.

The male chorus pieces seem to lie somewhere between the two operas, and Schoenberg uses vernacular media—the journalistic aphorism and the male chorus—to get his message out to the public, or at least to that part of the public with whom he felt comfortable. *Von heute auf morgen* and op. 35 are the only two pieces in which Schoenberg engaged the day-to-day social and political realities of the late Weimar Republic. The former addresses social issues, and its text was written by the composer's young second wife Gertrud, while the texts for op. 35, addressing political issues, were of course by the composer himself. The kind of "shirt sleeve" informality represented by op. 35 was perhaps only possible for Schoenberg in an all-male context, the only context in which politics could meaningfully be discussed in his milieu in 1930. Except for the triadic tonality of "Verbundenheit," the composer makes no concessions to the musical tastes prevalent in that social milieu, but he remains the only major modernist German composer of the day who associated himself directly with the *DASB*.

In "aiming" op. 35 as he did, though, Schoenberg opened up the possibility of a more pluralistic musical universe in which tonality, atonality and twelve-tone serialism could coexist, along with the increased range of both expression and potential appeal which this would allow. This almost postmodern pluralism is partly a concession to popular taste, and a leaning toward greater social relevance in the context of the already dying Weimar Republic. It was an experiment he would not repeat. From the historical perspective, it is even more interesting that each cycle progresses, or regresses, as it does, and not the other way around. Serialism, in other words, leads to conflict, violence, and death, whereas the opposite development leads (back) to triadic tonality, hope, and humanity. In the end, then, the piece conveys a veiled double message: hope lies in a return to human values based on individual responsibility, but by letting the cycle end in D minor, Schoenberg seems to be casting doubt even on this possibility.

NOTES

1. As this study was going to press, I became aware that Joseph H. Auner was working on a project that raises similar issues concerning op. 35. See "Schoenberg and His Public in 1930: The Six Pieces for Male Chorus, op. 35," in *Schoenberg and His World*, ed. Walter Frisch (Princeton: Princeton University Press, forthcoming).

2. See the discussion in Dietmar Klenke and Franz Walter, "Der Deutsche Arbeiter-Sängerbund: (d) Arbeitersänger zwischen Männerchören und gemischtem Gesang," in Dietmar Klenke, Franz Walter and Peter Lilje, *Arbeitersänger und Volksbühnen in der Weimarer Republik*, Forschungsinstitut der Friedrich-Ebert-Stiftung, Reihe: Politik- und Gesellschaftsgeschichte, Band 27, ed. Dieter Dowe (Bonn: J. H. W. Dietz Nachf., 1992), 47–49.

3. See R. John Specht, "Relationships between Text and Music in the Choral Works of Arnold Schoenberg" (Ph.D. diss., Case Western Reserve University, 1976), for Schoenberg's choral music generally, and pp. 10–60 for his activity as a choral conductor. For the latter, R. John Specht, "Schoenberg Among the Workers: Choral Conducting in Pre-1900 Vienna," *Journal of the Arnold Schoenberg Institute* X, 1 (June 1987): 28–37 is more accessible.

4. Gunter Mühl, "Das Verhältnis der Arbeiter-Sänger zum Bürgerlichen Gesangsvereinswesen bis 1933," *Illustrierte Geschichte der Arbeiterchöre*, ed. Rainer Noltenius (Essen: Klartext Verlag, 1992), 65, and Klenke and Walter, "Arbeitersänger," 34–46.

5. Schubert's pieces are found in *Franz Schuberts Werke: kritisch durchgesehene Gesamtausgabe,* ed. Eusebius Mandyczewski (Leipzig: Breitkopf und Härtel, 1884–97), *Serie IV*, no. 1–46; Mendelssohn's in *Friedrich Mendelssohn-Bartholdy Werke: kritisch durchgesehe Gesamtausgabe*, ed. Julius Rietz (Leipzig: Breitkopf und Härtel, 1874–77), Bd. XVII; Schumann's in *Robert Schumann's Werke,* ed. Clara Schumann (Leipzig: Breitkopf und Härtel, 1881–93), Bde. IX, X; Reger's in *Max Reger: Sämtliche Werke*, ed. Hermann Unger (Wiesbaden: Breitkopf und Härtel, 1954–), Bd. 27. Bruckner's male choruses are scattered throughout August Göllerich, *Anton Bruckner: Ein Lebens- und Schaffens-Bild,* 3 Bde. (Regensburg: Gustav Bosse Verlag, 1922–32).

6. *Paul Hindemith: Sämtliche Werke*, ed. Kurt von Fischer and Ludwig Finscher (Mainz: B. Schott's Söhne, 1979–), Bd. VII, 5, 121–65. I know of no evidence that any of Hindemith's male chorus pieces were ever performed in the context of the *DASB*, or that he had any contact with the organization.

7. See the list of works in Albrecht Betz, *Hanns Eisler: Political Musician*, trans. Bill Hopkins (Cambridge: Cambridge University Press, 1982), 297–98. See also Betz's discussion of Eisler's role in the choral movement 71ff., and

Eisler's own critical discussion of the *DASB* in his 1931 essay "Progress in the Workers' Music Movement," in *Hanns Eisler: A Rebel in Music. Selected Writings*, ed. Manfred Grebs, trans. Marjorie Meyer (New York: International Publishers, 1978), 32–35.

8. See the programs and repertory lists in Otto Rüb, "Die chorischen Organisationen (Gesangsvereine) der bürgerlich Mittel- und Unterschicht im Raum Frankfurt am Main von 1800 bis zur Gegenwart" (Ph.D. diss., Johann Wolfgang Goethe-Universität, Frankfurt am Main, 1964), 253–63 and Anita Dreischer, "Das Liedrepertoire von neun Ruhrgebiets-Arbeiterchöre 1898–1953," in Noltenius, *Illustrierte Geschichte der Arbeiterchöre*, 142–46.

9. See the letter from Schoenberg to Guttmann quoted in Specht, "Relationships," 51. "Verbundenheit" was completed on 19 April 1929, and "Glück" probably at about the same time, though no dated autograph source for it survives. The whole set was published by Bote & Bock (Berlin, 1930), and in *Arnold Schönberg: Sämtliche Werke* (Mainz: B. Schotts Söhne & Vienna: Universal Edition, 1966–), Reihe A, Bd. 18 (1980). The critical notes to the latter have not yet appeared.

10. See the discussion in Klenke and Walter, "Arbeitersänger," 102–08.

11. See Joan Evans, "New Light on the First Performances of Arnold Schoenberg's *Opera* 34 and 35," *Journal of the Arnold Schoenberg Institute* XI, 2 (November 1988): 163–73 for a full account. The name *Vorwärts* seems to have been a common one for workers' choral societies. A number of them, including this one, are listed in the appendix to Rüb, "Die chorischen," 248.

12. Evans, "New Light," 169.

13. The translations of the Bote & Bock edition are misleading at the very least. "Hemmung," for instance, is translated as "restraint," normally expressed in German as *Zurückhaltung*. "Ausdrucksweise" means more "manner" or "mode of expression," rather than "means," as in the published translation. "Glück" means both "happiness" and "luck," which neatly expresses the fortuitous character of the author's conception of happiness. "Obligation" in German is usually expressed as *Verpflichtung*, whereas "Verbundenheit" implies a mutual connection, rather than a duty. The pieces will be referred to subsequently by their German titles.

14. Specht, "Relationships," 255–336 is a thorough treatment of the individual pieces and their texts which I shall not attempt to duplicate here.

15. Willi Reich said that the texts ". . . all express some philosophical aphorism of a pessimistic nature." ("Schönberg's New Männerchor," *Modern Music* 9 [1932]: 63.) Aphorisms they certainly are, but they are equally certainly not all pessimistic.

16. William M. Johnston, "The Vienna School of Aphorists, 1880–1930," in *The Turn of the Century: German Literature and Art, 1890–1915,* ed. Gerald

Chapple and Hans H. Schulte (Bonn: Bouvier Verlag, 1981), 275–290. See also the bibliography in Klaus von Welser, *Die Sprache des Aphorismus,* Berliner Beiträge zur neueren deutschen Literaturgeschichte 8 (Frankfurt: Verlag Peter Lang, 1986). I am grateful to Charlotte Cross for drawing the article by Johnston to my attention.

17. *Die Musik XXXVI, 9ter Jhg.* (1909–10), 159–63. Two other sets of aphorisms are listed in Josef Rufer, ed., *Das Werk Arnold Schönbergs* (Kassel: Bärenreiter, 1959; with *Ergänzungen und Korrekturen,* 209ff, dated 1971), 152, no. 82 (1912), no. 84 [undated]. "Opera: Aphorisms," dated ca. 1930, is published in *Style and Idea: Selected Writings of Arnold Schoenberg,* ed. Leonard Stein, trans. Leo Black (London: Faber & Faber, 1975), 337–39. Although not labelled as such, the brief texts also published in *Style and Idea,* pp. 506–12 under the title "Human Rights," and dated 1947, must also be considered as aphorisms.

18. See Christian Wagenknecht, ed., *Aphorismen,* Schriften, Bd. 8 (Frankfurt am Main: Suhrkamp Verlag, 1986).

19. Published in *Aphorismen, Skizzen und Geschichten,* Bd. 1–2 (München: Carl Hansler Verlag, 1979).

20. The *Third String Quartet,* op. 30, is exceptional in that it uses a single row with three variant forms. Since all forms have the first five pitches in common, however, and one of the orderings clearly has priority over the others, the principle of a unifying single row still obtains.

21. Unnumbered item from the Arnold Schönberg Center, Vienna headed "Dich[tungen] 9–12." I wish to thank the R. Wayne Shoaf, archivist of the Arnold Schoenberg Institute when it was located at the University of Southern California in Los Angeles, for supplying me with photocopies of this and other documents related to op. 35.

22. Microfilm no. 633 of collection CASG85–C916, and Item CASG85–C914 respectively, from the archive of the Arnold Schönberg Center, Vienna.

23. In the typescript of the texts referred to above the title is "Landsknechte . . ." "The omission indicated by the ellipsis may be filled in with *-schicksal,* as in the text's final line, and as the title is shown on one of the musical sketches: "Landsknechteschicksal" [yeoman's fate; see microfilm no. 644 of the group of sketches labelled CASG85–C916 from the Arnold Schönberg Center]. Joseph N. Straus has also commented upon the unusual features of this piece, but his conclusions are very different from mine. See *Remaking the Past: Musical Modernism and the Influence of the Tonal Tradition* (Cambridge, Mass. and London, England: Harvard University Press, 1990), 83–6.

24. In Figure 5-1a, the lowest voice in the top brace has been shifted up an octave so that the chords fit on a single brace. In Figure 5-1b, a redundant voice has been eliminated in the bottom brace, m. 2, beat two, and some note spellings

have been changed in the interest of clarity. In the published score the composer has obscured the identity of some of the triads by mixing flats and sharps.

25. Schoenberg's practice in his late twelve-tone compositions was to devise the row in such a way that when its first six tones are combined with the first six of its inverted (I) form five (5) semitones (a perfect fourth) higher, the complete collection of twelve tones will result.

26. "My Attitude Toward Politics," in *Style and Idea*, 505–06.

27. Based on Specht, "Relationships," 138–40. Because it was unpublished at that time, Specht was not able to comment on the music. The piece is published in the same volume of the *Gesamtausgabe* as op. 35 (see note 8). Interestingly, this piece is not included in Pierre Boulez's recording of the complete choral music: *Sony Classical* S2K 44571.

28. "I did my duty enthusiastically as a true believer in the house of Hapsburg." ("My Attitude," 505).

29. In addition to Reich's article, there is an anonymous review in *Der Auftakt: Moderne Musikblätter* 10 (Prague, 1930): 294, and a more extensive one by Richard Petzold, "ARNOLD SCHÖNBERG: *Sechs Stücke für Männerchor*, op. 35," *Die Musik* XXIII (1930–31): 379. Hans F. Redlich devotes a paragraph to opus 35 in his "Die Kompositorische Situation von 1930," *Musikblätter des Anbruchs XII,* Heft 6 (Juni 1930): 187–90.

30. This discussion is based on Klenke and Walter, *Arbeitersänger*, especially 95–133.

31. Eisler, "Progress," 33. Is it only a coincidence that this article is exactly contemporary with the premiere of op. 35? Schoenberg is not mentioned in it, but the animosity between teacher and former pupil was both bitter and intense beginning in the mid-1920s.

32. The article is published in *Style and Idea: Selected Writings of Arnold Schoenberg*, ed. Leonard Stein (London: Faber & Faber, 1975), 96–99.

33. Pamela White, *Schoenberg and the God-Idea: The Opera "Moses und Aron"* (Ann Arbor: UMI Research Press, 1985), 85, 87.

CHAPTER 6

The Prophet and the Pitchman
Dramatic Structure and Its Musical Elucidation in *Moses und Aron,* Act 1, Scene 2

EDWARD D. LATHAM

According to Hans Stuckenschmidt, one of Schoenberg's pupils and his biographer, "the infinite is the underlying theme of [Schoenberg's] musical thinking, of his texts and of his religious imagery,"[1] and Schoenberg himself said that "there could be no art . . . not inspired by ethics, and there could be no human ethics not inspired by the spirit of Judaism."[2] Schoenberg's largest twelve-tone masterwork, the opera *Moses und Aron,* offers a good opportunity to explore the impact of his religious beliefs and their political correlations on his work, especially since it was conceived and composed in the years 1923–33, a time during which Schoenberg experienced persecution for his Jewish heritage at first hand. Moreover, the religious ideas expounded in the opera provide a window into Schoenberg's specifically Mosaic view of his purpose as a Jew and an artist.

THE OPERA AND ITS RELIGIOUS CONTEXT

Schoenberg's religious life has been a primary source of interest to several scholars, including Bluma Goldstein, Michael Mäckelmann, André Neher, and Alexander Ringer.[3] Though he was born Jewish and formally registered by his parents in the local synagogue in Vienna, he converted to Lutheran Protestantism immediately prior to his marriage to Mathilde von Zemlinsky, raising the question of whether his conversion was for spiritual or social reasons.[4] In 1933, as a result of events that had left him a refugee in Paris, Schoenberg expressed a desire to return to Judaism, signing a formal letter prepared by a local rabbi to acknowledge his "reconversion."[5]

Though the document itself was unnecessary (Judaism recognizes all those born to a Jewish mother as Jews, regardless of the status of their faith), it received wide publicity, and was thus a public statement of Schoenberg's religious convictions.[6]

Schoenberg's actual reconversion, according to his own letters, occurred much earlier. In a letter to Alban Berg, Schoenberg cited the Paris ceremony of 1933 as merely the official recognition of a process that had begun with the composition of "Du sollst nicht . . . du mußt" ["You should not . . . You must"], the second of the *Vier Stücke für gemischten Chor* [*Four Pieces for Mixed Choir*], op. 27, composed in 1925, as well as the libretto for *Moses und Aron* (1928) and his religious play, *Der biblische Weg* [*The Biblical Way* (1926–27)].[7] Schoenberg's turn toward religious subjects, and his reconversion to Judaism, must therefore be viewed at least partly as a reaction to his experience of World War I, as well as to events leading up to World War II, particularly since he composed the text for *Die Jakobsleiter* [*Jacob's Ladder*], his first strongly religious work, as early as 1915–17, during which time he served in the Austrian army.[8]

There are several issues connected to *Moses und Aron* that are clarified by an examination of Schoenberg's religious and political life. Schoenberg's failure to complete Act III, for example, has always been a source of interest to scholars and critics alike: why, when he had finished the bulk of the opera in 1932 (only the comparatively brief Act III remained to be set when Schoenberg left Berlin for good), did Schoenberg leave the work as a torso, even though he discussed finishing it right up until his death in 1951?[9] Politically, Schoenberg devoted increasing amounts of time after 1933 to the Jewish cause, as attested to by his father-in-law, Rudolph Kolisch, in a 1933 letter to George Alter:

> Don't count on Schoenberg for a recital in Prague. He no longer has a fixed address: now in Paris, now in Arcachon, now in Geneva . . . what he does have is an idee fixe: to help his Jewish brethren in distress, to help them get out of the German inferno. He no longer writes a note of music and has put himself entirely at the disposal of the World Jewish Congress which is being set up to prevent the worst. . . .[10]

Perhaps it was his inability, despite all his efforts, to prevent the horrors of the Holocaust that haunted Schoenberg, preventing him from completing the final act of his opera.[11] Like Moses, whose final words in Act II are "O Wort! Du Wort das mir fehlt!" [O word! Thou word that I lack!],[12] he lacked the means of effecting change: he had ideas about the salvation of the Jewish people but was unable to convince the necessary people to carry them out.[13]

An exploration of just what these ideas were reveals a strongly Mosaic aspect of Schoenberg's character. As he explains in a 1933 letter to the composer Ernst Toch:

> ... we must think of the tasks that have been placed on the Jew in his individual position as a people chosen by God; as the God [sic] which is singled out to maintain an idea; the idea of the unpresentable God.[14]

Taking up Theodor Herzl's Zionist call to arms, Schoenberg proposed to start a movement "which will unite the Jews again . . . in one people and bring them together in their own country to form a state."[15] He outlined his proposal in a four-point program, the slogan of which might be summarized as: Don't Fight! Unite and Take Flight![16] He even declared that he would be willing to become the president of this new state if necessary, a position for which he considered himself well qualified because of his hard-headed (i.e., Mosaic) qualities.[17]

The missing Act III might also be explained in religious terms, however. As Alexander Ringer notes in his book, *Arnold Schoenberg: The Composer as Jew*:

> His failure to compose the Third Act of *Moses und Aron*, an otherwise puzzling phenomenon, assumes cultural significance of a very special order as the subconscious concomitant of his axiomatic identification with a purely spiritual idea so all-encompassing that it "cannot and must not" be explicitly communicated.[18]

According to Neher, Schoenberg worked out his problems with praying to God in compositions like *Die Jakobsleiter* and *Moderne Psalmen*.[19] In these works, as well as in *Moses und Aron* and *Dreimal tausend Jahre* [*Three Times a Thousand Years*], the protagonist finishes the work on his knees, in a posture of prayer, searching for the right words to say.[20] Perhaps the ultimate prayer work was the music for *Kol Nidre* [*The Opening of the Gates*], the prayer that begins Yom Kippur, that Schoenberg composed and directed in a synagogue in Los Angeles on 4 October 1938, in response to the *Anschluss*.[21]

The religious significance of the incomplete Act III is twofold: not only does it emphasize, as Theodor Adorno put it, "the impossibility of aesthetic totality . . . by virtue of an absolute metaphysical content,"[22] the notion that the idea of God is essentially beyond completion, but it symbolizes the triumph of the idea (the spoken word of Moses) over the representation (the lyrical vocal line of Aron). In this sense, there is no other way that Act III could properly fulfill its obligations. In any case, both the political and religious perspectives on the incomplete opera point to a strong connection between the figure of Moses and Schoenberg himself.

In his view on the role of opera in society, Schoenberg was an idealist (again, like Moses). Unlike Kurt Weill, his contemporary who struck out in a markedly different direction, Schoenberg maintained that "the opera of the future cannot be art for the masses. . . ."[23] Declaring that cinema had usurped the popular role of opera, Schoenberg adopted a more elitist view, claiming that "the minority that can understand deeper things will never let itself be satisfied wholly and exclusively by what everyone can understand."[24]

Even so, the creator of the Golden Calf scene knew that idealism alone was not enough; there was also a bit of Aron in Schoenberg. As Ringer puts it, "Moses, the man of pure idea, and Aron, the communicator, reflect a spiritual dichotomy at the very roots of the Schoenbergian dialectic. . . ."[25] It was surely Schoenberg the communicator who produced the opera *Von heute auf morgen* [*From Today to Tomorrow*], op. 32, a direct response to Kurt Weill's *Der Dreigroschenoper* [*The Threepenny Opera*]. Compare Schoenberg's above-quoted statements about the opera of the future with this excerpt from a satirical, but serious, tract by Weill: "music is no longer a matter of the few . . . [it is] simpler, cleaner, and more transparent. It no longer wishes to represent philosophies. . . ."[26] In the end, however, the worldly and sarcastic tone adopted by Schoenberg in *Von heute auf morgen* proved to be the exception rather than the rule in his compositional output, and his later works did indeed "represent philosophies." Like Moses, Schoenberg believed that the idea was unavoidably and intentionally difficult; after *Von heute auf morgen* he left Aron's role to Weill.[27]

In light of the political and religious persona described by the preceding comments, it is hard to avoid claiming that Schoenberg strongly identified himself with Moses. In politics, he, like Moses, actively pursued a plan to lead the Jewish people into the wilderness toward a new home. In his artistic life he favored uncompromising idealism, turning increasingly to religious subjects for his texted works from 1915 onward, subjects that dealt specifically with Mosaic issues. In the text for *Die Jakobsleiter*, which was written in 1915–17, as well as those for *Der biblische Weg*

(1926–27), *Kol Nidre*, op. 39 (1938), *Dreimal tausend Jahre*, op. 50a (1949), and *Moderne Psalmen*, op. 50c (1951), Schoenberg confronted again and again the issues of comprehending the incomprehensible and prophesying to those unwilling or unable to heed the prophet's message, issues that occupied him spiritually, politically, and artistically throughout his life.[28]

Moses und Aron, then, can be seen as the ultimate statement of Schoenberg's personal creed, and the importance of the fact that he chose the operatic medium to convey this creed should not be underestimated. The challenge, of course, in discerning Schoenberg's message in the opera is to take both the music and the text into account, a challenge that has been met in various ways by previous writers, including Karl Wörner and Michael Cherlin.[29] One potentially fruitful avenue of inquiry that has been previously unexplored is the combination of a specific method of textual analysis with existing methods of musical analysis to arrive at a composite analysis of the opera. The method of dramatic analysis developed by the Russian dramaturg Constantin Stanislavsky (1863–1938) will be employed here as a means of discerning the motivations of the two primary characters, which will in turn shed light on Schoenberg's own motivations for writing the libretto and setting it.

STANISLAVSKY AND DRAMATIC STRUCTURE

Analyzing opera has always been a difficult task. If, as Joseph Kerman believes, "the relationship between . . . action and music is the perennial central problem of operatic dramaturgy,"[30] then Carolyn Abbate and Roger Parker are correct in saying that "'analyzing opera' should mean not only 'analyzing music' but simultaneously engaging with equal sophistication, the poetry and the drama."[31] In suggesting an examination of the construction of *Moses und Aron* based upon analyses of the drama, the libretto, and the music, this paper takes an initial step in that direction.

The Stanislavsky System

The concept of the *Osnovnaya Tsyel*, or "superobjective," is the cornerstone of Stanislavsky's dramatic theory, which is not to be confused with the "Stanislavsky method."[32] The System, as Stanislavsky originally conceived of it, was designed primarily to have two functions: (1) as a tool to be used in the analysis of "the score" of a role (internal preparation); and (2) as an organizing structure for the study of the physical and technical aspects of acting (external preparation). The complete system is laid out in *Building a Character*, the second of Stanislavsky's three major works devoted to acting. The distinction between internal and external preparation is preserved throughout the system, and Stanislavsky's famous dictum, "an actor prepares" (which served as the title of his first, and most important, discourse on acting), undergirds the entire system, covering both its internal and external aspects.[33]

In his third book on acting, *Creating a Role*, Stanislavsky defines the superobjective as the "overarching goal of a character."[34] The active attainment of the superobjective forms the "through-action" of the role; and the progression of the superobjective forms the "through-line," which is the "leitmotif of the entire work."[35] This superobjective represents the character's goal for the whole play or opera. It is then subdivided into "main objectives," goals for each scene in which the character appears, and "creative objectives," more localized goals that are aimed at achieving each main objective.

Stanislavsky's tripartite division of objectives is a hierarchical system, though not in the strict sense suggested by Richard Cohn and Doug Dempster, and it maintains a strong connection between its three levels.[36] It is also a linear system which depends on the progression of time for its fulfillment. As has often been noted, music and drama, as temporal arts, have a natural kinship; Stanislavsky's insistence on "progression," "active attainment," and the "through-line," or "through-action" emphasizes this temporality. In *An Actor Prepares*, he makes the active nature of the objective clear by referring to it as "a verb"; the dramatic "unit" that it represents he calls "a noun."[37]

Beyond being linear and hierarchical, the Stanislavsky system is also consciously musical. In *Creating a Role*, Stanislavsky refers to "the score of a role," which he defines as an outline of the character's objectives. One of the primary activities of an actor trained in the Stanislavsky method is consequently the "scoring" of his or her role, even before rehearsals begin.[38] Stanislavsky was inclined to think in musical terms, as he was trained as a singer before he became a director, and thereafter opera direction was one of his main occupations.[39] He even draws the analogy himself, when he says that "objectives are like the notes in music, they form the measures, which in turn produce the melody . . . the melody goes on to form an opera or a symphony, that is to say the life of a human spirit in a role, and that is what the soul of the actor sings."[40]

Stanislavsky instructs his students to analyze a role in several ways. Before creating the actual "score" of the role (i.e., the complete list of hierarchical objectives), there are several preliminary steps that can be taken to clarify the analyst's thoughts about the play, each of them involving the creation of a list. To begin with, there are the "external circumstances" or facts of the play (i.e., what actually happens in each scene). To clarify these circumstances, Stanislavsky might ask the analyst to provide a condensed outline of the actions that take place in the opera.[41] A second list might then be used to identify the "logic of feelings" (i.e., the sequential progression of actions that accompany the arousal of an emotion like love).[42] The ultimate goal of the actor, however, is always the scoring of the role, beginning with the superobjective and working down to creative objectives for each line spoken by the character.[43]

Applying Stanislavsky to *Moses und Aron*

This section applies the portion of Stanislavsky's system of dramatic analysis that involves the scoring of roles to the libretto of *Moses und Aron*, concentrating on the two title roles as the main protagonists of the opera. Due to the limited scope of this paper, each character's role has been analyzed only to the level of main objectives (i.e., the objectives for each scene), rather than line-by-line objectives. The score of Moses's role is shown in Figure 6–1a. His superobjective (labeled "SO" in Figure 6–1a) is to induce the people to worship the one true God. This superobjective, however, is only established as a result of his "conversation" with God in Act I, scene 1 (abbreviated as I/i and shown in boldface type at the

SO:	to induce the people to worship the true God	x
I/i:	to avoid the task the Lord has set for him	x
I/ii:	to convince Aron to give up idol worship	x
I/iv:	to convince the Volk to worship God directly	x
II/iv:	to banish the golden calf	/
II/v:	to convince Aron to give up idol worship	x
[**III/i**:	to banish Aron's form of idol worship	/]

Figure 6-1a. The score of Moses's role.

left in Figure 6–1a); this scene constitutes a preliminary development of the character of Moses who, at the outset of the opera, is unsure of his task. As the title of the scene ("The Calling of Moses") indicates, Moses is literally called by God who, in the guise of the burning bush, tells him that he must "be God's prophet" (p. 11). Moses's main objective in this scene is to avoid the task God has set out for him, and he tries to do so by offering five objections to God: namely, that he is too old, that the people are too blind, that he can offer no proof that he is a prophet, that no one will believe him, and that he is not a good speaker. God responds to his objections by offering Aron to him as his spokesperson. Moses, out of excuses, therefore fails to accomplish his goal in the scene and has to accept the new superobjective assigned to him by God.

He begins his struggle to achieve this new goal in scene 2 ("Moses meets Aron in the Wasteland"), where his main objective is to convince Aron to give up idol worship. Obviously, if he cannot even convince his salesman of the quality of the new product (i.e., abstract contemplative worship), it will never get sold. In order to accomplish this objective, he attempts to instruct Aron on the nature of God, whose grace, he says, "is granted through recognition" (p. 11). God, according to Moses, is "unimageable" and "can never be measured" (p. 12).

As scene 2 unfolds, however, it becomes clear that Aron has a different superobjective and attendant set of main objectives. Initially, it appears that Aron wants nothing more than to serve Moses, when he asks "My brother, did the almighty one give you me as his vessel?" (p. 11). When examined more closely, though, Aron's text clearly reveals his desire to lead the people himself. After Moses has presented the idea that God is invisible, a disbelieving Aron finds himself faced with a troubling fundamental question that he must ask of his people: "Folk chosen by the only one, can you worship what you dare not even conceive?" (p. 12). At this point in the scene, however, Aron's question is purely rhetorical; he has said previously that God is a "vision of highest fantasy" that has enticed fantasy to form Him, and has asserted that "love will surely not weary of image forming" (p. 12).

Aron's superobjective, then, is to bring the people their God in images they can understand. Figure 6-1b provides the score of Aron's role. His main objective for Act I, scene 2 is to accept God's call as he understands it (i.e., to affirm that God is to be worshipped through visible images). Moses and Aron become polarized, both dramatically and musically, after the turning point of the scene, each of them expounding their differing views of worship, but no longer communicating with each other. It is Aron who

SO:	to bring the Volk their God in images	/
I/ii:	to accept God's call as *he* understands it: to show the Volk their God in images	/
I/iv:	to convince the Volk to worship God (to astound the Volk with the three signs)	/
II/i:	to reassure the Elders	x
II/ii:	to please the Volk (to bring them gods)	/
II/iii:	to please the Volk (to bring them gods)	/
II/v:	to convince Moses of the necessity of images	/
[III/i:	to convince Moses of the necessity of images	x]

Figure 6-1b. The score of Aron's role.

prevails, however, as the end of the scene shows, since it is he that addresses God directly, praying already as the spokesperson of the people: "Almighty one, be the god of this people . . ." (p. 12). Moses, on the other hand, begins to doubt and question, asking God "to whom is the reward presented, him who wants or cannot want things else?" (p. 12). In this line, Moses is, in fact, asking God who is to be rewarded, himself or Aron; the answer, once so obvious to him, has become less apparent.

Aron continues to achieve his main objectives for the rest of his important scenes (I/4, II/2, II/3, and II/5, each marked with a slash in Figure 6–1b), convincing the people to worship God by amazing them with the three signs (I/4), pleasing the people by creating an image for them to worship (II/2, II/3), and convincing Moses of the necessity of images (II/5). Thus, if one ends the analysis of the libretto at the end of Act II—the point at which Schoenberg's musical setting ends—Aron achieves his superobjective and finishes the opera in triumph, proudly asserting that "through me has God given a signal to the people" (p. 21). If, however, one takes Act III into account, the reverse is true: Moses vanquishes Aron's form of idol worship and restores abstract contemplation of the "God-Idea" as the best form of worship.

In this case, it is best to separate the completed two-act opera as it stands from the three-act libretto. As Gertrud Schoenberg stated in her note accompanying the translation of Act III: "It suffices to understand and to experience the work in its present form. As it is, so was it to be."[44] Such a separation permits the examination of Schoenberg's musical setting of the libretto for its amplification of the dialogue of contrast between Moses and Aron, without requiring speculation on what form that setting would have taken for Act III. Within this limited context (i.e., the first two acts), then, it can be argued that the eventual triumph of Aron in Act II, scene 5 is already readily apparent in Act I, scene 2. To support this view, which is based upon the interpretation of the superobjectives for Moses and Aron discussed above, the aurally salient musical and poetic features of the scene will now be presented, along with the means by which they accentuate and confirm Aron's victory.

SCHOENBERG AND AURAL SALIENCE

Poetic Features

Allen Forte has discussed Schoenberg's libretto, for which he produced the English singing translation, in a brief essay entitled "Notes on the Historical Background of the Opera and on the Text," included in the liner notes of the original 1957 recording released on the Columbia Masterworks label.[45] In the essay, Forte recognizes that the contrast between Moses and Aron constitutes "the essential dualism of the drama . . . extended to all its dimensions," and he claims that it is on this oppositional basis that the drama unfolds.[46] He goes on to link this dramatic opposition to sonic elements in the libretto, identifying key word pairs that are linked aurally by the similarity of their vowel sounds. Claiming that each scene of the opera centers around a word pair, he offers the pairing of "Gott" and "Volk"—linked by their closed "o" sound—for the scene under discussion here.

The analysis of the text for the scene presented here takes Forte's notion of coherence and dramatic meaning through repetition of sound one step further, to include complete words and phrases. Figure 6-2 is a modified graph of the text for Act I, scene 2. It shows patterns of repetition, both local and long-range. A review of the word repetitions in the text confirms Forte's assertion that "Gott" and "Volk" are indeed the primary words of the scene: "Gott" receives eleven repetitions and "Volk" receives seven, while "Allmächtige," "Bild," "Liebe," "Einzige," "auserwählt," and "unvorstellbar" receive between four and six repetitions each.

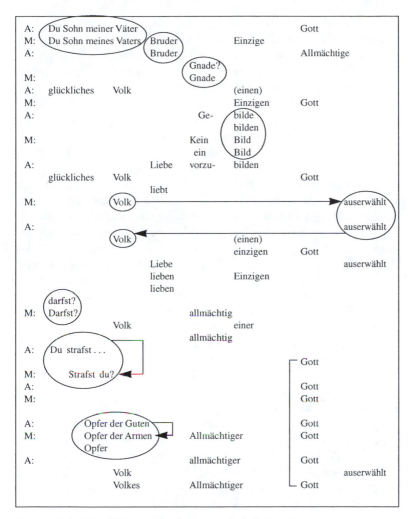

Figure 6-2. Word/Phrase Repetitions in Act I, scene 2.

Overall, the patterns of word repetition in the scene can be characterized by the use of two techniques. First, Schoenberg links the brothers
at the local, line-by-line level by repeating a single word or phrase in a
pair of lines. Since Aron usually initiates these pairs, he presents the
word or phrase first, as in the circled instance at the top left of Figure 6-2:
"Du Sohn meiner Väter" [son of my fathers]. Often, Schoenberg will
alter the phrase slightly, as he does in this case, or reverse it, to show its

different meaning for Moses. Here, Aron's plural "Fathers" becomes the singular "Father" for Moses, alluding to his conception of God as "Der Einzige" [the only one]. Another instance of alteration is shown in the bottom left corner of the graph where Aron's "Opfer der Guten" [offerings of the good] becomes "Opfer der Armen" [offerings of the poor] for Moses, de-emphasizing the inherent goodness of offerings. The reversal of a phrase, which literally represents the antithesis between the brothers, presents itself in the pairing of "Volk, auserwählt" and "Auserwähltes Volk," and also "du strafst" with "Strafst du," marked in the middle and the lower left of Figure 6-2, respectively.

The other element involved here is the intensification of the dramatic dialogue through the increase in repetitions, most evident in the passage immediately preceding the climactic turning point of the scene. In this passage, lines 7–11 (from "Gebilde" through "lieben") in Figure 6-2, Schoenberg overlaps four repeated-word groups: "Bild," "Liebe," "Volk," and "auserwählt," which translate as "image," "love," "people," and "chosen." These four words represent the fundamental conflict of the scene—the "Volk" have been "auserwählt," by God, but they can only love Him through a "Bild." Thus, the frantic rebuttal by Moses beginning with "Darfst?" is made all the more futile by the fact that the insurmountable obstacle of the scene is already in place by the time he begins. The futility of his argument is reflected by the fact that each character addresses God individually in lines 13–21, no longer communicating to each other but to God. The predominance of utterances of the word "Gott" in the last half of the dialogue, bracketed at the bottom right of Figure 6-2, reflects each brother's attempt to claim insight into God's plan for the people.

The gradually increasing tension between Moses and Aron, demonstrated by the increase in word repetitions, is also fueled by a series of shifts, or "beats," in the action. As Figure 6-3 shows, the scene revolves around a series of challenges posed by Aron and the responses to these by Moses. These are the "corrections," numbered 1 through 6. Each challenge raises the level of intensity in the scene, as Moses becomes increasingly agitated and begins to question his own conception of God. Thus, two dramatic strategies are at work in this scene: the development of the contrast between the two characters, and the gradual heightening of tension between them through the challenges and responses. In subsequent discussion, these two strategies will be referred to as the Principle of Contrast and the Principle of Intensification. The Principle of Contrast is played out in the local juxtaposition of lines linked by a common word, outlined in Figure 6-2, whereas the Principle of Intensification dic-

1. Moses and Aron meet.

2. Aron questions Moses.
   Moses corrects him (1st Correction).

3. Aron rejoices, but misunderstands.
   Moses corrects him again (2nd Correction).

4. Aron is obssessed with the idea of imaging God.
   Moses cautions him again (3rd Correction).

5. Aron continues to defend imaging.
   Moses corrects him yet again (4th Correction).

6. Aron shows his devotion to God (tries to speak Moses's language), but raises his fundamental question: can his beloved Volk love an intangible God?

   Moses is shaken by the question. He rebuffs Aron and blusters on about God (5th Correction).

7. They become polarized, each in his own world; they cannot communicate. Moses begins to have doubts about his methods.

8. Moses continues to have doubts. He tries to speak Aron's language (by abandoning *Sprechstimme* and singing) in order to turn him around (6th Correction). He fails.

9. Aron remains polarized, fixed on his own vision. He thanks God for showing him the proper way to worship Him (i.e., through images).

   Moses ends up defeated. He, too, holds fast to his own vision, and is unwilling to make further efforts to communicate with Aron.

Figure 6-3. A dramatic outline of Act I, scene 2.

tates the accentuation of the turning point of the scene, marked by the cluster of repetitions preceding "Darfst?" in Figure 6-2, and the multiple repetitions of the word "Gott" that follow. The ways in which these two strategies are sonically developed by Schoenberg in both the orchestra and the vocal parts form the subject of the final two sections.

Orchestral Features

In an opera, all musical elements, both abstract and audible, are inextricably linked to the drama. Or, to allow Milton Babbitt to put it more precisely, with regard to *Moses und Aron*:

> Among any events in the opera, coherence and continuity are effected through set forms, transpositional levels, melodic, harmonic, and rhythmic motivic elements, individual and composite rhythms, timbre, texture, and the interrelation of all these factors with the ideational and sonic structure of the text.[47]

Babbitt's interrelation, as it pertains to Act I, scene 2, will be the focus of this portion of the essay, which is divided into two sections devoted to orchestral features and vocal features, respectively. Each of these aspects of the scene will be examined for its individual contribution to the antithetical relationship between Moses and Aron, and it will be shown that the orchestral and vocal parts work together to accentuate Aron's attainment of his main objective for the scene.

An initial survey of some of the results obtained by comparing orchestral and vocal features with one another reveals a composite of aural and structural associations that is constructed for each character. Moses is associated aurally with low instruments, including the trombone, the tuba, and the contrabass, duple meter, low register, loud dynamics, and slow tempi. He is associated structurally with the major-second transpositional level of the row and its straightforward linear segments.[48] Aron, on the other hand, is associated aurally with higher, more lyrical instruments, such as the cello, flute, and violin, triple or irregular meter, high register, quiet dynamics, and faster tempi. Structurally, he is linked to the perfect-fifth transposition of the row and a division of the row into segments based on a selection of every other pitch in its sequence.[49]

Figure 6-4 charts six aurally salient features of the music that highlight the dialogue of contrast already present in Schoenberg's libretto, including texture, dynamics, tempo, meter, register, and timbre. The fourth and fifth columns, marked "Texture" and "Dynamics," represent the two features that dominate in the accentuation of this dialogue. The term "texture" is used here to denote a phenomenon that might be more familiar as "density." Here, texture is defined as the number of synchronic strands of music present at a given moment, including octave doublings. The strands employed yield a relative "thinness" or "thickness" of texture, depending on how many are present.

Sec.	Measures	Character/Drama	Texture	Dynamics
1	98 - 123	(instrumental intro.)	6 — 4 ╱	p — f
2	123 - 145	A/M: <u>1st correction</u>	1 — 3	f —
3	145 - 147	(inst. interlude)	7 — 7 ╱	—ppp
4	148 - 162	A/M: <u>2nd correction</u> <u>3rd correction</u> <u>4th correction</u>	3 — 10	p — ff
5	163 - 177	A: (shows devotion, but . . .)	11 — 16 ╱	mp — ff ╱
6	178 - 181	A: <u>Big Question</u>	10 — 0 ╱	pppp ╱
7	182	M: <u>Rebuttal</u>	(5) ╱	f ╱
8	183 - 186	M: <u>5th correction</u> (blustering)	11 — 0 ╱	pp — ff
9	187 - 207	A/M: separation M: <u>Big Question</u>	7 — 5	—f ╱
10	208 - 217	M: <u>6th correction</u>	5 — 3	p — ╱
11	218 - 233	A: Oblivious	6 — 12 ╱	—ff ╱
12	234 - 243	A: Devotion M: Defeat	5 — 5	pp—

Figure 6-4. Musical illustrations of the dialogue of contrast.

Seven of the twelve sections (which are marked 1–12 in the column on the far left labeled "SEC" for "Section") are defined texturally by a shift of three or more strands, indicated by diagonal lines in the "Texture" column. These twelve sections are adapted from the dramatic outline presented for reference in the "Character/Drama" Column; Sections 1 and 3, representing instrumental passages, are additions. The dramatic outline shows that the action of the scene is centered around six "corrections" by

Sec.	Measures	Tempo	Meter	Register	Timbre
1	98 - 123	= 66 a tempo	6 / 8	—$f^{\#2}$	A1
2	123 - 145	—	4/4, 12/8	—a^2	M1/A1
3	145 - 147	—	—	—	A1
4	148 - 162	= 84 more moving	3/4	$F^{\#}_1$—	A2'
5	163 - 177	= 132 lively, then slowing	5/4	—a^2	M2
6	178 - 181	very slow	6/4	E_1— e^3	A2"
7	182	—	2/4	—	M1'
8	183 - 186	= @58 a tempo	3/2	—	A1'
9	187 - 207	= 84 more moving	3/4	—	A1'
10	208 - 217	= 72 slower	4/4	—	M2'
11	218 - 233	= 132 faster	5/4	—	M2"
12	234 - 243	= 72 slower	3/4, 4/4	—	M1"

Figure 6-4 . (*continued*)

Moses, responses that he makes to Aron's misconceptions about God. In the most basic sense, then, the texture of the scene supports some of the dramatic shifts (or "beats" in Stanislavskian parlance) delineated by these corrections, carrying out the Principle of Intensification by emphasizing the building argument between Moses and Aron.

Beyond mere sectional support, texture assists in building dramatic tension in the scene through internal textural "crescendi" and "decrescendi" and the demarcation of climactic points in the drama. Section 6, the moment where Aron poses the fundamental question of the scene ("People . . . can you worship what you dare not even conceive?"), is marked in two ways. First, it encompasses the largest shift up to that point, a shift of six strands, from the sixteen-strand peak at the end of Section 5 to ten strands at the beginning of Section 6. Second, it involves the largest internal "textural dynamic" heard up to that point, a decrescendo from ten strands to none. These two factors have the effect of setting Section 6 in relief, marking it for the listener as the turning point of the scene.

Figure 6-5 is an amplification of the "Texture" column of Figure 6-4. It gives a clearer visual representation of the textural shifts just described. In the second row of the figure, the textural crescendo that begins at Section 4 can be plainly seen, culminating at the point marked with an arrow at m. 176. Just as striking is the rapid decrescendo following this textural peak: a texture that took Schoenberg 28 measures to build up is liquidated in 5, ending in silence at m. 181. The passage that immediately follows, mm. 181–87, can be considered a kind of textural coda, representing the frustrated rebuttal by Moses in Sections 7 and 8 (here I am referring back to Figure 6-4). Notably, this rebuttal now foreshadows his defeat, since it is short-lived from the textural perspective,

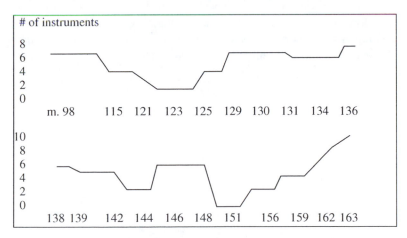

Figure 6-5. Textural shifts and crescendi.

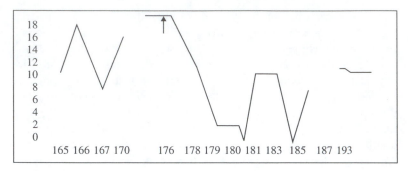

Figure 6-5. (*continued*)

dying out again at m. 187, and since it does not reach the heights of the previous sixteen-strand climax at m. 176.

In terms of dynamics, six of the twelve sections are emphasized by shifts from loud to soft (marked by diagonal lines in the "Dynamics" column of Figure 6-4). Just as in the case of texture, Section 6, as the climactic moment, is given the most dramatic shift (from *ff* to *pppp*), but the move is prepared and followed by large shifts both between and within Sections 4–8. In general, these two features, texture and dynamics, work together to form a pattern of fluctuation and contrast. Two places where they differ are interesting. In Section 6, the textural decrescendo has the effect of diminishing the quadruple-*piano* even further. Section 8, on the other hand, accentuates the futile blustering of Moses by decreasing the number of orchestra voices supporting his vocal line while he grows steadily louder in an effort to compensate for the lack of support. Clearly the orchestra is lending its support to Aron's side of the argument, and this is reinforced by the fact that it plays his timbre in this section, rather than that of Moses.

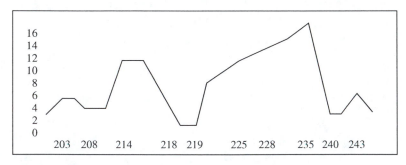

Figure 6-5. (*continued*)

The other features listed in Figure 6-4, with the exception of register, all fulfill the Principle of Contrast by building up a paradigmatic set of musical attributes for each character. As the "preview" given at the beginning of this section stated, Moses is associated aurally with slow tempi, duple meter, and low instruments; Aron with faster tempi, triple or irregular meter, and higher or more lyrical instruments. One of these three features—timbre—is particularly consistent in its association with each character. Figure 6-6 is an amplification of the "Timbre" column of Figure 6-4. It shows the primary timbral alternation of the scene, between Aron's two colors (Timbres A1 and A2) and those of Moses (Timbres M1 and M2). The alternation is marked by square brackets in the column headed "Timbre" in Figure 6-6 (A=Aron, M=Moses, and the apostrophes indicate a variation of the original timbre).

Vocal Features

Though Moses is only given specific, fixed pitches in one spot in the scene (and the entire opera), his *Sprechstimme* (a type of artificial vocal enunciation between speech and song) does have rhythm, register, and notes of differing durational value that can be examined in relation to the text. By m. 129, eighth-notes have become fairly standard and a quarter-note is used at cadences. Again in m. 145, a quarter-note is used for the end of a phrase. Up through m. 162, Moses's note values lengthen gradually, until, at m. 162, he reaches his highest, longest note thus far, a C on the word "denken." This moment coincides with the first peak in the tension between the two characters: the passage where Aron reveals his fundamental problem with his brother's abstract theology in mm. 163–81.

The next important moment for Moses is the beginning of his rebuttal of Aron's argument at m. 182, where he replies "Dare not?" Here his line reaches another high C on a quarter-note, marking this as one of his more important notes. Finally, in m. 185 (on the word "Einer"), Schoenberg places a fermata over another high C in Moses's vocal line, just before Aron begins a new phrase at m. 187 that will lead to Moses's voicing of self-doubt about his method of loving God. During this period of self-questioning, Moses's line ascends even higher to a D-flat in m. 201 on the words "to whom the reward?"

Running out of ways to get his point across to his brother, Moses tries to use Aron's own technique against him in m. 208; that is, he sings. He reaches his longest note of the piece at m. 213 on the word "Wahren," the last note of his sung line. Schoenberg's use of a sung line at this point

Timbre A1	Aron's opening color: flute, violins, harp (high inst.)
Timbre A2	Aron's second color: cellos (lyrical)
Timbre M1	Moses's color: contrabass, tromb., and tuba (low inst.)
Timbre M2	Moses's second color: the larger orch. (winds/strings)

Measure	Timbre
98	A1
115	A1
121	A1
123	M1
125	A1'
127	M1'
129	A1'
131	A2
133	A1'
138	M1
139	A2
140	A1"
142	M1'
144	A2'
145	A1'
148	A2'
163	M2
178	A2"
182	M1'
187	A1'
199	M1'
203	A2'
208	M2'
215	M1'
218	M2"
234	M1"

Figure 6-6. Timbral changes.

accentuates the importance of the dividing line between the two characters, in accordance with the Principle of Contrast: Moses will only cross
that line in desperation, as a last resort. This dividing line is enforced
throughout the scene as well. It is only when Aron hesitates briefly as he

poses his fundamental question that his lyrical vocal line falls into *recitativo* (pitched notes, but very detached ones), hovering close to the *Sprechstimme* used by Moses.

In his vocal line, then, Moses emphasizes the following words: "denken" [reflection], "Darfst" [dare not], and "Wahren" [righteous]. The musical singling-out of these words is appropriate, as they are the key concepts for Moses: for him, God is found through personal thought and reflection. He who follows this true path to God is righteous. And Moses is trying desperately to explain to Aron that it is not that he is forbidding the imaging of God so that the Volk will not dare to create their images; it is simply that God does not exist in those images in the first place. It is interesting, however, that his "highest note," as mentioned, occurs during the phrase "[Wem] Gebührt dem Lohn," or, "to whom the reward?" Obviously, it is this fear that plagues him, the fear that Aron may in fact be justified in his approach to the worship of God.

Finally, it is important to note that most of Moses's powerful vocal moments (mm. 162, 182, 185–86, 208) coincide with the sections mentioned previously (sections 5, 7, 9, and 10 of Figure 6-4, respectively), helping to further delineate them. Thus, Schoenberg's setting of Moses's text supports both the tension-building aspect of the scene (following the Principle of Intensification), by supporting the sectional divisions, and the paradigmatic contrasts between the two characters (following the Principle of Contrast), by creating a set of aurally prominent textual associations for Moses that support his side of the argument.

Aron's vocal line, like that of Moses, emphasizes three words through longer durational value: "Volk," "Gott," and "Liebe." These make sense for his character, because his love for the people and his desire to give them their God are the overwhelming influences in his life. As David Lewin has noted, in his love for the people Aron is closer in some ways to God than Moses (who does not love the people and would rather contemplate God alone).[50]

Aron's vocal line, charted in Figure 6-7, is complicated, however, by the fact that his registral peaks do not always coincide with his durational peaks. Two familiar principles govern Aron's registral movement: the Principle of Intensification, which governs the heightening of tension in the scene, and the Principle of Contrast, which necessitates the emphasis of the key words just outlined. Most of the important words, as illustrated on the right hand side of Figure 6-7, are set to pitches no lower than F. They thus fall in the top quarter of the tessitura and receive a commensurate amount of aural prominence. In general, however, though his line is constantly rising and falling, the top of Aron's range is continuously expanded as the scene progresses, musically increasing the tension in accordance with the drama and reflecting registrally his ideological polarization from Moses. In other words, as the scene is played out, Aron literally moves further and further away from Moses. This is shown on the left side of Figure 6-7, where a general rise in tessitura is marked with arrows, from G all the way up to B-natural, the putative top of the tenor range. Orchestral register also serves to increase the level of tension in the scene, culminating in the simultaneous arrival of the apex (e^3) and the nadir (E_1) in Section 6 (marked back in Figure 6-4).

CONCLUSION

This essay has demonstrated how all aspects of the scene are integrally linked together through the Principles of Contrast and Intensification. By illustrating how aurally salient features of both the text and the music emphasize the dialogue of contrast between Moses and Aron that leads to

Measure	Pitch	Measure	Word	Duration	Pitch
124	$c^\#$	130	Bruder	2 beats	-
126	g	134	Gefass	2 beats	-
129	e	137	Gnade	2+ beats	-
134	d	140	**Volk**	**3 beats**	**f**
138	$c^\#$	144	Macht	2 beats	-
155	Ⓖ	145	Besitzt	2 beats	-
161-2	G	163	**Volk**	**3 beats**	$f^\#$
164	Ⓖ$^\#$	166	**Gott**	**3 beats**	$f^\#$
167	Ⓐ-B$^\flat$	167-8	**Lieben**	**6 beats**	**B$^\flat$**
173	B$^\flat$-A	170	**Liebe**	**6 beats**	$g^\#$
176	g	172	Volker	2 beats	-
183	A-a$^\flat$	175-6	Lieben	2 beats	g
193	A	183	Gott	2 beats	-
197	a$^\flat$	194	Gott	2 beats	-
201	a$^\flat$	201	**Gott**	**3 beats**	a$^\flat$
204	a$^\flat$	219	**Gott**	**3 beats**	f
228	Ⓑ$^\flat$	222	**Volk**	**4 beats**	-
232	Ⓑ	240	Knechtshaft	3 beats	-
238	a$^\flat$				

Figure 6-7. Aron's vocal line: durational and registral peaks.

Aron's eventual dramatic triumph, and by identifying that triumph through a Stanislavskian analysis of the objectives of each character, I have worked to corroborate Abbate and Parker's thesis that " 'analyzing opera' should mean not only 'analyzing music' but simultaneously engaging with equal sophistication, the poetry and the drama." [51]

As mentioned in the introduction, however, there is a further conclusion to be drawn. That Schoenberg's setting of the opera breaks off at the moment when, at the end of Act II, Moses falls to his knees and cries "O Wort! Du Wort das mir fehlt!" is especially suggestive in light of the analysis of Moses's superobjective: to induce the people to worship the one true God. In his writings on the superobjective, Stanislavsky speaks not only of a superobjective for each character but also of a superobjective for an entire play or opera: the goal of the work. For *Moses und Aron*, one possibility for this superobjective might be to convince the audience of the essentially unrepresentable nature of the Idea. While it is true that the chorus of voices from the burning bush in Act I, scene 1 are meant to represent the voice of God, the singers are still invisible to the audience and they avoid the purely representational lyricism of Aron's vocal line.

If the superobjective of the opera can, to a certain extent, be considered the goal of the author in creating the work, then Schoenberg's goal is akin to that of Moses, and the opera becomes a "fundamental drama of communication," as Harry Halbreich puts it, written by "a profoundly religious man who regarded his art as a kind of priesthood." [52] What makes the opera so successful is the way in which Schoenberg uses all the textual, dramatic, and musical resources at his command to enable his people to comprehend the incomprehensibility of his greatest idea.

NOTES

1. Hans Heinz Stuckenschmidt, *Schoenberg: His Life, World and Work*, trans. Humphrey Searle (London: Calder, 1977), 152.

2. Arnold Schoenberg to Frank Pelleg and Oedoen Partos, 15 June 1951, cited in André Neher, *They Made Their Souls Anew*, trans. David Maisel (Albany: State University of New York Press, 1990), 163. Original source unspecified.

3. See Bluma Goldstein, *Reinscribing Moses: Heine, Kafka, Freud, and Schoenberg in a European Wilderness* (Cambridge, Mass: Harvard University Press, 1992); Michael Mäckelmann, *Schönberg und das Judentum: Der Komponist und sein religiöses, nationales, und politisches Selbstverständnis nach 1921*, Hamburger Beiträge zur Musikwissenschaft 28 (Hamburg: Verlag der Musikalienhandlung Karl Dieter Wagner, 1984); André Neher, *They Made Their*

Souls Anew; and Alexander Ringer, *Arnold Schoenberg: The Composer as Jew* (Oxford: Clarendon Press, 1990).

4. Neher puts forward the notion that Schoenberg's conversion to Lutheranism was "an act of purely social significance" (*They Made Their Souls Anew*, 150); Bluma Goldstein disagrees, noting that "being a Protestant in Catholic Austria was not an asset" (*Reinscribing Moses*, 138).

5. A facsimile of the original document (Arnold Schoenberg Institute 2282) may be found in Ringer, *Arnold Schoenberg: The Composer as Jew*, 135; a translation is included in Neher, *They Made Their Souls Anew*, 13.

6. According to Neher, the publicity surrounding the ceremony was the result of "awkward handling" by one of the two witnesses, a Dr. Marianoff. See Neher, *They Made Their Souls Anew*, 151.

7. Arnold Schoenberg to Alban Berg, 16 October 1933, quoted in Bluma Goldstein, *Reinscribing Moses,* 140. A translation of the letter may be found in *The Berg-Schoenberg Correspondence: Selected Letters*, ed. Juliane Brand, Christopher Hailey, and Donald Harris (New York: W. W. Norton, 1987), 446. Dating the libretto for *Moses und Aron* is difficult. Jan Maegaard's book, *Studien zur Entwicklung des dodekaphonen Satzes bei Arnold Schönberg* (Copenhagen: Wilhelm Hansen, 1972), one of the more recent authoritative sources for dating Schoenberg's works, dates the libretto to 1928. In the same 1933 letter to Berg, however, Schoenberg mentions 1928 as the year in which Berg learned of the work, but says it "goes back at least another five years" (*The Berg-Schoenberg Correspondence*, 446).

8. Hans Heinz Stuckenschmidt, *Arnold Schoenberg*, trans. Edith Temple Roberts and Humphrey Searle (New York: Grove, 1959), 74.

9. Scholars who have addressed this issue include Neher, *They Made Their Souls Anew*, 149; Goldstein, *Reinscribing Moses*, 149–52; and Alexander Ringer, *Arnold Schoenberg: The Composer as Jew*, 52–4.

10. Rudolf Kolisch to George Alter, 1933, Schönberg dossier, Georg Alter Archives, National Library, Jerusalem. Quoted in Neher, *They Made Their Souls Anew*, 158.

11. George Steiner, "Schoenberg's *Moses and Aron*," in *Language and Silence* (New York: Atheneum, 1967), 139, takes this view, noting that "events that were now come to pass in Europe were, quite literally, beyond words . . . that art can neither stem barbarism nor convey experience when experience becomes unspeakable." Quoted in Goldstein, *Reinscribing Moses*, 151.

12. Arnold Schoenberg, *Moses und Aron*, in Arnold Schönberg, *Sämtliche Werke*, Series A, vol. 8 (Mainz: B. Schott's Söhne, 1977). Allen Forte, "Moses and Aron," English singing translation of the libretto, in program notes to Arnold Schoenberg, *Moses und Aron*, BBC Singers and Symphony Orchestra, Pierre

Boulez, Columbia Masterworks M2 33594, 11–23, 21. All subsequent citations are taken from the Forte translation, and will be referenced by page numbers in parentheses at the appropriate points in the text of the paper. Excerpts from both the German and English translations of the libretto are used by permission of Mr. Lawrence Schoenberg, Belmont Music Publishers, Pacific Palisades, California 90272.

13. The complex set of circumstances that prevented Schoenberg from realizing his dreams for the Jewish people is discussed in detail in Alexander Ringer, *Arnold Schoenberg: The Composer as Jew*, 116–49 *passim*.

14. Arnold Schoenberg to Ernst Toch, 1933, quoted in Stuckenschmidt, *Schoenberg* (1977), 542.

15. Stuckenschmidt, *Schoenberg* (1977), 542. Herzl, the founder of modern Zionism, was an ardent advocate for the creation of a separate Jewish state on the African continent.

16. Arnold Schoenberg, "A Four-Point Program for Jewry," in Ringer, *Arnold Schoenberg: The Composer as Jew*, 230–44.

17. Goldstein, *Reinscribing Moses*, 166.

18. Ringer, *Arnold Schoenberg: The Composer as Jew*, 53.

19. Neher, *They Made Their Souls Anew*, 152.

20. Ringer, *Arnold Schoenberg: The Composer as Jew*, 176.

21. Neher, *They Made Their Souls Anew*, 165.

22. Theodor W. Adorno, "Sakrales Fragment: Über Schönbergs *Moses und Aron*, in *Quasi una Fantasia, Musikalische Schriften II* (Frankfurt am Main: Suhrkamp, 1963), 307. Quoted in Goldstein, *Reinscribing Moses*, 151.

23. Arnold Schoenberg, "The Future of the Opera," in *Style and Idea: Selected Writings of Arnold Schoenberg*, ed. Leonard Stein, trans. Leo Black (Berkeley: University of California Press, 1984), 337.

24. Schoenberg, "The Future of the Opera," 337.

25. Ringer, *Arnold Schoenberg: The Composer as Jew*, 40.

26. Kurt Weill, "The Musician Weill," *Der Berliner Tageblatt*, Christmas 1928. Quoted in Ringer, *Arnold Schoenberg: The Composer as Jew*, 90.

27. Even in *Von heute auf morgen*, Schoenberg was Moses trying to speak Aron's language: whereas *Die Dreigroschenoper* is an unapologetically tonal work, Schoenberg's opera is one of his early twelve-tone masterworks.

28. The dating of these works varies depending on the source. Where discrepancies between Josef Rufer, *Das Werk Arnold Schönbergs* (Basel: Bärenreiter Kassel, 1959), Jan Maegaard, *Entwicklung des Dodekaphonen Satzes bei Arnold Schönberg*, and Alexander Ringer, *Arnold Schoenberg: The Composer as Jew*, exist, I have chosen Ringer as the most recent available source.

29. See Karl Wörner, *Schoenberg's "Moses and Aron,"* trans. Paul Hamburger (London: Faber and Faber, 1963), and Michael Cherlin, *The Formal and Dramatic Organization of Schoenberg's "Moses und Aron"* (Ph.D. diss., Yale University, 1983). Other authors that have interpreted the opera include Pamela C. White, *Schoenberg and the God-Idea: The Opera "Moses und Aron"* (Ann Arbor: UMI Research Press, 1985) and Odil Steck, *"Moses und Aron": Die Oper Arnold Schönbergs und ihr biblischer Stoff* (Munich: Kaiser, 1981). For analyses that focus primarily on music-structural issues, see David Lewin, *"Moses und Aron*: Some General Remarks, and Analytic Notes for Act I, Scene 1," and Milton Babbitt, "Three Essays on Schoenberg," in *Perspectives on Schoenberg and Stravinsky*, ed. Benjamin Boretz and Edward T. Cone (Westport, Conn.: Greenwood Press, 1983), 61–77 and 53–60, respectively.

30. Joseph Kerman, *Opera as Drama*, 2nd ed. (Berkeley: University of California Press, 1988), 58.

31. Carolyn Abbate and Roger Parker, ed., *Analyzing Opera* (Berkeley: University of California Press, 1989), 4.

32. The "Stanislavsky method" is a Bloomian "mis"-appropriation of specific elements of Stanislavsky's system by several of his students, including Stella Adler and Lee Strasberg. In a manner that is strikingly similar to the reception of Heinrich Schenker's theoretical ideas in the United States, Stanislavsky's ideas were brought overseas by his students and disseminated from a headquarters in New York, which eventually became known as the Group Theater.

33. Constantin Stanislavsky, *An Actor Prepares*, trans. Elizabeth Reynolds Hapgood (New York: Theatre Arts Books, 1936). *An Actor Prepares* is the first volume of Stanislavsky's trilogy detailing all aspects of the actor's craft. The complete system is outlined in Constantin Stanislavsky, *Building a Character*, trans. Elizabeth Reynolds Hapgood (New York: Theatre Arts Books, 1949), 261–65.

34. Stanislavsky, *Creating a Role*, trans. Elizabeth Reynolds Hapgood (New York: Theatre Arts Books, 1961), 78.

35. Stanislavsky, *Creating a Role*, 78.

36. Richard Cohn and Douglas Dempster, "Hierarchical Unity, Plural Unities: Toward a Reconciliation," in *Disciplining Music: Musicology and Its Canons*, ed. Katherine Bergeron and Philip V. Bohlman (Chicago: University of Chicago Press, 1992), 156–81.

37. Stanislavsky, *An Actor Prepares*, 112.

38. Stanislavsky, *Creating a Role*, 56.

39. For specifics on Stanislavsky's involvement with opera, see Constantin Stanislavsky, *Stanislavsky on Opera* (New York: Theatre Arts Books, 1975).

40. Stanislavsky, *Creating a Role*, 51.

41. Stanislavsky presents an outline of the external circumstances of Griboyedov's *Woe from Wit* in *Creating a Role*, 14–16.

42. Stanislavsky includes an example of such a list in *Building a Character*, 270–72.

43. Stanislavsky's score for the role of Chatski in Griboyedev's *Woe from Wit* is reproduced in *Creating a Role*, 56–62 For didactic purposes, Stanislavsky considerably expands the basic list of objectives in this outline, adding commentary from the point of view of the character in order to help his students see how the outline relates to the progression of the drama in time. The upper-case letters, A to C, are the main objectives of the first section of the play. The lower-case letters indicate creative objectives used to achieve each main objective.

44. Gertrud Schoenberg, "Note to *Moses und Aron*, Act III," in program notes to Arnold Schoenberg, *Moses und Aron*, BBC Singers and Symphony Orchestra, Pierre Boulez, Columbia Masterworks M2 33594, 22.

45. A previous version of some material in this section of the paper was published in Edward D. Latham, "The Dialogue of Contrast in *Moses und Aron*, Act I, Scene ii: Drama, Pitch Structure, and Aural Salience," *Journal of the Music Graduate Society*, McGill University (Spring 1997).

46. Allen Forte, "Notes on the Historical Background of the Opera and on the Text," in program notes to Arnold Schoenberg, *Moses und Aron*, Orchestra and Chorus of the Norddeutscher Rundfunk, Hans Rosbaud, Columbia Masterworks K3L-241, 1–2.

47. Babbitt, "Three Essays on Schoenberg," 57–58.

48. A "row," in case the term is unfamiliar to the reader, is a compositionally predetermined ordering of the twelve notes of the chromatic scale; a "segment" is a portion of that row. Due to space limitations, and the fact that this essay is intended for a general readership, I will not undertake an analysis of the scene's structural features here. The most important element of the scene's structure is the alternation between two pairs of related row forms. Because the entire opera is based on a single row, repeated over and over again, the main techniques by which Schoenberg achieves variation in the pitch material are transposition (i.e., shifting the row up or down in pitch) and inversion (flipping the row upside down). By transposing the row and combining it with an inversionally related variant, Schoenberg creates a pitch-specific collection for each character. He then alternates these two collections to intensify the dialogue of contrast already created by the other musical features of the scene. As the musical equivalent of Aron's dramatic triumph at the end of the scene, Schoenberg's choice to keep the accompanying musical material within the collection associated with Aron's character is a powerful indicator that he was thinking in dramatic terms when he conceived the opera's musical structure. For a more detailed analysis of the

twelve-tone structure of the opera, see Latham, "The Dialogue of Contrast in *Moses und Aron*, Act I, Scene ii."

49. This division has been dubbed the "Odd/Even partition" and discussed in detail by Cherlin in "The Formal and Dramatic Organization of Schoenberg's *Moses und Aron*," 93–103.

50. David Lewin, "*Moses und Aron*," 62.

51. Abbate and Parker, *Analyzing Opera*, 4.

52. Harry Halbreich, "Schoenberg's Religious Thinking," in program notes to Arnold Schoenberg, *Moses und Aron*, BBC Singers and Symphony Orchestra, Pierre Boulez, Columbia Masterworks M2 33594, 3–4.

CHAPTER 7

Schoenberg's *Moses und Aron*
A Vanishing Biblical Nation

BLUMA GOLDSTEIN

In a previous reading of Arnold Schoenberg's opera *Moses und Aron* several years ago I understood the work as concerned generally with issues of representing what is inherently unrepresentable, specifically with the possibility of imparting the reality of a boundless, timeless God to his chosen people.[1] Given the conflict between Moses's uncompromising assessment of the inadequacy of language to communicate what was, for him, absolutely spiritual and Aron's linguistic fluency and ability to construct images that function for the people as external evidence of divine presence and power, the opera attempted to resolve the communicative dilemma of language—of word, image, symbol—to transmit the idea of an "eternal, invisible, unrepresentable God." In that reading I observed Schoenberg's Moses's unmitigated devotion to a metaphysical goal connected with the second commandment's prohibition against making graven images of God and also his complete indifference to the broader ethical and social condition of the people, which is so prominent in the biblical narrative. In fact, completely absent from the Moses of the opera was the biblical concern with liberation from Egyptian bondage and with the creation of an exemplary nation through adherence to commandments and law for the governance of communal life. It had not occurred to me, however, that the absence, indeed the erasure, of nation and the historical process of nation building in *Moses und Aron* was the result not of casual selectivity or inattention to the biblical text, but rather of systematic editing, restructuring, and rewriting the record of Moses's divine commission as liberator and architect of the nation Israel.

If this is indeed the case, and if Israel's nationhood or its absence informs the complex meanings of this opera and its aesthetic shape, as I believe it does, then the politics of nationhood or its exclusion may best be understood by exploring the relationship between Bible and opera and the implications of the textual decisions Schoenberg made.[2] This essay attempts first to examine a few salient revisions Schoenberg made and the ideational and ideological consequences of those changes; it will then shift its focus to a close reading of the libretto, concentrating on the intellectual and aesthetic structure of the opera; and finally try to explore and assess the larger social and perhaps political significance of revisions which, by eliding the historical and national significance of the exodus story, may be understood as a serious critique of the biblical narrative.

CONCEPTUAL TRANSFORMATIONS
OF THE BIBLICAL STORY

In 1923, just two years after Schoenberg (who had converted to Protestantism more than two decades earlier) suffered a traumatic anti-Semitic insult later identified as the impetus of his return to Judaism, he wrote his friend Wassily Kandinsky that he had turned down an invitation to join the Weimar Bauhaus cultural center because of rumors of anti-Semitism: "For what I was forced to learn in the course of the last year," he wrote, alluding to the earlier anti-Semitic incident, "I have finally understood and shall not yet again forget. Specifically, that I am no German, no European, indeed perhaps hardly a human being (at least the Europeans prefer the worst of their race to me), but that I am a Jew."[3] In that year he had already embarked on two major works on Jewish subjects: a drama, *Der biblische Weg* [*The Biblical Way*], unpublished in his lifetime and never performed,[4] and *Moses und Aron.* A 1933 letter from exile in Paris charts his return to Judaism along a Mosaic trail that, even in that fateful year, reveals a greater concern with theology than with the plight of the Jewish people: "As you surely noticed," he wrote Alban Berg, "my return to the Jewish religion took place long ago and can be recognized in my work, even in the published portions ('Du sollst nicht . . . Du mußt' [Thou shalt not . . . thou must . . .]) and in *Moses und Aron* about which you have known since 1928, but which goes back at least five years before that; but especially in my drama 'Der biblische Weg,' which was conceived at the latest in 1922 or 1923, though completed only in '26–'27."[5] "Du sollst nicht . . . du mußt . . . ," the second of *Vier Stücke für gemischten Chor* [*Four Pieces for Mixed Chorus*] composed in

1925,[6] refers specifically to the second commandment of the Decalogue prohibiting images of God, and is clearly related to major issues in both *Der biblische Weg* and *Moses und Aron*, but the drama also explores the possibility of escaping an intolerable situation in Europe and creating an African national homeland (a fictional realization of Theodor Herzl's "Uganda solution"), a modern Jewish state, a "new Palestine." Although while still working on the text of *Moses und Aron* Schoenberg experienced the increasingly perilous situation of European Jews—he had suffered humiliating anti-Semitic personal and professional insults in Germany, fled to Paris when the National Socialists came to power, and in 1934 emigrated to the United States—the opera exhibits small concern for the physical, social, or political welfare of the Israelites.

As an introduction to the scope and function of the biblical revisions in *Moses und Aron*, let me explore three interrelated substantive alterations to the biblical narrative that mark major conceptual transformations: replacing social and political liberation with spiritual or metaphysical deliverance; supplanting a God involved with, among other things, the Israelites' social and historical destiny by an abstract metaphysical entity seemingly exclusively interested in their spiritual devotion; and, finally, displacing the biblical God intimately involved with the people's life and welfare with one unconcerned with their physical well-being.

Liberation and Land[7]

Moses's concern, in *Moses und Aron*, is not with the actuality of Egyptian oppression and enslavement, but rather with the spiritual impoverishment of a people too preoccupied with the transitory and the quotidian; and the promised land—here associated not with a place or territory for settlement, but with a spiritual state of absolute devotion to an abstract deity—is divested of its reality as a discursive site of national identity in the biblical text. Indeed, in the opera, liberation requires neither a prolonged struggle with Pharaoh nor advance to a homeland, but can readily be realized by transferring one's attention from the commonplace and temporal to the transcendent and eternal.

In the Bible, Egypt and the promised land, Canaan, may be figured metaphorically as sites of enslavement and oppression and of plenitude, respectively, but they always retain a literal spatial, physical, and historical presence that is instrumental in the narrative of Israel's national formation. Indeed, almost as if to call attention to the historicity of Egypt and of Jewish life there, the Book of Exodus begins with a catalogue of the Israelites, previously detailed in Genesis, who had settled there and recounts the perilous changes that occurred after the accession of a new Pharaoh who was no longer obligated to Joseph. The change in the opera is significant. Alluding to Moses's first encounter with God in Exodus 3, *Moses und Aron* opens (after 6 Solo Voices sing the vowel "O" four times in the opening seven bars, no doubt suggesting the spiritual presence of the deity)[8] with Moses reciting the characteristics of his God— "Einziger, ewiger, allgegenwärtiger, unsichtbarer und unvorstellbarer Gott!" [Only, eternal, omnipresent, invisible, and unrepresentable God][9]—followed by the Voice, soon acknowledged as that of God, speaking out of the thornbush and commanding Moses first to preach or promulgate [*Verkünde!*], then to liberate his (that is, Moses's) people. While in the biblical text God openly declares that he wants the people liberated from Egyptian oppression, the mandate in *Moses und Aron* is equivocal and ambiguous. One need only compare the texts of Bible and opera to recognize critical differences:

> And the Lord continued, "I have marked well the plight of My peo-ple in Egypt and have heeded their outcry because of their taskmasters; yes, I am mindful of their sufferings. I have come down to rescue them from the Egyptians, and to bring them out of that land to a good and spacious land, a land flowing with milk and honey, the region of the Canaanites, the Hittites, the Amorites, the Perizzites, the Hivites, and the Jebusites. Now the cry of the Israelites has reached Me; moreover, I have seen how the Egyptians oppress them. Come, therefore, I will send you to the Pharaoh, and you shall free My people, the Israelites, from Egypt."[10]
>
> Exodus 3: 7–10

> Die Stimme:
> Du hast die Greuel gesehen, die Wahrheit
> erkannt; so kannst du nicht anders mehr:
> du mußt dein Volk daraus befreien!
> [The Voice:
> You have seen the horror, recognized
> the truth: so you can do nothing else any longer:
> you must liberate your people from that!](112)

The biblical citation above identifies quite specifically the privations the Israelites suffer, the lands from which they are to be liberated and to which they are to be brought, and the Israelites as God's own people

("My people" as opposed to the operatic "your [Moses's] people").[11] The substance and significance of God's words in *Moses und Aron*, however, are enigmatic and elusive: Just what does liberation signify here—from what and for what are these people to be liberated? What is the horror Moses has seen—is it a physical horror such as the beating of slaves or the moral horror of a spiritually degraded people? And what is the nature of this "truth" Moses is supposed to have recognized? Since to understand this utterance, one would have to know the referents of "horror" and "truth," it would seem that Moses either knows them or could attribute to these words whatever meanings he wished. Furthermore, two important aspects of the biblical text have been written out of the operatic one; that is, the voices of the people to which God responds and the recognition, in the Bible, that the promised land is not an abstract site or idea, but a territory filled with many different kinds of peoples.

God Dehistoricized

What, then, is the conception of God in *Moses und Aron*? And how does it differ from that in Exodus? In Exodus God refers to himself in several ways: He tells Moses to introduce him to the Pharaoh as "God of the Hebrews," identifies himself at times as the "God of Israel," at least four times as "the God of Abraham, the God of Isaac, and the God of Jacob," and when Moses inquires about his name, he answers in two ways: *Ehyeh-Asher-Ehyeh* (variously translated as "I Am Who I Am," "I Will Be What Will Be," etc.) and "Thus you shall say to the Israelites: '*Ehyeh* ["I Am" or "I Will Be"] sent me to you'" (Exodus 3: 14), emphasizing both that God is the ground of all being with no restrictions on anything and that he has a special relation with Israel.[12] Although traditional commentaries on Exodus 3:14 often refer to God as the "Eternal One," he does not, however, refer to himself as the Only God or Eternal One. It is also worth noting here that both versions of the Decalogue, which is the preamble to the covenant through which Israel became a people, are introduced by a God whose unique relationship with Israel is understood not only historically, but as specifically associated with liberation from Egyptian oppression: "I the Lord am your God who brought you out of the land of Egypt, the house of bondage" (Exodus 20: 2; Deuteronomy 5: 6). The Bible articulates a precarious tension in Israelite belief between a God that is both the exclusive creator of the world and one that nevertheless chose to conduct his project with humanity in relation to the historical destiny of a particular people and a particular land.

Even before he is enjoined to free his people in *Moses und Aron*, Moses enunciates two different views of God within moments of each other: "Only, eternal, omnipresent, invisible, and unrepresentable God" and "God of my fathers, God of Abraham, Isaac, and Jacob," a God involved in the history of the Israelites. Though these conceptions are neither necessarily contradictory nor mutually exclusive, Moses nevertheless adopts one to the exclusion of the other. Thus, the latter designation, which corresponds to the frequently recurring self-representation of God in Exodus, appears only once in the text (in Moses's second pronouncement in Act I, scene 1), whereas the former one, which is the first utterance in the opera and occurs repeatedly throughout, informs all of Moses's ideas and expectations. In opting for this one conception of God, however, Moses may not merely be pursuing his own idiosyncratic inclination for a God that is an ineffable idea, but in fact adopting God's expressed self-representation in the text. This God, whose pronouncements are clearly directed principally toward metaphysical existence, never identifies himself as the God of Abraham, Isaac, and Jacob, but only as "der Einzige" and "der Ewige" (114) and—after tersely noting that liberation requires rejecting the Pharoah—elaborates on the importance of renouncing the transitory and devoting oneself to a God that is unique and eternal:

> Moses:
> Wer bin ich, mich der Macht der Blindheit
> entgegenzustellen?
> Die Stimme:
> Dem einzigen Gott verbunden,
> mit Pharao entzweit!
> Moses:
> Was bezeugt dem Volk meinen Auftrag?
> Die Stimme:
> Des Einzigen Name!
> Der Ewige will es befreien, daß es nicht
> mehr Vergänglichem diene.
> . . . . . .
> Dieses Volk ist auserwählt,
> vor allen Völkern,
> das Volk des einzigen Gottes zu sein,
> daß es ihn erkenne
> und sich ihm allein ganz widme;
> . . . . . .
> Ich will euch dorthin führen,

wo ihr mit dem Ewigen einig
und allen Völkern ein Vorbild werdet.
[Moses:
Who am I to oppose the power of blindness?
The Voice:
Bound to the only God,
at one with you [singular/mit dir],
alienated from Pharaoh!
Moses:
What gives the people proof of my mandate?
The Voice:
The Name of the Only One!
The Eternal one wants to liberate it [the people], so that it no
longer serves what is transitory.
. . . . . .
This people is chosen,
before all peoples,
to be the people of the only [einzigen] God,
that it recognize Him
and devote itself to Him alone;
. . . . . .
I want to lead you [plural/euch, referring to Moses and his people]
      there,
where you will be united with the Eternal One,
and become a model for all peoples.](112–14)

Although initially Moses's list of divine attributes seems to be a response
to an audible yet undifferentiated utterance of the divine vowel sound,
the "O," his tenacious adherence thereafter to that same abstract conception of God throughout the opera seems related to the divine voice's articulated self-representation as unique and eternal.

God and His people? Moses's People?

By significantly refiguring the biblical event that is seminal for the formation of the nation Israel and its religion, namely, the commissioning of
Moses at the burning bush, the opening scene foregrounds the dominant
ideas and interests of the opera. In addition to the two major changes already mentioned—the transformation in the conceptions of liberation
and of God—there is a subtle yet significant shift from Bible to opera in
the relationship between God and the people. It involves a move from a

biblical God intimately involved with the life and welfare of the Israelites to a deity seemingly unconcerned with their social well-being.[13] Thus, in Exodus God refers to the people as "My people" whom he will deliver from Egyptian bondage because he himself has witnessed their misery, and Moses is the medium through which this will be accomplished: "I will send you to Pharaoh," God tells Moses, "and you shall free *My people*, the Israelites, from Egypt" (Exodus 3:10; emphasis added). Indeed, it is precisely this act of liberation that created a unique mutual bond between God and the people: "And I will take you to be My people," Moses is told to inform the people, "and I will be your God. And you shall know that I, the Lord, am your God who freed you from the labors of the Egyptians. I will bring you to the land which I swore to give to Abraham, Isaac, and Jacob, and I will give it you for a possession, I am the Lord" (Exodus 6:7–8). God's recognition of the Israelites as his own may have provided a model for Moses's later alliance of equality with his people when, for example, Moses speaks to God of "Your people and I" (Exodus 33:16). In *Moses und Aron*, however, God identifies the Israelites, on the one hand, as his own, as the chosen people of this "only God," yet, on the other, in relation to their particular predicament and practical needs, he refers to them not as his own, but as Moses's people: it is because *Moses* has "seen the horror, recognized the truth" that Moses must liberate *his*, that is, *Moses's* people. The detachment of God from the people is further accentuated when he and his voice disappear completely from the text after the opening scene.

Underscoring the remoteness of this God, this *deus absconditus*, in *Moses und Aron* is Moses's conception of the pillars of cloud and fire, which blatantly reverses their manifest function and significance in the Bible, where the pillars accompany the Israelites and constitute one recognizable way in which God abides continuously among the people and protects them: "The Lord went before them in a pillar of cloud by day and a pillar of fire by night, to give them light, that they may travel by day and night. The pillar of cloud by day and the pillar of fire by night did not depart from before the people" (Exodus 13: 21–22; see also Exodus 14: 19–20; Numbers 12:5, 14:14; and Deuteronomy 31:15). In the opera, however, after destroying the Golden Calf, Moses expresses horror when, confronted with the people following pillars of fire and cloud and condemning Aron's sanction of this activity, he dismisses the pillars as godless images, *Götzenbilder* [Idols] (194). When Aron explains that the pillars affirm the presence of God without revealing Him—"Gottes Zeichen, wie der glühende Dornbusch./ Darin zeigt der Ewige nicht sich,/

aber den Weg zu sich;/ und den Weg ins gelobte Land!" [God's sign, like the glowing thornbush./ Therein the Eternal One shows not Himself,/ but the way to Him;/ and the way to the promised land!] (194)—a despondent Moses collapses because of the people's spiritual degradation, which con- taminates the ineffable reality of an "Unvorstellbarer Gott! Unaussprech- licher, vieldeutiger Gedanke!" [Unrepresentable God! Inexpressible, ambiguous Idea!] (194) by bringing it into the worldly arena. Aron's ex- planation of the pillars' function, however, actually accords with the bibli- cal conception. Indeed, this is not the only instance in the opera in which Aron's views and insights conform more closely to the biblical text than do those of Moses; some of the more prominent ones include Aron's idea of emancipation as freedom from the Pharaoh's bondage (122, 152), his understanding of the promised land as an actual place where the people can settle happily (152), and his ongoing concern for the physical and so- cial needs of the people.

THE LIBRETTO: A CLOSER LOOK

At this juncture it must be obvious that rewritings of the biblical text (and there are more to come) are best elucidated within the context of the overall *Moses und Aron* libretto. Because they not only challenge crucial ideas of the biblical narrative about nationhood and religion, but also contribute mightily to the intellectual and aesthetic structure of the opera, I shall shift the focus to the ideational and aesthetic aspects of the opera as a whole.

The libretto to *Moses und Aron* was completed in October 1928 and consists of three acts. By August 1931 the score for the first act was com- plete, and in March of the following year the score of the second; lacking a musical score, act three remains incomplete. Textual revisions to the third act were made in 1934 and 1935 after Schoenberg emigrated to the United States, but in 1937 only sketches for a few measures of music were composed. Although there are indications to the year of his death in 1951 that he intended to finish the opera, that did not occur. I have dis- cussed elsewhere the many aesthetic and philosophical questions this un- finished text has raised among critics for almost half a century, but while the various arguments are interesting and important, this is not the place to recount them again. My own position remains unchanged, namely, to regard "the opera as one whose third act is spoken and to resist speculat- ing about the philosophical implications of an opera whose conclusion is without music."[14]

The overall tripartite structure of the opera concerns the dilemma of Moses's divine commission, that is, to impart to his people the nature of an ineffable, unrepresentable deity when any representation of such a deity could only falsify it. The first act includes the theophany at the burning bush; a dialogue between Moses and Aron about their mission and the nature of the deity; an insight into the needs and expectations of the people/ nation [Volk]; and finally, the encounter of Moses and Aron with the people. A very brief *"Zwischenspiel"* ["Interlude"] after Act 1, in which the people express their fear of having been abandoned by both Moses, who has been long absent, and his God, is followed by the second act, often considered the most "operatic" or "dramatic" part of the work because of the activity surrounding the creation of the Golden Calf and the ensuing wild orgy of sacrifice and jubilation at its altar. This act commences with the people's rebellion against an absent Moses and his God and concludes with a returning Moses who, bearing the Decalogue, immediately destroys the Golden Calf and later, in the course of a heated argument with Aron about their seemingly mutually exclusive assessments of tasks and achievements, smashes the tablets and finally collapses. In the third act, the mass of people is absent, but a totally silent group of elders and two warriors who are present to witness Moses's verbal avalanche all but obliterate Aron's explanations and insights; Aron, freed of his chains, collapses and dies, and for the first time in the opera Moses addresses the group directly.

Act One

Understanding the first act is crucial, in part, because it introduces the ways in which those deviations from and alterations of the biblical text that efface the evidence of nationhood and historicity are established, expanded, and corroborated within the libretto. The problematic role of the Bible in *Moses und Aron* becomes evident in this act, on the one hand, through diverse positions and ideas articulated by the voice from the burning bush, by Moses, Aron, and the people and, on the other, through the complex and powerful design of that articulation. Both of these aspects prepare for the ensuing conflicts in the opera and call attention to the major revisions to the biblical text. The act consists of four discrete scenes: scene one, the encounter between the voice from the burning bush, which Moses assumes is that of God, and Moses; scene two, a dialogue between Moses and Aron exposes the implications of their differing conceptions of God; scene three, a rather skeptical people airs its hopes and misgivings about Moses, Aron, and the new God; scene four, a prescient interaction between Moses, Aron, and the people about the kind of liberation and life this new God promises.

Conspicuous in the opening scene is the absence of definite location, indeed of any kind of discernible landscape whatsoever. Unlike the beginning of Exodus 3 which, at the site of the burning bush, situates Moses within a specific environment of family, country, and workplace—"Now Moses, tending the flock of his father-in-law Jethro, the priest of Midian, drove the flock into the wilderness, and came to Horeb, the mountain of God"—the first scene of the opera contains no such detail of social life; presented here is an isolated Moses in an amorphous, transcendent reality, one disclosed solely through a verbal interchange that recedes from concrete and mundane issues. In a previous reading of this scene, I had interpreted the revision of the biblical God's first utterance (after summoning Moses by name) not only as an expression of God's concern for Moses's bodily comfort, but also as an indication that the sacred and profane might not exclude each other as radically as Moses believes.[15] Schoenberg's insertion of a single phrase ("bist weit genug gegangen") [you have walked/gone far enough] into the biblical statement significantly alters the original text:

> Remove your shoes from your feet, for the place on which you stand is holy ground.
>
> (Exodus 3:5)

> Die Stimme:
> Lege die Schuhe ab:
> bist weit genug gegangen;
> du stehst auf heiligem Boden;
> [The Voice:
> Take your shoes off:
> you have walked/gone far enough;
> you are standing on holy ground;](112)

After all, it is no longer clear whether Moses is to remove his shoes because the ground is sacred or because of aching feet. This passage, however, may also indicate that rather than suggesting a shared space that the sacred and profane may inhabit, the significance of "walking/going" may actually be the target of the inserted clause, more specifically, the importance of "not walking/not going"; that is, that the sacred may indeed require the abrogation of all worldly activity, and thus "standing," not walking or going, may best befit one's relation to holiness. This interpretation of Schoenberg's revision and the absence of the elements of Moses's specific social environment suggest deliberate moves in the opera toward actually substituting a metaphysical milieu for one spatially and temporally defined.

The opposition between walking/going and spiritual being appears once again at the end of the third scene when the reality of Moses and Aron is perceived and understood by the people as numinous. There the chorus carefully observes the arrival of Moses and Aron, but seems unable to determine whether they are moving or standing, whether indeed their movements obey or defy the laws of nature:

Seht Moses und Aron!	[See Moses and Aron!
Moses' mächtiges Haupt	Moses' powerful head
Moses, den Stab in der Hand,	Moses, the rod in his hand,
schreitet langsam, bedächtig,	moves slowly, reflective
scheint fast zu stehn,	seems almost to stand,
bewegt sich kaum.	hardly moves.
Steht Moses oder geht er?	Is Moses standing or is he walking?
Moses steht!	Moses is standing!
Nein, er schreitet langsam!	No, he is moving slowly!
Er steht!	He is standing!
Nein, er geht!	No, he is walking/going!
Mächtig sein weißes Haupt,	Mighty his white head,
gewaltig sein Arm!	powerful his arm!
Gewaltig sein Haupt!	Powerful his head!
Seht!	See!
Aron, gewiß nicht mehr jung,	Aron, surely no longer young,
eilt, beschwingt, leichten Schrittes	rushes, speedily, with a light step
weit vor ihm her	far ahead of him
und steht doch nah bei ihm!	and yet stands close to him!
Steht Aron jetzt bei Moses?	Is Aron now standing close to Moses?
Nein, er eilt voran!	No, he is rushing ahead of him!
Geht Aron an Moses Seite?	Is Aron walking at Moses' side?
Vor oder hinter ihm?	In front of or behind him?
Sie bewegen sich nicht im Raum.	They are not moving in space
Sind näher,	Are nearer,
sind ferner,	are farther,
sind tiefer,	are deeper,

sind höher—	are higher—
verschwinden gänzlich!	disappear entirely!
Seht Moses! Seht Aron!	See Moses! See Aron!
Sie sind jetzt da!	They are now here!](132–4)

From the beginning of this extraordinary passage—"Seht Moses und Aron!"—the people's attention is focused on assessing the external appearance of the two approaching figures moving in space and time. In the final eight lines, however, Moses and Aron are displaced from a domain in which spatial and temporal factors govern behavior to a transcendent realm in which their physical aspect is effaced. Thus, beginning with the observation, "Sie bewegen sich nicht im Raum," Moses and Aron not only "disappear entirely," but assume, in the language of the chorus at least, a state of spiritual presence traditionally associated with the deity, that is, *Dasein*: "Sie *sind* jetzt *da*," the concluding line reads. "In the Buber/Rosenzweig translation of the Bible, when asked about His name God replies, 'Ich werde *dasein*, als der ich *dasein* werde' instead of the Luther rendition of 'Ich werde *sein*, der ich *sein* werde' [I shall be who I shall be] (Exodus 3:14)."[16] Although in *Moses und Aron*, the verb "*dasein*" refers not to God, but to Moses and Aron, later in this act the people overtly identify characteristics of Moses and Aron with those of the deity: "Ist Aron der Knecht dieses Moses,/ und Moses der Knecht seines Gottes,/ so muß es ein mächtiger Gott sein,/ da mächtige Knechte ihm dienen" [If Aron is the servant of Moses,/ and Moses is the servant of his God,/ then it must be a mighty God,/ since mighty servants serve him] (142). There is no evidence that Schoenberg knew the Buber/Rosenzweig translation, and Alexander Ringer claims that "the Bible in Martin Luther's translation had been his [Schoenberg's] steady companion even in his teens."[17] In any event, Luther's concept of "*Sein*" as "abstract Being" would actually seem more appropriate in *Moses und Aron* for Moses's conception of God, for he, along with the divine voice, consistently maintains the absolute spirituality and otherness of God. The Buber/Rosenzweig conception of "*Dasein*" (or the verb "*dasein*") in which the *presence*, albeit spiritual presence, of God is stressed, would be more acceptable to a people who want only a perceivable god and to Aron who can conceive of a completely spiritual and completely present God; furthermore, the form in which *dasein* appears here—"Sie sind jetzt da," as an inflected verb in which the "da" and "sein" are separated and the "da" [the "here" (or "there")] completes the entire passage—certainly seems to support the sense of presence articulated in the Buber/Rosenzweig translation.

Indeed, in Moses's understanding, the possibility of the deity's presence is so fundamentally inconceivable that when he hears Aron voice an idea of the spiritual presence of a God who might reward virtue and punish sin, whom people can love, Moses breaks out of the *Sprechstimme* he uses throughout to sing a brief but impassioned aria that may be a command or a plea to Aron: "Reinige dein Denken,/ lös es von Wertlosem,/ weihe es Wahrem. . . ." [Purify your thinking,/ free it from what is worthless,/ dedicate it to what is true. . .] (122). Soon thereafter each registers his contrary position: Moses utters an absolutely transcendent idea of the divine, Aron focuses on the deity's instrumentality in the social and historical life of the people:

Moses:	Moses:
Unerbittliches Denkgesetz,	Inexorable Law of thought
zwingt zur Erfüllung.	compels to fulfillment.
Aron:	Aron:
Allmächtiger!	Almighty one!
Sei der Gott dieses Volkes!	Be the God of this people!
Befrei es aus Pharaos	Free it from Pharaoh's
Knechtschaft!	bondage!(122)

The concluding scene of Act 1 is of considerable interest not merely for its demonstration of Aron's communicative dexterity—his flexibility at best, manipulative skill at worst—but for the display of the people's expectations and Aron's promises which, although condemned by Moses, actually have an affirmative significance in the biblical narrative. It is here when, for the first time, the brothers interact with the people that Aron attempts to traverse a trajectory between two seemingly inflexible poles. At one end there is Moses for whom God is almighty, ineffable, and unrepresentable; at the other, there are the people who want a visible god, one more powerful and tangibly useful than all other gods, one powerful enough to free them from Pharaoh's oppression and assure their future well-being. Because, however, in the opera Moses is presented as the most morally righteous figure, the one to whom God has chosen to speak and to invest with a divine mission, his condemnation of the views and values expressed by Aron and the people may also be interpreted as a critique of those aspects of the biblical story that resonate in their words and behavior.

The seriousness of this critique of the Bible may best be understood when one realizes just how extensively the revisions function to characterize, on the one hand, Moses as so completely spiritual that no trace of human error or earthly concern is permitted to mar either his ideas or actions; and, on the other hand, Aron as pragmatist and manipulator who—in order to attend to the physical well-being of the people and maintain them as a group—would falsify or betray God's being. Thus, in *Moses und Aron*, for example, Aron, not Moses, strikes the rock instead of speaking to it as God commanded, and Aron, not God, in Act 1 promises the people an *actual* land in which to settle. And in the last act it is Moses who sits in judgment on these actions of Aron:

> Moses:
> Da begehrest du leiblich, wirklich,
> mit Füssen zu betreten ein unwirkliches land,
> wo Milch und honig fließt.
> Da schlugst du auf den Felsen,
> statt zu ihm zu sprechen, wie dir befohlen,
> daß Wasser aus ihm fließe . . .
> Aus dem nackten Felsen sollte das Wort
> Erquickung schlagen . . .
> [Moses:
> Then you desired physically, actually,
> with your feet to enter the unreal land,
> where milk and honey flows.
> Then you struck the rock,
> instead of speaking to it, as you were ordered,
> so that the water would flow out of it . . .
> Out of the naked rock the word should have
> struck refreshment . . .] (198)

Two additional revisions of behavior affirmed in the Bible, but condemned by the operatic Moses are particularly significant in *Moses und Aron*: the denunciation of Aron's performance of wonders using the divine rod, and concern for the people's physical well-being as not a divine consideration.

Performance of wonders Moses's unrelenting and uncompromising disdain in the concluding scene of the first act for any worldly solutions actually contradicts the profound concern not only of both the biblical God and Moses for the people's survival and progress to nationhood, but even of the operatic God's interest in gaining the people's allegiance. The differences between opera and Bible may best be understood by comparing the representations of the divine wonders in the texts. In

Moses und Aron, the different modes of communication Aron uses—one linguistic, another performative—in order to assure the welfare and cohesiveness of the Israelites coincide, at least in part, with such efforts in the biblical narrative. Thus, when the people repudiate a God they cannot see, Aron tries to change their thinking first by shifting the meaning of "seeing" from visual perception to a kind of inner apprehension: "Schließet die Augen,/verstopfet die Ohren!/ So nur könnt ihr ihn sehen und hören!/ Kein Lebender sieht und hört ihn anders" [Close your eyes,/ stop up your ears!/ Only in that way can you see and hear him!/ No living person sees or hears him otherwise](136). This move inward coincides with the modernist rejection of impressionism and reliance on sense data and may function epistemologically as a measure of reality. But when that fails to convince the people and Moses responds to their recalcitrance with a cry of despair and retreats into the background— "Allmächtiger, meine Kraft ist zu Ende:/ Mein Gedanke ist machtlos/ in Arons Wort" [Almighty one, my strength is at an end:/ My idea is powerless/ in Aron's word!](138–40)—Aron takes the rod from Moses and performs the wonders God had granted Moses (in scene 1) for the purpose of persuading others of his power. The people, now convinced that Aron's feats are the visible signs of the invisible divine power that Moses knows, finally acknowledge the existence and supremacy of this God: "Durch Aron läßt Moses uns sehen,/ wie er seinen Gott selbst erschaut hat:/ so wird dieser Gott uns vorstellbar,/ den sichtbare Wunder bezeugen" [Through Aron, Moses lets us see,/ how he himself has seen his God,/ in this way, for us, this God becomes conceivable,/ whom visible wonders verify](146, 148).

This performance of wonders alludes to the beginning and end of Exodus 4, when Moses asks God "What if they [the Israelites] do not believe me and do not listen to me, but say: 'The Lord did not appear to you?'" God gives him the rod and the power to perform miraculous feats, which later Aron does enact before the Elders: "Aron repeated all the words that the Lord had spoken to Moses, and he performed the signs in the sight of the people, and the people were convinced" (Exodus 4: 1, 30–31). The Bible notwithstanding, in the final act of *Moses und Aron*, Moses accuses Aron of sacrilege because, in his view, the exhibition of the wonders drew attention to the power of the act, not to their divine origin:

> Moses:
> Dem Ursprung, dem Gedanken entfremdet,
>   genügt dir dann weder das Wort noch das Bild . . .
> Aron: (unterbrechend)

... sichtbare Wunder, sollte ich tun,

wo das Wort und das Bild des Mundes versagten . . .!

Moses:

... da genügte dir nur mehr die Tat, die Handlung?

Da machtest du den Stab zum Führer,

meine Kraft zum Befreier,

und Nilwasser beglaubigte die Allmacht . . .

[Moses:

Alienated from the source, from the idea,

neither the word nor the image satisfied you then . . .

Aron: (interrupting)

... visible marvels I was supposed to perform,

where the word and the spoken image failed . . .

Moses:

... then only the deed, the act satisfied you?

then you made the rod into a leader,

my strength into a liberator,

and the water of the Nile attested to the supreme power . . .](198)

Even within the opera text, however, this condemnation is problematic, as Aron's behavior seems to conform to God's stated reasons for extending this opportunity to Moses. It would seem, at least from God's words regarding the wonders, that Moses may have adopted a conception of the deity far more abstract and rigid than the deity himself holds; and that Moses's demands of conformity to his ideas exceeds even God's expectations. Consider God's directive to Moses, in the opera's opening scene, about how to influence a group of unbelievers who admire cleverness, strength, and miracles:[18]

Moses:

Niemand wird mir glauben!

Die Stimme:

Vor ihren Ohren wirst du Wunder tun.

Ihre Augen werden sie anerkennen.

Von deinem Stab werden sie hören;

deine Klugheit bewundern.

Von deiner Hand

an deine Kraft glauben.

Vom Wasser des Nil

fühlen, was ihrem Blut befohlen.

[Moses:

No one will believe me!
The Voice:
Before their ears you will perform wonders.
Their eyes will recognize them.
From your rod they will hear;
admire your cleverness.
From your hand
believe in your strength.
From the water of the Nile
feel, what was dictated to their blood.] (114)

Clearly aware of the difficulties involved in transforming an enslaved people "daß es nicht/ mehr Vergänglichem diene" [so that it no/ longer serves what is transitory] (114), this God directs Moses to present the people with wonders that may gratify their need for sensory verification, their desire for a crafty and powerful leader, and their admiration for the power of magic and miracles. Moses's immediate response to God's pronouncement—"meine Zunge ist ungelenk" [my tongue is clumsy] (114)—indicates that his speech problem will hinder him from performing the wonders, but his subsequent condemnation of Aron's performance suggests that Moses may in fact interpret God's directive as inappropriate, that his demands on the people are far more stringent than those of the deity himself.

The Israelite's physical well-being In the final moments of Act 1 there is yet another situation in which Aron's interests and activity, harshly censured by Moses at opera's end, in fact reflect those of the biblical Moses. Having accepted their new God and satisfied that he will liberate them from bondage, the people in *Moses und Aron* are prepared to proceed into the wilderness when a priest questions whether the wilderness can supply them with sustenance. Moses, who had long been silent, responds with a very terse, imperious statement, once again stressing the necessity of purity of thought: "In der Wüste wird euch die Reinheit/ des Denkens nähren, erhalten und entwickeln . . ." [In the wilderness the purity/ of thinking will nourish, sustain, and develop/enhance you] (150). Both God and Moses in the biblical narrative know that it will take more than purity of thinking to nourish and sustain this people in the wilderness. Thus, at the beginning of the exodus from Egypt, God advises them to take their flocks and herds with them (Exodus 12:34), and at other times, God complies with Moses's pleas to God for help in allaying the people's hunger and thirst (see Exodus 15, 16, 17).

The opera, however, takes a different turn. Apparently alarmed by Moses's comment and recognizing the fragility and anxiety of the people, Aron makes a long, impassioned speech to counteract Moses's contention that purity of thinking alone will fulfill all needs. He assures the people that God understands that they are still children—in the Luther translation of Exodus they are repeatedly referred to as "die Kinder Israel" [children of Israel][19]—who cannot be expected to do what adults can; that they will be given time to develop wisdom; that they will not want for food in the wilderness; that God—as they had already witnessed—can perform wonders; that they and their families will be liberated from "Fron und Plage" [compulsory labor and torment]; and finally that God will lead them to a promised land: "Er wird euch führen in das Land,/ wo Milch und Honig fließt;/ und ihr sollt genießen *leiblich,*/ was euren Vätern verheißen *geistig* [He will lead you into the land,/ where milk and honey flows;/ and you shall enjoy *bodily,*/ what your fathers were promised *spiritually*](emphasis added, 152). Aron's conception of a God who is concerned about the Israelites' welfare and involved with their future surely mirrors the devotion and commitment of the biblical God in the Exodus narrative. It is clear from Act 1's concluding aria that although Aron may have been able to maintain the cohesiveness of the group, its religious understanding is wanting: thus, the people essentially still retain polytheistic beliefs— "Allmächtiger, du bist stärker/ als Ägyptens Götter,/ Pharao und seine Knechte schlägst du nieder" [Almighty one, you are stronger/ than Egypt's gods,/ you will beat down Pharaoh and his servants](152)—and have not yet transformed their thinking, nor progressed from a conception of liberation as the negation of oppression (*freedom from*) to an affirmation of a substantive social or moral agenda (*freedom to* or *for*).

Act 2: The Golden Calf

There are in the second act, which is largely occupied with the events surrounding the construction of the Golden Calf and its altar, some very significant revisions of the biblical narrative, including one that actually enhances Aron's stature. Thus, although in Exodus 32 Aaron unhesitatingly sets about making the molten calf when asked by the people for a god to replace the absent leader Moses, in *Moses und Aron* a very reluctant Aron yields to the will of the people and the panic of the Elders only after a bellowing crowd, enraged by Moses's absence and impossible to placate, threatens "to tear apart" the Elders. This decision in the opera to concede to the people's wishes seems a very difficult one for Aron to make, caught as he is between a rock and a hard place, between performing a perfidious act and losing the confidence of the people. His distress becomes apparent at the beginning of Act 2, scene 3, after the construction of the Calf and altar, when Aron, who is usually very voluble, speaks only very briefly and then disappears completely during the ensuing wild orgy of drunkenness, dance, sex, murder, and human sacrifice. The orgy continues for a long while until a single command from Moses, who has arrived with the Decalogue, causes the Golden Calf to disappear: "Vergeh, du Abbild des Unvermögens,/ das Grenzenlose in ein Bild zu fassen! (*Das Goldene Kalb vergeht; das Volk weicht zurück und verschwindet rasch von der Bühne*)" [Disappear, you image of powerlessness,/ to contain the boundless in an image! (*The Golden Calf disappears; the people retreats and quickly vanishes from the stage*] (182).

The difference in the depictions of the Calf's destruction here and in the Bible illuminates major philosophical, religious, and aesthetic concerns of the opera; namely, the question of the insubstantiality of images and the dilemma of the relationship between an unrepresentable, ineffable deity and its representation, between idea and image, word and image, or more generally between spirituality and materiality. In the two biblical versions of the Calf's destruction (Exodus 32:19–20, Deuteronomy 9:21), Moses physically burns it, grinds it to bits, strews the remains on the water, and, in Exodus, makes the people drink of it, thereby, in my reading, ensuring the integration of the Calf's substance into their physical environment or body. There are, of course, differing interpretations of this event. Some biblical interpreters have understood the act of imbibing the remains of the Calf as one method for determining the guilt of a sinner;[20] or as a "sign of the total destruction of the cursed image in which Israel participates to her shame."[21] The internalization of the Calf's residue, it seems to me, may also signify that a lasting imprint or memory of the blasphemous act persists and functions as an indelible part of the record of the nation Israel's history, to which the very existence of the biblical account may attest.

The importance of this change in *Moses und Aron* cannot be overestimated, because it presents a seminal instantiation of Moses's insistence on the supreme power of the word identified with idea/divine idea [*Gottesgedanke*] and on its absolute dissociation from image, be it "Bild," "Abbild," or "Sinnbild." To an adamant, unforgiving Moses his destruction of the Golden Calf signifies the absolute power of the word: "Dein Bild verblich vor meinem Wort!" [Your image faded at my word!](184), is his rejoinder to Aron's explanation that communication with the people requires a language they know, namely, the language of images. For Aron, the act of destroying the Calf by means of the word constitutes merely another image, but for Moses it was a spiritual act of absolute divine power, divine law: "Gottes Ewigkeit vernichtet Göttergegenwart!/ Das ist kein Bild, kein Wunder!/ Das ist das Gesetz./ Das Unvergängliche, sag es,/ wie die Tafeln, vergänglich; / in der Sprache deines Mundes!" [God's eternity destroys the presence of gods!/ That is no image, no miracle!/ That is the Law./ The imperishable, say it (once spoken),/ like these tablets, perishable;/ in the language of your mouth!](186). Thus, the substantiality of the Calf, whose physical being can and does disappear completely at the sound of the word, is called into question; and its total erasure certainly suggests that, unlike the biblical instance, the heinous incident will leave behind no trace and have no historical moment. On the other hand, the biblical narrative may indicate that this act was indeed meant to be part of the nation's history not to be forgotten, not to be eradicated.

After the destruction of the Golden Calf, Moses and Aron enter into a lengthy, intense interchange that circles unrelentingly around the same issues, namely, Moses's conception of the absolute mutual exclusivity of word and image, of God and representation, and Aron's insistence that images are an appropriate way to communicate the idea of God to a people who comprehend only what is graspable. This dialogic event departs radically from the biblical account in which, after a very brief inquiry about the reasons for making the Golden Calf and Aron's rather perfunctory explanation, Moses immediately turns his attention to gaining control over an unruly, rebellious people. The long philosophical dialogue, which is wholly Schoenberg's innovation, elaborates not only upon opposing views about the possibility or impossibility of representing the unrepresentable, but also upon the difficulty Moses would face should he attempt to communicate with a people who, though chosen by God, was not yet capable of "thinking" God. After all, in Moses's *Weltanschauung* "thinking" is of the essence, the idea—like the "word"—being identified with spirit, with God. Unlike the biblical Moses who complains that he is "slow of speech and slow of tongue" (Exodus 4: 10), the operatic one tells God, "Meine Zunge ist ungelenk:/ ich kann denken,/ aber nicht reden" [My tongue is clumsy:/ I can think,/ but not talk](114). Moses's consummate devotion to idea and Aron's dedication to the welfare of the people are reflected, during their argument in Act 2, in the clear articulation of their convictions:

> Aron:
> Ich liebe dieses Volk,
> ich lebe für es
> und will es erhalten!

Moses:

Um des Gedankens willen

Ich liebe meinen Gedanken und lebe für ihn!

[Aron:

I love this people,

I live for them

and want to sustain them!

Moses:

For the sake of the idea

I love my idea and live for it!](186)

When Aron maintains that images, be they thornbush, pillars of cloud and fire, or tablets, represent a way of approaching the deity— "Gottes Zeichen, wie der glühende Dornbusch/ Darin zeigt der Ewige nicht sich,/ aber den Weg zu sich;/ und den Weg ins gelobte Land!" [God's sign, like the glowing thornbush/ Therein the Eternal One shows not Himself,/ but the way to him;/ and the way to the promised land!] (194)—Moses concedes defeat. It is, however, Aron's declaration that the tablets, too, are no idea, as Moses would have it, but merely "an image, a part of an idea" (190) that causes Moses to smash the tablets— unlike his biblical namesake who destroyed the Decalogue on first viewing the revelry around the Calf. Unable to bear either Aron's valorization of the image or the people praising their God as "stronger than Egypt's gods," a devastated Moses collapses:

Moses:

Unvorstellbarer Gott!

Unaussprechlicher, vieldeutiger Gedanke!

Läßt du diese Auslegung zu?

Darf Aron, mein Mund, dieses Bild machen?

So habe ich mir ein Bild gemacht, falsch,

wie ein Bild nur sein kann!

So bin ich geschlagen!

So war alles Wahnsinn, was ich

gedacht habe,

und kann und darf nicht gesagt werden!

O Wort, du Wort, das mir fehlt!

[Moses:

Unrepresentable God!

Inexpressible, multivalent idea!

Do you permit this explanation?

> May Aron, my mouth, make this image?
> Then I have made for myself an image, false,
> as only an image can be!
> Then I am defeated!
> Then everything was madness, which I
> have thought, and can and must not be said!
> O word, you word, that I lack!] (194)

Clearly, Moses's dedication to the mutual exclusivity of idea, word, and image has imprisoned him in a conception of unmitigated aniconism and austerity; and if his understanding of God as ineffable idea were to be merely an image of his own making, as Aron suggests, then he is indeed defeated. What remains ambiguous is whether the word he lacks is God's word, his own, or perhaps both.

Act 3: Finale

I have previously discussed this third act in some detail, focusing on Moses's new recognition of the validity of those images that not only originate in the word (as do all images), but also retain the idea and obey the word.[22] Here I want to concentrate on the ways in which the characteristics of the Moses figure and the critique of biblical imagery alluded to earlier contribute to a metaphysical environment that significantly elides the historical and national significance of the biblical narrative. The very brief third and final act takes place in the wilderness and seems to replicate a court of justice in which Moses, once again confident of his divine mission, functions as inquisitor, judge, and jury; while Aron, a prisoner in chains, is cast in the role of accused desecrator. Also present are the two warriors who dragged Aron on stage and seventy Elders—in the Bible they constitute a kind of judicial council—whom Moses addresses directly for the first time in the closing moments of the opera. The people/chorus who represent the constituents of the nation are completely absent, however, when Moses finally takes direct control, revalues the status of the image and the possibility of communicating the divine idea, and becomes something more or other than a completely distant leader who speaks through another.

The biblical Moses, who has never experienced life in a homeland, was also the liberator who helped free the Israelites from Egyptian oppression and through the receipt and delivery of legislation—ethical and ritual, civil and criminal—created the foundation for a lawful society in their future homeland. It is, in fact, this impending historical event of liberation from Pharaoh and the promise of the land that is the bedrock of a covenant between God and the people that Moses is to communicate to the people:

> Say, therefore, to the Israelite people: I am the Lord. I will free you from the labors of the Egyptians and deliver you from their bondage. I will redeem you with an outstretched arm and through extraordinary chastisements. And I will take you to be My people, and I will be your God. And you shall know that I, the Lord, am your God who freed you from the labors of the Egyptians. I will bring you into the land which I swore to give to Abraham, Isaac, and Joseph, and I will give it to you for a possession, I the Lord. (Exodus 6: 6–8)

The importance of Israel's history for this covenant is highlighted by the repeated references to historical data which bracket the actual covenant ("And I will take you to be My people, and I will be your God"): namely, liberation from Egypt mentioned twice and the guarantee of a land, which had already been pledged to the Patriarchs. This divine message promises the Israelites the end of oppression, the end of struggling with a wilderness, the end of exile in a permanent homeland, which God had previously indicated would be "a good and spacious land, a land flowing with milk and honey" (Exodus 3:8).

In the finale of *Moses und Aron,* however, Moses communicates a significantly different message, one that actually controverts, even subverts the biblical covenant and promise. Before addressing the assembled Elders and warriors, Moses first blames Aron for the detrimental effects of his use of images, which, apparently because of their reliance on the world of the senses, deprive others of what their soul needs for eternal life, namely, the ability to renounce desire:

> Moses:
> . . . . .
> denn du weißt, daß der Felsen ein Bild,
> wie die Wüste und der Dornbusch:
> drei, die dem Leib nicht geben,
> was er braucht gegen den Geist,
> der Seele, was deren Wunschlosigkeit
> zu ewigem Leben genug ist.
> [Moses:
> . . . . . .
> for you know that the rock is an image
> like the wilderness and the thornbush:

> three that do not give to the body,
> what it needs for the spirit,
> [nor give] to the soul what of its freedom from craving
> is sufficient for eternal life.](200)

To Aron's laconic response that he had hoped thereby to secure freedom for the people so that they might become a people/nation ("Für seine
Freiheit, daß es ein Volk werde!"), Moses—adding the Golden Calf and
pillars of cloud and fire to his previous catalogue of images—castigates
him for misrepresenting God as an image of impotence and dependence
while elevating the people to omnipotence and independence (200–2).

It is only after charging Aron with sacrilege and betrayal of the divine
mission that Moses delivers what he considers to be the message his God
has entrusted him to proclaim, but his understanding of that message may
be wanting. God had, after all, enjoined the people to dedicate themselves
completely to him, but here Moses offers the people the freedom to serve
not God, but the *idea* of God—"Dienen, dem Gottesgedanken zu dienen,/
ist die Freiheit, zu der/ dieses Volk auserwählt ist." [To serve, to serve the
idea of God,/ is the freedom for which/ the people has been chosen](200).
In Moses's view this would require an everlasting austere wilderness existence. After warning this audience of warriors and Elders that, should they
abandon the "Wunschlosigkeit der Wüste" [the wilderness' freedom from
craving] and misuse their talents for worldly purposes, they will be thrown
back into the wilderness, Moses finally reminds them that power will issue
only from devotion to a permanent ascetic existence: "Aber in der Wüste
seid ihr unüberwindlich/ und werdet das Ziel erreichen:/ Vereinigt mit
Gott." [But in the wilderness you are invincible/ and will reach the goal:/
United with God] (204). Thus, this wilderness, in which life is characterized primarily by renunciation of desire and by unrelenting dedication to
an abstract idea of God, is the site of the promised land as eternal homeless
existence. What remains in this "promised land," however, are Moses and a
totally silenced *vox populi*—two virtually silent warriors, a group of mute,
quiescent Elders, and an absent people. Ilana Pardes notes that the unique-
ness of national drama in the Bible lies in how extensively it personifies
and dramatizes the nation which, after all, "has a voice (represented at
times in a singular mode); it moans and groans, cries, is euphoric at times,
complains frequently, and rebels against Moses and God time and again."[23]
That nation has, however, vanished from the operatic text; and it is very
difficult to imagine that such a social grouping, exclusively male, completely submissive, and acquiescing—at least tacitly—to a wholly ascetic
spiritualism, will ever be able to produce or reproduce itself as a nation. In-

deed, this social grouping, which seems to resemble the authoritarian *Führer-Volk* structure of all-powerful leader and submissive followers united in a lifelong abstract spiritual mission, virtually displaces nation and the social, ethical, and cultural project of creating it.

REFLECTIONS ON SCHOENBERG'S REVISIONS/ CRITIQUE OF THE BIBLICAL NARRATIVE

At opera's end questions about how to interpret and assess the significance of the biblical revisions in *Moses und Aron* abound. One wonders why Schoenberg would have written a work in which the adaptation of the biblical narrative so decisively excluded all references to the Israelites' historical struggles, to nationhood, and the importance of material existence. After all, not only did a devastating anti-Semitic incident he experienced precipitate his intense preoccupation with Judaism in general and the Moses figure in particular; but the Nazi's increasingly vicious attacks on Jews had left him deeply wounded personally and professionally. To try to understand the absence of the Israelites' history and concern with their physical needs in the opera, let me focus on just three interrelated perplexing questions: What imperatives inform the construction of such a rigid and absolute aniconism when the Bible presents views of God both as an invisible, incorporeal being and as visible and corporeal? How, when so many people were struggling with the agony of actual exile, could an existence of perpetual homelessness propounded by this operatic Moses have found such a privileged place in the text? Why, at a time when totalitarianism was repressing all contrary and differing viewpoints and when the *Führer-Volk* ideology [all-powerful leader-submissive people] was menacing Europe, would one reconstitute such an authoritarian paradigm in a text concerned with liberation? Although conclusive answers to these quandaries would be hard to come by, a closer look at some of the implications of the issues they raise may help to illuminate some of the more resistant aspects of the text and its cultural context.

One of the dominant ideas in *Moses und Aron* is Moses's stubborn insistence on an uncompromising aniconic conception of God, in this instance an invisible, unrepresentable deity who can evidently be aurally apprehended (his voice is heard by Moses), but not represented in visual images. There is, to be sure, a long tradition of understanding Jewish thought and culture as monotheistic and auditory especially in contrast to Greek thought and culture, which was regarded as pagan and visual. In this opposition, visuality is figured as spatial and external, while the auditory, in Elliot R. Wolfson's formulation, "implies a sense of phenomenological immediacy without necessitating spatial or worldly exteriority,"[24] thus supporting the position of the Deuteronomist for whom God's absolute otherness did not, however, disallow his voice to be represented: "The Lord spoke to you out of the fire; you heard the sound of words but perceived no shape—nothing but a voice . . . For your own sake, therefore, be most careful—since you saw no shape when the Lord spoke to you at Horeb out of the fire—not to act wickedly and make for yourself a sculptured image in any likeness whatever . . ." (Deuteronomy 4: 12; 15). Of course, there are in the Bible also clear instances of God's visibility; take Exodus 24: 9–11 for example: "Then Moses and Aaron, Nadab and Abihu, and seventy Elders of Israel ascended; and they saw the God of Israel: under His feet there was the likeness of a pavement of sapphire, like the very cloud for purity. Yet He did not raise His hand against the leaders of the Israelites; they beheld God, and they ate and drank." Wolfson contends that although such contradictions in representation and views of the deity may not be convincingly resolved, they can be accepted as two points of view inhabiting the same text and informing Jewish tradition.[25] One wonders why, despite these differing conceptions of the deity and despite the fact that the biblical Moses had seen God several times, Schoenberg should have constructed a Moses figure that insisted so adamantly on his absolute immateriality and invisibility. Several possible explanations seem plausible.

The three works Schoenberg identifies as markers on his road back from Christianity to the "Jewish religion"—"Du sollst nicht, du mußt," *Der biblische Weg*, and *Moses und Aron*—focus on the confluence of an ineffable God and his chosen people and on aspects of the Mosaic tradition, particularly the second commandment's prohibition of graven images, which in these texts pertain exclusively to images of the deity. The stringent aniconic position in *Moses und Aron* may be an attempt to represent Judaism as superior to a Christianity which—in its preoccupation with sacraments, symbols, and the incarnation of God in Christ—is figured as closer to paganism. Paradoxically, however, by transcending all worldly considerations and by eliding almost all references to both the history of the Israelites and the giving of the Law which, in large part, identifies the distinctiveness of the nation, Moses's conception of God and religion may avoid the particularism of Christianity, but certainly not the universalism associated with it. The fact that this universalism insists on sameness and equality, which become oppressive and perhaps lethal when they permit no contrary viewpoints, may also explain why *Moses und Aron* concludes with a Moses who—with the elimination of Aron and the rebellious populace—becomes the sole ruler and voice of a totally submissive and silenced group of the elites (warriors and Elders). In addition to dissociation from past Christian affiliation, Schoenberg's persistent interest in aniconism and universalism during this period may also signify a reaction to the Nazi's preoccupation with images and symbols and with particularism that proved so devastating to him personally and professionally and to his compatriots and colleagues. An unpublished letter to Alma Mahler written on 19 January 1929 suggests that because of bitter encounters with anti-Semitism, Schoenberg may have associated Christianity and National Socialism. Referring to a traumatic anti-Semitic experience in a metaphor that merges the burden of the Christian cross [*Kreuz*] with the terror of the Nazi swastika [*Hakenkreuz*, literally "cross with hooks"], Schoenberg complains that his compositions, unlike those of Alban Berg who was not a Jew, can no longer be performed undisturbed, and adds: "denn mit mir ist es ein Hakenkreuz: ich bin ein schuftiger, unverständlicher Jude" [for in my case it is a swastika: I am a mean, incomprehensible Jew][26]—the *Kreuz*/cross he now bears is the *Hakenkreuz*/swastika.

The significance of eternal homelessness in *Moses und Aron* needs yet to be explored; and a recent discussion about diaspora and diasporic identities by Daniel and Jonathan Boyarin may elucidate important aspects of exile and diaspora. In their essay "Diaspora: Generation and Ground of Jewish Identity," the privileging of diaspora is grounded in the continuously renewed productive coexistence and interaction of peoples in which their "cultures are not preserved by being protected from 'mixing' but probably can only continue to exist as a product of such mixing. Cultures, as well as identities, are constantly being remade."[27] Two possible alternatives to diasporic existence which the Boyarins reject are: a spiritualized universalism, associated with Paul, which they view as having a tendency, especially when allied with power, to produce "imperialism and cultural annihilation";[28] and the attachment of the people "to their natural land," to an autochthonic nationalism, which may result in an oppressive "national self-determinism" that excludes those with counterclaims to the land. From this perspective, Moses's conception of a permanent wilderness existence, identified as it is with neither a specific location nor culture but merely with universal spiritualized devotion, actually corresponds to the Paulinian alternative. The fact that the promise of spiritual liberation applies only to a chosen people, however, does call into question the authenticity of this universalism. On the other hand, the rejection of any claim to an actual land in *Moses und Aron* is also not a move toward a diasporic interactive condition, but rather merely an augmentation of Moses's position on spiritual universalism. After all, this Moses and the Israelites, seemingly alone and immobilized in their transcendence, will apparently spend their entire lives in a wilderness without undergoing the cultural and social development that the people in the biblical narrative achieve. Of course it is possible, as Sidra DeKoven Ezrahi suggests, that "monotheism evolved into a strategy for making the world into one's home, preparing the way for eliminating exile altogether as a category of experience,"[29] but such "nonterritoriality" might not necessarily eventuate in a socially or culturally integrated diaspora.

Clearly, for Schoenberg—and not only in *Moses und Aron*—social, political, or genealogical factors may not have been determining characteristics of nationhood. Because, for him, Jews as individuals and nation were solely defined by an ascetic monotheism, the nation could seemingly survive best not in an integrative intercultural situation where it would have to contend with other peoples and cultures, but rather in a metaphysical state of being in which all worldly connections were severed or renounced. Similar views appear in Schoenberg's "Four-Point Program for Jewry,"[30] a curious document completed in 1938 that was to be the manifesto of the Jewish Unity Party he was seriously planning to organize and lead. The largest portion of this tract is devoted to an attempt to convince Jews to discontinue their boycott of German products and their fight against anti-Semitism, both of which efforts he regarded as useless because they were directed against others and not focused directly on self-preservation. Indeed, for him self-preservation was a religious duty that "God's chosen people" were obligated to fulfill because they "were chosen to survive, to endure through the centuries, to refute the laws of nature."[31] Thus, twentieth-century European Jews, who have been divinely elected to preserve the idea of God and whose spiritual mission sets them apart from others, actually mirror the Israelites and their metaphysical imperative in *Moses und Aron*.

Among Schoenberg's most troubling characteristics, especially given what he suffered as a result of fascist rule, were his antidemocratic and authoritarian predilections and solutions, blatantly apparent in Moses's autocratic rule over the Israelites at the conclusion of *Moses und Aron*, in the authoritarian organizational structure planned for the Jewish Unity Party, and elsewhere as well. Witness, for example, his involvement with the *Verein für musikalische Privataufführungen* [Society for Private Musical Performances],[32] which he founded in 1918 and later, in the "Four-Point Program," boasted about running like a "kind of dictator." It seems that when opposition to his plans for the Society arose, he admits he "did something which under other circumstances could be called illegal," namely, dissolved the group and created one that would adhere only to his principles; "these principles," he says, "were my country"[33]—an echo perhaps of his Moses's "spiritual wilderness" as the promised land. The Jewish Unity Party was apparently also to be organized along authoritarian lines with an autocratic leader because, as Schoenberg notes, "history had always shown that the great men, standing alone, persecuted, unsupported, eventually achieved victory and were proved right."[34] And in a letter of 13 June 1933 to Jakob Klatzkin, he articulated the undemocratic structure he had in mind:

> If I could have my own preference, and wanted to create a new Party, a new sect, it would have to be nationalchauvinistic to the highest degree, based in the religious sense on the idea of the chosen people, militant, aggressive, opposed to any pacifism, to any internationalism. These are my personal convictions, and I shall not deny that I would be strongly engaged in winning sympathizers for these methods, for these very fighting methods.[35]

Not unlike Freud who, during this same period—in *Totem und Tabu* [*Totem and Taboo*], *Massenpsychologie und die Ich-Analyse* [*Mass Psychology and the Analysis of the Ego*], and *Der Mann Mose und die monotheistische Religion* [*Moses and Monotheism*]—maintained that society needs a superior individual ("the great man") to lead inferior group members, Schoenberg openly affirmed completely undemocratic principles.[36] It is very disturbing and difficult to fathom how, when Hitler was putting into practice his pernicious *Führerprinzip* [leader with absolute power], Schoenberg and other persecuted intellectuals could valorize a model of leadership comparable to that of the National Socialists. There is more than a margin of truth to Richard Taruskin's assessment of "Schoenberg's personality . . . as absolutist and despotic as any dictator's," and of the broader social and political implications of such antidemocratic positions. "The legacy of fascism," Taruskin asserts, "is an inherent and, in the West, largely unacknowledged, facet of the anti-democratic legacy of modernism."[37] It should be noted, however, that the antidemocratic aspect of modernism was but one strand of an extensive, very diverse, and complex movement. Arguments in support of Schoenberg's authoritarian positions either in his political efforts or in *Moses und Aron* are neither very convincing nor easy to justify. One can only hope that his pronouncements and solutions were merely a gauge of the despair and helplessness experienced in response to a world that seemed to be reeling out of control.

There is perhaps a salutary dimension to Schoenberg's transformation of the biblical narrative about the struggle for liberation—a struggle that needs not only to be remembered, but repeatedly rehearsed—into a kind of psychodrama about "inner freedom" amidst external oppression. In choosing to write not an original text, as he did in *Der biblische Weg*, but to revise and reform the biblical one, Schoenberg inscribed himself as interpreter into the bedrock of Jewish history and tradition, thereby provoking his audience to return to the biblical narrative, perhaps to remember it once again.

NOTES

I am deeply grateful to Chana Kronfeld, Richard Hecht, and Erich Gruen for reading a draft of this paper with great care; their criticisms, insights, and suggestions were enormously helpful. I also want to thank Robert Alter, Gerard Caspary, and John Schott for their illuminating comments on issues with which I had difficulties.

1. Bluma Goldstein, *Reinscribing Moses: Heine, Kafka, Freud, and Schoenberg in a European Wilderness* (Cambridge: Harvard University Press, 1992), 137–67.

2. The one comprehensive study of the relationship of *Moses und Aron* and the Bible is Odil Hannes Steck, "Moses und Aron": die Oper Arnold Schönbergs und ihr biblischer Stoff [*"Moses und Aron": Arnold Schoenberg's Opera and its Biblical Material*] (München: Chr. Kaiser Verlag, 1981) in which he maintains that while the omissions and revisions suggest that this is "a biblical-unbiblical opera," they in fact support the basic intention of the "innermost substance of the Old Testament"; that is, to present "das absolue Prae Gottes, das Gottsein Gottes" [the absolute *Prae* of God, the divine Being of God] (48). Thus, he maintains that the purport of Schoenberg's opera is fundamentally the same as that of the Old Testament (see 48–50). My own reading of the texts of the opera and of the Bible questions these conclusions.

3. Letter to Wassily Kandinsky, 20 April 1923, Arnold Schönberg, *Ausgewählte Briefe*, ed. Erwin Stein (Mainz: B. Schott's Söhne, 1958), 90. Hereafter cited as *Briefe*. Arnold Schoenberg, *Selected Letters,* trans. Eithne Wilkins and Ernst Kaiser, ed. Erwin Stein (Berkeley: University of California Press, 1964), 88. The translations from the *Briefe,* however, are mine.

4. Arnold Schoenberg, *Der biblische Weg/The Biblical Way*, trans. Moshe Lazar, *Journal of the Arnold Schoenberg Institute* 17, Nos. 1&2 (June & November 1994): 162–329. (Bilingual edition)

5. Letter to Alban Berg, 16 October 1933, *Briefe*, 200–01; *Letters*, 184.

6. Arnold Schoenberg, *Vier Stücke für gemischten Chor*, op. 27.

7. "Land" here refers both to Egypt and Canaan, but it should be noted that it is the exodus from Egypt and the covenant in the wilderness that is the basis of the relationship between God and Israel. "The covenant became binding on Israel before they took possession of the land." Moshe Greenberg, *Understanding Exodus* (New York, Behrman House: 1969), 14. Also Peter Machinist, "Distinctiveness in Ancient Israel: An Essay," *Studies in Assyrian History and Ancient Near Eastern Historiography: Presented to Hayim Tadmor*, ed. Mordechai Cogan and Israel Eph'al (Jerusalem: Magnes Press, 1991), Vol. 33 of *Scripta Hierosolymitana*, 208–09 notes that although the land promised to the Israelites is of central importance, "Israel can exist apart from the land, as the experiences in Egypt and later Babylonia demonstrate."

8. See Michael Cherlin's very interesting and convincing analysis of the opening segment, "Schoenberg's Representation of the Divine in Moses und Aron," *Journal of the Arnold Schoenberg Institute* 9, no. 1 (1986): 210–16.

9. Karl H. Wörner, *Schoenberg's "Moses and Aaron,"* trans. Paul Hamburger (London: Faber, 1963), 112. This volume contains the libretto with an English translation. Because the English translation is problematic, I have translated all the passages quoted here. I have also relied on the edition of the *Moses und Aron* opera text, ed. Christian Martin Schmidt (London: Ernst Eulenburg Ltd., 1958) to correct punctuation and typographical errors. Hereafter, references to the opera will appear in parentheses in the text. Quotations from the libretto of *Moses und Aron* are used by permission of Belmont Music Publishers, Pacific Palisades, California 90272.

10. Passages from the Bible refer to *Tanakh/The Holy Scriptures: The New Jewish Publication Society Translation According to the Traditional Hebrew Text* (Philadelphia: The Jewish Publication Society, 1988).

11. I shall return to the significance of this difference later.

12. See footnote a to Exodus 3: 14 of JPS Translation: "Meaning of Heb. uncertain; variously translated: 'I Am That I Am'; 'I Am Who I Am'; 'I Will Be What I Will Be'; etc.," See also Moshe Greenberg, *Understanding Exodus*, 81–84; U. Cassuto, *A Commentary on the Book of Exodus* (Jerusalem: The Magnus Press, 1967), 37–39; Elias Auerbach, Moses, trans. and ed. Robert A. Barclay and Israel O. Lehman (Detroit: Wayne State University Press, 1975), 37–38. I shall return to the significance of *Ehyeh-Asher-Ehyeh* in another context.

13. Machinist, "Distinctiveness in Ancient Israel," 205.

14. Goldstein, *Reinscribing Moses,* 150–52. For other views, see Michael Mäckelmann, *Arnold Schoenberg und das Judentum: Der Komponist und sein religiöses, nationales und politisches Selbstverständnis nach 1921* (Hamburg: Musikhandlung Wagner, 1984), 167–90; Theodor W. Adorno, "Sakrales Fragment: Über Schönbergs *Moses und Aron,*" in *Quasi una Fantasia, Musikalische Schriften II* (Frankfurt am Main: Suhrkamp, 1963), 307; Daniel Albright, *Representation and the Imagination: Beckett, Kafka, Nabokov, and Schoenberg* (Chicago: University of Chicago Press, 1981), 43–44; Monika Lichtenfeld, "Über Schoenbergs *Moses und Aron,*" in *Arnold Schönberg: Gedenkausstellung 1974,* ed. Ernst Hilmar (Vienna: Universal Edition, 1974), 134.

15. Goldstein, *Reinscribing Moses,* 153–54.

16. The chapter "Facing the Forest Ridge: The Hebrew Bible in the German Horizon" in Peter E. Gordon, "Under One Trade Wind: Philosophical Expressionism from Rosenzweig to Heidegger" (Ph.D. diss., University of California, Berkeley, 1997) on the Buber/Rosenzweig translation of the Bible, was especially illuminating in exploring the philosophical implications of the choice of *dasein* (over *sein*) to translate the Hebrew *Ehyeh-Asher-Ehyeh.*

17. Alexander L. Ringer, *Arnold Schoenberg: The Composer as Jew* (Oxford: Clarendon Press, 1990), 7.

18. Steck, *Moses und Aron,* 33, maintains that references here to eyes and ears "emphasize the spiritual (!) significance of the wonders for the ear and visual cognition," in contrast to Aron's performance. This observation strikes me as very problematic, especially as Aron himself stresses the importance of "seeing" during the performance: for example, his aria begins with "Seht Moses' Hand," and ends with "Seht!"; and this emphasis on "seeing" is repeated throughout (pp. 146–48). In addition, God's directive, with its emphasis on the senses, on "cleverness," and "strength," and His expected results do not suggest to me anything substantially different from what Aron accomplishes.

19. In the Hebrew, the term is "b'nai Israel," meaning "the sons (or descendents) of Israel," but Luther's translation is "die Kinder Israel" (the King James English translation is "the children of Israel").

20. See, for example, Nahum M. Sarna, *Exploring Exodus: The Origins of Biblical Israel* (New York: Schocken, 1996), 219–20. Sarna connects drinking the Calf's remains with Numbers 5:11–31, in which a potion of sacral water mixed with dust from the floor of the tabernacle is used to determine whether or not a wife was unfaithful; also Cassuto, *A Commentary,* 419; Auerbach, Moses, 127.

21. Brevard S. Childs, *The Book of Exodus* (Philadelphia: The Westminster Press, 1974), 569.

22. Goldstein, *Reinscribing Moses,* 161–64.

23. Ilana Pardes, "The Biography of Ancient Israel: Imagining the Birth of a Nation," *Comparative Literature* 49, no. 1 (1977): 26.

24. Elliot R. Wolfson, *Through a Speculum That Shines: Vision and Imagination in Medieval Jewish Mysticism* (Princeton: Princeton University Press, 1994), 15. Also see the first chapter, esp. 13–28.

25. Ibid., 28.

26. Cited in Reinhold Brinkmann, "Arnold Schoenberg the Contemporary: A View from Behind," in *Constructive Dissonance: Arnold Schoenberg and the Transformations of Twentieth-Century Culture,* ed. Juliane Brand and Christopher Hailey (Cambridge: Harvard University Press, 1997), 210. See his illuminating explication of the complexities of the metaphor.

27. Daniel Boyarin and Jonathan Boyarin, "Diaspora: Generation and the Ground of Jewish Identity," *Critical Inquiry* 19, no.4 (1993): 721.

28. Boyarin and Boyarin, "Diaspora," 707.

29. Sidra DeKoven Ezrahi, "Our Homeland, the Text . . . Our Text the Homeland: Exile and Homecoming in the Modern Jewish Imagination," *Michigan Quarterly Review* 31, no. 4 (1992): 471.

30. Arnold Schoenberg, "Four-Point Program for Jewry," *Journal of the Arnold Schoenberg Institute* 7, no. 1 (1979): 49–67.

31. Schoenberg, "Four-Point Program," 51.

32. H. H. Stuckenschmidt, *Schoenberg: His Life, World and Work,* trans. Humphrey Searle (London: John Calder, 1977), 254ff.

33. Schoenberg, "Four-Point Program," 55.

34. Ibid., 57.

35. Arnold Schoenberg, quoted in Moshe Lazar, "Arnold Schoenberg and His Doubles: A Psychodramatic Journey to His Roots," *Journal of the Arnold Schoenberg Institute* 17, nos. 1&2 (1994): 105.

36. See, for example, Ringer, *Arnold Schoenberg* 142, n. 59: Schoenberg notes that "(a) democracy must lead to corruption, since those rising from below want the wealth without which there is no power; (b) in a democracy only the will of him who flatters the masses can exert itself. By the same token, democracy will never permit the ideas of truly great men to prevail."

37. Richard Taruskin, "The Dark Side of Modern Music: The Sins of Toscanini, Stravinsky, Schoenberg . . . ," *The New Republic* (5 September, 1988): 33, 34.

CHAPTER 8

Schoenberg Rewrites His Will
A Survivor from Warsaw, Op. 46

DAVID ISADORE LIEBERMAN

In June of 1921, Arnold Schoenberg traveled with his family and a group of his students to the Austrian resort of Mattsee where, freed from the distractions of daily life in Vienna, he planned to spend the summer composing. The vacationers had not been in Mattsee long when Schoenberg received a postcard addressed to "the famous composer A. Schoenberg, unfortunately at present in Mattsee." The card called his attention to an anti-Semitic screed printed in the local newspaper, and was signed "an Aryan vacationer."[1] After members of the town council subsequently informed him that the resort was closed to Jews, the composer and his party left Mattsee, finding alternative accommodations at Traunkirchen am Traunsee.[2] Josef Rufer, one of the students who had witnessed the incident at Mattsee, recalled in 1974 an exchange he had with Schoenberg after the relocation to Traunkirchen.

> When in the summer of 1921—it was in Traunkirchen on the Traun Lake—I picked him up for our customary evening walk and the conversation turned to his work, he remarked: "Today I have succeeded in something by which I have assured the dominance of German music for the next century." At that time Schoenberg had finalized and tried out in his compositions his "Method of Composition with Twelve Tones which are related only to One Another."[3]

Considered together, these two episodes serve to define Schoenberg's mature development. Two of the principal preoccupations of his last three decades thus emerge as twinned explorations, both begun in the early 1920s: the development of serial technique and the rediscovery of his own Jewish identity.[4] They inevitably intertwined, achieving a kind of symbiosis some ten years after their inception in the incomplete opera *Moses und Aron* (1927–32). During that intervening decade, the already palpable strain of anti-Semitism Schoenberg had confronted in Mattsee became increasingly pervasive in the politics and culture of German-speaking countries,[5] a development that would seem to complicate his assessment of his role as the guarantor of German musical dominance. But if he felt any contradiction between his artistic language and his self-definition as a Jew in the years before the Second World War, his music offers no clear evidence of it. Only after the near extermination of European Jewry, when the forced opposition of identities between German and Jew had come to seem permanently cemented, did Schoenberg seek a means of isolating and resolving that apparent opposition in his own work. The site of this attempted resolution is the cantata *A Survivor from Warsaw*, op. 46.

Composed in August 1947, *A Survivor from Warsaw* belongs to a group of late compositions whose stylistic multivalence has perplexed and intrigued scholars and critics. Works from this period, including the *Kol Nidre*, op. 39 (1938), the Variations on a Recitative for Organ, op. 40 (1941), *Ode to Napoleon*, op. 41 (1942), the Piano Concerto, op. 42 (1942), and the *String Trio*, op. 45 (1946), draw on a wide variety of styles, ranging from the twelve-tone serial technique to what Carl Dahlhaus describes as "a partial return to tonality."[6] The stylistic disparity that marks the late works taken as a group also functions within individual works, as Christian Martin Schmidt has observed of *A Survivor from Warsaw*, "in which two periods of Schoenberg's composition collide."[7] Schmidt edited *A Survivor from Warsaw* for the edition of Schoenberg's complete musical works published by Universal Edition and B. Schott's Söhne, and his 1976 musical analysis of it remains definitive. For him the stylistic collision in *A Survivor from Warsaw* constitutes a metamusical gesture, generating "music about the music of two crucial periods in [Schoenberg's] development."[8] He identifies these two periods as, first, the freely atonal or expressionist period, of which the most relevant example is the monodrama *Erwartung [Expectation]*, op. 17 (1909), and second, the period of twelve-tone serialism, bracketed by the Woodwind Quintet, op. 26 (1923–24) and the Prelude "Genesis," op. 44 (1945).[9]

My critique of *A Survivor from Warsaw* takes Schmidt's as its point of departure. I believe his argument that this work draws meaning from the clash of distinctive musical styles is essentially correct, but I disagree with his interpretation of that meaning, which, if it is to address the work's autobiographical import, requires a fuller engagement with the facts of Schoenberg's biography, as well as with the text of the work itself, than Schmidt's analysis offers. I will return to Schmidt's conclusions when I reach my own, but first it will be necessary to examine each of the two explorations I have mentioned as crucial to an understanding of *A Survivor from Warsaw*: the development of serial technique and Schoenberg's rediscovery of his Jewish identity.

SERIAL TECHNIQUE AND THE CRISIS IN GERMAN MUSIC

Serial technique emerged as the solution to a creative dilemma that by 1921 had been developing in Schoenberg's work for twelve years. Charles Rosen has identified the chief concerns that motivated the turn to serialism.

> Schoenberg's most pressing concern, after World War I, was to return to the great central tradition of Western music. Not only had the existence of this civilized tradition been made precarious by the war's devastation, but its coherence had been threatened by the revolutionary developments of the preceding years. . . .

The problem was, above all, to integrate the advances of 1908–1913 with the inheritance of the eighteenth and nineteenth centuries. When Schoenberg in 1921 privately confided to a friend that his invention of serialism would guarantee the supremacy of German music for centuries to come, his claim is not merely an example of that arrogant Prussian chauvinism characteristic of the non-Prussian citizens of the border states. The central tradition was, indeed, German, and the rising influence of French and Russian music was as great a menace to its integrity as the innovations of Schoenberg and his school. The aim was to reconstitute and preserve that integrity.[10]

For Schoenberg, the German character of the central tradition was more than a simple aggregate of works by German-speaking composers; it was an evolving legacy he had an obligation to perpetuate. This conviction finds its fullest written expression many years after the first serial compositions of the 1920s, indirectly in Schoenberg's 1933 radio lecture on Johannes Brahms,[11] substantially revised as "Brahms the Progressive" in 1947,[12] more directly in such essays as the two-part "National Music" from 1931,[13] the 1941 "Composition with Twelve Tones" (the earlier of two essays published under this title),[14] and "My Evolution"

(1949).[15] But even a work as early as the first edition of his textbook *Harmonielehre* [*Theory of Harmony*] (1911) contains statements that clearly suggest his evolutionary conception of music history. Although nearly contemporaneous with Schoenberg's first atonal compositions, the *Harmonielehre* is primarily concerned with providing the student of composition with a thorough understanding of the harmonic practice of the eighteenth and nineteenth centuries. It also betrays its author's deep concern to show that his own apparently revolutionary practice in fact had its roots in that same tradition.

> One of the foremost tasks of instruction is to awaken in the pupil a sense of the past and at the same time to open up to him prospects for the future. Thus instruction may proceed historically, by making the connections between what was, what is, and what is likely to be. The historian can be productive if he sets forth, not merely historical data, but an understanding of history, if he does not confine himself simply to enumerating, but tries to read the future in the past.
>
> Applied to our present concern, that means: Let the pupil learn the laws and effects of tonality just as if they still prevailed, but let him know of the tendencies that are leading to their annulment.[16]

Although the annulment of the laws of tonality appears in this passage as a phenomenon in progress, it could be argued that Schoenberg himself had already fully (and publicly) enacted that annulment. By 1911 there had been performances of three of the major works announcing and confirming his departure from tonality: the String Quartet no. 2 in F# minor, op. 10 was first performed on December 21, 1908, and the song cycle on poems by Stefan George *Das Buch der hängenden Gärten* [*The Book of the Hanging Gardens*], op. 15 and the Three Piano Pieces, op. 11 were premiered on January 14, 1910.[17] For the latter concert he prepared a program note in which he anticipated, correctly, listeners' resistance to his new direction.

> With the George songs [op. 15] I have for the first time succeeded in approaching an ideal of expression and form which has been in my mind for years. Until now, I lacked the strength and confidence to make it a reality. But now that I have set out along this path once and for all, I am conscious of having broken through every restriction of a bygone aesthetic; and though the goal towards which I am striving appears to me a certain one, I am, nonetheless, already feeling the resis-

tance I shall have to overcome; I feel how hotly even the least of tem-
peraments will rise in revolt, and suspect that even those who have so
far believed in me will not want to acknowledge the necessary nature
of this development.[18]

His pessimistic expectations were well founded; even critics favorably
disposed to Schoenberg found this new music incomprehensible.[19]

Schoenberg's *Harmonielehre*, then, appeared in the wake of the un-
welcoming reception accorded his newest works. In such an atmosphere,
it should hardly be surprising that a passage such as the program note
quoted above, insisting that this music represented the realization of
tonality's inherent tendencies, functions more by assertion than by persuasion.[20] In the later essays, removed by a distance of decades from the
first passions aroused by his apparent radicalism, Schoenberg is better
able to assess the evolutionary impulses that had driven him to the abandonment of tonality.

The later writings make clear that Schoenberg saw his work as the
logical culmination of an exclusively German tradition, even if, from
essay to essay, the relative importance of individual German composers
seems to be measured on a sliding scale. In the second part of the 1931
essay "National Music," for instance, he lists as his most important influences the tradition's earliest representatives, Johann Sebastian Bach and
Wolfgang Amadeus Mozart, giving secondary status to Ludwig van
Beethoven, Johannes Brahms, and Richard Wagner, and honorable mentions to Franz Schubert, Gustav Mahler, Richard Strauss, and Max
Reger.[21] But it emerges in other essays that he saw the legacy that passed
into his own hands at the turn of the century as having been principally
shaped by Brahms and Wagner, the two composers whom, he claims,
polemicists of an earlier generation had divided by an "impassable
gulf."[22] In "Brahms the Progressive" Schoenberg disputes the prevailing
perception that viewed Wagner as "the progressive, the innovator," and
Brahms as "the academician, the classicist."[23] In fact, the generation of
composers immediately preceding his own, including Mahler, Strauss,
and Reger, had already demonstrated that it was possible to include "the
qualities of both [Wagner and Brahms] in one work."[24] To Schoenberg
himself, however, fell the task of demonstrating that the styles of Wagner
and Brahms were not only compatible, but that they were actually more
fundamentally similar than the conventional wisdom allowed. If Wagner's
progressivism rested on his advanced harmonic practice, an example from
Brahms's String Quartet in C minor, op. 51, no.1 proved "[h]ow great an

innovator Brahms was in respect to harmony."[25] If Brahms's reputation for academic conservatism rested on his interest in formal organization in music, it should also be remembered that Wagner's "'Leitmotiv' technique represents the grandiose intention of unification of the thematic material of an entire opera, and even of an entire tetralogy [i.e., Wagner's four-opera *Ring* cycle]," and that "this organization is also formalistic."[26] In other words, that both composers stemmed from a single tradition—the German tradition—and participated in its continuing evolution superseded the stylistic idiosyncrasies that separated them in the minds of more superficial observers.

But if Schoenberg was prepared to challenge received wisdom on the issue of Brahms's conservatism as opposed to Wagner's progressivism, in one important respect he retained the received wisdom's premises, even if in a significantly modified form. He continued to see German music as responding to two drives: a progressive impulse realized in tonal expansion through increasing chromaticism, and a traditionalist impulse, embodied in part in the concern for formal organization suggested above and in an interest in the developmental practice associated with Mozart and Brahms.

The essay "My Evolution," an artistic autobiography written in 1949, demonstrates clearly that the broadening of harmonic possibilities always retained progressive connotations for Schoenberg. Here the exploration of ever more dissonant relationships and expanding chromaticism serves as the organizing principle for the seventy-five-year-old composer's sketch of his early career, framed explicitly as his "advance in the direction of extended tonality."[27] So the symphonic poem *Pelleas und Melisande*, op. 5 (1902–03) contains melodies whose "extratonal intervals demand extravagant movement of the harmony,"[28] and the Chamber Symphony no. 1, op. 9 (1906), by connecting "remote relations of the tonality into a perfect unity, . . . make[s] great progress in the direction of the emancipation of the dissonance."[29] By the time of the String Quartet no. 2, op. 10 (1907–08), the tension between chromatic expansion and the stability required for the retention of a tonal center had become insurmountable, for "the overwhelming multitude of dissonances [could not] be counterbalanced any longer by occasional returns to such tonal triads as represent a key."[30] *Das Buch der hängenden Gärten*, op.15 (1908–09) and the Three Piano Pieces, op. 11 (1909), represent the "first step" in the new direction of music without reference to a tonal center, a move which "brought about accusations of anarchy and revolution," but which was in fact "distinctly a product of evolution, and no more revolutionary than any other development in the history of music."[31]

Not long after he embarked on this new path, however, Schoenberg found himself mired in a creative crisis, to which he hints obliquely in "My Evolution."

> Intoxicated by the enthusiasm of having freed myself from the shackles of tonality, I had thought to find further liberty of expression. In fact, I myself and my pupils . . . believed that now music could renounce motivic features and remain coherent and comprehensible.[32]

Although the subjunctive phrasing implies that Schoenberg is about to declare this renunciation of motivic features to have proven a dead end, he does not. What remains only a subtle implication in "My Evolution," however, receives fuller attention in the 1941 essay "Composition with Twelve Tones." Here, as in "My Evolution," Schoenberg identifies the "emancipation of the dissonance" enacted in his music around 1908 as the culmination of a process of harmonic expansion begun in the works of Richard Wagner.[33] But he goes on to say that the "extreme expressiveness" made possible by this new style came at a high price: the loss of the tonal devices that enabled "harmonic variation" to establish a work's formal structure, without which "it seemed at first impossible to compose pieces of complicated organization or of great length." The solution to this problem readiest at hand was to join the music to a literary text and allow the structure of the text to determine the structure of the music.[34] Although Schoenberg does not identify any particular work as an example, the 1909 monodrama *Erwartung*, which, as noted above, Christian Martin Schmidt identifies as the most relevant of the early atonal works for understanding *A Survivor from Warsaw*, clearly meets the description.

The text of *Erwartung* was prepared at Schoenberg's request by Marie Pappenheim, a medical student who had become part of his circle.[35] Its dramatic action is minimal: a woman, lost at night in a forest where she was apparently to meet her lover, stumbles upon a corpse that is perhaps that of the lover, whom she herself may have murdered. The string of uncertainties is central; it is impossible to say how much of the woman's monologue is "reliable," with its lurches from visions of a romantic idyll to enraged suspicions of betrayal. Evidence of her madness comes not only from her wild, shifting emotions, but from the disintegration of her memory into tenuously interconnected fragments, shorn of coherent sequence.[36] Schoenberg's setting of this nightmarish text certainly matches its emotional extremity, but much of its impact derives from its depiction of the faculty of memory in a state of collapse. The music unfolds in a continuous present, taking up motives and then dropping them after a few iterations, frustrating the listener's expectation of the sort of audible coherence normally established by the repetition of identifiable motives or themes. As Charles Rosen has put it, in *Erwartung* "Schoenberg did away with all the traditional means [by] which music was supposed to make itself intelligible."[37] Indeed, nothing could be further from the tonal tradition's complexes of interconnection and differentiation than the evaporating past of *Erwartung*, with its insistent denial of satisfaction to any order-imposing faculty of recollection. Like the woman whose helpless dementia it expresses, the music has lost the ability to make sense of memory, allowing only fragmentary, distorted glimpses of the lost tonal tradition.

The sense of music's disconnection from its own past implied in *Erwartung* finds more explicit confirmation in the 1912 *Pierrot lunaire*, op. 21. Described by Malcolm MacDonald as "an ironic epilogue to the works since 1907,"[38] this "cycle of poems declaimed with the accompaniment of chamber orchestra" draws on texts by the French poet Albert Giraud as translated by Otto Erich Hartleben.[39] The poems share with the text of *Erwartung* a nightmarish quality, but filtered through the persona of the luckless *commedia dell'arte* clown Pierrot, the mood shades into gruesome satire rather than psychosis.[40]

Pierrot lunaire emphasizes discontinuity with the musical past not, as in *Erwartung*, by an emphatic breakdown of the faculty of memory, but by overdetermined or problematized references to past musical forms. One such reference is all but demanded by the title of the poem, "Valse de Chopin," ["Chopin Waltz"] (no. 5). But as Jonathan Dunsby observes, "Schoenberg seems to introduce little Chopin" into the music; the means available to a "post-tonal composer" for invoking the "Chopinesque" are limited by the insufficient common ground between Schoenberg's style, on the one hand, and Frédéric Chopin's on the other.[41] Schoenberg's identification of "Nacht" ["Night"] (no. 8) as a "Passacaglia"[42] is another historicizing gesture. The passacaglia is a form associated with music of the Baroque era based on the systematic repetition of a brief melodic pattern, usually in the bass.[43] "Nacht" meets and exceeds the expectations raised by its designation as a passacaglia, as variants of its recurring three-note motive gradually saturate the whole musical texture.[44] "Parodie" (no. 17) and "Der Mondfleck" ["The Moonfleck"] (no. 18) make prominent use of canon and fugue, compositional methods based on echo effects between polyphonic voices that share with the passacaglia a distinctly archaic flavor. "Der Mondfleck," like

"Nacht," seems bent on overdetermination, with its simultaneous fugue and two canons. At the midpoint of "Der Mondfleck," the piccolo, clarinet, violin, and cello begin an almost note-for-note retrograde, retracing the music of the first half of the piece backwards through the second half.[45] These self-consciously excessive nods to history heighten the exaggeration of the grotesque in *Pierrot lunaire*,[46] but they also suggest Schoenberg's growing discomfort with the gap the break with tonality had placed between himself and the artistic tradition in which he had been raised.[47]

Between 1907 and 1912, then, Schoenberg explored the ramifications of his fulfillment of what he construed as the evolutionary imperative to break free of tonality. The invocations of the musical past in *Pierrot lunaire* suggest that during this time the complementary traditionalist impulse had begun to press with increasing urgency, leading him to what he described in 1941 as "the conviction that these new sounds [must] obey the laws of nature and of our manner of thinking— the conviction that order, logic, comprehensibility and form cannot be present without such laws."[48] As he had in 1911 with the *Harmonielehre*, Schoenberg responded to this compositional crisis by organizing his thoughts into a theoretical treatise, an unpublished manuscript he drafted in April of 1917: *Zusammenhang, Kontrapunkt, Instrumentation, Formenlehre* [*Coherence, Counterpoint, Instrumentation, Instruction in Form*].[49] Although the treatise remains fragmentary, it makes clear the extent to which Schoenberg linked aspects of compositional practice with the continuation of musical tradition. The manuscript marks the first articulation of the concept of "developing variation,"[50] a conception of thematic derivation and compositional process that became a key feature of his later writing.[51] As Ethan Haimo has observed, "Almost all of Schoenberg's remarks about developing variation are couched in discussions of the music of eighteenth- and nineteenth-century composers,"[52] and, indeed, in the 1917 manuscript Schoenberg introduces the concept with an example from Mozart's String Quartet in C major, K. 465, in which he demonstrates that the theme's final motive is derived through the gradual alteration of an initially subordinate gesture.[53] That this concern with motivic procedures had implications for large-scale formal conception may be gleaned from the opening sentence of the section "Instruction in Form": "The first instructions about the (motivic) construction and the organization of ideas are already contained in the counterpoint {text}."[54] In other words, motivic development is the first issue that comes to Schoenberg's mind as he begins his discussion of large-scale formal organization, implying that an understanding of the process of motivic development is necessary not only to an understanding of the construction of thematic materials, but of the construction of whole formal units as well.

In "Composition with Twelve Tones (1)" Schoenberg casts serial technique as the specific solution to the dilemma that overtook him after *Pierrot lunaire*: "After many unsuccessful attempts during a period of approximately twelve years, I laid the foundations for a new procedure in musical construction which seemed fitted to replace those structural differentiations provided formerly by tonal harmonies."[55] This new procedure enabled him to reconnect with the specific practices of the German musical tradition. In constructing a serial row the composer establishes a fixed order for the presentation of the twelve pitches of the chromatic scale, which he then subjects to precisely the same principles of reversal and mirroring employed by the Renaissance and Baroque masters of counterpoint. Through the subdivision of the row into segments deployed as primarily melodic or harmonic units, serialism also provided Schoenberg with the conceptual framework he needed to apply developmental practice in an atonal environment, inasmuch as "the distribution [of the tones of the row] may be varied or developed according to circumstances. . . ."[56] Ethan Haimo argues that Schoenberg's "reconciliation of serial ordering and developing variation" required a lengthy process of acclimation to the new technique during the 1920s, and that he only conceived of uniting them after he had already begun composing with the serial technique.[57] But in the 1917 manuscript, as described above, Schoenberg had already connected formal structure with motivic construction and motivic construction with the German musical tradition as represented by Mozart's C major string quartet. The solution to the problem of form could hardly have appeared to be much of a solution, and certainly not one which would guarantee another century of German musical dominance, if it did not already hold the promise of bringing formal structure and developing variation together into what he had contended as early as 1912 must be a "complete organism."[58]

Serialism, in short, restored the faculty of memory to music by enabling the restoration of the principle of developing variation. Within the individual work, developing variation enabled the construction of thematic components that evolve through a tissue of connections linking what is heard *now* with what was heard *before*,[59] as opposed to the moment-to-moment, continuous present evoked in *Erwartung*. Serialism thereby also enabled music to recover its own historical awareness; *Pier-*

rot lunaire could sharpen its satirical edge with arch references to an apparently calcified musical past, but serial technique offered a means of validating a work's position within a vital, continuing, developmentally oriented tradition.[60]

SCHOENBERG'S JEWISH AWAKENING

That the catalyst for his exploration of Jewish identity was a personal confrontation with anti-Semitism hardly makes Schoenberg unique; such experiences were not uncommon for assimilated, German-speaking Jews in the latter decades of Jewish emancipation.[61] What is striking is the intensity of Schoenberg's reaction: after the Mattsee incident, an explicit concern with his own Jewishness began to move to the center of his life and work.

Schoenberg's biographer Hans Heinz Stuckenschmidt locates the foundation of his subject's personality in the lively intellectual and religious tension that prevailed in his parents' household. Schoenberg's mother Pauline was a daughter of one of Prague's oldest Jewish families, and adhered to the Orthodox traditions in which she had been raised, while her husband Samuel, according to her nephew Hans Nachod, was "a sort of anarchistic wit."[62] Pauline's brother, Schoenberg's Uncle Fritz, a lover of Friedrich Schiller's poetry and a sometime poet himself, took on the role of intellectual mentor after Samuel's early death. Stuckenschmidt's portrait of the adult Schoenberg reflects these conflicting parental inclinations toward conservatism and progressivism: "In his mature character we find the strict preservationist and in his later years the pious Jewish feelings of his mother together with the stimulating views of his father, who took a critical standpoint on all matters. . . ."[63]

Whatever the nature of Samuel Schönberg's doubts, he and his wife entered their son's name into the register of the Viennese Jewish community and, in accordance with Jewish law, had him circumcised eight days after his birth.[64] The earliest surviving record of Arnold's own thinking on spiritual matters appears in a letter to his cousin Malvina Goldschmied, dated May 25, 1891, in which the sixteen-year-old declares himself an "unbeliever" but identifies scripture as a repository of valuable wisdom.[65] He made his next significant religious statement in 1898, when at the age of twenty-three he left the Jewish community and converted to Lutheranism in a ceremony at Vienna's Dorotheerkirche.[66]

Whether and to what extent Schoenberg's conversion may have been motivated by a sense of professional necessity has never been satisfactorily settled. Pamela White has succinctly reviewed the issues involved and influences at play. Although his decision to convert to Lutheranism in Catholic Vienna has seemed problematic, she writes, it was in fact not an uncommon choice. Protestantism may have represented the lesser betrayal for Jews who, even in the latter days of the nineteenth-century emancipation, saw conversion as a necessary prerequisite to success in the middle-class professions, a step taken with misgivings and therefore to be mitigated as much as circumstances allowed.[67]

In Schoenberg's individual case, however, there are a variety of alternative circumstances that soften the apparent pragmatism implied by this explanation. Following Stuckenschmidt, White mentions the probable influence of the singer Walter Pieau, who was active in the young composer's circle and is recorded as godfather at his baptism.[68] She also offers Alexander Ringer's account of Schoenberg's experience as the conductor of a worker's chorus, through which he was exposed to their distrust of the Roman Catholic Church.[69] Ringer has elsewhere defended Schoenberg's conversion against charges of professional opportunism by emphasizing the inadequacy of his early Jewish education.

> Paradoxically, Schoenberg had forsaken Judaism as a formal religion not, like many others, under secularizing or assimilationist influences, but rather because, virtually untutored in Jewish values, he looked for other vessels to quench his spiritual thirst.[70]

White herself offers an explanation derived from developmental psychology: "[T]he apparent mystery of Schoenberg's conversion may be explained as a change in loyalties from an earlier adolescent affiliation with values in the home—his 'free-thinking' father—to a young adult's affiliation with peers."[71] But whatever motivated Schoenberg to convert, his active life as a Protestant was, as White observes, short-lived. Although he and his first wife Mathilde Zemlinsky (also of Jewish descent) confirmed their marriage by civil ceremony with a second ceremony in the Dorotheerkirche in 1901, his interest in the church appears to have waned after they moved to Berlin in 1902.[72]

The incomplete oratorio *Die Jakobsleiter* [*Jacob's Ladder*] suggests the complex interweaving of issues of religious belief, literary influence, and artistic development in Schoenberg's spiritual maturation. *Die Jakobsleiter* occupied Schoenberg from 1915 to 1922, the years of protracted creative crisis, with interruptions for his periods of military service during the First World War.[73] The initial idea for a work on the struggle for religious faith emerged as early as 1911, when he conceived of a composition inspired by the novelist August Strindberg's autobiographical fragment *Jakob ringt* [*Jacob Wrestles*] and Honoré de Balzac's novel *Séraphita*, both of which reflect the influence of the mystical theosophy of Emanuel Swedenborg.[74] In 1912 he wrote to the poet Richard Dehmel, upon whose *Verklärte Nacht* he had based his own 1899 sextet of the same title, hoping to interest Dehmel in preparing a text for "an oratorio on the following subject: modern man, having passed through materialism, socialism, and anarchy and, despite having been an atheist, still having in him some residue of ancient faith (in the form of superstition), wrestles with God (see also Strindberg's *Jakob ringt*) and finally succeeds in finding God and becoming religious. Learning to pray!"[75] Dehmel's religious perspective, however, turned out to be incompatible with his own, and Schoenberg ultimately wrote the text himself.[76]

Pamela White identifies the period of the inception of *Die Jakobsleiter* as "a clearly new stage of development in Schoenberg's religious faith," marked by the synthesis of his philosophical and literary interests with "the rekindling of interest in Judaism via Old Testament images."[77] But as the title of Strindberg's fragment suggests, the Old Testament imagery came already bundled with the literary sources: in *Jakob ringt*, the Biblical story of Jacob wrestling with the angel serves as a metaphor for Strindberg's own religious crisis, and Jacob's vision of the ladder to heaven appears in Balzac's *Séraphita*.[78] Nor, as Jean Christensen reminds us, is *Die Jakobsleiter* lacking in ideas derived from the New Testament, particularly from Christ's Sermon on the Mount.[79] White is surely correct to say that *Die Jakobsleiter* is an expression of Schoenberg's deepening spiritual awareness, but given the variety of traditions he melds in its text, it is difficult to see the oratorio as clear evidence of a rekindled interest in Judaism, much less as evidence, as Alexander Ringer asserts, that Schoenberg remained "an unreformed Jew at heart."[80]

Schoenberg completed the text of *Die Jakobsleiter* in 1917; work on its music occupied him for over four years, from 1917 to 1922, the period during which he also developed serial technique as the solution to the crisis brought on by the abandonment of tonality.[81] Looking back on his unfinished oratorio in 1948, Schoenberg pointed to it as an important step in the development of twelve-tone serialism.[82] Its status as a transitional work between the free atonality of *Erwartung* or *Pierrot lunaire* and fully realized serial technique may explain why it remained unfinished, but as Michael Mäckelmann points out, it should also be remembered that in the early 1920s Schoenberg's religious convictions underwent a change as profound as that in his compositional practice. As he came fully to embrace his Jewish identity, the mystical theosophy of *Die Jakobsleiter* became increasingly untenable as a spiritual orientation.[83]

Schoenberg revealed the governing principles of his idiosyncratic engagement with Jewish issues in a 1923 exchange of letters with his long-time friend, the painter Wassily Kandinsky. Kandinsky had asked Schoenberg to join him at Weimar, where he hoped to found an intellectual center associated with the Bauhaus. Rumors had recently reached Schoenberg that the Bauhaus artists, and perhaps even Kandinsky himself, had given voice to anti-Semitic sentiments,[84] and he rejected the offer with an impassioned assertion of his own Jewishness.

> For I have at last learnt the lesson that has been forced upon me during this year, and I shall not ever forget it. It is that I am not a German, not a European, indeed perhaps scarcely a human being (at least, the Europeans prefer the worst of their race to me), but I am a Jew.[85]

Kandinsky expressed his confusion and denied the charge of anti-Semitism in a conciliatory reply,[86] but Schoenberg, willfully misinterpreting Kandinsky's endorsement of a society blind to ethnic differences, responded on May 4 with a lengthy, two-part diatribe. After venting his lingering outrage over the expulsion from Mattsee two years earlier, he called attention to the growing appeal of anti-Semitism on the German political stage.

> [W]hen I walk along the street and each person looks at me to see whether I'm a Jew or a Christian, I can't very well tell them that I'm the one that Kandinsky and some others make an exception of, although that man Hitler is not of their opinion.[87]

The first part of the letter concludes with a chilling prediction, a full ten years before Hitler's rise to power, and nearly twenty before he set the machinery of the Final Solution in motion.

> But what is anti-Semitism to lead to if not to acts of violence? Is it so difficult to imagine that? You are perhaps satisfied with depriving Jews of their civil rights. Then certainly Einstein, Mahler, I and many others will have been got rid of. But one thing is certain: they will not be able to exterminate those much tougher elements thanks to whose en-

durance Jewry has maintained itself unaided against the whole of mankind for 20 centuries. For these are evidently so constituted that they can accomplish the task that their God has imposed on them: To survive in exile, uncorrupted and unbroken, until the hour of salvation comes![88]

Schoenberg's anticipation of an anti-Semitic will to extermination associated with the growing prominence of Adolf Hitler, stated several months before Hitler's own failed coup attempt in November 1923, must surely have been one of the earliest articulations of this possibility.[89] But what is particularly striking is Schoenberg's embedding of that vision of attempted extermination in an expression of fierce resistance, emphasizing his absolute certainty that no matter how ferociously attacked, Judaism would endure.

The second part of the letter completes the foundation for Schoenberg's developing vision of Jewish identity. He broke off writing for a few days, and upon returning to the letter, claimed to see his lengthy argument against anti-Semitism as "morally and tactically . . . a very great mistake."[90] He continued with the following explanation, in which it becomes clear that he believed the separation between Jew and anti-Semite to be insurmountable by reason or argument, making continued discussion pointless.

> I was arguing! I was defending a position!
>
> I forgot that it *is not a matter* of right and wrong, of truth and untruth, of understanding and blindness, but of power; and in such matters everyone seems to be blind, in hatred as blind as in love.
>
> I forgot, it's no use arguing because of course I won't be listened to; because there is no will to understand, but only one not to hear what the other says.
>
> If you will, read what I have written; but I do ask that you will not send me an argumentative answer. Don't make the same mistake as I made. I am trying to keep you from it by telling you:
>
> I shall not understand you; I cannot understand you.[91]

Schoenberg's growing preoccupation with the issue of Jewish identity kept pace with the acceleration of anti-Semitism as a political force. Even as it impinged on his social contacts and professional choices, it found its way into the stuff of his work. In 1926 he moved to Berlin to accept a position at the Prussian Academy of the Arts, after an ugly public debate in which his fitness for the position was challenged on anti-Semitic grounds.[92] Later that year he began his first Zionist manifesto, the play *Der biblische Weg* [*The Biblical Path*], which ties the achievement of a Jewish homeland to the Jews' readiness to use force, to meet the brutality of anti-Semitism on its own terms. The play links the cause of Jewish survival explicitly with the need to reinvigorate the Jewish mission: to accept the possibility of martyrdom in the name of truth, defined as the thought of God the all-powerful and unknowable. It is an allegory of the Exodus from Egypt played in twentieth-century terms, its central figure, Max Aruns, an amalgamation of the biblical figures Moses and Aaron, both receiver and transmitter of the God-idea.[93]

The ideas addressed in partial allegory in *Der biblische Weg* received fuller exploration in a work initially conceived as the play was nearing completion in the mid-1920s.[94] In the opera *Moses und Aron*, Schoenberg turned directly to the biblical story that formed the background for the drama of twentieth-century politics in *Der biblische Weg*, the moment of the Jews' selection to bring the idea of the "one, eternal, omnipresent, imperceptible, and inconceivable God" to the rest of humanity.[95] As he had for *Die Jakobsleiter*, Schoenberg wrote his own libretto for *Moses und Aron*, a project which was substantially completed by 1930, when he began work on the music.[96] By now his command of serial technique had become sufficiently sophisticated that he was prepared to base the entire opera on a single twelve-tone pitch set.[97] Thus he wed the text of *Moses und Aron*, which reflects his working out of the spiritual and political implications of his decision to embrace Jewish identity, to a musical language that he had designed expressly in order to sustain the German musical tradition.

Experiences like the expulsion from Mattsee in 1921 and the debate over his appointment to the Prussian Academy in 1925 could hardly have left Schoenberg unaware that some Germans were barely willing to allow him a position in the German tradition, much less to concede that his work should be the model for its continuation. This awareness seems reflected in the two-part essay "National Music" he drafted in 1931, while he was still at work on the music of *Moses und Aron*. In the first part, where a concern with national "hegemony" in art echoes his remark to Rufer in the summer of 1921, Schoenberg posits a "strong hold exerted on art by race and nationality."[98] German musical superiority, which had determined "the way things developed" for the past two hundred years, rested on the success of German composers in finding "predominantly German ways to express themselves."[99] Now German music

stood at a turning point, not unlike the one it had faced in the eighteenth
century, when J. S. Bach had established the groundwork for the suc-
ceeding two centuries of German musical dominance.

> So if at the climax of contrapuntal art, in Bach, something quite new si-
> multaneously begins—the art of development through motivic varia-
> tion—and in our time, at the climax of art based on harmonic
> relationships, the art of composing with "twelve tones related only to
> each other" begins, one sees that the epochs are very similar.[100]

In the second part of "National Music" he outlines the artistic genealogy
mentioned earlier, emphasizing the importance of the music of Bach,
Mozart, Beethoven, Brahms, and Wagner to his own musical development in order to illustrate something which, "remarkably, nobody has yet
appreciated[:] that my music, produced on German soil, without foreign
influences, is a living example of an art able most effectively to oppose
Latin and Slav hopes of hegemony and derived through and through
from the traditions of German music."[101]

A fragment that also dates from 1931 strongly suggests that asser-
tions of his own fundamentally German musical identity arose in response to challenges on this very score. In the draft preface for a music
treatise he had been developing, Schoenberg acknowledges the growing
division between himself and German music in a gloomy concession, although, as the rather telegraphic sketch reveals, he clearly continues to
hope that the tradition will one day reclaim him.

> German music will not take my path, the path I have pointed out.
>
> Prepared to release myself from it, but not without having settled
> my debt to it, I wish as thanks to show it the path it has taken.
>
> Until I am near [to it again].
>
> And if by widening the interval until this separation is annulled I
> have blurred the point at which I have stood, I wish to emphasize that
> much more clearly the point at which it [German music] stands and
> will stand, until someone whose guidance it will accept leads it for-
> ward.[102]

It would take a significantly more drastic attack than anything he had yet
experienced to convince Schoenberg that, as a Jew, he might never be
permitted the relationship to the German musical tradition he believed
his work had earned.

On March 1, 1933, the president of the Prussian Academy announced before the assembled faculty that the newly installed Nazi government had demanded the elimination of Jewish influence in the Academy. Declaring that he never stayed where he was not wanted, Schoenberg stormed out of the meeting.[103] Less than two months later he left with his family for Paris, where he participated in a "reconversion" ceremony confirming his return to Judaism. Galvanized by his second experience with expulsion, he wrote on August 4 to Anton von Webern of the development of his Jewish consciousness and his plans for the future.

> For fourteen years I have been prepared for what has now happened. During that time I was able to prepare myself for it thoroughly, and have finally cut myself off for good—even though with difficulty, and a good deal of vacillation—from all that tied me to the Occident. I have long since resolved to be a Jew. . . . And now, as from a week ago, I have also returned officially to the Jewish religious community; indeed, we do not differ in the matter of religion (my *Moses and Aaron* will show this), though we do when it comes to my views on the need for the church to adapt itself to the demands of the modern way of life. It is my intention to take an active part in endeavors of this kind. I regard that as more important than my art, and am determined—if I am suited to such activities—to do nothing in future but work for the Jewish national cause. . . . My immediate plan is for a long tour of America, which could perhaps turn into a world tour, to persuade people to help the Jews of Germany.[104]

Earlier, in a letter written on June 13 to Jacob Klatzkin, the Jewish philosopher with whom he had shared his developing Zionist vision, he had dealt rather more bluntly with the issue of relations between Jews and Europeans: "We are Asians and nothing of real substance connects us with the West."[105]

Few perceived the threat to European Jewry as clearly and as early as Schoenberg. After emigrating to the United States in 1933, he began a campaign of agitating on their behalf, delivering speeches and drawing up plans of action that culminated in his second Zionist manifesto, the 1938 call-to-arms "A Four-Point Program for Jewry."[106] In this essay, as he had in the 1923 letter to Kandinsky, Schoenberg accurately anticipated the impact the war that now threatened Europe would have on the Jews there: "Is there room in the world for almost 7,000,000 people? Are they condemned to doom? Will they become extinct? Famished? Butchered?"[107]

But as Moshe Lazar has observed, Schoenberg pursued his program in effective isolation, addressing himself "to individuals (writers, artists, friends) who could not in any way have assisted in such a complex political and international issue," while ignoring "the Zionist leaders who were certainly representative of all existing political trends in World Jewry."[108] Despite the almost uncanny accuracy of his assessment of the situation, his agenda for averting the looming disaster in Germany showed little interest in political reality, and stood no chance of affecting the course of world events.

GERMAN MUSIC AND THE JEWISH SELF: *A SURVIVOR FROM WARSAW,* OP. 46

Schoenberg's declarations severing his ties with "the West" could easily be taken, and perhaps dismissed, as impassioned rhetoric inspired by the extremity of the historical moment. In his work, after all, he continued to draw upon the paradigmatically Western German musical tradition, even in the liturgically conceived *Kol Nidre*, op. 39 (1938).[109] Indeed, it is difficult to imagine a composer who turned sixty in 1934 turning his back on a lifetime of aesthetic conviction and artistic practice in order to assert an overtly Jewish musical identity. The search for evidence in Schoenberg's music of a personal withdrawal from the West in general and Germany in particular will be fruitless if it insists on the abandonment of German musical practice as its single satisfactory criterion. The result will be significantly different, however, if such evidence may also include an assessment of German culture carried out within a musical work, and particularly one that is carried out side-by-side with an assessment of Jewish culture.

No single event could have provided Schoenberg a better opportunity to comment on the state of German culture than the Second World War, and indeed, references to the war do emerge in his late works. The *Ode to Napoleon*, op. 41 (1942),[110] for instance, offers a sarcastic allegory of Hitler through a setting of Lord Byron's bitter poem, and the epigrammatic section headings he gave to the Piano Concerto, op. 42, another 1942 composition, seem to tie progress in the concerto to the progress of recent world history ("Life was so easy," "But suddenly hatred broke out," "A serious situation was created," "But life goes on").[111] But only one of the late compositions deals explicitly with the attempted extermination of Europe's Jews, the final proof for Schoenberg of the irreconcilable enmity between German and Jew. In *A Survivor from Warsaw* he substantially redefines the opposition Nazism had decisively established between the German culture in which he had been raised and rejected and the Jewish identity he had so aggressively reclaimed. Here, Schoenberg effectively rewrites his will, withdrawing from German music the right to inherit that which he considered his most enduring legacy, and which he had developed specifically for the benefit of German music: the method of composing with twelve tones related only to one another.

The composition of *A Survivor from Warsaw* took Schoenberg just two weeks during the middle of August 1947. The first inspiration for a composition about the Holocaust, however, had come earlier in the year, through a commission that had provided him with the work's dramatic scene. This project quickly foundered on the issue of Schoenberg's fee, but he did not abandon the original idea. When the Koussevitzky Foundation contacted him early in July to remind him of its standing offer to commission a new work, he accepted immediately, proposing a composition for small orchestra, two narrators, and men's chorus. Schoenberg was nearly seventy-four in the summer of 1947, and his eyesight was failing. He prepared the manuscript in condensed score on specially printed, oversized music paper, penciling in the instrumentation rather than writing out each instrumental part on an independent staff. Under Schoenberg's direction, the conductor René Leibowitz prepared the full orchestral score.[112] In its final form, the work calls for standard orchestra, a single narrator, and a men's chorus. The narrator delivers the first portion of the text in *Sprechstimme*, the rhythmically regulated speech Schoenberg had used in *Pierrot lunaire* and for the part of Moses in *Moses und Aron*. The chorus sings the concluding portion of the text, a setting of the central prayer of the Jewish liturgy, the *Shema Yisrael*.

A Survivor from Warsaw draws meaning from processes of disjuncture and disruption, establishing frames of narrative, language, and musical style only to shatter them by the intrusion of radically dissimilar elements that refuse assimilation. The very identity of the work rests on one such disjuncture, the discontinuity between title and text, or between name and object. The event described in the text could have taken place at almost any moment during the Holocaust: condemned Jews bursting into spontaneous, collective prayer before being sent to death. The title and the narrator's single reference to having lived in Warsaw's sewers have usually been understood to place the event at the Warsaw ghetto, where on April 19, 1943, Jews launched an armed resistance against the Nazis that lasted for three weeks.[113] Even such authoritative commentators as René Leibowitz and Christian Martin Schmidt have shared this assumption.[114]

But as Michael Strasser has argued, to deduce the work's dramatic setting from the title is to miss an important aspect of its meaning.[115] If Schoenberg did indeed intend to depict a particular moment in the history of the uprising (presumably its collapse, since the Nazis are clearly in charge), then it must be conceded that his information appears to have been inaccurate. I have been able to find no independent confirmation that any such event as he describes took place on May 15, when the Nazis officially declared the ghetto resistance to have been crushed,[116] or at any other moment in the aftermath of the uprising. To expect absolute historical accuracy, however, begs the question of how much Schoenberg actually knew about the uprising when he composed *A Survivor from Warsaw*; he may very will have intended to depict the particular event but gotten the facts wrong.

Strasser calls attention to evidence drawn from the text itself, which also argues against setting the scene at the ghetto. The day of the event, the narrator tells us, begins "as usual," and the Jews know precisely what is expected of them, responding to Reveille, falling into military formation and following orders to count off, all bespeaking acclimation to a hideous routine. Clearly, this is not the confusion following the collapse of armed resistance at Warsaw, but the regimented existence of a concentration camp. From this evidence Strasser concludes that "when Schoenberg constructed his text he sought to dissociate the story from a specific incident, deliberately obscuring details of time and place in order to emphasize its symbolic character."[117] Reference to Warsaw continues to function, however, as a symbolic reminder of the ghetto uprising.[118]

By placing the scene in an unnamed camp, then, Schoenberg gives the narrative a mythic status; through the shown but unnamed concentration camp Holocaust history becomes Holocaust trope. The same dynamic works in reverse with respect to Warsaw, named but not shown and thus raised as a competing trope. The disjuncture between title and content reverses the usual relationship between the Warsaw resistance and the Holocaust as a whole. Instead of appearing as a single, exceptional event in a bleak progression of annihilation, the Warsaw trope here encloses the Holocaust, enabling the uprising to define the meaning of the larger history. It is a dramatic enactment of the reversal Schoenberg had asserted twenty-four years earlier in his letter to Kandinsky.

During the span of its approximately seven minutes *A Survivor from Warsaw* employs three different languages, leaping from English to German and finally to Hebrew. This could be understood as an attempt at verisimilitude, but the text resists an interpretation of its multilingual character as a simple scene-setting device. Just as the fissure between title and dramatic scene forces both into the sphere of the mythic, the abrupt, calculated shifts of language complicate the listener's relationship to the text, loading additional layers of meaning onto language itself.

The opening sentences establish English as the linguistic frame. On practical grounds, this was clearly an inevitable choice; Schoenberg had been living in the United States for fourteen years, and *A Survivor from Warsaw* was composed as an American commission for performance before an American audience. Michael Mäckelmann sees the English text as occupying a "neutral place" between the passages in German and Hebrew,[119] but the static quality this implies misses the richer purpose Schoenberg invests in the English-language narrative.

> I cannot remember ev'rything. I must have been unconscious most of the time. —I remember only the grandiose moment when they all started to sing, as if prearranged, the old prayer they had neglected for so many years—the forgotten creed! But I have no recollection how I got to live underground in the sewers of Warsaw for so long a time.[120]

With his first words the Survivor thus establishes the narrative frame as well, distancing the listener from his story. His admissions emphasize the fragmentation of his recollections, as does the slippage between his memories of the Warsaw sewers and of the concentration camp. As the agent of memory, he intervenes between the listener and the events he describes, establishing distance in time. That this Survivor from Warsaw gives his narrative in English strongly suggests geographic distance, although this can be fully established only retrospectively (i.e., when another language intrudes). The dialogic context also implies a role for the listener as a character partially *within* the work, whose presence exerts a necessary pressure on the telling of the Survivor's story; a shadow figure, presumably an American, for whose benefit the narrative is rendered into English.

Changes in address and verb tense signal the shift from the introduction to the narrated sequence of events. The narrator's introduction has established a sharp division between first person/present tense and third person/past tense—between the agent of memory and the contents of memory. Now, as he recounts the worries of the prisoners spilling from their bunks in response to a bugle call, the narrator's address shifts to second person and veers toward the present tense, placing the listener in the prisoners' place and compelling sympathy with their fears: "You had been separated from your children, from your wife, from your parents; you don't know what happened to them—how could you sleep?"[121]

In the subsequent sentences, which describe the Jews assembling before the Nazi soldiers, the unstable verb tense undermines an attempt to reassert dramatic distance through the resumption of third person address: "They came out. . . . They fear the sergeant. They hurry as much as they can."[122] At this point language itself becomes an additional device for extending the listener's identification with the Jews, who have the first quoted speech to appear in the narrative: "'Get out! The sergeant will be furious!'"[123] The speech is given in English, perhaps the least likely of all European languages to have been native to Jews in a Nazi concentration camp, dispelling the possibility that a concern for realism alone motivates the later shifts of language. Translating the Jews' speech (from Yiddish? Polish? German?) embraces the narrator, the listener, and the Jews in a community that retains the principle of communication, a community whose borders are drawn by the sudden intrusion of the sergeant's spoken German.

> Achtung! Stilljestanden! Na wirds mal? Oder soll ich mit dem Jew-
> ehrkolben nachhelfen? Na jutt; wenn ihr's durchaus haben wollt!
> [Attention! Be silent! Are you ready yet? Or should I assist you with
> my riflebutt? All right then, if that's what you really want!][124]

And after having beaten the Jews and ordered them to count off:

> Rascher! Nochmal von vorn anfangen! In einer Minute will ich wissen
> wieviele ich zur Gaskammer abliefere! Abzählen!
> [Faster! Begin again from the front! In a minute I'll know how many
> I'm sending to the gas chamber! Count off!][125]

The sergeant speaks only in German, and only the sergeant speaks German; linguistically, he is entirely isolated. This initial disruption of the linguistic frame forces upon the listener an awareness of the split between the meaning of the words and the means of their transmission. German language acts as a sign, calling attention to the sergeant's Germanness. In fact, language is the only cultural signifier deployed in the text of *A Survivor from Warsaw*. Not once does the narrator name the prisoners as Jews or the soldiers as Nazis or Germans. In the universe of this brief work, moreover, the condition of being German offers sharply limited possibilities. Closed to translation and therefore excluded from the community of civilized discourse, the sergeant can speak only of beatings and gas chambers, and can act only with savagery.

Although the intrusion of German text necessarily disrupts the linguistic frame, it leaves the narrative frame intact. The free oscillation between English and German in the Survivor's speech does not offend against the dialogic context; the listener's distance from the events safely contained within the Survivor's memory continues undisturbed. The explosion of the narrative frame occurs as the Jews, in the accelerating frenzy of their counting-off, suddenly unite in the singing of the *Shema Yisrael*. In effect, they burst from the Survivor's memory, collapsing time and space in order to assert unmediated dramatic presence.

If the sergeant's German text points to German identity, the Hebrew prayer inevitably points to Jewish identity, and the text of the prayer confirms the latter's absolute, irreconcilable opposition to the former. The *Shema Yisrael*, Judaism's central prayer and proclamation, is drawn from the book of Deuteronomy.

> Hear, O Israel! The Lord our God is one Lord; and you shall love the Lord your God with all your heart and with all your soul and with all your might. And these words which I command you this day shall be upon your heart; and you shall teach them diligently to your children, and shall talk of them when you sit in your house, and when you walk by the way, and when you lie down, and when you rise.[126]

The text commands an awareness of God that pervades all the activities of daily living, and the vehicle for that awareness is the text itself, "these words which I command you this day." The principle of communicable meaning, of language as the token of civilization implied by the narrator's selective translations, now becomes explicit. Moreover, the prayer highlights the stark opposition between the routines of civilized living and the routines of the concentration camp, between a society that prizes the education of its children and one that separates them from their parents to send them to an unknown fate. Locked in memory and therefore confined to the past, German identity distills into savagery; Jewish identity, forcefully refusing confinement to the past, insists on the continuity of human civilization in general and the Jewish mission in particular.

While the linguistic and narrative components of *A Survivor from Warsaw* sort out the disposition of entire social orders, its musical elements join these monumental issues to an individual composer's personal assessment of his work and its place in history. The bifurcation of musical style in *A Survivor from Warsaw* is one of its most striking features; the music that accompanies the Survivor's narrative differs sharply from the setting of the Hebrew prayer. The work is a serial composition, organizing note-by-note succession according to a twelve-tone row, but during the narrative, the music evades the construction of extended themes, one of the goals for which Schoenberg developed serial technique. Instead, musical progress in the first part of *A Survivor from Warsaw* consists of the stringing together of brief motives rarely more than a few beats in duration, a style whose closest analog, as both Theodor Adorno and Christian Martin Schmidt have observed, is that of the 1909 expressionist monodrama *Erwartung*.[127]

The association of *Erwartung* with the Survivor's narrative is entirely appropriate, perhaps even inevitable; few works have given so compelling a voice to the terror born of the collapse of perceived reality. But as Schmidt argues, the invocation of a style Schoenberg had developed and ultimately rejected as an artistic dead-end nearly thirty years earlier cannot help but raise autobiographical overtones.[128] Moreover, if in *Erwartung* the musical agenda rested on the disabling of musical memory, in *A Survivor from Warsaw* the texture is flooded with gestures that link decisively to the past. One of these, the melodic half-step used as a "sighing" motive to depict the suffering of the imprisoned Jews,[129] has a lengthy pedigree.[130] It appears most prominently in accompaniment to the text "It was painful to hear them moaning and groaning," after the Jews have been beaten.[131]

A recurring bugle call representing the Nazis is another motive with overtly historical associations. Schmidt describes the bugle calls as musically "deformed" in order to depict military brutality, a gesture he associates with the music of Gustav Mahler.[132] But in Mahler as in Schoenberg, such gestures inevitably recall the identification of brass fanfares with Germanic heroism in the music dramas of Richard Wagner, which, as Schoenberg could hardly have been unaware, the Nazis made centrally important to their propaganda.[133] Schmidt also argues that this fanfare motive is progressively neutralized during the course of the piece, becoming dispersed throughout the orchestra and losing its distinctively military color.[134] What seems at least equally striking about this motive, however, is the extent to which it retains its distinctive identity, reappearing several times either with precisely the same pitches or in exact transposition to another pitch level.[135] Schmidt's contention is surely correct that these literal repetitions have a textual basis, portraying the repeated bugle calls described in the narrative, and, as he also notes, the motive does undergo

significant transformation in other manifestations.[136] But the obstinate retention of an all-but-unchanging form of the motive carries connotations
peculiar to Schoenberg's musical language, in which, as we have seen, the
principle of developing variation, of the immediate modification of a
stated idea, is a key determinant of artistic worth. A motive that resists development in this way reveals itself to be frozen in the past, becoming increasingly irrelevant as the music progresses.

The choral setting of the *Shema Yisrael* overturns the quasi-expres-
sionist musical style of the narrative, replacing it with an extended
melodic line comprised of several statements of the serial row. Schmidt's
analysis outlines the theme's ABA' formal structure, in which a modified
version of the opening melodic material returns at the conclusion, and
calls attention to the development in the B section of material presented
in the first A section. This reclamation of formal and motivic structural
processes aligns the second section of *A Survivor from Warsaw* with
compositions of Schoenberg's twelve-tone period.[137] The mission of serialism to enable the construction of coherent themes through the process
of developing variation, which had been frustrated during that portion of
the work in which an explicitly German sensibility dictated the course of
events, reaches fulfillment only with the statement of Judaism's central
proclamation.

As Schmidt also points out, the first section's opposing motives, the
sighing melodic half-step and the fanfare, undergo substantial redefinition in the second section.[138] His assertion that this redefinition consists
of the subordination of the motives' expressive associations to their role
in a structure of pure musical form, however, seems to miss an important
point. The melodic half-step, previously symbolic of the Jews' suffering,
now forms the foundation of their collective prayer, appearing throughout the prayer melody itself, most prominently as its opening and closing
gestures, and saturating its orchestral accompaniment.[139] The expression
of Jewish faith grows precisely from the expression of Jewish pain; it
would be difficult to imagine a more compelling musical realization of
Schoenberg's conviction that Jewish belief and Jewish suffering are intimately connected, that "[o]nce convinced by an ideal the Jew is ready to
suffer or die for it."[140] Similarly, in the final three measures, strings and
brass restate the opening bugle call with overlapping entries, but in a varied form that gives prominence to its own melodic half steps. The fanfare's original military character is thus subordinated to its resemblance
to the prayer melody, even as the Nazi design to exterminate Jewry is
overwhelmed by the persistence of Jewish faith.[141]

By breaking forcefully from the style of the first section of the piece, the prayer setting serves the distinctive function of making music conscious of itself as music, even as the text's interplay of languages calls attention to them as languages. Music becomes an object for its own consideration, bringing into sharp focus the juxtaposition of the earlier, athematic expressionist style against the later, fully thematic serial style. Herein lies Schmidt's metamusical gesture, which for him is ultimately about resolving the anxiety of isolation through collective action. *A Survivor from Warsaw* communicates the anxiety of isolation by the invocation of the style of *Erwartung* and by the sergeant's attempts to impose upon the Jews the fragmenting ritual of counting-off; collective action is represented by their spontaneous eruption into group prayer. The interplay of first, second, and third person address in the Survivor's narrative also emphasizes the shift from the individual to the collective.[142] This undoubtedly forms a part of Schoenberg's intent; his Zionist writings reveal his conviction that a unified front, enforced "with all means," is indispensable to the task of ensuring Jewish survival.[143] But by resting on largely abstract, ideological issues, Schmidt fails to confront the ways in which the specific history of Schoenberg's subject matter interacts with the impulse to musical autobiography.

Michael Strasser also argues for an autobiographical reading of *A Survivor from Warsaw* but where Schmidt's emphasis is on political or ideological issues, Strasser's is on the spiritual. The condemned Jews find strength when they remember "the old prayer they had neglected for so many years," and claim for themselves a share in the spirit of the Warsaw ghetto uprising. Like Schoenberg's, their assertion of Jewish identity is a return, a self-recognition that dawns in the face of the most extreme manifestation of anti-Semitism.[144] This, too, commands a portion of the truth, but neglects Schoenberg's deliberate opposition between what he construes as the condition of being German and the condition of being Jewish.

If, as Michael Mäckelmann has argued, Schoenberg's return to Judaism in the early 1920s complicated his relationship to the unfinished oratorio *Die Jakobsleiter*, contributing to his inability to complete the work,[145] the extent to which he had bound serial technique from its inception to his vision of the future of German music may well have raised an analogous problem in the 1930s. The redefinition of serialism enacted in the 1947 *A Survivor from Warsaw*, then, could offer insight into the troublesome issue of Schoenberg's multivalent late style, raised at the beginning of this discussion. The incompletion of *Moses und Aron*, for instance, can be understood in part as a function of the difficulty of telling the funda-mental Jewish story in a thoroughly German musical language, once the opposition between German and Jewish was made to seem insurmount-able by Hitler's rise to power in 1933. Similarly, the variegated works Schoenberg composed after his emigration to the United States, marked by an apparent determination "[t]o keep the choice between tonality and atonality open on principle,"[146] would reflect the discomfort equally atten-dant upon either devoting himself wholly to a style which had come to seem tainted, or abandoning the fruit of a lifetime of artistic development. Only by confirming his worst expectations did German culture provide Schoenberg the means to release himself from its grasp on his imagination.

The affirmations Schmidt, Strasser, and others have rightly found in *A Survivor from Warsaw* are necessarily bound to and contingent upon an equally powerful repudiation.[147] Schoenberg's invocation of the musical past points explicitly to a specific passage in his own artistic development; as he composed *Erwartung* he was beginning to perceive the collapse of the German musical tradition, at the moment when a ruthless commit-ment to his own aesthetic vision had led him to the abandonment of tonal-ity, but before the development of serial technique enabled him to overcome the crisis that abandonment had created. The disorientation ex-pressed in *Erwartung* in 1909 mirrored its composer's own. In the 1947 *A Survivor from Warsaw* the expressionist style projects the collapse of meaning onto German culture as a whole, and forbids German culture from participating in the renewal promised by the turn to serialism.

NOTES

This paper grew out of a research project suggested by Professor Thomas Noblitt of the Indiana University Department of Musicology for a course on the composers of the Second Viennese School he taught in the fall of 1993. I am grateful to Professors Allan Keiler and Eric Chafe of the Brandeis University De-partment of Musicology, the editors of this volume, and my wife, Tanya Tupper, for comments, advice, and support.

1. Josef Rufer, "Hommage à Schoenberg," in *Arnold Schoenberg Corre-spondence: A Collection of Translated and Annotated Letters Exchanged with Guido Adler, Pablo Casals, Emanuel Feuermann, and Olin Downes*, ed. and trans. Egbert M. Ennulat (Metuchen, NJ: Scarecrow, 1991), 9.

2. Malcolm MacDonald, *Schoenberg* (London: J.M. Dent, 1976), 34.

3. Rufer, "Hommage à Schoenberg," 2.

4. Several scholars have called attention to the close chronological pairing between the genesis of serialism and Schoenberg's return to Judaism. See

Pamela C. White, *Schoenberg and the God-Idea: The Opera "Moses und Aron"* (Ann Arbor: UMI Research Press, 1983), 55; Alexander Ringer, "Introduction: Composer and Jew," in *Arnold Schoenberg: The Composer as Jew* (Oxford: Clarendon, 1990), 19 [subsequent citations to *Arnold Schoenberg: The Composer as Jew* are to this edition]; Michael C. Strasser, "'A Survivor from Warsaw' as Personal Parable," *Music and Letters* 76 (1995): 63.

5. For a study of the rise of anti-Semitism in German political life in this period, see Anthony Kauders, *German Politics and the Jews* (Oxford: Clarendon, 1996). Kauders focuses primarily on the cities of Düsseldorf and Nuremberg, but as he argues in his conclusion, his detailed study of anti-Semitism at the local level in the period 1910–33 has implications for the wider culture; see pp.182–91.

6. Carl Dahlhaus, "Schoenberg's Late Works," in *Schoenberg and the New Music*, trans. Derrick Puffett and Alfred Clayton (Cambridge: Cambridge University Press, 1987; reprint, Cambridge: Cambridge University Press, 1990), 158.

7. Christian Martin Schmidt, "Schönbergs Kantate 'Ein Überlebender aus Warschau' op. 46," *Archiv für Musikwissenschaft* 33 (1976): 180. Translation mine.

8. Ibid., 175. Translation mine.

9. Ibid., 277.

10. Charles Rosen, *Arnold Schoenberg* (New York: Viking, 1975; reprint, with a new preface, Chicago: University of Chicago Press, 1996), 70–71.

11. Arnold Schoenberg, "Lecture to Be Delivered in Frankfurt am Main, February 12, 1933," ed. and trans. Thomas McGeary, in Thomas McGeary, "Schoenberg's Brahms Lecture of 1933," *Journal of the Arnold Schoenberg Institute* 15 (1992): 22–87.

12. Arnold Schoenberg, "Brahms the Progressive (1947)," in *Style and Idea: Selected Writings of Arnold Schoenberg*, ed. Leonard Stein, trans. Leo Black (New York: St. Martin's, 1975), 398–441. Subsequent citations of essays from *Style and Idea* refer to this edition.

13. Arnold Schoenberg, "National Music (1) (1931)," in *Style and Idea*, 169–72; Arnold Schoenberg, "National Music (2) (1931)," in *Style and Idea*, 172–74.

14. Arnold Schoenberg, "Composition with Twelve Tones (I) (1941)," in *Style and Idea*, 214–45.

15. Arnold Schoenberg, "My Evolution (1949)," in *Style and Idea*, 79–92.

16. Arnold Schoenberg, *Theory of Harmony*, trans. Roy E. Carter (Berkeley: University of California Press, 1978), 29; originally *Harmonielehre*, 3rd ed. (Vienna: Universal-Edition, 1922). The 1922 third edition, upon which Carter bases his translation, retains the cited passage as it appeared in the first edition of 1911. See Arnold Schoenberg, *Harmonielehre* (Leipzig: Universal-Edition, 1911), 30–31.

17. Hans Heinz Stuckenschmidt, *Schoenberg: His Life, World and Work*, trans. Humphrey Searle (London: John Calder, 1977), 558–59.

18. Arnold Schoenberg, program notes for the concert at the Verein für Kunst und Kultur, January 14, 1910, in Willi Reich, *Schoenberg: A Critical Biography*, trans. Leo Black (London: Longman, 1971), 49.

19. Reich, *Schoenberg*, 50.

20. That Schoenberg published his *Harmonielehre* at least in part as a response to his critics seems clear from his discussion of it in a 1937 essay: "The *Harmonielehre* endowed me with the respect of many former adversaries who hitherto had considered me a wild man, a savage, an illegitimate intruder into musical culture." Arnold Schoenberg, "How One Becomes Lonely (1937)," in *Style and Idea*, 50.

21. Schoenberg, "National Music (2) (1931)," 172–74.

22. Schoenberg, "Brahms the Progressive (1947)," 399.

23. Ibid., 398.

24. Ibid., 399.

25. Ibid., 402.

26. Ibid., 405.

27. Schoenberg, "My Evolution (1949)," 82.

28. Ibid., 82.

29. Ibid., 84.

30. Ibid., 86. For a critical survey of Schoenberg's development up to the brink of his abandonment of tonality, see Walter Frisch, *The Early Works of Arnold Schoenberg, 1893–1908* (Berkeley: University of California Press, 1993).

31. Schoenberg, "My Evolution (1949)," 86.

32. Ibid., 88.

33. Schoenberg, "Composition with Twelve Tones (1) (1941)," 216.

34. Ibid., 217–18.

35. Stuckenschmidt, *Schoenberg: His Life, World and Work*, 119.

36. For a more detailed synopsis of the text of *Erwartung*, see MacDonald, *Schoenberg*, 183.

37. Rosen, *Arnold Schoenberg*, 39.

38. MacDonald, *Schoenberg*, 13.

39. For the quoted description of *Pierrot lunaire* see Arnold Schoenberg, "How One Becomes Lonely (1937)," 51; Arnold Schoenberg, *Driemal sieben Gedichte aus Albert Girauds "Pierrot lunaire" (Deutsch von Otto Erich Hartleben),* op. 21, ed. Reinhold Brinkmann, in *Melodramen und Lieder mit Instrumenten*, Abteilung VI, Reihe A, Band 24 of *Arnold Schönberg: Sämtliche Werke* (Mainz: Schott Musik International; Vienna: Universal Edition, 1996).

40. For a lucid discussion of *Pierrot lunaire* see Jonathan Dunsby, *Schoenberg: "Pierrot lunaire,"* Cambridge Music Handbooks, ed. Julian Rushton (Cambridge: Cambridge University Press, 1992).

41. Ibid., 40.

42. Arnold Schoenberg, *Pierrot lunaire, op. 21,* 40.

43. *New Harvard Dictionary of Music*, s.v. "Passacaglia."

44. Stuckenschmidt, *Schoenberg: His Life, World and Work*, 198.

45. Dunsby, *Schoenberg: "Pierrot lunaire,"* 66.

46. Gabriele Beinhorn, *Das Groteske in der Musik: Arnold Schönbergs "Pierrot lunaire,"* Musikwissenschaftlichen Studien, no. 11, ser. ed. Hans Heinrich Eggebrecht (Pfaffenweiler: Centaurus, 1988), 201.

47. Rudolf Stephan argues that the passacaglia in "Die Nacht" represents an attempt to recover the ability to sustain large, integrated forms. See Rudolf Stephan, "Schönberg und der Klassizismus," in *Die Wiener Schule*, ed. Rudolf Stephan (Darmstadt: Wissenschaftliche Buchgesellschaft, 1989), 162.

48. Schoenberg, "Composition with Twelve Tones (1) (1941)," 218.

49. Severine Neff, introduction to Arnold Schoenberg, *Coherence, Counterpoint, Instrumentation, Instruction in Form,* ed. Severine Neff, trans. Charlotte M. Cross and Severine Neff (Lincoln, Neb.: University of Nebraska Press, 1994), xxv–xxvi. Neff calls attention to "a major feature of Schoenberg's lifework: the correspondence of significant theoretical activity with crucial turning points in his compositional development."

50. Ibid., xxv.

51. Ethan Haimo, "Developing Variation and Schoenberg's Serial Music," *Music Analysis* 16 (1997): 350.

52. Ibid.

53. Schoenberg, *Coherence, Counterpoint, Instrumentation, Instruction in Form*, 41–43.

54. Ibid., 103. In fact, the discussion cited above concerning motivic construction through developing variation appears not in the "Counterpoint" section but in that on "Coherence."

55. Schoenberg, "Composition with Twelve Tones (1) (1941)," 218.

56. Ibid., 226.

57. Haimo, "Developing Variation and Schoenberg's Serial Music," 354–55.

58. Arnold Schoenberg, "The Relationship to the Text (1912)," in *Style and Idea*, 144.

59. Haimo, "Developing Variation in Schoenberg's Serial Music," 363. Haimo describes the process as one by which "Schoenberg reaches back to the material he has created and recycles it for further use."

60. It could be argued with some justification that in *Pierrot lunaire* Schoenberg makes fully effective use of developing variation technique, for instance in "Nacht" (no. 8), and that the retrograde passage in "Der Mondfleck" (no. 18) demonstrates that sophisticated contrapuntal practices need not be grounded in a serial framework—in other words, that Schoenberg's own work undermines his insistence that serialism "grew out of a necessity"; Schoenberg, "Composition with Twelve Tones (1)," 216. Indeed, Carl Dahlhaus contends that Schoenberg's arguments in defense of his compositional decisions are less than convincing; Carl Dahlhaus, "Schoenberg's Aesthetic Ideology," in *Schoenberg and the New Music*, 88. For the present purpose, however, the goal is to establish what Schoenberg believed about his own work, rather than to evaluate his convictions. His belief that without benefit of serial ordering atonal music was unable to provide structural organization is more germane here than whether or not such was actually the case. The discussion by Stuckenschmidt cited above emphasizes the application of developing variation technique in *Pierrot lunaire*; Stuckenschmidt, *Schoenberg: His Life, World and Work*, 198.

61. As another example of this phenomenon, see Jakob Wassermann, *My Life as German and Jew*, trans. Salomea Neumark Brainin (New York: Coward-McCann, 1933), 72–74.

62. Stuckenschmidt, *Schoenberg: His Life, World and Work*, 16–17.

63. Ibid., 18.

64. Ibid., 16.

65. Ibid., 25–26.

66. Ibid., 34.

67. White, *Schoenberg and the God-Idea*, 53.

68. Ibid., 53; Stuckenschmidt, *Schoenberg: His Life, World, and Work*, 34.

69. White, *Schoenberg and the God-Idea*, 53; Alexander Ringer, "Arnold Schoenberg and the Prophetic Image in Music," *Journal of the Arnold Schoenberg Institute* 1 (1976): 30.

70. Ringer, "Introduction: Composer and Jew," in *Arnold Schoenberg: The Composer as Jew*, 7.

71. White, *Schoenberg and the God-Idea*, 54.

72. Ibid., 54.

73. Michael Mäckelmann, "Auf der Suche nach dem Gottesgedanken: Zum geistigen Hintergrund von Arnold Schönbergs unvollendetem Oratorium *Die Jakobsleiter*," in *Musikkulturgeschichte: Festschrift für Constantin Floros zum 60. Geburtstag*, ed. Peter Petersen (Wiesbaden: Breitkopf & Härtel, 1990), 402. Mäckelmann's dating of Schoenberg's work on the text of *Die Jakobsleiter* follows that in Josef Rufer's catalog; see Josef Rufer, *The Works of Arnold Schoenberg*, trans. Dika Newlin (New York: Free Press of Glencoe, 1963), 120, 153–54.

Schoenberg Rewrites His Will   225

For a slightly modified interpretation of Rufer's data, see Jean Christensen, "Arnold Schoenberg's Oratorio *Die Jakobsleiter*," vol. 1 (Ph.D. diss., University of California, 1979), 19–21.

74. Mäckelmann, "Auf der Suche nach dem Gottesgedanken: Zum geistigen Hintergrund von Arnold Schönbergs unvollendetem Oratorium *Die Jakobsleiter*," 399–400.

75. Arnold Schoenberg to Richard Dehmel, Berlin-Zehlendorf, 13 December 1912, *Arnold Schoenberg Letters*, ed. Erwin Stein, trans. Eithne Wilkins and Ernst Kaiser (New York: St. Martin's Press, 1965), 35.

76. Alexander Ringer, "Faith and Symbol," in *Arnold Schoenberg: The Composer as Jew*, 177–78.

77. White, *Schoenberg and the God-Idea*, 66.

78. Mäckelmann, "Auf der Suche nach dem Gottesgedanken," 403.

79. Jean Christensen, "Arnold Schoenberg's Oratorio *Die Jakobsleiter*," vol. 1, 60–63.

80. Ringer, "Faith and Symbol," 178.

81. Mäckelmann, "Auf der Suche nach dem Gottesgedanken," 402.

82. Arnold Schoenberg, "Composition with Twelve Tones (2) (1948)," in *Style and Idea*, 247–48.

83. Mäckelmann, "Auf der Suche nach dem Gottesgedanken," 413.

84. Stuckenschmidt, *Schoenberg: His Life, World and Work*, 290.

85. Arnold Schoenberg to Wassily Kandinsky, Mödling, 20 April 1923, *Arnold Schoenberg Letters*, 88.

86. Wassily Kandinsky to Arnold Schoenberg, Weimar, 24 April 1923, *Arnold Schönberg - Wassily Kandinsky: Briefe, Bilder und Dokumente einer außergewöhnlichen Begegnung*, ed. Jelena Hahl-Koch (Salzburg: Residenz Verlag, 1980), 91–93.

87. Arnold Schoenberg to Wassily Kandinsky, Mödling, 4 May 1923, *Arnold Schoenberg Letters*, 89.

88. Ibid., 92–93.

89. Conditioned by long experience with "casual" anti-Semitism, especially in its political manifestation, most German Jews failed to recognize its transformation in Hitler's hands into something substantially more dangerous until it was far too late. See Robert Weltsch, "Entscheidigungsjahr 1932: Die Endphase der Weimarer Republic," in *Die deutsche Judenfrage: Ein kritischer Rückblick* (Königstein/Ts.: Jüdischer Verlag, 1981), 45–72; see also Shulamit Volkov, "Antisemitismus als kultureller Code," in *Jüdisches Leben und Antisemitismus im 19. und 20. Jahrhundert* (Munich: C.H. Beck, 1990), 36.

90. Schoenberg to Kandinsky, 4 May 1923, *Arnold Schoenberg Letters*, 93.

91. Ibid., 93.

92. See in particular Alfred Heuss, "Arnold Schönberg—Prussian Teacher of Composition," trans. Alexander Ringer, in Alexander Ringer, *Arnold Schoenberg: The Composer as Jew*, 224–26; originally published as "Arnold Schönberg, Preußischer Kompositionslehrer," *Neue Zeitschrift für Musik* 92 (1925): 583–85.

93. My synopsis of *Der biblische Weg* is indebted to Alexander Ringer's discussion of the play; see Alexander Ringer, "Idea and Realization," in *Arnold Schoenberg: The Composer as Jew*, 58–64. The play itself has been published in the original German with a side-by-side English translation; see Arnold Schoenberg, *Der biblische Weg*, trans. Moshe Lazar, in *Journal of the Arnold Schoenberg Institute* 17 (1994): 162–329.

94. White, *Schoenberg and the God-Idea*, 8–9.

95. Arnold Schönberg, *"Moses und Aron": Oper in drei Akten,* ed. Christian Martin Schmidt, Abteilung III, Reihe A, Band 8, Teil 1 of *Arnold Schönberg: Sämtliche Werke* (Mainz: B. Schott's Söhne; Vienna: Universal Edition, 1977), 8. Translation mine.

96. White, *Schoenberg and the God-Idea*, 9.

97. Schoenberg, "Composition with Twelve Tones (1) (1941)," 224.

98. Schoenberg, "National Music (1) (1931)," 169.

99. Ibid., 170.

100. Ibid., 171.

101. Schoenberg, "National Music (2) (1931)," 173.

102. Arnold Schoenberg, *The Musical Idea and the Logic, Technique, and Art of its Presentation*, ed. and trans. Patricia Carpenter and Severine Neff (New York: Columbia University Press, 1995), 422. I am indebted to Charlotte Cross for bringing this passage to my attention and to Crystal Mazur Ockenfuss for help with the translation.

103. MacDonald, *Schoenberg*, 41.

104. Arnold Schoenberg to Anton von Webern, Paris, 4 August 1933, in Reich, *Schoenberg*, 189–90.

105. Arnold Schoenberg to Jacob Klatzkin, Paris, 13 June 1933, in Alexander Ringer, "Unity and Strength," in *Arnold Schoenberg: The Composer as Jew*, 129.

106. Arnold Schoenberg, "Two Speeches on the Jewish Situation (1934 and 1935)," in *Style and Idea*, 501–05; Arnold Schoenberg, "A Four-Point Program for Jewry," in Alexander Ringer, *Arnold Schoenberg: The Composer as Jew*, 230–44.

107. Arnold Schoenberg, "A Four-Point Program for Jewry," 230.

108. Moshe Lazar, "Arnold Schoenberg and His Doubles: A Psychodramatic Journey to His Roots," *Journal of the Arnold Schoenberg Institute* 17 (1992): 107.

109. Hartmut Luck, "Arnold Schönbergs *Kol Nidre*: Ein Werk des antifaschistischen Widerstandes?" *Österreichische Musikzeitschrift* 48 (1993): 143–44.

110. Arnold Schoenberg, *Ode to Napoleon, op. 41*, ed. Reinhold Brinkmann, in *Melodramen und Lieder mit Instrumenten*, 97–166.

111. Reich, *Schoenberg*, 213.

112. For a fuller discussion of the genesis of *A Survivor from Warsaw*, see Strasser, "'A Survivor from Warsaw' as Personal Parable," 52–57.

113. Leni Yahil, *The Holocaust: The Fate of European Jewry*, trans. Ina Friedman and Haya Galai (New York: Oxford University Press, 1990), 482.

114. René Leibowitz, *Introduction a la musique de douze sons* (Paris: L'Arche, 1949), 323; Schmidt, "Schönbergs Kantate," 179.

115. Strasser, "'A Survivor from Warsaw' as Personal Parable," 59.

116. Yahil, *The Holocaust*, 482–83.

117. Strasser. "'A Survivor from Warsaw' as Personal Parable," 58–59.

118. Ibid., 61.

119. Michael Mäckelmann, *Arnold Schönberg und das Judentum: Das Komponist und sein religiöses, nationales und politisches Selbstverständnis nach 1921*, Hamburger Beiträge zur Musikwissenschaft, no. 28, ed. Constantin Floros (Hamburg: Verlag der Musikalienhandlung K.D. Wagner, 1984). 482.

120. Arnold Schoenberg, *A Survivor from Warsaw, op. 46*, in Schmidt, "Schönberg's Kantate," 175. In his analytical article on *A Survivor from Warsaw* Schmidt provides the text as he edited it for publication in the complete works, including his transliteration of the Hebrew prayer. Subsequent citations of the text of *A Survivor from Warsaw* are from this publication unless otherwise indicated. The copyright for *A Survivor from Warsaw* was issued in 1949 to Bomart Music Publications, Inc.; in 1955 it was assigned to Boelke-Bomart, Inc. The revised edition was copyright in 1974 by Boelke-Bomart, Inc. Reprinted by permission.

121. Ibid.

122. Ibid.

123. Ibid. I base my argument that this passage is to be understood as quoted speech on the 1949 edition of *A Survivor from Warsaw* published by Boelke-Bomart, where it does indeed appear in quotation marks. Punctuation in Christian Martin Schmidt's edition of *A Survivor from Warsaw* for the collected works relies primarily on that in Schoenberg's short score, which differs substantially from the Boelke-Bomart edition. Schmidt bases this decision on the transmission process leading to the 1949 publication. In preparing the full score from Schoenberg's short score, René Leibowitz omitted much of Schoenberg's original punctuation. Since Leibowitz's score served as the basis for the Boelke-Bomart publication,

Boelke-Bomart editors had to supply the necessary punctuation without reference to the autograph source. But Schmidt also notes that there exists a copy of the Boelke-Bomart edition with Schoenberg's own corrections, among which Schmidt lists corrections in the narrator's text [i.e., the respelling of German words: "Still gestanden!" to "Stilljestann!" and "Gewehrkolben" to "Yewehrkolben"]. That Schoenberg took the trouble to correct details of spelling but left the inauthentic punctuation untouched suggests to me that even if he did not provide the quotation marks himself, they did not violate the spirit of the text as he understood it. On punctuation issues, see Christian Martin Schmidt, *Chorwerke II: Kritischer Bericht, Skizzen, Fragment*, Abteilung V, Reihe B, Band 19 of *Arnold Schönberg: Sämtliche Werke* (Mainz: B. Schott's Söhne, Universal Edition, 1977), 72; on corrections in Schoenberg's copy of the printed edition, see ibid., 64. For the text as it appears in the first publication see Arnold Schoenberg, *A Survivor from Warsaw, op. 46* (Hillsdale, NY: Boelke-Bomart, 1949), ii.

124. Schoenberg, *A Survivor from Warsaw, op. 46*, in Schmidt, "Schönbergs Kantate," 175. Translation mine.

125. Ibid., 175. Translation mine.

126. Deut. 6:4–7.

127. Theodor Adorno, "Arnold Schoenberg 1874–1951," in *Prisms*, trans. Samuel Weber and Sherry Weber (Cambridge, Mass: MIT Press, 1981), 172; Schmidt, "Schönbergs Kantate," 277.

128. Schmidt, "Schönbergs Kantate," 174.

129. Ibid., 261.

130. As an example see Johann Sebastian Bach, *Weinen, Klagen, Sorgen, Zagen*, BWV 12, in *Kantaten zum Sonntag Jubilate*, Serie I, Band 11.2 of *Neue Ausgabe Sämtliche Werke* (Kassel: Bärenreiter, 1989), 7. Bach's setting of this particularly anguished text includes frequent melodic half-steps in the vocal parts and a repeating bass pattern consisting primarily of a scalar descent by half-steps.

131. Arnold Schoenberg, *A Survivor from Warsaw, op. 46*, ed. Christian Martin Schmidt, in *Chorwerke II*, Abteilung V, Reihe A, Band 19 of *Arnold Schönberg: Sämtliche Werke* (Mainz: B. Schott's Söhne, Universal Edition, 1975), 105. The cited passage appears in measures 44–45. Subsequent citations of the score of *A Survivor from Warsaw* refer to this edition.

132. Schmidt, "Schönbergs Kantate," 261.

133. For the importance of Wagner to the Nazis, see Michael H. Kater, *The Twisted Muse: Musicians and Their Music in the Third Reich* (New York: Oxford University Press, 1997), 34–39.

134. Schmidt, "Schönbergs Kantate," 262.

135. Schoenberg, *A Survivor from Warsaw, op. 46*, in *Arnold Schönberg: Sämtliche Werke*. The trumpet restates the opening motive literally once in mea-

sure 25 (p. 99) and twice in measure 32 (p. 101); low strings state the motive in exact transposition in measure 33 as do the woodwinds in the following measure (p. 102).

136. Schmidt, "Schönbergs Kantate," 262.

137. Ibid., 270–72.

138. Ibid, 274–75.

139. Schoenberg, *A Survivor from Warsaw, op. 46,* in *Arnold Schönberg: Sämtliche Werke*. The prayer melody begins on a rising half step in measures 80 and 81 (p. 114) and closes on a falling half step in measure 97 (p. 120); half steps in the orchestral accompaniment are particularly prominent in measures 80 through 85 (pp. 114–16).

140. Schoenberg, "A Four-Point Program for Jewry," 232.

141. Schoenberg, *A Survivor from Warsaw, op. 46,* in *Arnold Schönberg: Sämtliche Werke*. See measures 97–99 (p. 120).

142. Schmidt, "Schönbergs Kantate," 277.

143. Schoenberg, "A Four-Point Program for Jewry," 238.

144. Strasser, "'A Survivor from Warsaw' as Personal Parable," 59–60.

145. Mäckelmann, "Auf der Suche nach dem Gottesgedanken," 413.

146. Dahlhaus, "Schoenberg's Late Works," 168.

147. Michael Mäckelmann also finds the prayer-setting to be a ringing affirmation in the face of barbarism. Adorno, characteristically, gives the greater weight to the brutality depicted in the narrative, but even he grudgingly concedes that "[t]he Jewish song . . . is music as the protest of mankind against myth." Mäckelmann, *Arnold Schönberg und das Judentum*, 490–91; Adorno, "Arnold Schoenberg 1874–1951," 172.

CHAPTER 9

Texts and Contexts of
A Survivor from Warsaw, Op. 46

CAMILLE CRITTENDEN

> *This text is based partly upon reports which*
> *I have received directly or indirectly.*[1]
> — ARNOLD SCHOENBERG

With this epigraph Schoenberg prefaced one of his most dramatic and emotionally moving works, *A Survivor from Warsaw*. Written in the span of thirteen days, this testament to the experience of European Jews under the Nazis demonstrates Schoenberg's galvanization of his creative forces to convey the terror and strength of his coreligionists. The *Survivor*'s main themes are both political and religious, two well-trodden approaches to Schoenberg scholarship, yet the work occupies only a small fraction of the vast Schoenberg bibliography. Often mentioned only in passing, most commentators have cited the piece as evidence of Schoenberg's deep commitment to Judaism and his abiding empathy with those unable to escape the tragic consequences of the Third Reich.[2] However, Schoenberg's correspondence with Holocaust survivors and sources relevant to the work's compositional history suggest that *A Survivor from Warsaw*, masterly though it is, represents an artistic response common to many émigrés and one inspired more by Schoenberg's immediate material concerns than by an urgent personal desire to create a monument to his faith. This essay will offer new, previously unpublished materials as possible sources for Schoenberg's text, examine the work itself for its text-music relationships, and explore the significance of the work for its composer.[3]

The story of *A Survivor from Warsaw*, narrated by a single male voice, relates a horrific wartime event. The narrator begins in the present tense, noting that he cannot remember everything, "only the grandiose moment when they all started to sing . . . the old prayer," then returns to the events that preceded that stirring moment. He recalls the illness and despair of the prisoners and their harsh treatment at the hands of the commanding sergeant. At reveille the sergeant demanded that they appear before him in order to count off, and when they did not accomplish this task to his satisfaction, he and his subordinates beat the victims with their weapons. As the narrator lay still, he could hear the sergeant ordering his minions "to do away with [them]," and the prisoners counted off once again: "They began again, first slowly: one, two, three, four, became faster and faster, so fast that it finally sounded like a stampede of wild horses." Suddenly, in a moment of strength and solidarity, the group broke into the ancient Hebrew creed, the *Sch'ma Israel* ["Hear, O Israel, the Lord is our God, the Lord is one"].

Possible sources for the text of *A Survivor from Warsaw* have been a matter of speculation over the years. According to Walter Rubsamen, Schoenberg's work was inspired by the news that his niece had been shot in a concentration camp.[4] Schoenberg's student Winfried Zillig asserted that the text was based on a letter that was smuggled out of the Warsaw Ghetto.[5] Willi Reich reports René Leibowitz's recollection that a Holocaust survivor came to visit Schoenberg, and the composer wrote down his story, using it almost verbatim as the text to *Survivor*.[6] Nuria Schoenberg Nono, Schoenberg's daughter, also remembers a letter of some kind, but one that was sent to Alma Mahler or another friend, not to Schoenberg himself.[7] Only Michael Strasser mentions the central role played by Schoenberg's brief contact with dancer Corinne Chochem and her suggestion of incorporating a Hebrew melody into a work set in the Warsaw Ghetto.[8] It remains puzzling that Schoenberg, who carefully documented so much of his life and thought, left no clearer trace to the origins of this moving work.

As direct sources, none of these explanations is entirely satisfactory: Schoenberg's niece was not shot in Warsaw or in a camp but rather in the woods near Dresden,[9] and the text is too heavily flavored by Schoenberg's own idiosyncratic English to be the words of anyone else.[10] The text itself suggests that Warsaw serves more as a symbolic than a realistic setting, for all specific time references have been removed, and the site of the action is only implied. The title alludes to the Warsaw ghetto uprising, yet events such as trumpet reveille and lining up for the gas chamber suggest the barracks of a concentration camp.[11] This mixture of elements is, however, typical of traumatic memories; the whole nightmarish experience, from relocation to deportation to the camps, is compressed into a single moment. Schoenberg himself admitted, "We should never forget [what has been done to the Jews], even if such things have not been done in the manner in which I describe in the *Survivor.* This does not matter. The main thing is, that I saw it in my imagination."[12] A letter or more specific documentation describing the scene may yet come to light, but it seems far more likely that Schoenberg assembled his various impressions of the Jewish ghettos, Nazi occupation, and the concentration camps to arrive at his own dramatic synthesis of the experience. Correspondence with friends, former students, and family members remaining in Vienna after the *Anschluß* of 1938 provided a foundation for Schoenberg's conception of life under the Third Reich.

Schoenberg left Germany in 1933, a time when Nazi agitation against Jews was ominous but not yet physically violent. Five years later, however, his daughter, Gertrud Greissle (Figure 9-1), feared for her life

Figure 9-1. Gertrud Greissle (early 1940s). This photo shows Schoenberg's first daughter a few years after arriving in the United States. Used by permission of Belmont Music Publishers, Pacific Palisades, California 90272.

and tried desperately to escape from Vienna with her husband Felix and their two sons. As early as February 1938 she insisted:

> We absolutely must leave this place. So many acquaintances have found positions in America, it *must* also be possible for us, if we were only supported. . . . Now the situation is so: until just recently we could still live well and comfortably here when we get well-paid work from America. Today the whole situation is different, new and unbearable difficulties remove peace and concentration from any work.[13]

By April almost all their documents were in order, and they were especially anxious to leave because of a recent SS attack on Felix, which they tried to pass off as a traffic accident. They arrived the following month in the United States, and only once they were safely on American shores could the Greissles describe the events of the last few months without fear of censorship or Gestapo retaliation.

In a letter to Schoenberg after their arrival in New York, Felix elaborated on his attempts to secure the necessary paperwork and on changes in the political atmosphere of Vienna:

> I don't feel up to writing about everything we went through in Austria, but I will try to give a short report. The persecution in Austria has increased to an extent that defies all imagination. The measures taken in good old Germany are child's play in comparison. . . . What I had to go through before I could get permission to leave the country (about 50 trips within 6 weeks to about 10 offices) simply cannot be described. The party from whom I needed the "Declaration of Non-Suspicion" really put me through the third degree. Since I had to admit the truth at least partially, I "confessed" that we were going to visit you, to which I received the answer (NB from a high official): "What? You wanna visit Arnold Schoenberg? If he were still here, we would've locked him up a long time ago."[14]

The continuation of Felix's story illustrates the idiosyncrasies of the newly installed regime in Vienna immediately after the *Anschluß:*

> Before I could come out with my business, first I had to cautiously feel out with every official how he really felt, if he was a true or only a feigned Nazi, anti-Semitic or not, a man who expected something from the new regime or one who feared it and worried about his position.

> Everyone, everyone wears masks. Every position decides arbitrarily and almost independent of each other. I had to play the Yes of the one against the No of the other, never saying the whole truth and never a whole falsehood, mix things that could be checked with those that couldn't, so that no devil (yes, really *devil*) could ever make his way out. Our particular difficulty lay in the fact that our passport had unfortunately just expired and an extension would certainly not be granted, especially since Trudi [Gertrud Greissle] would count as a full-blooded Jew—actually a mixed marriage is especially unfortunate in this respect. I decided therefore to produce an Aryan certificate for Frau Greissle, neé Schönbergerr, which was successful—and I am really proud of this trick—thanks to the fact that for now there is not yet a Race Bureau in Austria.[15]

Felix elaborated on the "traffic accident" that catalyzed their departure: at the scene of a "Jewish boycott" (when Nazis pulled Jewish merchants out of their homes and businesses and forced them to paint *Saujude* [filthy Jew] over their own business signs), Felix commented that an officer's blow to an old woman was "unnecessarily brutal." The next thing he knew, he had been hit from behind with such force that it displaced his jaw, knocked out several teeth, and tore the skin under his chin such that he needed stitches. In the contemporary Viennese atmosphere, anyone with wounds of this kind was immediately suspected of being Jewish and was then vulnerable to further abuse. Felix explained: "I told *no one* the true story of this event, not even my closest friends, because I was afraid that it would circulate and become public, and then with this excuse the SA would know why they beat me up and then take away my passport."[16] Not even his children were told the truth until they reached America.

In the same letter, Felix reported news of friends and family still in Austria: Schoenberg's brother Heinrich, immediately evicted from his home in Salzburg, was forced into hiding in Vienna for three weeks until his wife found a place for him; Schoenberg's cousin Hans Nachod, an opera singer, was forced to scrub floors and toilets daily in an SA barracks across the street from his home; one of Felix's friends, a Jewish doctor, was imprisoned for no apparent reason and taken away to the cemetery in a sealed coffin a week later. In the first days after the *Anschluß*, Felix and Gertrud themselves tried to take a walk, but neighbors spat at them and cried "Saujuden." Felix described a Vienna resembling an army camp, overflowing with troops of all kinds, where even in the small suburb of Mödling the new regime had stationed four hundred tanks.[17]

A month after arriving in America, Gertrud expressed to her father her unabated terror:

> Still *today* I'm afraid I'll wake up in my bed in Mödling. We suffered terrible fear, every time someone came up the stairs, my heart was in my throat with fear: Are they coming for us? Who? What will they want? 100 times a day and worst at night because everyone knew that one day they would "get through."[18]

Felix continued:

> Nevertheless, we are naturally very happy to be here. Just in the past few days we received indirectly more terrible news from Vienna. A friend of mine was sent to Dachau on account of a triviality, indeed the whole situation is such that the same thing could easily have happened to me.[19]

Despite the details of their experiences in Vienna, Schoenberg was loath to believe the urgency of their departure. Before leaving Austria, the Greissles were busy copying scores and parts for Schoenberg's Violin Concerto, op. 36, and Schoenberg's letters to them are often more those of a demanding employer than of a solicitous father. He felt they should have waited for an affidavit he sent them, but after waiting two months for the document, they felt compelled to leave immediately if they were to leave at all. Felix wrote (3 June 1938), "we had to risk it"; Gertrud insisted (11 June), "Apparently I must explain once again the reason we left without an affidavit"; and a month later (10 July), "As always: We *had* to leave"; and still again (4 November), "it was not possible to wait any longer." Felix reconciled Schoenberg's disbelief (11 June): "Surely you cannot understand everything because you did not go through it yourself, and your personal sense of justice certainly rebels against believing such a thing, but these things can be explained with one sentence: Germany is no longer a republic."[20] Schoenberg's position is paradoxical, for on the one hand, he foresaw the violence to which anti-Semitism could lead many years before the Nazi party came to power,[21] yet he could hardly conceive of the immediate physical danger facing Jews in Nazi Vienna.[22]

After the war, Schoenberg received accounts from his sister Ottilie Blumauer and his sister-in-law Bertel Ott Schoenberg that his niece, Inge Blumauer (Figure 9-2), had died tragically. Bertel reported:

Figure 9-2. Inge Blumauer and husband (mid-1930s). Schoenberg's niece and her husband were shot by the Nazi SA in the woods near Dresden. Used by permission of Belmont Music Publishers, Pacific Palisades, California 90272.

A terrible misfortune befell Inge. They (she and her husband) wanted to leave with a group of refugees on 1 May [1945] from Elstra, where they ran their business in a smithy (artistic iron work for export), since this area was to become a war zone. On the day before, four SS or SA men came to their home and said they should both come with them, promising that nothing would happen to them. Trusting them, the pair followed and were driven in the car about an hour to a stony brook. There the SA men, without saying another word, shot down Inge and her husband. Werner was dead immediately, and Inge was left to lie with two lung wounds, one stomach wound, and an arm shot through from 11 pm until 8 am the next morning, when she could drag herself to the street and then was found and brought to the Dresden hospital.[23]

Although Inge survived long enough to see her mother again, she soon died from the gunshot wounds.[24] According to Rubsamen, this story served as the foundation for Survivor, but although it undoubtedly influenced Schoenberg's conception of the piece, it was only one of many accounts he heard of personal hardship and terror under the Nazis.

In addition to reports from his family members, Schoenberg also received accounts of the situation in Vienna from former students and friends. Josef Polnauer, a railroad executive, former student and supporter of Schoenberg, wrote the most explicit descriptions of his experiences as a Jew in post-*Anschluß* Vienna.[25] He had not been able to organize the documents necessary to leave, but with the help of his Aryan wife, he survived in hiding during the war. He wrote to Schoenberg about his government pension being cut "for political reasons," about being evicted from his apartment building and forced to live in an overcrowded building for Jews only, and about how the only bright moments in his days came from time spent with friends like Erwin Ratz (another Schoenberg pupil) and Anton Webern.[26] In his final letter to Schoenberg before going into hiding, Polnauer thanked him:

> Unfortunately, it is not unfounded when I have really dark thoughts about my fate. And when for that reason I look over the course of my life, it becomes—certainly not for the first time—but today with the most powerful intensity of consciousness, so clear, how much I owe everything beautiful and worthwhile in my life to you, dear Herr Schönberg! An inescapable feeling urges me to tell you that now and to give you as a modest birthday present my heartfelt thanks for everything I have received. Who knows if I will have such a chance to do so again.[27]

On that despairing note, the letters stop for almost four years.

Polnauer's account of his dramatic rescue ("truly a counterpart to the surprise ending of *Fidelio*") suggests a source for Schoenberg's portrayal of the sergeant in *A Survivor from Warsaw*:

> Our apartment house, a corner house on an intersection, had been occupied by the SS as a battalion armory shortly before [our rescue] and the tenants had to stay in the basement the whole time. . . . When the Russians were already fairly close, the commandant ordered that everyone be accounted for and called up to defend. There were about 40 people in the basement. The inspection of documents began—I had none and hid myself in the back. But finally I, too, had to get in line. Then an SS man dashed down the basement stairs and yelled: "Everyone out! The Russians have broken through, they're coming down the Brückengasse—get out, get out!" The whole crowd stormed out of the basement and out of the house—I was saved![28]

Two elements link this letter, which Polnauer wrote in April 1946, to Schoenberg's work of a year later. For one, he reports the officer crying "'raus, 'raus!" [Get out!], a phrase shouted twice in the course of *A Survivor from Warsaw*. Polnauer's imitation of the SS officer's speech is also mirrored in Schoenberg's piece; his letter reads, "der Russe ist durchjebrochen," substituting the soft "y" sound for the harder "g" as is common to the Prussian dialect. Schoenberg makes the same linguistic gesture when the sergeant shouts, "Stilljestanden!" and "Na jut."

However remarkable Schoenberg's work may be, the impulse to compose such a memorial was not. Many Jewish European émigrés, from artists and writers to film makers and actors, sought to come to terms with their experiences and those of their families left behind through creative outlets. Indeed, Schoenberg's own wife wrote a fictional account of Nazi terrorism, a screenplay entitled, "Where There Is a Will, There Is a Way."[29] Gertrud Schoenberg (née Kolisch), a creative and well-educated woman, wrote several plays and screenplays, as well as the libretto to Schoenberg's *Von heute auf morgen* [*From One Day to the Next*].[30] Although she developed no substantial literary career of her own, she had studied theater arts in Austria at Max Reinhardt's school, and she maintained a lively interest in theater, film, and radio throughout her life.[31] In the fall of 1943, only a few months after the Warsaw Ghetto uprising and several years before Schoenberg began working on *A Survivor from Warsaw*, Gertrud wrote her screenplay about a different kind of survivor.

Her work tells the story of a young girl and her brother who disguised themselves and escaped from Europe after their parents, American and English spies, were killed by the Nazis. Gertrud submitted her story, without success, to many of the major film studios in Los Angeles, including Columbia and MGM.[32] She also sent it to Charlotte Dieterle, fellow émigré and wife of director William Dieterle, who acknowledged: "I have read it and find the form very interesting and unique, even if the content once again revolves around one of the terrible Hitler stories."[33] The form upon which Dieterle commented is that of a framing story: the girl relates the story's main events while making her confession to a priest before leaving Europe for America. A few years later Schoenberg chose the same narrative structure for his *Survivor from Warsaw*.

In addition to similarities in form, Gertrud's story shares its religious tone with Schoenberg's work. In the screenplay, characters refer repeatedly to God and their religious faith, a theme established immediately at the beginning of the story with the fourteen-year-old Maria's prayers in a Catholic church, "Oh my God! I am heartily sorry for having offended Thee and I detest all my sins because I dread the loss of heaven and the pains of hell."[34] Gertrud's story begins just as Schoenberg's work ends, with a fervent prayer for salvation, the obvious difference being between Gertrud's Catholic faith (encompassing heaven and hell) and Schoenberg's expression of Judaism.

As the screenplay continues, at mid-afternoon the only sound comes from an organist practicing in the church: "And now, interrupted only by the sound of the organ, which rises like the trombones on doomsday, when little Maria confesses her great sins, the timid voice is heard."[35] This sentimental description is notable for its relationship to Schoenberg's work, for in his portrayal of "doomsday," the trombone is the sole instrument reinforcing the chorus's prayer. Trombones are also the only instruments accompanying the narrator's first entrance (m. 12); their sustained chord, like that of an organ, recalls the opening scene described in Gertrud's play. Gertrud's suggestion is not unique, of course; the trombone has been a traditional symbol of death and lament since the Renaissance, but in her mind at least, and that of her husband as well, the trombone is specifically associated with tragic death.

No documentary evidence survives of Gertrud's participation in the creation of *A Survivor from Warsaw*, but the coincidence of both Schoenbergs' creative efforts on a similar topic suggests a mutual influence.[36] Gertrud's fictional "Maria" and her younger brother "Rudi" were the children of American and English parents, but the story takes them to many of the same places the Schoenbergs had lived and visited before coming to America: Vienna, Ostende, Paris, Iberia. At the time Gertrud wrote the screenplay, her children (Nuria Dorothea *Maria* and *Rudolf* Ronald) were only somewhat younger than the children portrayed in the story. (The children's names also suggests Gertrud's own siblings, her sister Maria "Mitzi" and her brother Rudolf "Rudi" Kolisch.)[37] Like the fictional children who took action against the Nazis, Nuria and Ronald Schoenberg also contributed to the war effort by participating in an anti-Nazi film made by 20th-Century Fox entitled "Prelude to War." They, along with other (mostly Jewish) émigré children, portrayed Aryan German children singing Hitler songs.[38] Schoenberg's work, as complex and original as it is, must be regarded as one of many creative responses to the atrocities of World War II.

LANGUAGE

In no other single work does Schoenberg use three different languages. The combination of English and German reflects his own linguistic background,[39] but his use of Hebrew is unprecedented in his oeuvre. *A Survivor from Warsaw* is not only the first work but, except for "De Profundis" ["Out of the Deep"], op. 50b (1950), it is the only work in which Schoenberg used an extensive Hebrew text. Although he hoped the *Kol Nidre*, op. 39 (1938) would be used in Temple services,[40] he chose to compose it almost exclusively in English. For both the *Survivor* and the *Kol Nidre*, Schoenberg relied heavily on advice from Rabbi Jacob Sonderling, a prominent Jewish leader in Los Angeles, who wrote out for him the complete text of the *Sch'ma* prayer found in *Survivor*.[41] Sonderling included a detailed phonetic guide, suggesting that not only was the text of the common prayer unfamiliar to Schoenberg, but the pronunciation of Hebrew was foreign as well.[42]

A Survivor from Warsaw is also the only complete work for which Schoenberg wrote an original text in English. Of his two other complete works in English, the *Kol Nidre* was in part translated from Hebrew and in part newly composed by Rabbi Jacob Sonderling, and the *Ode to Napoleon* uses Lord Byron's text. Vocal works following the *Survivor* are either in Hebrew (op. 50b) or in German, except for the fragment he composed at the end of his life, "Israel Exists Again." In both this fragment and in *A Survivor from Warsaw* the English language is linked to the fate of European Judaism.

Schoenberg uses the three languages to various ends within the piece. First, language is linked to time perception: English is used for the narration of past events and is spoken; German, also spoken, is used in present tense for the sense of immediate action; Hebrew, the only language that is sung, is used for ritual prayer. It symbolizes the ancient past and distant future and creates a timeless space, apart from the modern languages. Second, the choice of language delineates political entities: (Prussian) German is the language of the oppressor; English is the language of the refugee and the oppressed; Hebrew is for the chosen people, a collective that triumphs in the face of adversity. In performance, a narrator whose English is colored by a German accent is most effective, for it replicates the sound of a German refugee recounting his experience from American or English exile. Although Schoenberg lived in the United States for many years, his spoken English remained heavily accented and his written English highly idiosyncratic until the end of his life.[43]

In addition to its unusual linguistic features (use of Hebrew and original English), the tone of *A Survivor from Warsaw* differs from any other Schoenberg work. Although the narrative style is poetic and the location of events is ambiguous, the story is actually quite straightforward and realistic compared to other works with a single narrator, such as *Erwartung* [*Expectation*], or works using *Sprechstimme* [speech-song], like *Pierrot lunaire* [*Moonstruck Pierrot*] and *Moses und Aron*. In its treatment of contemporary themes and its use of modern language, *Survivor* comes closest to the text of *Von heute auf morgen*.

The dramatic style of *A Survivor from Warsaw* is clearly influenced by the story-telling conventions of contemporary film and radio. Schoenberg scorned Hollywood composers and performance practices,[44] yet he borrowed some aspects of their musical language to appeal to a modern audience. Schoenberg's narrator serves as a voice-over for the vivid illustration of events in the music. During his introduction ("I remember only the grandiose moment when they all started to sing, as if prearranged, the old prayer") a muted horn plays the beginning of the *Sch'ma*, the old prayer, which later serves as the climax of the piece. In a similar way, a character might "remember" a melody significant to a story about to be recounted.

After the narrator's introductory frame, the instrumental music fades as the speaker says, "But I have no recollection how I got underground to live in the sewers of Warsaw for so long a time." The muted strings decrescendo from *pianissimo* [sic], then stop before the speaker begins his story ("The day began as usual."). With this technique, the music articulates disjunctions in the narrative. The trumpet reveille, the opening phrase of the piece, is repeated at measure 25, "Reveille when it was still dark." The text draws attention to the music both here and a few measures later when the trumpets sound again, this time accompanied by a military drum, as the narrator cries, "The trumpets again." What had been background accompaniment (nondiegetic) becomes momentarily source music (diegetic), an event that occurs again at the end of the piece when the choir sings in chorale style the row upon which the work is built. For this brief but intense work, Schoenberg summoned all musical conventions at his disposal to convey the drama of the scene.[45]

TEXT-MUSIC RELATIONS

Schoenberg's twelve-tone compositions are often considered complex and cerebral, more appealing to the brain than to the heart, but an examination of the close relationship between text and music in this dramatic work demonstrates Schoenberg's masterly ability to engage both simultaneously.[46] This tightly packaged piece reflects the sentiment Schoenberg had expressed almost thirty-five years earlier in "The Relationship to the Text": "Thence it became clear to me that the work of art is like every other complete organism. It is so homogeneous in its composition that in every little detail it reveals its truest, inmost essence."[47] Each of the ninety-nine measures in this piece reflects some facet of Schoenberg's text.

Schoenberg composed the central role not for a singer but for a speaker, a compositional choice he had made for his overtly political work, *Ode to Napoleon*, and for his religious opera, *Moses und Aron*. He insisted that the narrator's part actually be spoken at all times. In a letter to René Leibowitz he emphasized: "As I said—never sing. This is very important because singing produces motives and motives must be carried out, motives produce obligations which I do not fulfill."[48] However, he carefully notated the *Sprechstimme* on a (one-line) staff with relative pitches, creating twenty-five different "notes." Although he claimed he did not want to create motivic obligations, occasionally the *Sprechstimme* reflects the musical contours of the row. Klaus Schweizer has pointed out similarities in rhythm and melodic shape between the *Sch'ma* melody and the phrase, "the old prayer they had neglected for so many years—the forgotten creed!" (mm. 19–20).[49] A striking similarity may also be found between the speaker's unaccompanied words "I heard it" (m. 46) and the rising trumpet call at the beginning of the work. While Schoenberg insisted upon the spoken word, his notation suggests that certain phrases, at least, were strongly associated with the melodic shape of the row.

Schoenberg brought to this work years of experience composing for orchestra and a well-practiced skill for setting text. His command of instrumental range and expressive possibilities is evident in his incorporation of a wide variety of instrumental techniques: *col legno battuto, sul ponticello,* harmonics, solo *divisi* alternating with *tutti,* flutter tongue, pizzicato, and mutes. He had a distinct aural expectation for each of these techniques and gave explicit instructions to the performer, specifying, for example: "ponticello is not merely *near* the bridge, but directly on the bridge, in order to give this immaterial sound."[50]

Schoenberg created drama through unusual instrumentation and instrumental effects, but he also recognized the power of silence. In one sketch of the sergeant's text, before the sergeant orders the prisoners to count off, Schoenberg indicated: "Moaning, cries, calm - fearful. Quiet with tension."[51] He uses silence to create dramatic tension at significant moments when the narrator's part is unaccompanied: "As if prearranged [m. 18] . . . The day began as usual [m.25] . . . Get out! [m. 27] . . . Get out! [m. 33] . . . Wenn ihrs durchaus haben wollt! [m. 42] . . . I heard it though I had been hit very hard [m. 46] . . . I must have been unconscious [m. 54] . . . whereupon the sergeant ordered to do away with us [m. 56] . . . Then I heard the sergeant shouting [m. 62]."

When the speaker first mentions "the old prayer" (m. 19), he is accompanied only by harp, solo strings, and the horn playing the cantus firmus *Sch'ma,* which reappears at the end of the piece. The harp and string parts are static and repetitive, providing a background to the speaker and the horn. Sketches show that Schoenberg composed the violin material specifically for that instrument (labelling their lines "vl."), but he wrote the text under what became the horn part, suggesting that his initial idea might either have been for the chorus to sing softly under the narrator at the beginning of the piece or for the violin material to accompany the first bars of the prayer again at the end.[52]

Schoenberg emphasizes the work's rounded form by repeating the phrase, "I must have been unconscious," both at the beginning and before the final scene. The idea of memory is raised by the first line: "I cannot remember everything." Many who suffer some kind of traumatic shock also experience temporary amnesia before the unpleasant memories return.[53] Schoenberg had created a similar effect in *Erwartung* when the sole narrator is unsure how long she has been in the woods and how (or if) her lover has died. In both works fragmentary sentences also contribute to the feeling of spatial and temporal disjunction. After the presumed-dead had been ordered away in *Survivor,* the narrator's thoughts and sentences become incomplete: "There I lay aside—half-conscious. It had become very still—fear and pain."

Schoenberg depicts the prisoners coming out slowly at first, then faster, with staccato winds and cello playing *col legno battuto*. These instruments alternate quickly, reflecting the halting, nervous steps of the prisoners ("They came out; . . . They hurry as much as they can."). At the words "In vain!" the percussion section takes over with hocket playing between the military drum and bass drum, depicting "Much too much noise, much too much commotion!" The xylophone repeats a three-note pattern in a rhythm and contour evocative of the final movement of Beethoven's Sixth Symphony. However, if this was a deliberate allusion on Schoenberg's part, it was a deeply ironic one; Beethoven's movement is entitled "Frohe und dankbare Gefühle nach dem Sturm" ["Happy and grateful feelings after the storm"], but for Schoenberg's victims, the storm is far from over.[54]

Just as Schoenberg's use of the trombone reflects a centuries-old musical convention for bereavement, his use of the descending minor second partakes of a similar trope of lament. He built the minor second into the row itself, and the sighing fall is found throughout the work. Schoenberg depicts the "groaning and moaning" (mm. 44–45) with a tremolo augmented chord in the violas and the descending minor second high in the range of the oboes and clarinets. Two measures later the bassoon takes over the figure high in its range (mm. 46–47). The sighing lament returns again (this time marked *molto espressivo*, for oboes and violas) at the words "They are all dead!"

The central moment of this dramatic work is the unison entrance of the men's chorus. The gradual climax leading up to the prayer, mm. 74 through the first half of 80, was carefully worked out in the sketches.[55] Schoenberg precisely calculated the temporal duration of each measure, assigning a metronome marking to each, in order for the passage to accelerate gradually within a total time of fifteen seconds.[56] The drama of this climax is aided by incremental increases in instrumentation, a "terraced" addition of instruments similar to an organ's ability to add stops.[57] Finally, Schoenberg shortened the note values in some instruments from triplet eighths to sixteenths, and as the violins and flutes move steadily higher in their range, the orchestra breaks off for a split second as the choir makes its powerful unison entrance.

The concluding prayer is the most straightforward presentation of the row from which the piece was composed, and it reflects the prayer's text in several ways.[58] The opening *forte* sixteenth-half note pattern

("*Sch'ma*") acts as a battle cry against the injustices suffered by those who pray, a choral parallel to the trumpet call of the oppressor that opens the piece. The first line of the choral prayer, "Hear, O Israel, the Lord is our God," calls attention to the fact both that it is sung aloud ("Hear") and to the fact that it is sung by a collective ("*our* God"). Schoenberg also created narrative closure by reviving the violin pattern that accompanied the prayer melody at the beginning of the piece. The final phrase reflects both the literal meaning of the text ("when thou risest up") and the sense of strength and rebellion in its sharply rising contour.

PERSONAL SIGNIFICANCE

Schoenberg's use of the Hebrew prayer has encouraged biographers to regard the work as a public expression of his renewed faith. Yet, as concerned as he was about the political fate of European Jews, he did not practice his faith at home.[59] He neither attended temple services nor celebrated Jewish holidays with his family.[60] His wife Gertrud was Catholic, and their children were raised in the Catholic faith.[61] There is scant evidence that Schoenberg ever learned Hebrew,[62] and the *Sch'ma*, a prayer often recited before going to bed at night, as well as in the moments before death, was not entirely familiar to him.[63]

Indeed, an exchange between Gertrud Schoenberg and George Rochberg suggests that Schoenberg's Judaism was less important to him than some scholars have hoped and implied.[64] Rochberg wrote her in October 1962 regarding a biographical article he was preparing and asked, "Would you accept as basically correct my inference that the link between the religious works and those with political overtones—*Ode to Napoleon* and *Survivor from Warsaw*—is Schoenberg's reconversion to Judaism? And also that Schoenberg's reconversion to Judaism was at least in part his answer to the Nazis?"[65] As was her custom, Gertrud glossed the original letter in preparing her reply, and beside the first question she wrote and underlined a large "NO," beside the second question, a smaller "yes." In her reply she explained, "Of course, the reconversion to Judaism was, in fact, an answer to the Nazis—which was greatly publicized, very much to the distaste of Schoenberg—and could be mentioned rather in a short foot-note than is [*sic*] a big event in Schoenberg's life."[66] This comment of course represents Gertrud's perspective, not Schoenberg's own. Still, it bears directly on the prominence that scholars after Schoenberg's death have granted to his Jewish identity, a prominence perhaps greater than Schoenberg himself would have allowed.

A Survivor from Warsaw has been described as "one of [Schoenberg's] most personal expressions"[67] and as a "personal parable."[68] Yet, like many works from the last decade of his life, the impetus for its composition came more from immediate external circumstances than from an intrinsic imperative to create such a piece. For several months before beginning work on the *Survivor*, Schoenberg had been contemplating using traditional Jewish melodies in a depiction of the Warsaw Ghetto uprising; the idea had been suggested to him by Corinne Chochem, a dancer from New York who had originally considered commissioning the work.[69] Schoenberg wrote to her about the piece he had in mind: "I plan to make it this scene—*which you described*—in the Warsaw Ghetto, how the doomed Jews started singing, before going to die."[70] He mentions neither here nor elsewhere a more personal motivation for this particular scenario; although he knew several Holocaust victims, none of his friends or family members witnessed the specific event of the Warsaw Ghetto uprising.[71] Schoenberg's negotiations with Chochem regarding the commission for this work ran aground when she could not raise the fee he asked ($1000). Despite her appeals to his generosity for the sake of Jewish cultural life, Schoenberg insisted, "I have done throughout my whole life so much for idealistic ends (and so little has to be [*sic*] returned to me in kind) that I have done my duty."[72] Facing rising costs of living and dwindling means, Schoenberg was limited in his compositional choices to a work for which he could count on remuneration.[73]

Such an opportunity presented itself in the form of a grant from the Koussevitzky Foundation. The Foundation had offered Schoenberg a $1000 grant already in 1944, but they insisted upon a new work, not one already in progress. Schoenberg had hoped to complete *Moses und Aron* and *Die Jakobsleiter* [*Jacob's Ladder*], but he realized they would not be easily finished and their fragments would not fulfill the conditions of the grant. The Foundation renewed its offer in July 1947, and Schoenberg accepted, sending them the manuscript score of *Survivor* on August 24. Despite the composer's efficiency in fulfilling the commission, he did not receive a check until mid-October, a delay that caused him great alarm and distress. For, as Schoenberg wrote Koussevitzky, the reasons he finally accepted the commission and composed *A Survivor from Warsaw* were his failing health and financial exigencies.[74] Although he wanted to finish his large-scale religious opera or to see his Zionist play, *Der biblische Weg* [*The Biblical Way*], produced, his declining physical condition provided incentive for him to launch a project that he knew he could finish, one that required only moderate forces for performance, and for which he would be sufficiently paid.[75] With a five-member family to support, Schoenberg, as the sole provider, had every reason for concern.

The subject of *A Survivor from Warsaw* was a natural choice for a composer who had been driven out of Germany by Nazism and who had once pledged "to do nothing in the future but work for the Jewish national cause."[76] Like many of Schoenberg's most engaging works, the composer has woven his own musical and religious world view into the fabric of the piece. As he asserted in "Brahms the Progressive," "The language in which musical ideas are expressed in tones parallels the language which expresses feelings or thoughts in words."[77] Schoenberg formulated this statement the same year as he composed *A Survivor from Warsaw*, a piece in which he reserves the most strict, linear exposition of the twelve-tone row for the *Sch'ma Israel*. By setting the *Sch'ma*, sung by the chorus in unison, to the foundation of the entire work, Schoenberg equates faith and salvation with twelve-tone music. As the creator of the twelve-tone method of composition, Schoenberg once again assumes the role of prophet and divinely inspired creator, just as he had in the overtly autobiographical leading roles in *Moses und Aron* and *Der biblische Weg*.[78] Schoenberg's musical law is as strict as God's moral law expressed in the most direct terms (Hebrew). Both are redemptive and eternal, for God will assure the security of his Chosen People, and Schoenberg's twelve-tone method will "assure the hegemony of German music."[79]

Schoenberg explained to Peter Gradenwitz his views on "the contradiction between principle and policy, between the pure God-Idea and the primitive popular experience. As for me, in this struggle, only the Idea can be victorious."[80] In *A Survivor from Warsaw*, Schoenberg represents the tragic "popular experience" through the narrator's story and the victory of the "pure God-Idea" through the chorus's *Sch'ma* set in the pure statement of the twelve-tone row. The Idea is revealed in its purest form only at the conclusion, yet it undergirds every measure of the work.

Even as the piece attests to Schoenberg's tremendous creative powers, its compositional history also reflects the bitterness and disappointment that characterized many moments of his final years. His attempts to earn a living solely through his compositions were frequently thwarted; he had most recently been rejected for a fellowship from the Guggenheim Foundation in 1945. Although he enjoyed teaching, Schoenberg resented the fact that his music was not more financially rewarding, unlike that of his colleagues in the movie industry. Koussevitzky bore his share of Schoenberg's frustrations when Schoenberg's commission payment for *Survivor* was delayed. Indignant, but defensive about the work's final shape, Schoenberg began the new year with this reproach:

> That the piece is not extremely long should not worry you: would I write like my contemporaries—repeating every little bit of an idea four to eight times—the piece might have become 25 minutes longer, without a greater profusion of ideas.[81]

Schoenberg continued proudly:

> I am accustomed to surpass the generosity of people with whom I have to deal. Thus, instead of taking revenge, for the unfair treatment, I decided I should improve the external looks of my score by binding it "manu propria" and adding a copy of the traditional score, which has been executed by my friend, the eminent French composer, conductor and lecturer Mr. René Leibowitz. I hope you appreciate it now more.[82]

Leibowitz wrote out the fair copy score of *A Survivor from Warsaw* under supervision of the composer, whose failing eyesight consigned him to working on large-staff paper; he composed his late works in a detailed particell, which could later be transcribed onto conventional orchestral staves.[83] On the last page of the score, Leibowitz wrote lengthwise "Score Made by René Leibowitz—Hollywood, December 1947." Schoenberg later angrily crossed through "Made" and commented below it: "This is one of Leibowitz's lies. He has not *made* the score, but only *copied it.*"[84] Schoenberg's ire could be explained by his poor understanding of English, perhaps thinking to himself in German, "Leibowitz hat die Partitur nicht gemacht, sondern nur kopiert." (Schoenberg still thought and composed primarily in German; sketches for the text of *Survivor* are in German, which he then translated himself.)[85] But he had already lived in the United States for fourteen years, and the few who might have been privy to the manuscript score at the time (or the musicians and scholars who might examine it after his death) would hardly have misunderstood Leibowitz's remark. That Schoenberg treated the one "survivor from Warsaw" whom he knew personally with such jealousy and suspicion is a paradoxical aspect of this work's compositional history.

Although Schoenberg did not experience the camps or the atrocities of Nazi occupation first hand, he effectively recreated the terror and accompanying feeling of community among the persecuted Jews in *A Survivor from Warsaw*. In a review of a radio performance in 1951 Hans Keller, himself a survivor of Nazi brutality, acknowledged: "What higher praise can the *Survivor* receive than a musician-survivor's confession that never since his escape from the Nazis did he feel, at the same time, so terrifyingly near and so redeemingly far from the memory of his experiences?"[86] Despite the complexities of Schoenberg's attitude toward the conventions of his faith and toward his own Jewish family members and students, the piece remains a memorial of solidarity in the face of evil, as well as a powerful tribute to Schoenberg's career as a lonely, but visionary, survivor.

NOTES

1. Arnold Schoenberg, Preface to *A Survivor from Warsaw*, ed. Jacques-Louis Monod (Vienna and London: Universal Edition; Boelke-Bomart, Inc., 1979), iii. The introduction provided includes the complete text and explanatory notes in English, German, and French.

2. In addition to works cited in ensuing notes, scholarship on *A Survivor from Warsaw* includes the following: Peter Gradenwitz, "The Religious Works of Arnold Schoenberg," *The Music Review* (February 1960): 19–29; Hanns-Werner Heister, "Zum politischen Engagement des Unpolitischen," in *Herausforderung Schönberg: Was die Musik des Jahrhunderts Veränderte*, ed. Ulrich Dibelius (Munich: Carl Hanser Verlag, 1974); Michael Mäckelmann, *Arnold Schönberg und das Judentum: Der Komponist und sein religiöses, nationales und politisches Selbstverständnis nach 1921* (Hamburg: Verlag der Musikalienhandlung Karl Dieter Wagner, 1984); Dika Newlin, "Self-Revelation and the Law: Arnold Schoenberg in His Religious Works," in *Yuval: Studies of the Jewish Music Research Centre*, ed. Israël Adler (Jerusalem: Magnes Press, The Hebrew University, 1968): 204–20; Alexander Ringer, *Arnold Schoenberg: The Composer as Jew* (Oxford: Oxford University Press, 1990); Robert John Specht, Jr. "Relationships Between Text and Music in the Choral Works of Arnold Schoenberg" (Ph.D. diss., Case Western Reserve University, 1976).

3. I would like to acknowledge and thank Marilyn McCoy, formerly Assistant Archivist at the Arnold Schoenberg Institute (ASI), for her work on the Gertrud Greissle correspondence (Gertrud Schönberg Greissle was the daughter of Schoenberg and his first wife, Mathilde Zemlinsky). Through careful study of the internal evidence, Ms. McCoy was able to date the many undated letters in this collection. These letters offer invaluable, but until now unavailable, insight into many details of Schoenberg's family life, as well as copious information regarding the performance and publication of his works. Excerpts from the letters of Arnold and Gertrud Schoenberg are used by permission of Belmont Music Publishers, Pacific Palisades, California 90272.

4. Walter H. Rubsamen, "Schoenberg in America," *The Musical Quarterly* 37/4 (October 1951): 482.

5. Winfried Zillig, *Variationen über neue Musik* (Munich: Nymphenburger Verlagshandlung, 1959), 101.

6. Willi Reich, *Schoenberg: A Critical Biography*, trans. Leo Black (New York and Washington: Praeger Publishers, 1971), 221–23.

7. Nuria Schoenberg Nono, interview with the author, 13 November 1996. I would like to thank Nuria Schoenberg Nono and Lawrence Schoenberg (who, along with Ronald Schoenberg, are the children of Schoenberg and his second wife, Gertrud Kolisch) for sharing their recollections of their father with me.

8. Michael Strasser, "'A Survivor from Warsaw' as Personal Parable," *Music and Letters* 76/1 (February 1995): 52–63.

9. Her story is described below.

10. Schoenberg's English remained colored by German word order, vocabulary, and spelling until the end of his life, as demonstrated by quotations from his letters given in the body of this essay, as well as in the notes below.

11. Strasser elaborates on Schoenberg's conflation of the ghetto with the concentration camp, "'A Survivor from Warsaw' as Personal Parable," 58–59.

12. Arnold Schoenberg to Kurt List, 1 November 1948, ASI L3 L1 (copy). Nuria Schoenberg Nono, ed., *Arnold Schoenberg Self-Portrait* (Pacific Palisades: Belmont Music Publishers, 1988), 105.

13. Gertrud Greissle to Arnold Schoenberg, 26 February 1938, ASI L14b G21 (copy). All translations from correspondence originally in German are my own.

14. Felix Greissle to Arnold Schoenberg, 3 June 1938, ASI L14b G21 (copy).

15. Felix Greissle to Arnold Schoenberg, 3 June 1938, ASI L14b G21 (copy).

16. Felix Greissle to Arnold Schoenberg, 11 June 1938, ASI L14b G21 (copy).

17. Schoenberg had lived in Mödling from 1918 until 1926 when he moved to Berlin.

18. Felix and Gertrud Greissle to Arnold Schoenberg, 10 July 1938, ASI L14b G21 (copy).

19. Ibid.

20. Felix Greissle to Arnold Schoenberg, 11 June 1938, ASI L14b G21 (copy).

21. In a letter to Wassily Kandinsky of 4 May 1923 Schoenberg wrote, "But what is anti-Semitism to lead to if not to acts of violence?" *Arnold Schoenberg-Wassily Kandinsky: Letters, Pictures and Documents*, ed. Jelena Hahl-Koch, trans. John C. Crawford (London and Boston: Faber & Faber, 1984), 81. In his "Four-Point Program for Jewry" (November 1938) Schoenberg predicted still more explicitly: "Is there room in the world for almost 7,000,000 [Jewish] people?

Are they condemned to doom? Will they become extinct? Famished? Butchered? . . . What have [our Jewish leaders] done to find a place for the first 500,000 people who must migrate or die?" Arnold Schoenberg, "A Four-Point Program for Jewry," *Journal of the Arnold Schoenberg Institute* 3 (March 1979): 49–67.

22. Schoenberg's reluctance to accept the situation's urgency is further demonstrated in correspondence with his cousin Hans Nachod (ASI L3 N1, copies). Schoenberg tried repeatedly to help his wayward son Georg escape from Vienna, where he lived with his wife and daughter. Nachod had made plans to flee to England, and he was to deliver money and an affidavit to Schoenberg's son before leaving; however, Georg never appeared at the prearranged rendezvous, and Nachod had to leave without giving him the documents. Schoenberg wrote several irate letters to Nachod after that, excoriating him for leaving without tracking down Georg. He was, of course, concerned for the safety of his son, but he also did not seem to realize (for Nachod's sake) that the chances for escaping safely were slim and becoming narrower every day.

23. Bertel Ott Schönberg to Arnold and Gertrud Schoenberg, 9 June 1946, ASI L24a S16 (copy).

24. Ottilie Schönberg Blumauer to Arnold and Gertrud Schoenberg, 28 July 1946, ASI L10 B11 (copy).

25. See letters from Josef Polnauer to Arnold Schoenberg of 14 December 1938, 28 December 1938, 27 March 1939, 20 July 1939, and 24 August 1939, ASI L21 P7 (copies).

26. Josef Polnauer to Arnold Schoenberg, 20 July 1939, ASI L21 P7 (copy).

27. Josef Polnauer to Arnold Schoenberg, 14 August 1941, ASI L21 P7 (copy). Schoenberg's birthday was a month later, 13 September.

28. Josef Polnauer to Arnold Schoenberg, 16 April 1946, ASI L21 P7 (copy).

29. ASI, Gertrud Schoenberg Satellite Collection, GSX6 (original written in English).

30. For more on Gertrud's contribution to this opera see Juliane Brand, "Of Authorship and Partnership: The Libretto of *Von heute auf morgen*," *Journal of the Arnold Schoenberg Institute* 14 (November 1991): 153–240, and Brand, "A Short History of *Von heute auf morgen* with Letters and Documents," ibid.: 241–70.

31. Nuria Schoenberg Nono, interview with the author, 13 November 1996.

32. Gertrud received conflicting reasons for the rejection of her screenplay. Story editor John Mock at Columbia wrote: "Thank you very much for allowing us to consider your original story WHERE THERE IS A WILL THERE IS A WAY. I regret, however, that the subject matter is so grim and fantastic that it would be difficult to translate it into credible terms for the screen" (John Mock to

Gertrud Schoenberg, 7 September 1943, ASI Gertrud Schoenberg Satellite Collection, Correspondence [GSV011]). On the other hand, story editor Marjorie Thorson at Metro-Goldwyn-Mayer wrote to Gertrud's friend and Hollywood agent Charlotte Dieterle: "This material failed to arouse studio interest mainly because it deals with the war and spies, and this particular type of story has been done so often in the past that it is considered out-dated as far as the motion picture industry is concerned" (Letter filed with Correspondence from Charlotte Dieterle to Gertrud Schoenberg, 18 December 1943, ASI Gertrud Schoenberg Satellite Collection [GSXIV29]).

33. Charlotte Dieterle to Gertrud Schoenberg, 26 October 1943, ASI, Gertrud Schoenberg Satellite Collection, Correspondence (GSXIII419).

34. G. Schoenberg, "Where There Is a Will," 1.

35. G. Schoenberg, "Where There Is a Will," 2.

36. The Schoenbergs continued to enjoy a creative collaborative relationship well into the 1940s. Another screenplay (or operetta libretto) drafted by Gertrud (ASI Gertrud Schoenberg Satellite Collection [GSXA16]) shows evidence of Schoenberg's hand in planning the musical numbers where he made notes about what kind of meter would be most suitable. The work remained untitled, but the story concerned a pair of professional tennis players.

37. I would like to thank E. Randol Schoenberg for pointing out the extent of these similarities and for his enthusiastic and knowledgeable discussion of Schoenberg and Judaism (interview with the author, 12 July 1997).

38. A short clip of this film is included in the video *City of Strangers: A Sense of Difference* (British Broadcasting Corporation, 1992). Schoenberg had little to do with his children's brief participation in the film, but Nuria Schoenberg Nono recalls that he made small wooden frames for the 50–cent pieces they each received, commemorating their first earnings (interview with the author, 13 November 1996). Gertrud Schoenberg also recorded the event in her diary for August 1942, "Nuria and Ronny earn their first cts 50" (ASI, Gertrud Schoenberg Satellite Collection, Diaries 1941–1950).

39. At the top of the particell score Schoenberg wrote "Begonnen 11. August 1947," and at the end, "finished August 23. 1947" (ASI Box 50); the progression from German to English supports Strasser's conception of the piece as a personal parable (see Strasser, " 'A Survivor from Warsaw' as Personal Parable").

40. See Schoenberg's letter to Paul Dessau, 22 November 1941: "Ich glaube, daß es [*Kol Nidre*] sowohl im Tempel als auch im Konzert von großer Wirkung sein muß." *Arnold Schönberg, Sämtliche Werke, Abteilung V: Chorwerke, Reihe B, Band 19, Kritischer Bericht*, ed. Christian Martin Schmidt (Mainz: B. Schott's Söhne; Vienna: Universal Edition AG, 1977), xii.

41. Letter, Jacob Sonderling to Arnold Schoenberg, ASI L25 S29 (copy). Sonderling had commissioned Schoenberg's *Kol Nidre*, for which he wrote and translated the text.

42. Schoenberg made a similar request regarding the composition of op. 50b when he asked Chemjo Vinaver, who had commissioned the work, to "write the English equivalent, verbally, indicating stressed and accented syllables by a comma; and unstressed, unaccented syllables by a semicircle" under the Hebrew text of Psalm 130. Arnold Schoenberg to Chemjo Vinaver, 2 June 1950, ASI, L3 J1 (copy). After finishing the composition Schoenberg explained to Vinaver, "It was terribly difficult for me to deal with the right accentuation of the Hebrew words. Especially because of the many unaccented syllables. This is why it took—after the first preparations of a few days—almost two weeks to finish the composition." Schoenberg further recommended, "I would prefer, if below the Hebrew letters there would be written in English letters the pronunciation so that at least people who want to know how it sounds can read it." Arnold Schoenberg to Chemjo Vinaver, 24 July 1950, ASI, L3 J1 (copy).

43. Voice recordings in the ASI, as well as the recollection of his children, testify to his German-inflected speech.

44. Several letters from Schoenberg's California years bear witness to the frustration he experienced by his occasional contacts with the Hollywood musical world. A letter to Oskar Kokoschka from 3 July 1946 is representative: "You complain of lack of culture in this amusement-arcade world. I wonder what you'd say to the world in which I nearly die of disgust. I don't only mean the 'movies'." *Arnold Schoenberg: Letters*, ed. Erwin Stein, trans. Eithne Wilkins and Ernst Kaiser (Berkeley and Los Angeles: University of California Press, 1987), 242.

45. Richard Taruskin has also noted the work's debt to the film idiom, in less-than-complimentary terms: "Were the name of [*A Survivor from Warsaw*'s] composer not surrounded by a historiographical aureole, were its musical idiom not safeguarded by its inscrutability, its B-movie clichés—the Erich von Stroheim Nazi barking 'Achtung,' the kitsch-triumphalism of the climactic, suddenly tonal singing of the Jewish credo—would be painfully obvious." (See "A Sturdy Musical Bridge to the 21st Century," *New York Times*, 24 August 1997.) Taruskin makes a surprising but significant miscalculation in citing the twelve-tone *Sch'ma* as "tonal singing." By trivializing Schoenberg's modernism, he can more conveniently juxtapose the postmodernism of Steve Reich's "Different Trains," the main thrust of his review. I would like to thank Therese Muxeneder for calling this review to my attention.

46. Schoenberg had clearly been thinking about the differences between cerebral and emotional composition during the year before composing *A Survivor from Warsaw*. See Arnold Schoenberg, "Heart and Brain in Music (1946)"

in *Style and Idea: Selected Writings of Arnold Schoenberg*, ed. Leonard Stein, trans. Leo Black (Berkeley and Los Angeles: University of California Press, 1984), 53–76.

47. Essay written in 1912. Published in *Style and Idea*, 141–45.

48. Arnold Schoenberg to René Leibowitz, 12 November 1948, ASI L3 L2 (copy).

49. Klaus Schweizer, *"Ein Überlebender aus Warschau* für Sprecher, Männerchor und Orchester von Arnold Schönberg," *Melos* VI (1974): 367.

50. *Arnold Schönberg, Sämtliche Werke*, 62.

51. ASI Box 50, mfl. 948v. "Stöhnen, Wehklagen, Ruhe - Angstvoll. Stille mit Spannung."

52. ASI Box 50, mfl. 949.

53. C.B. Scrignar, M.D., *Post-Traumatic Stress Disorder: Diagnosis, Treatment, and Legal Issues* (New York: Praeger Publishers, 1984), 61.

54. This Beethoven Symphony was on Schoenberg's mind not long before he was composing the *Survivor*, for he mentions the fourth movement specifically in "Criteria for the Evaluation of Music" (1946) in *Style and Idea*, 124–36. I would like to thank John Palmer for calling this similarity to my attention.

55. ASI Box 50, mfl. 956.

56. Paradoxically, Schoenberg advised at the beginning of the published score: "The metronome-marks need not be taken literally—primarily they should give a fair idea of the tempo in respect to the character of each section in all its changes." Arnold Schoenberg, *A Survivor from Warsaw*, iii.

57. Schoenberg had composed the *Variations on a Recitative for Organ*, op. 40, only a few years before.

58. Schoenberg probably composed the row with the final climax in mind; however, sketches for the row and its permutations do not include text (see ASI Box 50).

59. Moshe Lazar points out that even Schoenberg's political concern for the establishment of a Jewish state became increasingly a matter of daydream, for although he was aware of the Jewish colonization of Palestine after World War II, he continued to plan for a new Jewish colony with himself as ruler (see Arnold Schoenberg, "Jewish Government in Exile," ASI T56.19). Moreover, the names of postwar Jewish politicians and Zionist leaders are almost completely absent from his writings. See Moshe Lazar, "Arnold Schoenberg and His Doubles: A Psychodramatic Journey to His Roots," *Journal of the Arnold Schoenberg Institute* 17 (1994): 8–115.

60. Lawrence Schoenberg, interview with the author, 24 October 1996, and Nuria Schoenberg Nono, interview with the author, 13 November 1996.

61. Recollections of Nuria Schoenberg Nono suggest that formal religion of any kind played little role in Schoenberg family life. She tells a story of walking home after school one day when she was about eight years old (c. 1940), and some schoolchildren were teasing a boy for being Catholic. This scene bothered her because she thought, "Wait, I think I'm Catholic." When she arrived home, she asked her parents, "What's Catholic?" They responded that it was a religion, along with Judaism and Protestantism, any one of which people might choose to believe and follow. Arnold and Gertrud must have decided soon after this question that the children should have a more solid religious background, for they sent Nuria's younger brothers to Catholic schools. Nuria Schoenberg Nono and Lawrence Schoenberg, interview with the author, 13 November 1996.

62. Gertrud Schoenberg admitted: "It is unlikely that [Schoenberg] had any Jewish education." See Lucy S. Dawidowicz, "Musical Hebraism," *Commentary* 1/44 (July 1967): 73–77. See also Schoenberg's comment to Rabbi Samuel Abrams soon after arriving in the United States: "I would have used the occasion, to come in the Temple at the occasion of a divine service. But there is a difficulty: I don't understand enough English (I beg your pardon for the poor English, I am writing) and also not Hebrew." Arnold Schoenberg to Samuel J. Abrams, 23 February 1934, ASI, L1, A1 (copy).

63. The prayer was unfamiliar to him at least in Hebrew; it is possible that he was familiar with it in German.

64. Alexander Ringer and Michael Mäckelmann, among others, have made claims for the significance of Judaism in Schoenberg's personal life. See Ringer, *Arnold Schoenberg: The Composer as Jew* and Mäckelmann, *Arnold Schönberg und das Judentum: Der Komponist und sein religiöses, nationales und politisches Selbstverständnis nach 1921.*

65. George Rochberg to Gertrud Schoenberg, 24 October 1962, ASI, Gertrud Schoenberg Satellite Collection, Correspondence (GSXV208b).

66. Gertrud Schoenberg to George Rochberg, 26 November 1962, ASI Gertrud Schoenberg Satellite Collection, Correspondence (GSXV208a).

67. Rubsamen, "Schoenberg in America," 432.

68. Strasser, "'A Survivor from Warsaw' as Personal Parable," 52.

69. For further details and correspondence regarding the work's genesis, see Strasser, "'A Survivor from Warsaw' as Personal Parable," 52–55.

70. Arnold Schoenberg to Corinne Chochem, 20 April 1947, ASI L2a C1 (copy). My italics.

71. Several members of his extended family died in camps in Poland, but no details of their abduction or death remain (see letter from Bertel Ott Schoenberg, 9 June 1946). René Leibowitz, Schoenberg's student who helped him write out the score to *Survivor*, was born in Warsaw (1913) but moved to Paris in 1933.

With the help of Georges Bataille, Leibowitz went into hiding in 1943 and survived the war.

72. Arnold Schoenberg to Corinne Chochem, 23 April 1947, ASI L2a C1 (copy).

73. Schoenberg reviewed his financial situation with Professor Paul Dodd of UCLA in a letter of 12 May 1948 in which he stated "Unless I succeed in forcing exploiters of my works, publishers, performers etc., to pay what they owe me, I would have to live on $29.60 [per month, his pension from UCLA] with a wife and 3 small children (ages 16, 11, and 7). It has often enough occurred that I had for months no other income." *Arnold Schoenberg: Letters*, 254. In Schoenberg's correspondence with Chochem (cited above), with Chemjo Vinaver (cited below), and with the Koussevitzky Foundation (cited below) Schoenberg insists upon his need for his compositions to provide income.

74. Arnold Schoenberg to the Koussevitzky Foundation, 1 January 1948, ASI L3 K3 (copy). "When, at the end of August, I sent you the piece 'Survivor from Warsaw,' which you had commissioned, I was sick and needed the money urgently. These were also the reasons why I accepted your commission and, why the score did not look as beautifull [*sic*] as one is accostumed [*sic*] from me."

75. He was similarly motivated to complete the chorus "De Profundis," op. 50b. As he wrote to Chemjo Vinaver, "I am sorry; I cannot work two weeks for the honor only, of which I have got enough, but only for money of which I have not enough." Arnold Schoenberg to Chemjo Vinaver, 1 July 1950, ASI, LF J1 (copy).

76. Arnold Schoenberg to Anton Webern, 4 August 1933. Quoted in Reich, *Schoenberg*, 189–190.

77. *Style and Idea*, 399.

78. See Alexander L. Ringer, "Arnold Schoenberg and the Prophetic Image in Music," *Journal of the Arnold Schoenberg Institute* 1/1 (October 1976): 26–38.

79. Schoenberg allegedly made this comment to his student Josef Rufer in the summer of 1922. H. H. Stuckenschmidt reports it in his biography, *Arnold Schoenberg*, trans. Edith Temple Roberts and Humphrey Searle (New York: Grove Press, 1959), 82.

80. Arnold Schoenberg to Peter Gradenwitz, n.d., ASI, L2 G2 (copy).

81. Arnold Schoenberg to the Koussevitzky Foundation, 1 January 1948, ASI L3 K3 (copy). The concept of efficiently communicating a musical idea was uppermost in Schoenberg's mind during these years. In the essay "New Music, Outmoded Music, Style and Idea" (1946) he wrote, "In a manifold sense, music uses time. It uses my time, it uses your time, it uses its own time. It would be most annoying if it did not aim to say the most important things in the most concentrated manner in every fraction of this time." *Style and Idea*, 116.

82. Arnold Schoenberg to the Koussevitzky Foundation, 1 January 1948, ASI L3 K3 (copy).

83. See original particelli for the String Trio, op. 45 (ASI Box 49), the *Survivor* (ASI Box 50), and the Phantasy for Violin, op. 49 (ASI Box 51). Schoenberg commented on the unusual dimensions of the *Survivor* autograph in a letter to the work's publisher, Margot Tietzt, at Bomart Music Publications: "What they [the Koussevitzky Foundation] call the sketch is my original manuscript and it is in this way, as I am forced by my nervous eye trouble, to write my scores at present. As you probably have already seen with the Trio." Arnold Schoenberg to Margot Tietzt, 13 April 1949, ASI, L1 B2.

84. Although this comment is written on a primary source (C) used to make the critical edition, it is not mentioned in the Kritischer Bericht. Leibowitz's comment (and every other physical detail of the document) is reported, but not Schoenberg's caustic note. See *Arnold Schönberg, Sämtliche Werke*, 63.

85. See sketches, ASI Box 50, mfl. 948.

86. Hans Keller, "Schoenberg: *A Survivor from Warsaw*," in *Hans Keller: Essays on Music*, ed. Christopher Wintle (Cambridge: Cambridge University Press, 1994), 81.

CHAPTER 10

Returning to a Homeland
Religion and Political Context
in Schoenberg's *Dreimal tausend Jahre*

NAOMI ANDRÉ

Scholars have paid little attention to Arnold Schoenberg's op. 50a
"Dreimal tausend Jahre" ["Three Times a Thousand Years"], except to
mention briefly that it is one of his last finished compositions.[1] This is
perhaps because of the work's relatively small scale: a four-voice
(SATB) a cappella choral piece that is only twenty-five measures long.
But the miniature is also an example of Schoenberg's latest artistic creed:
it is based on a poem with a religious subject and it employs the technique of composing with twelve tones in a specific way.

The sparse commentary is probably not fully unmerited. The handling of the serial technique seems, after all, rather straightforward, in
particular when contrasted with two other works based on religious
themes—Schoenberg's masterly use of one row in the two completed acts
of his opera *Moses und Aron* [*Moses and Aron*], or the blending of his serial method and the Hebrew melody "Shema Yisroel" in *A Survivor from
Warsaw*. Furthermore, throughout his career, Schoenberg's works based
on religious themes comprised some of his most ambitious ventures—
large-scale compositions with traditional and frequently nontraditional
performing forces (usually including the presence of a speaker)—in
which a heightened spiritual experience is conveyed through the combination of various dramatic elements. This is not true of "Dreimal tausend
Jahre," where the theatrical and the daring seem to be actively shunned. In
this work, Schoenberg achieves a sophisticated musical expression
through modest and conventional means. In addition, op. 50a reveals how
Schoenberg kept the musical construction, the relationship of the music to

the text, and the interaction between his artistic life and his Jewish identity in balance to encompass a unified whole.

SCHOENBERG'S FINAL PERIOD

The autograph manuscript for "Dreimal tausend Jahre" is dated 20 April 1949. The work first appeared in the fall of 1949 in the Swedish journal *Prisma* as a special seventy-fifth birthday tribute to Schoenberg. The editors of the journal had asked the composer for a short composition and published the chorus as a facsimile reproduction of Schoenberg's manuscript. It remains unclear, however, whether the work was composed for this specific occasion or whether it was written independently and already finished before the request.[2] "Dreimal tausend Jahre" received its first performance in Fylklingen, Sweden by the Lilla Chamber Chorus under the direction of Eric Ericson on October 29, 1949. In 1955, the piece was posthumously published by B. Schott's Söhne in Mainz.[3]

"Dreimal tausend Jahre" was not originally numbered op. 50a. When it was published in *Prisma*, Schoenberg numbered it op. 49b. In order to fully understand how it was given its final opus number, it is necessary to discuss briefly the complicated history of op. 49. In the late 1920s, Schoenberg was commissioned by the Prussian government to arrange some German folksongs for inclusion in a book of folksongs for young people that appeared, with Schoenberg's arrangements, in 1930. Schoenberg's contributions included three mixed choral settings and four solo voice and piano arrangements. Many years later, in June 1948, Schoenberg returned to three of the folksongs from the German commission, arranged them for four-voice a cappella choir, and published them without an opus number.[4] The German folksongs date from the fifteenth and sixteenth centuries and both of Schoenberg's settings (from 1928–29 and 1948) follow a basic tonal plan with allowances for the old church modes of the original melodies.

A pragmatic explanation for the original numbering of "Dreimal tausend Jahre" is that in April of 1949 when Schoenberg dated the "Dreimal tausend Jahre" manuscript (only ten months after he had reset three of the German folksongs), he probably felt the similarity in genre (four-voice a cappella choral pieces) justified grouping the three folksongs and "Dreimal tausend Jahre" together. Thus, he gave the "Three Folksongs" the opus number 49a and "Dreimal tausend Jahre" the number op. 49b. But combining "Dreimal tausend Jahre" with settings of folksongs is also a statement about the type and character of his original composition: it indicates that the setting of this religious choral piece has a kind of folksong character.

The final opus number assignment took place, most likely, no later than the summer of 1950. At work on "De Profundis" ["Out of the Depths"], a setting of Psalm 130 in Hebrew for six-part chorus (SSATBB), Schoenberg decided to extract "Dreimal tausend Jahre" from op. 49 and create an op. 50 (Schoenberg's last assigned opus number). Schoenberg wrote "De Profundis" in June and July of 1950 at the request of choral conductor Chemjo Vinaver for inclusion in his *Anthology of Jewish Music*.[5] A few months later, Schoenberg suggested this piece to Sergei Koussevitzky when asked to contribute a work for the "King David Festival," a celebration of Israel that was to be held in Jerusalem. Schoenberg dedicated the composition to the newly-formed country of Israel.[6] This setting of the biblical Psalm 130 provides a connecting link to Schoenberg's next and final composition on religious themes, his Modern Psalms project, for which he wrote several psalm texts, yet only set the first musically.[7] Schoenberg intended his modern psalms to follow in the biblical tradition, as evidenced by his early labeling of his first psalm as 151, as if to proceed from the last biblical psalm, 150.[8] Thus, by the end of 1950, "Dreimal tausend Jahre," "De Profundis," and the "Modern Psalms" constituted op. 50 a–c; all choral works based on religious themes, and all works using the twelve-tone method.[9] The new neighborhood of "De Profundis" and the "Modern Psalms" gives the small piece op. 50a a higher aesthetic rank. Instead of being grouped in op. 49 with three tonal folksongs that are reminiscent of the German commission, it now is recontextualized as an integral part of his artistic activities for the Jewish cause and for the state of Israel.

Schoenberg's final compositional efforts illustrate his ardent commitment to writing music with religious associations. The establishment of Israel, to which Schoenberg was strongly attached,[10] led him at the end of his career to two completed compositions ("Dreimal tausend Jahre," op. 50a and "De Profundis," op. 50b) and two larger unfinished projects. In addition to the unfinished "Modern Psalms" collection (mentioned above), Schoenberg also worked on the orchestrated choral work "Israel Exists Again," another composition that he never completed. Schoenberg's advanced age and poor health as well as the large scope of these projects probably contributed to the unfinished and fragmented results.

Schoenberg's difficulty with finishing large-scale works that were closely tied to religious themes has precedent in two major earlier works, the oratorio *Die Jakobsleiter* [*Jacob's Ladder*], which Schoenberg worked on from June 1917 through July 1922 and to which he returned in October 1944, and his opera *Moses und Aron*, of which he set the first two acts between May 1930 and March 1932.[11] While not all his religious projects remained unfinished, it seems as though Schoenberg placed particularly high demands on himself for such works and set expectations that he frequently had difficulty in meeting.

Schoenberg's decision to set "Dreimal tausend Jahre" as a four-part a cappella choral piece reflects his increased interest in choral works during his career in the United States. Though he did write choral pieces in Germany, these pieces were not at the center of his compositional output.[12] Instead, he preferred setting texts as solo songs. Schoenberg's song production from his earliest years of composing up through 1916 far exceeded his works in any other genre at that or any other point in his career.

Using a text provided Schoenberg with a means for musical organization and structure during the development of his compositional style away from a tonally based harmony, through atonality, and finally to his method of composing with twelve tones. In his essay "Composition with Twelve Tones" (1941), Schoenberg wrote about the evolution of his compositional style. Of the period soon after 1908 he states:

> I discovered how to construct larger forms by following a text or a poem. The differences in size and shape of its parts and the change in character and mood were mirrored in the shape and size of the composition, in its dynamics and tempo, figuration and accentuation, instrumentation and orchestration. Thus, the parts were differentiated as clearly as they had formerly been by the tonal and structural functions of harmony.[13]

While the use of a text could imply works for either a solo voice or chorus (or a combination of both, such as in opera or oratorio), Schoenberg's emphasis on works for solo voice at this time is striking. The association of the genre of the song with his evolving musical style is further borne out by the relatively few works for solo voices that he wrote after this period.[14] After Schoenberg left Germany, his writing for solo voice all but ended. It is singularly represented by "Ode to Napoleon," op. 41 (1942), an unconventional work which uses a speaking-singing style similar to *Sprechstimme*, which Schoenberg first explored in *Gurrelieder* (begun, 1900; completed with orchestration, 1911) and further developed in *Pierrot lunaire* [*Pierrot of the Moon*] op. 21 (1912). "Ode to Napoleon" employs a reciter accompanied by an ensemble of piano and string quartet or string orchestra.

As mentioned above, Schoenberg's final musical projects were choral compositions and, with the exception of the Three Folksongs of op. 49, were based upon religious subjects. But even before he focused exclusively upon religious subjects, these themes were already prominent in his artistic output. In 1938, Schoenberg wrote the *Kol Nidre*, op. 39, which he adapted from Jewish liturgy; in 1944 he made an unsuccessful attempt to finish *Die Jakobsleiter*; and in 1945 he composed the "Prelude" to the orchestrated choral suite *Genesis*.[15] In this light, it is not difficult to see two parallel situations in Schoenberg's earlier and later career: a focus on the solo song at a relatively early stage in his compositional output (circa 1908 through 1916) and a focus on choral works at the end of his career (late 1930s through 1951). No other two points in Schoenberg's career so closely resemble each other in terms of compositional emphasis on specific vocal genres. But the representational distinction is important. The solo song is the lyrical utterance of a single, individual voice, whereas the choral music is a collective expression of a group of multiple voices. Thus the change in preference from the solo song to choral music reflects Schoenberg's development away from the subjectivism characteristic of his Vienna years in the late nineteenth and early twentieth centuries toward the religious-political engagement of his late American works.

SCHOENBERG AND JEWISH IDENTITY

The emphasis on a single topic area of inquiry—in this case, religious themes—in Schoenberg's later works deserves further attention. While the early interest in text-based works (notably solo songs) is explained as a response to his compositional development, a corresponding explanation for focusing on choral settings—primarily on religious subjects—at the end of his career may be less straightforward, but it is not elusive. In order to provide a larger context for this issue, it is most helpful at this point to briefly turn to the topic of Schoenberg and Judaism.

As early as the 1920s, Schoenberg recognized that his identity as a Jew in Germany during the rise of Hitler's fascism and Nazi regime would pose problems for his creative development as well as his artistic and physical survival.[16] From his experience of anti-Semitism at Mattsee (an Austrian resort area) during the summer of 1921, where he and his vacationing family were forced to leave because Jews were not tolerated,[17] and his later dismissal from his teaching position at the Prussian Academy of Arts in Berlin in 1933 when the government announced its plan to remove all Jewish constituents from the school, Schoenberg was convinced that the conditions of Jews in Germany would only continue to worsen.[18]

Schoenberg addressed issues pertaining to his religious identity in both his correspondence and his musical compositions. (As a background context, it is important to keep in mind that Schoenberg was born into a Jewish family, but he did not receive a rigorous religious upbringing.[19] In 1898, he converted to Protestantism.)[20] In 1922, when he was living in the recovering yet still war-torn Vienna, Schoenberg wrote to Wassily Kandinsky[21] about a crisis of re-evaluation and search for direction that he felt characterized the time for both the Viennese and for himself personally and artistically. In these comments, his conception of religion emerges as an element that provides guidance and personal sustenance.

> I expect you know we've had our trials here too: famine! It really was pretty awful! But perhaps—for we Viennese seem to be a patient lot— perhaps the worst was after all the overturning of everything one has believed in. That was probably the most grievous thing of all.
>
> When one's been used, where one's own work was concerned, to clearing away all obstacles often by means of one immense intellectual effort and in those 8 years found oneself constantly faced with new obstacles against which all thinking, all power of invention, all energy, all ideas, proved helpless, for a man for whom ideas have been everything it means nothing less than the total collapse of things, unless he has come to find support, in ever increasing measure, in belief in something higher, beyond. You would, I think, see what I mean best from my libretto "Jacob's Ladder" (an oratorio): what I mean is—even though without any organizational fetters—religion. This was my one and only support during those years—here let this be said for the first time.[22]

By citing *Die Jakobsleiter* as an early locus for working out and illustrating his "belief in something higher, beyond," Schoenberg set his own precedent for bringing together several themes that would continue to be linked throughout his career: his expression of religious faith, his ventures in choral music, and his developing musical language and style.[23]

The next year, on 20 April 1923, in another letter to Kandinsky, Schoenberg addressed the growing tide of anti-Semitism and how this influenced his conception of his own identity.

> For I have at least learnt the lesson that has been forced upon me during this year, and I shall not ever forget it. It is that I am not a German,

not a European, indeed perhaps scarcely even a human being (at least, the Europeans prefer the worst of their race to me), but I am a Jew.

I am content that it should be so![24]

Encompassing racial, religious, political, and national identities, this statement shows that even Schoenberg's earlier religious venture into another faith could not eclipse the religious and ethnic affiliations of his family, especially in a country that was increasingly relying upon such criteria as a basis for discrimination. Seen in connection with his experience at Mattsee two years before and his expression of religious guidance in his letter to Kandinsky the previous year, this declaration forms the foundation for Schoenberg's personal identity for the rest of his life. These words mark a critical point in what will eventually lead to Schoenberg's formal return to the Jewish faith.

Schoenberg's decision to leave Germany on 17 May 1933 and emigrate to America exhibited both profound religious conviction as well as concern for his and his family's survival.[25] Additionally, once he left Germany, he began a period in his life characterized by a great affirmation in his efforts to align himself with the Jewish community as an active member working for its continued existence. Two major indicators of Schoenberg's commitment are the ceremony in which he reclaimed his Jewish roots and his prose writings, which took on a tone of strong political activism for the problems facing the Jews in Germany.

On 24 July 1933, shortly after Schoenberg left Germany, he participated in a ceremony that officially marked his re-entry into the Jewish faith. At a small gathering in Paris, with Marc Chagall as one of the witnesses, Schoenberg publicly declared his return to the community of Israel.[26] Though this ceremony came ten years after Schoenberg professed his Jewish identity in his letter to Kandinsky, this re-entry marked, above all, an important symbolic gesture for Schoenberg.[27] At this time in his life, after he had fled from the religious persecution of Germany and was just embarking on a writing campaign that was intended to ensure the survival of German Jews and promote Jewish unity worldwide, practically all of Schoenberg's activities—personal, artistic, and political—centered on his reaffirmation of his commitment to Judaism.

For the person who is mainly familiar with Schoenberg's artistic side, his efforts for and writings on the situation of the Jews in the 1930s may come as a surprise. On more than one occasion in the months following Schoenberg's departure from Germany in 1933, his involvement and passion for the Jewish cause so engrossed him that he expressed his willingness to completely devote himself to it, even at the expense of his composing. In a letter to Anton Webern dated 4 August 1933, Schoenberg expressed this sentiment after briefly outlining how his spiritual development, one stage of which was given expression in his play *Der biblische Weg* [*The Biblical Way* (1927)], had evolved due to the recent events in his life:

> I have long since been resolved to be a Jew, and you will also have sometimes heard me talk about a play (*The Biblical Way*); I could not say more about it at that time, but in it I have shown the ways in which a national Zionism can become active. And now, as from a week ago, I have also returned officially to the Jewish religious community. . . . It is my intention to take an active part in endeavors of this kind. I regard that as more important than my art, and I am determined—if I am suited to such activities—to do nothing in the future but work for the Jewish national cause.[28]

In October of the same year he reiterated these thoughts when, in the same document in which he outlined his plan for the resettlement of the German Jews, he wrote: "I offer the sacrifice of my art to the Jewish cause. And I bring my offer enthusiastically, because for me nothing stands above my people."[29]

Tormented by his prophetic vision of the Holocaust, Schoenberg's letters and writings from the months he spent in Paris and the early years in America are dominated by his deep concern for the political situation of the Jews. His writings on this subject include his plans for the formation of an activist political group—the Jewish Unity Party—which would be "a new party, a new sect . . . nationalistic-chauvinistic to the highest degree, in the religious sense, based on the notion of the chosen people, militant, aggressive, against all pacifism, against all internationalism."[30] In addition, he outlined an extensive evacuation plan for the relocation of German Jews: "I intend to engage in large scale propaganda among all of Jewry in the United States and also later in other countries, designed first of all to get them to produce the financial means sufficient to pay for the gradual emigration of the Jews from Germany."[31]

There is one other specific element related to Schoenberg and Judaism that will provide a further contextual basis for analyzing the text and music of "Dreimal tausend Jahre." Outlined most thoroughly in his extended essay "A Four-Point Program for Jewry," Schoenberg articulates an idea that became centrally connected to his plans for the Jews.[32]

Schoenberg's titles for the four points of this essay are as follows: (1) "The fight against anti-Semitism must be stopped,"[33] (2) "A united Jewish party must be created," (3) "Unanimity in Jewry must be enforced with all means," and (4) "Ways must be prepared to obtain a place to erect an independent Jewish state." In specific reference to the fourth point, Schoenberg discusses the proposed Uganda project (that Uganda would be made a Jewish colony) that was rejected by the Zionist Congress at the beginning of the century and emphasizes the immediate importance of designating a place, a geographic location, for the return of Jews to a homeland. The concern for the creation of a modern-day homeland for the Jews is a theme that is carried into op. 50a, "Dreimal tausend Jahre."

In summary, though Schoenberg's youth was not marked by a strongly practiced religious faith, and even included a temporary conversion to Protestantism, his letters show that by the 1920s religious themes were a source of guidance for him in both personal and artistic matters. By 1933, Schoenberg's view of what was already happening and was most likely going to happen in Germany prompted him to act on his religious faith and leave his homeland indefinitely. His religious convictions motivated his early activities after he left Germany: he focused his efforts primarily on helping the Jews left in Germany. In his re-entry into the Jewish community (in the Paris ceremony in 1933) and his writings about the necessity for creating a Jewish homeland for modern times, the idea of "returning" characterizes both his own religious journey as well as his aspirations for Jewish people to have a newly created homeland. These issues provide a fuller context for understanding Schoenberg's religious background—on both personal and political levels—and pave the way for a more encompassing analysis of "Dreimal tausend Jahre."

AN ANALYSIS OF THE TEXT OF OP. 50A

The text for op. 50a is Schoenberg's adaptation of Dagobert David Runes's poem, "Gottes Wiederkehr" ["God's Return"], the first selection in a volume of poetry by Runes entitled *Jordan Lieder: Frühe Gedichte* [*Jordan Songs: Early Poems*] which had been published by the Philosophical Library of New York in 1948. At that time, Runes was the president of the publishing house. He was also active as an author and editor of books. In addition to his publications on philosophy, Goethe, tyranny, and Soviet issues, the New York Philosophical Library published *Jordan Lieder* as well as his other books on Jewish subjects: *The Hebrew Impact on Western Civilization* (a collection of essays he edited, 1951),[34] the

Concise Dictionary of Judaism (1959) and *The War Against the Jew* (1968). Shortly after his *Jordan Lieder* was published, Runes sent a copy to Schoenberg. In February of 1949, Schoenberg thanked Runes for the poems and also mentioned that he was considering setting one for chorus. Later that year in August, Schoenberg let Runes know that he had set the poem and it would appear in the Swedish magazine, *Prisma*. Schoenberg also expressed the hope that Runes would not object to his altering some of the words in the poem. Schoenberg finally sent Runes a copy of the completed chorus on 13 March 1950 and apologized for the misspelling of the poet's name (Runer, instead of Runes).[35]

During this same time, Schoenberg and Runes were also in contact about the publishing of *Style and Idea*. Although the preparation of the first edition of *Style and Idea* was initiated in 1943 (before Runes was president of the publishing house), the actual publication did not appear until 1950 due to difficult negotiations between Schoenberg and the Philosophical Library about essay selection and the translation of the essays from German into English (some of the essays were written in German, most of the later ones written after Schoenberg came to America were in English). Though their letters concerning "Gottes Wiederkehr"/"Dreimal tausend Jahre" were cordial, a few years later, by April 1951, Schoenberg was on less amicable terms with Runes. Schoenberg accused him of withholding royalties for *Style and Idea*, to which Runes replied angrily and severed further correspondence.[36]

Schoenberg's alterations to Runes's poem were slight, yet not inconsequential. Changing the title, adding new capitalization and punctuation, reconfiguring the form of the poem, and slightly adjusting the text all illustrate the care and effort Schoenberg put into this work.[37] If these modifications are examined individually, they reflect subtle, seemingly insignificant, levels of change. Viewed all together, however, they illuminate his personal reading of the poem and are enhanced by his musical setting.

(The italicized portions are my addition to highlight the places where Schoenberg altered Runes's text.)

Figure 10-1a. Text of "Gottes Wiederkehr"
by Dagobert David Runes[38]

> Dreimal tausend Jahre,
> Seit ich *Dich* gesehn,
> Tempel in Jerusalem,
> Tempel meiner *Wehn.*

Und ihr Jordanwellen—
Silbern Wüstenband;
Gärten und Gelände
Grünen, neues Uferland.

Und mir ists als rauschten
Leise von den Bergen her
Deine *alt* verschollnen Lieder
Flüsternd Gottes Wiederkehr.

Figure 10-1b. Text to Schoenberg's "Dreimal tausend Jahre"[39]

Dreimal tausend Jahre seit ich *dich* gesehn,
Tempel in Jerusalem, Tempel meiner *Wehn!*
Und ihr Jordanwellen, silbern Wüstenband,
Gärten und Gelände grünen, neues Uferland.
Und man hört es klingen leise von den Bergen her,
Deine *all*verschollnen Lieder künden Gottes Wiederkehr.

Figure 10-1c. Translation of Schoenberg's version[40]

Three times a thousand years passed since I saw you go,
Temple of Jerusalem, Temple of my *woe*!
And you waves of Jordan, the desert's silver band
Gardens and broad meadows, richly spread across the shoreland.
And one hears them sounding softly from the mountains there,
All your *long*-forgotten songs, *announcing* God's return.

Figure 10-1d. Translation of the last quatrain of Runes's "Gottes Wiederkehr"

And to me it seems that they *murmur*
Softly from the mountains there,
All your *old*-forgotten songs,
Whispering God's return.

Schoenberg dropped Runes's title "Gottes Wiederkehr," which comes from the last line of the poem, and instead used the first line of the poem, "Dreimal tausend Jahre," for the title. [41] Thus, he reserved the words *God's return* for the very end, where they will be the last impression taken away. Given Schoenberg's own return to Judaism in 1933 and his quest for the re-establishment of a Jewish homeland, it becomes more clear why these words are given special emphasis; the theme of "returning" reflects issues that were very personal for him.

On a more subtle structural level, Schoenberg changed the form of Runes's poem from three quatrains into a single strophe of six lines; thus Schoenberg created three couplets by compounding every two lines into one, and also transformed the rhyme scheme (see Figures 10-1a-d). Schoenberg's version simplifies the form of the poem to three rhyming couplets, whereas Runes's version has a less explicit structure in which the second and fourth lines of each quatrain are paired and the first and third lines are separate and do not rhyme.[42] By consolidating the text into a smaller form overall, Schoenberg gave himself more flexibility in terms of the musical realization. His reworking of the poem's three-quatrain strophic structure gave him the freedom to set each couplet independently and to expand specific sections for added emphasis—an option he followed in the second and, most notably, the third stanzas.

Schoenberg's minor revisions to Runes's text include changing the initial capital on the word *Dich* [you] in Runes's second line to a lower case, most likely in order to refer specifically to the temple of Jerusalem and to reserve the implied reference to a deified agent for God alone. Another alteration in punctuation occurs where Schoenberg added emotional emphasis to the end of his first couplet by changing the period after *Wehn* [woe] to an exclamation point. The modifications to the text, where Schoenberg replaces some of Runes's words, all take place in the final quatrain/couplet. Schoenberg strengthened the last quatrain by changing the first line and the first word of the last line to make a bolder impression. The emphasis shifts from a subjective comment, to a more affirmative statement.

> Runes's version: "Und mir ists als rauschten . . . Flüsternd Gottes Wiederkehr."
> [And to me it seems that they murmur . . . whispering God's return.]
> Schoenberg's version: "Und man hört es klingen . . . Künden Gottes Wiederkehr."
> [And one hears them sounding . . . announcing God's return.]

The slight change in Schoenberg's last line from Runes's *alt verschollnen* to *allverschollnen* reduces the antiquity and outdatedness implied in the *old-forgotten songs* of the distant past. Instead, Schoenberg calls them *long-forgotten songs*; though they have been forgotten, their relevance to the present is still intact. Viewed together, the adjustments in punctuation and wording increase the emotional energy of the text; expanded extremes in affect are created by the emphasis given to *woe!*, the forgotten songs of the past deserve to be remembered, and further excitement is provided by adding power to the presentation of the final words—*God's return*—which are *sounding*, rather than *murmuring*, and *announcing* instead of *whispering*. Schoenberg's deliberate use of the word *künden* is especially revealing; in addition to indicating a more forceful presentation of the text, this word in German is associated with prophetic messages and adds a messianic aspect, a call for deliverance, to the poem's meaning.

Schoenberg's revisions to the text show his sensitivity to recognizing and addressing the similarity Runes's poem had to the style of early romantic German poetry. A few of the lines call to mind similar lines in poems by the nineteenth-century poet Joseph Eichendorff. By way of illustration, the word *rauschten* and the use of the subjunctive by Runes (particularly in the line: "und mir ists als rauschten") are both very reminiscent of Eichendorff's style. Several similar examples may be found in Eichendorff's poems set by Schumann in his 1840 song cycle *Liederkreis*, op. 39; "ist mir's doch, als könnt's nicht sein!" [it seems to me it can not be!] and "und im Traume rauscht's der Hain" [and the woods rustle in a dream] from the final song of this cycle, "Frühlingsnacht" ["Spring Night"], are just two instances.[43]

Schoenberg's primary changes to Runes's poem focus on reserving the climactic feeling for the end of the work and imbue the text with a more triumphal and heroic tone. Given the religious and political meaning Schoenberg was investing in his choral compositions at the end of his career, such revisions reflect the strong statement he wanted to convey about Israel's recreation. His alterations to Runes's poem show a careful blending of a respect for the past with an optimistic prophetic vision for the future.

The text of the poem celebrates the creation (or recreation) of the country of Israel as illuminated in the metaphor of God's return. Runes illustrates this event with the visual image of the temple's destruction in the opening lines and the aural image of the reappearance of the "long-forgotten anthems" in the final lines. The time encompassed spans from the three thousand years in the past (with the destruction of the temple of Jerusalem) through the present (indicated by the present tense in the final lines), and even into the future which incorporates the ambiguous, although immanent, time of God's return. There is a cyclical element in the opening and closing lines with the destruction of the temple of Jerusalem three thousand years ago and the reappearance of the long-forgotten songs signaling God's return. This cyclical element emphasizes both the visual and aural memories of Israel; the place of worship as well as the accompanying music.

MUSICAL ANALYSIS OF "DREIMAL TAUSEND JAHRE"

In 1923, Schoenberg wrote: "In twelve-tone composition consonances (major and minor triads) and also the simpler dissonances (diminished triads and seventh chords)—in fact almost everything that used to make up the ebb and flow of harmony—are, as far as possible, avoided."[44] Though Schoenberg explicitly avoided tonal references in his early twelve-tone works, he slightly modified this approach later in his career. The music of "Dreimal tausend Jahre" is an example of this later handling of the technique with greater freedom.

In Schoenberg's employment of his serial technique in "Dreimal tausend Jahre" the row frequently is divided into its two hexachords.[45] Unlike his early serial works, in "Dreimal tausend Jahre" Schoenberg periodically repeats notes before stating a full row, or hexachord, completely.[46] As the piece progresses, the row material is distributed among two, three, and sometimes all four voices, and unlike his earlier serial compositions, rarely does a full row appear in its entirety in one voice. In this composition only two basic rows are used: the Prime row, the row in its original form (P0), and the Inversion of the Prime row that begins five half steps above P0 (which will be referred to as I5)[47] (see Figures 10-2a and 10-2b). Besides using the Inversion, these two row forms (and hexachords from these rows) are also presented as Retrogrades.[48]

The row has an added feature; it is combinatorial.[49] In op. 50a, the first hexachord of P0 and the second hexachord of I5—as well as the second hexachord of P0 and the first of I5 respectively—have the same pitch class content. Thus, the first hexachords of both P0 and I5 together include all twelve pitch classes, as do the second hexachord of P0 and I5 together, respectively (see Figures 10-2a and 10-2b).

There are moments when "tonal" sonorities break through the surface, which can be seen in an ideological and practical context. Conceptually, the tonal references lend a fairly simple and folk-like character to the work. Logistically, the tonal allusions were built-in features that Schoenberg created in his construction of the row and suggested in his handling of it throughout the piece. Twelve pitches distributed among four simultaneously sounding voices create a situation in which it is difficult to juggle all possible combinations of vertical sonorities and avoid

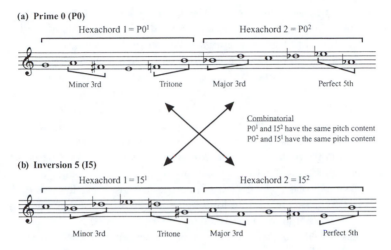

Figure 10-2a. The original or "prime" form of the row used in "Dreimal tausend Jahre." The O signifies that this is the prime form of the row at its original transposition level. The numbers in superscript following the designation of the row form indicate the first and second hexachord or division of the twelve-tone row into two segments of six tones.

Figure 10-2b. The inversion of the prime row of "Dreimal tausend Jahre," beginning five half-steps above the original.

unison or octave doublings. A consequence of this difficulty is seen in the first measure of the piece, where both the alto and tenor parts are missing one note for each of their hexachords (Figure 10-3). The alto's second hexachord of P0 is missing the B-flat (most likely to avoid doubling the B-flat in the bass) and the tenor's second hexachord of I5 is missing a B-natural (most likely to avoid doubling the B-natural in the soprano).[50]

Additionally, vertical intervals of thirds, sixths, and fifths appear and contribute to the composition's quasi-tonal sound.[51] Examples of this appear at the very beginning in Schoenberg's distribution of the row throughout all four voices (in the second beat of the first measure there is a minor seventh chord sonority—G-B-flat-D-F, Figure 10-3), at the end with the repeated C in the bass (last two measures, Figure 10-5), and the outlined (horizontally) E major chord in the soprano (the last iteration of

"Gottes Wiederkehr" in the last two measures of Figure 10-5). Further-more, the melodic contour of the row incorporates both tonal and atonal elements; along with whole and half steps, there are intervals of thirds, a perfect fifth, and a tritone (Figures 10-2a and 10-2b).

In addition to the quasi-tonal allusions in Schoenberg's handling of the row and its construction, there are moments of word painting—in-stances when the meaning of the text is reflected in the music. The two most notable cases occur in the setting of the third couplet. The first in-stance appears at the beginning of the stanza (Figure 10-4) with the "softly sounding" songs represented by very soft dynamic markings (*pi-anissimo* in the men's parts and *pianississimo* in the women's parts) and the echo effects created by the repetition in the rhythmic canons between the two men's and women's parts (to be discussed further later on in the analysis). The second case follows in the last measures of the work with the repetition of the word *return* (*Wiederkehr*, Figure 10-5).

Runes's simple poetic form (condensed further by Schoenberg) com-bined with the vivid and lyrical imagery in the text lend the poem an al-most old-fashioned and nostalgic tone; a desire of things past and hope for the future. In addition to harkening back to Schoenberg's earlier settings of German folksongs, the nature of the poem is reflected in the character of the musical setting. The musical elements contribute to the "Romantic" character of this work; the nostalgic imagery, quasi-tonal allusions, and text painting create a connection to, or reminiscence of, the nineteenth-century German choral lied. Combined with the moderate range for all four vocal parts, this work is challenging, yet does not present an overly demanding situation for the singers. It is accessible both for performers as well as for audiences. The careful blending of musical, textual, and for-mal elements from the past and the present provide a fitting commentary on Schoenberg's aspirations for the newly recreated Israel.

Though the poetic form of three rhymed couplets could have easily led to a strophic musical form, where the same music is repeated for each verse (in this case, each couplet), Schoenberg did not do this (a practice mainly reserved for tonal compositions); instead he composed new music for each strophe—therefore leading to three through-composed stanzas and thus reflecting the meaning in the opening line: "Three times a thousand years." The musical settings of the three stanzas are not of equal length; through text repetition and the use of longer note values, they grow increasingly longer. The proportions of the three stanzas to each other is yet another feature Schoenberg used to illustrate the impor-tance of the third strophe, especially in his setting with the repetition of the last words, "God's return." The first stanza is four measures long; the second stanza is twice the length of the first, a full eight measures; and the third stanza is thirteen measures long, one measure longer than the first and second stanzas combined and slightly longer than half the total length of the piece.[52] Thus, the dramatic weight shifts from the first to the second stanza, and then finally to the third stanza which acts as the culmination for the entire work.

Schoenberg's conflation of Runes's two lines of text into one serves a musical purpose that underlies his concentration on the theme of return. Schoenberg uses the mirror principle (also known as a musical palindrome),[53] a procedure—not uncommon in Schoenberg's twelve-tone music—of stating a hexachord and then immediately following it by its retrograde. In this way the first six notes stated are then restated backwards, so that the hexachordal material immediately returns (albeit reversed) once it is first presented. He employs this technique throughout all four voices in the first verse. The one exception is in the bass voice in the very beginning ("Dreimal tausend Jahre seit ich dich gesehen"); however, by the middle of the stanza ("Tempel in Jerusalem") the bass also incorporates the mirror principle (Figure 10-3).

One trend that is seen over the course of the work is that the interaction between the four voices becomes increasingly integrated in terms of sharing the same rhythms, text, and row material. In the first stanza, the four voices are the most rhythmically and thematically independent. Each voice in the first stanza uses a different hexachord. Though the opening rhythm (dotted quarter-note plus three eighth-notes followed by a longer note value), which is first presented in the soprano in the beginning of Figure 10-3 ("Dreimal tausend Jahre"), is used throughout the first stanza in each voice, it serves to keep the four voices contrapuntally independent rather than rhythmically aligned (as will be seen later on).[54] The text is presented separately throughout, except for the simultaneous declaration of the last word *Wehn!* [Woe!]

In the second stanza the voices become more interdependent. For most of the first half of this stanza, the lower voices, tenor and bass, are paired; for most of the second half of the stanza, the outer voices, soprano and bass, and inner voices, alto and tenor, are paired. The shared rhythms further ally the voices aurally because each pair of voices simultaneously presents both the same rhythmic patterns and text declamation. By the end of this stanza, all four voices divide the same inverted form of the row.[55]

The third stanza continues the trend of the second stanza and increases the degree of interrelatedness among the four voices by extending

Figure 10-3. "Dreimal tausend Jahre," stanza 1 (mm. 1–4 with annotations). Used by permission of Belmont Music Publishers, Pacific Palisades, California 90272.

the same procedures: rhythmic pairings, shared row material, and simultaneous text declamation. However, a new element is added to the first four and a half measures of this stanza: two extended two-part rhythmic canons (between the two upper voices and the two lower voices), which are imitative throughout.[56] Towards the end of both canons, the two pairs of voices also each share the same hexachordal material. In both canons, the imitative rhythm links each of the two parts aurally, yet both lines in each canon maintain a level of independence because they proceed in contrary motion.[57]

The first canon, between the tenor and the bass, begins at "Und man hört es klingen" (Figure 10-4).[58] A unique feature of the first two measures of this canon is that the mirror principle, which was seen in the opening measures of the first verse at the beginning of the work, is taken up again. In the text, the reference to the temple's destruction in the opening lines and the "long-forgotten songs" that "one hears from the far hills" in the last stanza are both elements from the past that are rekindled by the image of God's return. Using the mirror principle, Schoenberg musically links both references of recurrence on two complementary levels. First, on a small scale, the musical material of the palindrome is repeated in the beginnings of both stanzas one and three. Second, in a broader manner, this mirror technique is strategically used two times in the composition—both for images closely associated with God's return. In a similar fashion to the first stanza, the tenor and bass, in the beginning of the third stanza, each state their own hexachord (the first halves of the I5 and the P0, respectively) and then, in palindromic fashion, present these notes again in reverse order.

In the second half of the last stanza, the row and hexachords are handled with increasing freedom. Three and sometimes all four voices share the same row material. Additionally, a part of a hexachord will be stated and then its retrograde will follow before all six notes appear.[59] By the last four measures, the distribution of the row material becomes less clear. Though every note can still be placed into a hexachord, an increased amount of borrowing of pitches between vocal parts to complete these configurations becomes necessary. Thus, by the end of the work, the four voices become almost fully dependent on each other for a complete presentation of a row, or hexachord.[60]

The last three words of the text, "künden Gottes Wiederkehr," make their first appearance in the men's voices in the penultimate measure of Figure 10-4 and, by the second half of the next measure, all voices repeat these words through the last eight measures of the work. Additionally,

Figure 10-4. "Dreimal tausend Jahre," first half of stanza 3 (mm. 13–17 with annotations). Used by permission of Belmont Music Publishers, Pacific Palisades, California 90272.

Figure 10-4. (*continued*)

Schoenberg gave these words further weight by slowing down the note values and elongating the phrase structure. These final words, proclaiming God's return, are given the strongest emphasis in the text and form the primary climactic point in the composition. As was mentioned above in the discussion of the text, this image, that of returning, was a critical issue for Schoenberg in terms of his own religious experience as well as for his aspirations for the re-establishment of a homeland where the Jews of Germany and the world could return and be united.

THE REALIZATION OF A GOAL

Schoenberg's religious works always occupied an extremely meaningful and intensely personal position in his life, and his setting of "Dreimal tausend Jahre" embodies a sophisticated assortment of elements which illuminate his distinctive reading of Runes's poem "Gottes Wiederkehr." In his choice of Runes's poem, along with his slight alterations, Schoenberg emphasized the celebratory nature of the text and treated it along the lines of a choral anthem to the new Jewish nation. The concept of returning is represented musically on a couple of levels: the mirror technique (musical palindrome) for the presentation of hexachordal material in the first and third stanzas as well as the prominence given to the text "Gottes

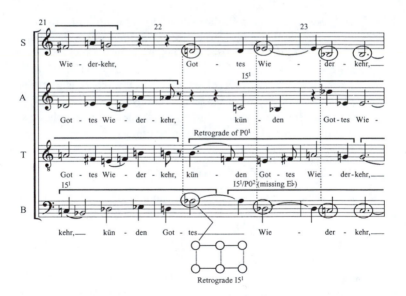

Figure 10-5. "Dreimal tausend Jahre," second half of stanza 3 (mm. 18–25 with annotations). Used by permission of Belmont Music Publishers, Pacific Palisades, California 90272.

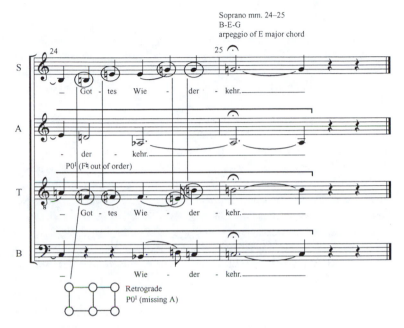

Figure 10-5. (*continued*)

Wiederkehr" at the end of the third stanza through the number of measures, repetition, and metric weight these words receive in the score.

Through his handling of the row, his use of hexachords, and the integration of the voices in shared pitch and rhythmic material, we see a late
treatment of his serial technique that also metaphorically expresses the
themes of renewal and resurgence; sentiments Schoenberg strongly felt
for the newly created Israel. Positioned as the first of only two compositions on religious subjects that Schoenberg completed after the creation
of the country of Israel, "Dreimal tausend Jahre" can be seen as a commentary on the realization of a goal that had occupied his thinking since
the early 1930s. In this light, the increase in shared hexachordal material
and general interrelatedness between the voices as the work progresses
could take on a metaphorical meaning to express the unity and solidarity
Schoenberg hoped the formation of Israel would bring. The tight organization of this short choral work which shows Schoenberg's mastery of
clarity and control is a fitting statement for the fulfillment of such a
quest.

NOTES

An earlier version of this essay originated in a graduate seminar on Schoenberg in America given by Reinhold Brinkmann at Harvard University in the fall of 1991. I am especially grateful to Professor Brinkmann for many helpful suggestions and encouraging comments as I revised and expanded this text into its current form.

1. The bibliography for "Dreimal tausend Jahre" includes: Peter Gradenwitz, "The Religious Works of Arnold Schoenberg," *The Music Review* 21/1 (1960): 24; André Neher, *They Made Their Souls Anew*, trans. David Maisel (New York: State University of New York Press, 1990), 159, 161 ("Dreimal tausend Jahre" is mistakenly referred to as a cantata); Oliver Neighbour, "Arnold Schoenberg," in *The New Grove Second Viennese School: Schoenberg, Webern, Berg*, ed. Stanley Sadie (New York: W.W. Norton & Company, 1988), 66; Willi Reich, *Schoenberg: A Critical Biography*, trans. Leo Black (New York: Praeger, 1971), 230; Alexander L. Ringer, *Arnold Schoenberg: The Composer as Jew* (Oxford: Clarendon Press, 1990), 176, 204; Walter H. Rubsamen, "Schoenberg in America," *The Musical Quarterly* 37/4 (1951): 486; *Arnold Schönberg Sämtliche Werke*, Abteilung 5: Chorwerke II, Reihe A, Band 19, ed. Josef Rufer and Christian Martin Schmidt (Mainz: B. Schott's Söhne; Vienna: Universal Edition, 1975), 135–38; *Arnold Schönberg Sämtliche Werke*, Abteilung 5: Chorwerke II Kritischer Bericht, Skizzen, Fragment, Reihe B, Band 19, ed. Christian Martin Schmidt (Mainz: B. Schott's Söhne; Vienna: Universal Edition, 1977), 94–99; Claudio Spies, "Dreimal tausend Jahre, op. 50a," in "Articles, Pictures, Texts and a Recording of Schoenberg's Voice," liner notes for *The Music of Schoenberg*, vol. 3, Columbia Records M2L 309/M25 709, 44–48; Hans Heinz Stuckenschmidt, *Arnold Schoenberg*, trans. Edith Temple Roberts and Humphrey Searle (Westport, Connecticut: Greenwood Press, 1979), 142–43, 155.

2. Rubsamen, "Schoenberg in America," 486. The tribute to Schoenberg appeared in *Prisma*, no. 4 (Stockholm: n.p., 1949), 40–46. For a discussion of the autograph manuscript, sketches, and *Prisma* edition, see *Arnold Schönberg Sämtliche Werke*, Abteilung 5: Reihe B, 95.

3. Neighbour, "Schoenberg," 69.

4. The most current and comprehensive information about Schoenberg's folksong settings (for both the *Volksliederbuch für die Jugend* [*Book of Folksongs for Youth*] and op. 49) is in *Arnold Schönberg Sämtliche Werke*, Abteilung 5: Chorwerke I, Reihe B, Band 18, Teil 1, ed. Tadeusz Okuljar and Martina Sichardt (Mainz: B. Schott's Söhne; Vienna: Universal Edition, 1991), XXIX–XXXI.

5. Ringer, *Arnold Schoenberg*, 204.

6. Gradenwitz, "Religious Works of Arnold Schoenberg," 25 and Ringer, *Arnold Schoenberg*, 204.

7. Gradenwitz, "Religious Works of Arnold Schoenberg," 26.

8. On the manuscript dated 29 September 1950, Schoenberg wrote "Der 151. Psalm." This title was later crossed out and changed to "A Psalm" (Gradenwitz, "Religious Works of Arnold Schoenberg," 25). For a full account of the several titles Schoenberg gave to this work, see *Arnold Schönberg Sämtliche Werke*, Abteilung 5: Reihe B, 119.

9. The numbering of the "Three Folksongs" and "Dreimal tausend Jahre" and the separate grouping of the tonal folksongs and "Dreimal tausend Jahre" with "De Profundis" is briefly discussed in Josef Rufer, *The Works of Arnold Schoenberg: A Catalogue of His Compositions, Writings and Paintings*, trans. Dika Newlin (London: Faber and Faber, 1962), 75–76.

10. Schoenberg's concern with the situation of the Jews and his commitment to the establishment of a homeland for the Jews after he left Germany in 1933 will be discussed in the upcoming section "Schoenberg and Judaism."

11. Neighbour, "Schoenberg," 69.

12. Completed choral works with opus numbers written in Germany include: *Friede auf Erden* [*Peace on Earth*], op. 13, for eight-part chorus (1907); Four Pieces, op. 27, for SATB and instrumental accompaniment (1925); Three Satires, op. 28, with instrumental accompaniment (1925); and Six Pieces, op. 35, as choral settings for men's voices, op. 35, (1929–30). For a comprehensive list of Schoenberg's choral works of this period, including works without opus numbers, see Neighbour, "Schoenberg," 69–85.

13. *Style and Idea: Selected Writings of Arnold Schoenberg*, ed. Leonard Stein, trans. Leo Black (Berkeley: University of California Press, 1984), 217–18.

14. Reinhold Brinkmann has written about Schoenberg's concentration on lyrical genres (namely the Lied) during this time period. See "The Lyric as Paradigm: Poetry and the Foundation of Arnold Schoenberg's New Music," in *German Literature and Music: An Aesthetic Fusion: 1890–1989*, ed. Claus Reschke and Howard Pollack (Munich: Wilhelm Fink Verlag, 1992), 95–129, esp. 112–13 and "Schoenberg the Contemporary: A View from Behind," in *Constructive Dissonance: Arnold Schoenberg and the Transformations of Twentieth-Century Culture*, ed. Juliane Brand and Christopher Hailey (Berkeley: University of California Press, 1997), 196–219, esp. 200.

15. The role of religion in Schoenberg's compositions and his emphasis on religion at the end of his life are discussed in Gradenwitz, "Religious Works of Arnold Schoenberg," 19–29.

16. A selective bibliography on Schoenberg and Judaism includes: Gradenwitz, "Religious Works of Arnold Schoenberg," 19–29; Michael Mäckelmann, *Arnold Schönberg und das Judentum*, Hamburger Beiträge zur Musikwissenschaft 28 (Hamburg: Verlag Karl Dieter Wagner, 1984); Dika Newlin, "Self-Revelation

and the Law: Arnold Schoenberg in His Religious Works," *Yuval I: Studies of the Jewish Music Research Center*, ed. Israël Adler (Jerusalem: Magnes Press, The Hebrew University, 1986), 204–20; Ringer, *Arnold Schoenberg*; and David Schiff, "Jewish and Musical Tradition in the Music of Mahler and Schoenberg," *Journal of the Arnold Schoenberg Institute* 9 (June 1986): 217–31.

17. See Ringer, *Arnold Schoenberg*, 3.

18. On 1 March 1933, Schoenberg attended a meeting of the Academy's Senate at which it was announced that the Academy would be ridding itself of all Jewish connections and associations. Seeing the rapid deterioration of the stability of his teaching position (though his contract was not subject to renewal for another twenty-three months), Schoenberg decided to leave Berlin with his family on 17 May 1933. On 23 May 1933, his official dismissal from the Academy was sent to him. For more information on Schoenberg and the Prussian Academy of the Arts, see Rufer, *Works of Arnold Schoenberg*, 207–09. See also Reich, *Schoenberg*, 187–88 and Stuckenschmidt, *Arnold Schoenberg*, 109.

19. Ringer, *Arnold Schoenberg*, 7.

20. Ibid., 26.

21. Wassily Kandinsky, the artist, was one of Schoenberg's friends, but there were points of tension between them due to Kandinsky's hesitation in distancing himself from anti-Semitic sentiments. See Schoenberg's letters to Kandinsky, 20 April and 4 May 1923 in *Arnold Schoenberg Letters*, ed. Erwin Stein, trans. Eithne Wilkins and Ernst Kaiser (London: Faber and Faber, 1964), 88–93.

22. Schoenberg to Kandinsky, 20 July 1922 in *Arnold Schoenberg Letters*, 70–71.

23. In the early 1920s, Schoenberg was developing his method of composing with twelve tones and his first compositions using this method appeared.

24. Schoenberg to Kandinsky, 20 April 1923 in *Arnold Schoenberg Letters*, 88.

25. See note 18.

26. Marc Chagall, the painter, was an acquaintance of Schoenberg. Their paths crossed again when Chagall, at the request of Chemjo Vinaver, contributed the frontispiece to the *Anthology of Jewish Music*—the same collection for which Schoenberg wrote the chorus "De Profundis," op. 50b. See Neher, *They Made Their Souls Anew*, 149–51 and Ringer, *Arnold Schoenberg*, 204. For a translation of the document drafted by Rabbi Louis-Germa Lévy and signed by Schoenberg and his two witnesses, Chagall and Dr. Marianoff, see Neher, *They Made Their Souls Anew*, 13.

27. In a letter to Alban Berg dated 16 October 1933, Schoenberg commented that his official return to Judaism took place earlier and was evident in a few of his published works, which he cites as "Du sollst nicht, du musst," op. 27, no. 2, (1925); *Moses und Aron* (which he claims to have begun as early as 1923);

and *Der biblische Weg* (conceived in 1922 or 1923 and finished in 1927). See *Arnold Schoenberg Letters*, 184.

28. Schoenberg to Webern, 4 August 1933 in Reich, *Schoenberg*, 189. Cf. Ringer, *Arnold Schoenberg*, 116.

29. Ringer, *Arnold Schoenberg*, 137.

30. Schoenberg to Jakob Klatzkin, 13 June 1933 (Ringer, *Arnold Schoenberg*, 128).

31. Ringer, *Arnold Schoenberg*, 135. The outline for the realization of his plan is presented in Schoenberg's completed document, which is a typed copy marked "G 4" and is dated from the last week in October, 1933—just before Schoenberg and his family left France for the United States.

32. The essay, "A Four-Point Program for Jewry," is reprinted in full as "Appendix C" in Ringer, *Arnold Schoenberg*, 230–44. Schoenberg's other activities (lectures and writings) from the early 1930s include: "Forward to a Jewish Unitary Party," "We young jewish [*sic*] Austrians," "The Jewish Question," "Notes on Jewish Politics," and "The Jewish Government in Exile" (as listed in Rufer, *Works of Arnold Schoenberg*, 156, 174).

33. The title of Point 1 is misleading. In this portion of the essay, Schoenberg expresses his feelings that it is useless to fight the negative, anti-Semitism, and more productive to put efforts into the positive cause: "We have not to fight against anti-Semitism or nazism, but *for* something; for the existence of a Jewish nation." Quoted from Schoenberg, "A Four-Point Program for Jewry," in Ringer, *Arnold Schoenberg*, 231.

34. An indication of Runes's sensitivity and connection to music is shown in the contents of this collection, which includes an essay by musicologist Paul Nettl entitled "Judaism and Music."

35. Thomas McGeary, "The Publishing History of *Style and Idea*," *Journal of the Arnold Schoenberg Institute* 9 (November 1986): 180–209, esp. 201. Schoenberg's changes to the text of the poem will be discussed below.

36. Ibid., 180–209.

37. Ibid., 209. McGeary briefly reports some of the changes that Schoenberg made to Runes's poem (new title, text alterations, and the repunctuation of the poem from 3 quatrains to 6 lines). I am particularly interested in the question of how they reflect Schoenberg's reading of the poem.

38. Ibid., 209. Text taken from "Appendix II: Schoenberg's Alterations to 'Gottes Wiederkehr' ('Dreimal tausend Jahre')." Runes's poem is reprinted with permission from Philosophical Library, New York.

39. The German text is taken from *Arnold Schönberg Sämtliche Werke*, Abteilung 5: Reihe B, 95. Used by permission of Belmont Music Publishers, Pacific Palisades, California 90272.

40. The English translations of Figure 10-1c and 10-1d are my own; they are adapted from the one in Spies, "'Dreimal tausend Jahre,' op. 50a," 48.

41. The title was changed in Schoenberg's autograph manuscript. Some later printed editions of the work have retained "Gottes Wiederkehr" as a subtitle (though this was probably not Schoenberg's intention).

42. A simple diagrammatic representation of Runes's rhyme scheme is as follows: a b c b, d e f e, g h i h.

43. The author gratefully acknowledges Reinhold Brinkmann's sensitivity to Schoenberg's reading of Runes and his bringing to my attention the connections between Eichendorff and the prophetic connotations embedded in "künden."

44. Arnold Schoenberg, "Twelve-Tone Composition (1923)," in *Style and Idea*, 207.

45. In twelve-tone analysis, a hexachord refers to either the first half of the tone row (the first six pitches) or the second half of the row (the last six pitches).

46. The most strict application of the serial technique prohibits the repetition of a pitch before all other eleven pitches of a chromatic scale are sounded in order to insure an equal handling of all pitches and to avoid the predominance of one or a few pitches above the others.

47. The Prime form of the row is the original order of the row and can be replicated on (or transposed to) all the other eleven pitches. The Inversion form of the row takes each ascending interval of the Prime row and changes it into the corresponding descending interval, and vice versa. The Retrograde form presents the notes of a Prime version of the row in reverse order. It is also possible to present the notes of the Inversion in reverse order to produce the Retrograde Inversion.

48. Schoenberg notated the Prime (P0) and the Inversion transposed up five half-steps (I5) forms of the row in his sketches for "Dreimal tausend Jahre," which are reproduced in the commentary to the critical edition. See Sketches A4 and A9 in *Arnold Schönberg Sämtliche Werke*, Abteilung 5: Reihe B, 97. Claudio Spies offers an analysis of this work in his liner notes (Spies, "'Dreimal tausend Jahre,' op. 50a") which mentions the theme of "returning" in the construction of the row and the text (which will be further discussed in this essay below).

49. In a combinatorial row, certain subsets, usually hexachords, of some row forms can be combined with other subsets (hexachords) of other row forms to produce all twelve pitch classes.

50. This situation occurs again in the third measure of Figure 10-3 when the tenor's second hexachord of I5 is missing A-natural (most likely to avoid doubling the A-natural in the alto) and the bass's second hexachord of P0 is missing A-flat (most likely to avoid doubling the A-flat in the soprano).

51. One of the principles of Schoenberg's method of composing with twelve tones prohibits overt references to tonality caused by sounding the intervals of

octaves, thirds, sixths, and fifths—intervals on which traditional harmony is so dependent.

52. Ironically the number thirteen is important here in this work: the third stanza begins in measure 13 and the stanza is thirteen measures long. Schoenberg was notoriously superstitious when it came to the number thirteen and even went as far as to label this measure "12a" instead of "13" in the autograph manuscript copy of this score (see *Arnold Schönberg Sämtliche Werke*, Abteilung 5: B, 94).

53. Like a verbal palindrome in which a word or phrase reads the same forwards and backwards (e.g., madam), a musical palindrome presents notes in the same way (e.g., A B C B A)

54. The recurring rhythmic motive of stanza 1 may be seen in Figure 10-3— in the soprano (measures 1, 3, and 4), the alto (measure 2), the tenor (measure 3), and bass (measure 3, where the eighth-notes are immediately followed by two more eighth-notes, rather than a longer note value).

55. In terms of rhythmic pairing, the tenor and bass share the same basic rhythm (with one slight deviation) for "Und ihr Jordan." "Gärten und Gelände" illustrates rhythmic pairing between the outer (soprano and bass) and inner (alto and tenor) voices. Row sharing is a feature that also occurs earlier in the stanza: in the first four measures the bass, tenor, and soprano all share the same retrograde form of the row (retrograde of P0). For the text "Gärten und Gelände grünen, neues Uferland," the bottom three voices share the same rows (I5 and the retrograde of the second hexachord of P0). It is I5 that is stated in all four voices at the end of the stanza; the lower voices present the first hexachord and the upper voices share the second hexachord. (The second stanza is not given as a musical example.)

56. A musical canon is based on the idea of repetition between two or more voices with an element of a fixed time delay between the entrances of the different voices. In tonal music, frequently the interval at which the musical imitation appears is chosen to best facilitate an easy harmonic combination, such as at the octave, the unison, the fifth, the fourth, etc. In twentieth-century music, the canon is not uncommonly used as a structural element to aid in the internal organization of a composition.

57. A loose type of inversion principle between the two voices in each canon is used. The resulting contrary motion refers to the directions in which the lines move—i.e., when the tenor descends, the bass ascends; when the tenor ascends, the bass descends.

58. Since the compositional techniques of the first canon encompass and go beyond those used in the second canon, the following discussion will focus on the first canon.

59. Examples of this type of palindrome can be seen in the second and third measures of Figure 10-5 in the bass where only the first four notes of the first half

of I5 appear in forward and then retrograde form. A similar case appears in the soprano (the third and fourth measures of Figure 10-5) where the first four notes of the first hexachord of P0 also appear in forward and then retrograde forms.

60. The one exception is the alto line that presents the first hexachord of I5 in the second half of the third and fourth measures and again in the last four measure of Figure 10-5.

CHAPTER 11

Schoenberg's *Modern Psalm,* Op. 50c and the Unattainable Ending

MARK P. RISINGER

In a 1957 book review of the facsimile edition of Schoenberg's last work, *Moderne Psalmen* [*Modern Psalms*], Hans Keller begins with a description of "Schoenberg's last and very fragmentary work . . . whose completion was prevented by his death." After discussing the musical setting of the first text, "Psalm no. 1" (op. 50c), he concludes by referring to ". . . the fact that [Schoenberg's] death prevented him from completing the piece."[1] This explanation of the work's unfinished condition conveys a perfectly reasonable assumption that has stood largely unchallenged for the last forty years. Furthermore, Keller's assumption is undoubtedly true if one considers "the work" to comprise all sixteen texts that Schoenberg had written between 29 September 1950 and 3 July 1951.[2] The composer had entitled each of the individual texts either "Psalm" or "Moderner Psalm" and given them the collective title of *Moderne Psalmen*, presumably with the intention of setting them to music; at the time of his death on 13 July 1951, however, he had composed music only for the first text, now simply referred to as "Modern Psalm" (op. 50c).[3] The music of this setting, like the texts themselves, remained incomplete. Considerations of "the work" aside, however, Keller's assertion about "the piece"—the music of the first "Modern Psalm"—is problematic, as it implies that Schoenberg was still actively engaged in composing music for his first text some nine months after he had begun; as we shall see, certain aspects of the composition suggest that he had intentionally and permanently ceased composing at some earlier point. The intellectual and spiritual struggle embodied in the text, as well as shifting patterns of text setting in the last section of music composed, indicate that Schoenberg had reached an impasse in his attempt to express the inexpressible through music. He therefore made the same decision he had made on two previous occasions when confronted with the same problem: he left the work without ending it.

Schoenberg related the full title of his work-in-progress to Oskar Adler in a letter dated 23 April 1951: "Psalmen, Gebete und andere Gespräche mit und über Gott" [Psalms, Prayers and other Discourses with and about God].[4] The latitude implicit in this title gave Schoenberg the freedom to cover a wide variety of topics in his Psalms, including prayer, the granting of prayers, requests to God to punish offenders, the Chosen People of Israel, the Ten Commandments as the basis of morality, Jesus as the most noble of men, and the maintenance of the Jewish race through intermarriage.[5] The pseudo-Biblical orientation of these texts was undoubtedly an outgrowth of the two works he had completed just prior to embarking on the *Modern Psalms*, the a cappella choral pieces *Dreimal tausend Jahre* [Three Times a Thousand Years, op. 50a] and "De Profundis" ["Out of the Depths," op. 50b]. The former is a setting of a poem by Dagobert Runes, and the latter is a Hebrew-language setting of Psalm 130.[6] The influence of "De Profundis" on Schoenberg as he began work on his own "Psalm" is most readily seen in the manuscript of the text, which he originally titled "Der 131 Psalm."[7] He subsequently altered the "3" to make it a "5," thereby numbering his work to take up where the Psalmist of the Old Testament had left off, but he ultimately rejected such numberings altogether; he drew a line through "Der 151" and preceded it with the indefinite article, leaving the final form of the title "A Psalm" and in the upper right corner adding the designation "No. 1."[8] However direct the influence of these two preceding pieces may have been, the central issue that Schoenberg confronted in the text and music of "Modern Psalm," the search for unity with God, had been a part of his artistic consciousness for the greater part of his creative life. Therefore, following an examination of the text of "Modern Psalm," a brief overview of earlier works dealing with religious topics will provide us with the backdrop necessary to an understanding of Schoenberg's final attempt to grasp the eternal and unattainable.

Schoenberg's text for op. 50c encompasses both direct address to God as well as discourse about God, just as the title related to Adler describes. Whereas the text of Psalm 130 begins as an individual voice crying out to God ("Out of the depths I cry to thee, O Lord!") and ends with an emphasis on communal worship ("O Israel, hope in the Lord! For with the Lord there is steadfast love, and with him is plenteous redemption"),[9] Schoenberg's "Modern Psalm" takes the opposite approach, beginning from a stance of confidence in communal worship before turning to troubling questions about the efficacy of individual prayer and the possibility of union with God:

> *Der Erste Psalm*
>
> O, du mein Gott: alle Völker preisen dich
> und versichern dich ihrer Ergebenheit.
> Was aber kann es dir bedeuten, ob ich das
> auch tue oder nicht?
> Wer bin ich, dass ich glauben soll, mein   5
> Gebet sei eine Notwendigkeit?
> Wenn ich Gott sage, weiss ich, dass ich damit
> von dem Einzigen, Ewigen, Allmächtigen, All-
> wissenden und Unvorstellbaren spreche, von dem ich
> mir ein Bild weder machen kann noch soll.   10
> An den ich keinen Anspruch erheben darf oder
> kann, der mein heissestes Gebet erfüllen oder
> nicht beachten wird.
> Und trotzdem bete ich, wie alles Lebende
> betet; trotzdem erbitte ich Gnaden und Wunder;   15
> Erfüllungen.
> Trotzdem bete ich, denn ich will nicht des
> beseligenden Gefühls der Einigkeit, der Ver-
> einigung mit dir, verlustig werden.
> O du mein Gott, deine Gnade hat uns das Gebet   20
> gelassen, als eine Verbindung, eine
> beseligende Verbindung mit Dir. Als eine
> Seligkeit, die uns mehr gibt, als jede Erfüllung.[10]
>
> *[The First Psalm*
>
> O, you my God: all people praise you
> And assure you of their devotion.
> But what can it signify to you, whether I
> Do likewise or not?
> Who am I, that I should believe my
> Prayer to be a necessity?
> When I say "God," I speak thereby
> Of the Only, Eternal, Omnipotent
> Omniscient and Unimaginable, of whom I
> Neither can nor should make myself an image.

> On whom I may not and cannot make any claim,
> Who my most fervent prayer will either fulfill
> or disregard.
> And yet I pray, as all living things
> pray; Yet ask I for grace and miracles;
> Fulfillment.
> Yet I pray because I do not want to lose
> The sublime feeling of unity, Of union with you.
> O you my God, your grace has granted unto us the prayer,
> as a bond, a
> sublime bond with you. As a
> Bliss that gives to us more than any fulfillment.][11]

Schoenberg composed eighty-six measures of music for this text, music whose texture alternates between a Speaker (using "Sprechstimme" or "speaking voice") and a six-voice chorus, accompanied by orchestra.[12] The Speaker's text includes lines 1–19 and the sung text lines 1–16, but the final four lines, which reaffirm the possibility of a consummated union with and fulfillment from God, were never set at all. The decision to leave such lines alone, without setting them to music, provides a reminiscence of Schoenberg's noncompletion of two other sacred works, *Die Jakobsleiter* [*Jacob's Ladder*] and *Moses und Aron*, whose protagonists are unable to find fulfillment through prayer.

An attempt to understand the emphasis on prayer and its attendant problems in "Modern Psalm," as well as in the other two works just mentioned, must begin with a letter Schoenberg wrote to Richard Dehmel, dated 11 December 1912:

> . . . for a long time I have been wanting to write an oratorio on the following theme: how the man of today, who has passed through materialism, socialism, and anarchy, who was an atheist but has still preserved a remnant of ancient beliefs (in the form of superstition)—how this modern man struggles with God (see also *Jakob ringt* by Strindberg) and finally arrives at the point of finding God and becoming religious. How to learn to pray! This change should not be caused by any actions, by blows of fate, or by a love affair. Or, at least, such things should be merely hinted at, kept in the background as motivations. And above all: the text must mirror the speech, thought and expression of the man of today; it should deal with the problems which press upon us. For those who struggle with God in the Bible also express themselves as men of their time, speak of their own concerns and remain at their own social

and spiritual level. Therefore, they are artistically strong, but cannot be put into music by a composer of today who fulfills his obligations. At first I had intended to write this myself. Now, I do not trust my own capacity to do so. Then I thought of arranging Strindberg's *Jakob ringt* for my purposes. Finally, I decided to begin with positive religiosity, and I plan to rework the final chapter ("Journey to Heaven") of Balzac's *Seraphita*. But I could not get rid of the idea of "The Prayer of the Man of Today"; and I often thought "If only Dehmel . . ."[13]

In his original libretto to *Die Jakobsleiter*, completed in 1917, Schoenberg makes the voice of Gabriel the vehicle for his further thoughts on "the prayer of the man of today":

Lernet beten: "Wer betet, ist mit Gott eins worden" (Balzac: *Seraphita*). Nur seine Wünsche trennen ihn noch von seiner Aufgabe.
Aber die Vereinigung muss nicht aufhören, wird nicht durch Schuld unter-brochen. Der Ewige, euer Gott, ist kein eifernder Gott, der rächt, sondern ein Gott, der mit eurer Unvollkommenheit rechnet, dem eure Unzulänglichkeit bekannt ist, der weiss, dass ihr versagen müsst und dass euer Weg weit ist.
Er erhört euch, gewährt euch im Sinne eures Weges, ihr seid ewig in seines Hand, trotz freiem Willen geführt, behütet und beschützt, trotz böser Lust zur Sünde mit ihm Verbunden, von ihm geliebt, wenn ihr zu beten vermögt.
Lernet beten: Klopfet an, so wird euch aufgetan![14]
[Learn to pray: for "he who prays has become one with God" (quoted from *Seraphita*). Only his wishes separate him still from his goal. But this union must not cease, and will not be invalidated by your faults. The Eternal One, your God, is no jealous God of revenge, but a God who reckons with your imperfections, to whom your inadequacy is known, who realizes that you must falter and that your road is long.
He listens to you, protects you on your way; you are eternally in His hand, guided, watched over and protected in spite of your free will, bound to Him in spite of your evil desire for sin, loved by Him—if you know how to pray.
Learn to pray: Knock, and the door will be opened unto you!][15]

Having once quoted *Seraphita* and asserted that "he who prays has become one with God" in *Die Jakobsleiter*, it seems odd that Schoenberg should have turned so doubtful in regard to the efficacy of prayer by the

time of "Modern Psalm": "Wer bin ich, dass ich glauben soll, mein/
Gebet sei eine Notwendigkeit?" [Who am I, that I should believe my/
Prayer to be a necessity?] These thoughts convey a tension in Schoenberg's belief system between the need for unity with God and the fear
that God may not be listening. Schoenberg's concept of God is unques-
tionably modeled on the Old Testament descriptions of the God of Abraham and Moses, as becomes clear through his repeated use of the
formulation "dem Einzigen, Ewigen, Allmächtigen" [the Only, Eternal,
Omnipotent] in several subsequent texts of the *Modern Psalms* (nos. 5, 8,
and 9). He expresses a further sense of identification with the Mosaic
concept of God in the lines just following the phrase quoted above (lines
7–10). Line 10, paraphrasing the second commandment of the Decalogue, embodies yet another source of conflict for the artist and composer, since a God who is "unimaginable" cannot be represented without
being diminished to some degree, and music that is meant to represent
complete unity with this God is doomed to fail of its purpose from the
outset. Thus the final four lines of Schoenberg's text for "Modern
Psalm," which speak of this unity and fulfillment as an accomplished
fact, were left with no music composed for them at all. Just as there are
antecedents in Schoenberg's works that discuss the importance of prayer,
there is an antecedent that stresses the prohibition against representations
of God. In the second of his *Vier Stücke für gemischten Chor* [*Four
Pieces for Mixed Chorus*], op. 27 (1925), Schoenberg wrote a text that
takes the second commandment as its point of departure:

Du Sollst Nicht, Du Musst
Du sollst dir kein Bild machen!
Denn ein Bild schränkt ein,
begrenzt, fasst,
was unbegrenzt und unvorstellbar bleiben soll.
Ein Bild will Namen haben:
Du kannst ihn nur vom Kleinen nehmen;
Du sollst das Kleine nicht verehren!
Du musst an den Geist glauben!
Unmittelbar, gefühllos
und selbstlos.
Du musst, Auserwählter, musst, willst du's
bleiben!¹⁶

[You should not, you must
You should make for yourself no image!

Because an image limits,
Restricts, lays hold of
What should remain unrestricted and unimaginable.
An image wants a name:
You can take it only from that which is insignificant;
You should not revere the insignificant!
You must believe in the Spirit!
Immediate, unfeeling
And self-sacrificing.
You must, Chosen one, must, if you wish to
remain so!][17]

Hence, the reference in *Modern Psalm* to the problem of representing God is but the last comment in an ongoing conversation that Schoenberg had been having with himself for many years. A final word on this topic from David Schiff provides a helpful summary of the problem:

> Schoenberg's concept of Judaism was as idiosyncratic and complex as his music. It turned on the idea of the unrepresentable God. If God is formless, every work of art which aspires to the spiritual is a Golden Calf, a false idol. And yet all art is a representation—is it all thus inherently false? Every artist is thus both Moses and Aron distorting thought in the very act of giving it shape. . . . Schoenberg's mosaic critique represents a basic and probably unanswerable question about the nature of musical expression.[18]

While we cannot hope to reconstruct or understand every facet of the relationship between Schoenberg's religious ideology and his compositional practice, the music of *Modern Psalm* and its relationship to the text illustrates the "mosaic critique" to which Schiff refers, a critique which in all likelihood has more to do with why Schoenberg never finished the piece than did his death. Understanding something of the background to the text, we should now turn our attention to the music of "Modern Psalm" in order to see how its relationship to the text compares with Schoenberg's other approaches to the same topic.

Schoenberg made his first compositional steps in "Modern Psalm" by preparing a chart showing his original twelve-tone "row," the melody on which the piece is based and in which no pitch is repeated until all the remaining pitches have been used. He divided this twelve-note sequence into two groups of six notes, labeled A[ntecedent] and C[onsequent], each of which is referred to as a "hexachord." On the next line, he began a perfect fifth lower than the original and wrote the inversion of the row, in which the distance from one pitch to the next is the same, but moving in the opposite direction of the original, thereby producing a mirror image of the original (Figure 11-1). Using five more pairs of staves, Schoenberg wrote out five more versions of the row and its inversion, each beginning a whole tone lower than the one before. After filling the page in this way, he made the following marginal notes across the top and down the side:

> Die Wunder-Reihe [The Miracle Set]
>   As usual, the inversion in the lower fifth of the antecedent furnishes the remaining six tones. It occurred miraculously that the six tones of the inversion in another order (C2) became the retrograde of the antecedent A(1). The retrograde of this C appears to be the transposition of the antecedent A, a whole tone lower. See 2a.— The same procedure applied to A3 furnishes 4a, consisting of the *same* six notes in another order. In the same manner the As (5), (7) (9) and (11) and the Cs (6), (8), (10), and (12) are produced. The advantage of this miracle set is that the six antecedents offer the same intervallic relationship, though they consist all of the same six tones. Similarly the remaining five consequents consist of the same tones in a different order as C2. Furthermore, so as A(1) can be accompanied by *A(1)inv.* or C(2), all the other 5 antecedents have the same choice. Moreover: every A can be accompanied by every C, by every inversion of every A, and by every A. This offers a greater variety than double counterpoint of all sorts. Of course, you have to invent your themes as ordinarily, but you have more possibilities of producing strongly related configurations, which will [*sic*] in sound are essentially different.[19]

At the end of this passage, Schoenberg signed his name and added the date, October 1950. The most striking aspect of this set, the "miracle" to which Schoenberg refers, is that the "C" hexachord reproduces the se-

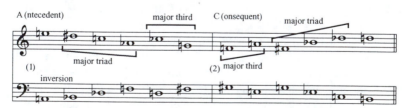

Figure 11-1. The tone-row and its inversion for "Modern Psalm."

quence of intervals in the "A" hexachord in reverse order, or in retrograde. This fact probably inspired one of the most common musical gestures in "Modern Psalm," which is the use of a hexachord followed immediately by its retrograde.

The most important musical patterns that Schoenberg employs, at least for the purposes of this discussion, can be summarized as follows:

1. A hexachord is often followed immediately by its retrograde (Figure 11-2).
2. The "prime" (original) form of a hexachord in one voice part is often coupled with the inversion form in another part (Figure 11-3).
3. Orchestral lines are frequently written *colla parte* [in unison] with vocal lines.
4. The pitches of a single hexachord are often distributed between multiple instrumental or vocal lines to form a "hexachordal set" (Figure 11-4).

The construction of the tone-row itself, containing two major triads and two other major thirds (labeled in Figure 11-1), makes it possible for Schoenberg to compose passages with particular tonal tendencies, such as the suggestion of A-flat major and E minor in the first eight measures of the piece, which are somewhat unusual in a twelve-tone composition. Because Schoenberg chooses to use only whole-tone transpositions of the original row, there appear throughout the piece only two different groups of six tones that make up the twenty-four hexachords on the chart, making it possible to follow the use of particular hexachords with relative ease. Such tracing of hexachordal usage makes it further possible to identify patterns or what we might call "hexachordal clustering," in which certain hexachords tend to appear in conjunction with certain others. For instance, there is a marked tendency for the A11 hexachord to appear in close proximity to A3; having noticed this tendency, we might well consider whether two passages that share this "hexachordal cluster" might share other traits as well, such as the repetition of text from one passage in another. While we should avoid any analysis that seeks merely to identify row forms (bearing in mind Schoenberg's insistence on the "what" of a piece rather than the "how"),[20] nevertheless a certain amount of row identification is necessary in order to see how Schoenberg approached the setting of his text and to see where he was in the compositional process when he stopped composing.

The opening section of "Modern Psalm" is the only passage in the music that simultaneously combines all forces: spoken, choral, and orchestral. The pitches of both the choral and orchestral parts remain within a single hexachord, A1, for the first eight measures of the piece; this passage is the only part of the work that employs the original A hexachord for an extended length of time and in which a single hexachord is allowed to dominate the pitch content for more than a measure or two. Throughout the remainder of the work, Schoenberg uses hexachords in combination with each other, rather than in isolation. Another unusual aspect of this opening, pointed out by Ringer, is Schoenberg's reduction of the six-part choral texture in mm. 1–8 to only four parts for the remainder of the piece. While it is not unusual to expand the texture (i.e., the number of vocal lines) for climactic purposes, there is almost no precedent for reducing the choral texture in this way after so short a passage.[21] By utilizing all of his forces at the beginning, including an expanded choral texture, Schoenberg illustrates quite vividly the opening affirmation of the text, "alle Völker preisen dich" [all peoples praise You], before turning to more individual questions and concerns. Such careful planning at the beginning establishes a pattern for the use of hexachords and the exposition of text throughout the remainder of the piece that warrants close analysis and attention to compositional details. The musical characteristics enumerated above, which Schoenberg establishes in the first part of the piece, provide a point of comparison with the last section, in which his approach is quite different.

The procedure in the alto line illustrated in Figure 11-2 is one of the most common in the work: the use of a hexachord followed immediately by its retrograde, thus creating a kind of musical palindrome. Such a pattern is logical, as it resembles the construction of the original twelve-

Figure 11-2. "Modern Psalm," alto line of mm. 3–7, showing use of A(1) hexachord and its retrograde. Used by permission of Belmont Music Publishers, Pacific Palisades, California 90272.

tone row whose second half is a retrograde of the first, transposed down a whole-tone. In the case of the alto line, the g on the syllable "-chern" serves as both the final note of the hexachord A1 and as the first note of the retrograde. Such is not always the case, for in numerous other passages, Schoenberg repeats the final note to provide a beginning for the retrograde form.

A second pattern emerges early in the piece, demonstrated by soprano and tenor lines beginning in Figure 11-3. At this point, we find C2 beginning in the soprano on the syllable "-chern" and continuing through the beginning of m. 10. The tenor entrance beginning one measure later uses the inversion of hexachord C2, "C2inv," thus coupling the original form with the inversion form as a counterpoint. The bass entrance that follows the tenor duplicates the soprano's use of C2, though several of the intervallic relationships are inverted. Thus the pitches and their order follow the pattern of the C2 hexachord without duplicating the melodic shape of the soprano line. Both tenor and bass immediately follow the initial statements of their hexachords with the retrogrades of those hexachords, just as in the alto line of Figure 11-2.

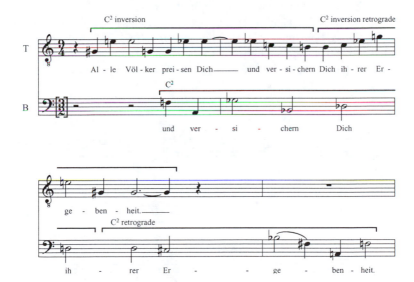

Figure 11-3. "Modern Psalm," tenor and bass lines, mm. 9–12, showing use of C(2) hexachord coupled with its inversion. Used by permission of Belmont Music Publishers, Pacific Palisades, California 90272.

One further point must be made concerning the instrumental parts. Much of the orchestral writing in "Modern Psalm" is written *colla parte* [in unison] with the vocal lines. In the passage just discussed, for instance, we find duplication of lines between the soprano and English horn; between the tenor, bassoon, and viola; and between the bass, contrabass, and violoncello. In addition, the violins, oboe, and E-flat clarinet share a line as well. The reasons for composing in this way are potentially several: as support for the vocal lines, as a means of composing faster (considering Schoenberg's deteriorating health at the time), or as timbral contrast to particular vocal sounds. All three of these considerations may have played a role in the disposition of instruments. This preponderance of *colla parte* writing has one other effect as well: in the instances where Schoenberg chooses to use a solo instrument for a particular text-related purpose, the effect is heightened to a considerable degree by his use of the instrument alone, apart from the voices.

Finally, one should be aware that there are instrumental and choral passages in which the individual lines do not represent straightforward, recognizable versions of any one hexachord; instead, the pitch content of several adjacent lines combines to form what might be called a "hexachordal set" of pitches. For example, in the passage illustrated in Figure 11-4, the oboe, E-flat and B-flat clarinets, and violins combine to form the set of pitches belonging to the C2 hexachord, or "C2set," if we trace the order of pitches from the oboe's F to the E-flat clarinet's simultaneous A back to the oboe's G-flat, and so forth. This technique occurs in both

Figure 11-4. "Modern Psalm," mm. 9–10, individual pitches of C(2) hexachord distributed among different instruments to form a "hexachordal set." Used by permission of Belmont Music Publishers, Pacific Palisades, California 90272.

choral and orchestral parts, but it is more prevalent in the orchestra until the final few bars. The shift to a choral texture comprised almost exclusively of hexachordal sets in the last five measures is another aspect of this passage that sets it apart from the rest of the piece, with ramifications to which we shall return below.

From this point, we may look at other musical characteristics that help define the overall shape of the work and that have less relation to purely technical concerns and more to the response of music to text. Schoenberg's decision to set the text of *Modern Psalm* using a speaker in addition to a chorus brings this work into an association with earlier works—some on religious topics, others on political themes—that employ *Sprechstimme* as an expressive device. Of particular relevance are *Die Jakobsleiter*, in which the angel Gabriel alternates between sung pitches and pitched speech; *Moses und Aron*, with its choral *Sprechstimme* to represent the voice of God; and Schoenberg's last completed work, "De Profundis," which employs choral *Sprechstimme* simultaneously with choral singing throughout to reiterate and reinforce the sense of the text. The *Sprechstimme* in "Modern Psalm" is notated using conventional note values placed above and below a single line with bass clef, apparently intended for a male speaker. While the opening section begins with chorus and *Sprechstimme* singing and speaking simultaneously (just as in "De Profundis"), throughout much of the remainder of the work Schoenberg alternates between sung and spoken passages, often allowing the chorus to repeat text that has already been spoken. Ultimately, however, the Speaker is allowed to say more than the chorus sings, since the spoken text extends through line 19, which speaks of the fear of losing a feeling of unity with God, while the sung text breaks off after line 16, which asserts the continuing desire for grace and fulfillment. Schoenberg seems to have been unwilling—or perhaps unable—to approach setting the most confident and affirming part of the text, the final four lines that speak of prayer as a sublime bond with God, as "a Bliss that gives to us more than any fulfillment." Instead, the final words sung by the chorus, the words that end the work, are the searching and yearning words of line 14: "Und trotzdem bete ich" [And yet I pray].

I have already pointed out that Schoenberg uses all three parts—the speaker, the six-part chorus, and the orchestra—for the opening passage asserting that "alle Völker preisen dich" [all peoples praise you]. There appears to be tension, however, between the certainty of this collective consciousness and the individual uncertainty of the questions to which he immediately turns: "Was aber kann es dir bedeuten, ob ich das auch tue oder nicht?" [But what can it signify to you, whether I do likewise or not?]

The choral passage at this point is a two-part canon (soprano and alto in unison, followed by tenor and bass) using the hexachord "C2inv" immediately followed by its retrograde. The tonal implications of the original row and its various forms are never clearer than at this point, which sounds like the key of C-minor, the tonality that returns very clearly as Schoenberg's closing gesture at the end. Thus, the uncertainty expressed early in the piece through the use of C-minor may foreshadow similar uncertainty at the point where the music breaks off. As the canon ends in m. 18, the speaker continues with line 5, asking the question central to the entire piece: "Wer bin ich . . . ?" [Who am I . . . ?] The chorus picks up these words immediately and emphatically in a series of overlapping entries from bass to soprano using A11 and A3 in alternation; the Speaker repeats them one final time before he continues in m. 20. As he does so, the string writing that accompanies him continues the use of A3 and A11 from the choral parts in m. 19. This passage, however, provides the perfect illustration and validation of Schoenberg's insistence on the "what" of a piece rather than the "how," for although the pitch content of the string parts is the same as in the choral passage immediately preceding, the musical character of the two could not be more different. As the Speaker completes his question, "Wer bin ich dass ich glauben soll, mein Gebet sei eine Notwendigkeit?" [Who am I, that I should believe my prayer to be a necessity?], Schoenberg marks the string writing "am Steg" [on the bridge], creating an instrumental color that conveys a sense of mystery, of the numinous. He continues the use of this color, gradually adding high woodwinds, as the Speaker begins to describe the import of speaking God's name, of speaking about the "Only, Eternal, Omnipotent, Omniscient, and Unimaginable," in short, the characteristics of God that are most troubling. The orchestral support underneath the spoken text grows until the climax of this section at the words "der mein heissestes Gebet erfüllen oder nicht beachten wird" [who my most fervent prayer will either fulfill or disregard] and then subsides completely until it grows silent, leaving both the Speaker and listener to ponder the deepest dilemma of faith.

In the section that follows, the choir re-enters after an absence of twelve measures, taking up the same text just spoken, and once again the sound of gently undulating vocal lines is a marked contrast to what has come before. At the same time, however, the musical lines are familiar to us because the mirror-canon in the tenor and bass has already been presented in m. 24, as mentioned above. Without employing any radically different procedure, Schoenberg uses one hexachord to fulfill two pre-established patterns: he follows the initial row form with its retrograde and at the same time combines the original form in one part (bass) with its inversion (tenor). Following the completion of this canon in tenor and bass, the alto and soprano join them to complete the restatement of lines 7–13.

All of the orchestral parts are written *colla parte* with the voices throughout this passage, with the single exception of the flute. Its solo line in this passage employs the same hexachords being sung in the alto vocal line, though Schoenberg creates a completely different melody from them. This extensive solo, as well as a later violin solo, represents something of the solitude in the text, the single voice searching and striving for a unity with God that eludes its grasp. In a sense, the solo instrument is a part of the musical landscape because it follows the hexachordal patterns of other voices, and yet it is not integrated to the same degree as all the other instruments. The flute solo accompanies the lines from the text that describe God and his characteristics (lines 7–13). These lines recall the passage quoted earlier from op. 27, no. 2: "Thou shalt make for thyself no image!/ For an image creates limitations,/Places bounds on what should be limitless and inconceivable." One cannot help but wonder whether, in Schoenberg's view, he might not have been violating his own prohibition by an attempt to create in musical terms a work of art that comprehended knowledge of and union with God. This conflict may well hold the key to the question of why this work was never finished: Schoenberg may simply have been unable to reconcile himself to the realization of such spiritual aspirations in his art, since the very act of completion would place limits and boundaries on something that is limitless and give expression to that which is inexpressible.

One of the two orchestral interludes in the piece follows the end of this canon between soprano and alto, just before the turning point in the text in which the poet first says "Und trotzdem bete ich. . . ." [And yet I pray]. Marked "pesante," [weighty] this interlude contains an aggressive build-up to a brief but emphatic trombone solo, leading to the return of an Adagio marking as the Speaker resumes at line 14. The accompaniment throughout this section is much more fragmentary in its construction than any passage heard thus far. Though Schoenberg continues to use identifiable hexachords in most parts, the sense of a continuous line decreases considerably and gives way to shorter bursts of sound. All of this occurs as the Speaker states the reasons why he still prays, possibly the most critical part of the text to Schoenberg, wishing to disclose his own desire for unity and a sense of oneness with God.

The second orchestral interlude interrupts the Speaker just before he reaches the line of text that recalls the beginning: "O, du mein Gott" (line 20), a line of affirmation that never appears in the composition. Instead, through this interlude Schoenberg builds to another climactic unison in the orchestra, leading to a fermata and providing a sense of closure before the re-entry of the chorus. Instead of moving ahead into the next section of text (lines 20–23), the chorus returns to line 14 and begins to sing text that we have already heard spoken. This procedure mirrors earlier passages, such as that involving lines 7–10, in which spoken text is followed by a repetition that is sung. From this point to the end of the piece, however, a transformation of compositional procedure begins to unfold. In the last measures that Schoenberg composed, there is a noticeable thinning of texture, particularly in the orchestral writing. While this thinning is due partly to Schoenberg's desire for a different sound, which he also approaches in the vocal lines, the last several measures remain blank in some orchestral parts, suggesting that they had not been completed. In other words, Schoenberg may not have intended to leave those measures permanently empty, as he did not write in the rests that we would normally expect to find if those instruments were meant to remain silent. Both m. 83 of the violoncello/contrabass line and m. 86 of the tenor have smaller pieces of paper glued over them to cover whatever he had written, and the whole page is extended by the addition of a leaf over m. 86. All of this makes for a somewhat confusing puzzle, but it provides evidence to suggest that the composition through m. 86 was by no means completed. The change that occurs in the choral parts at this point consists of using hexachordal sets rather than straightforward hexachords in the last five bars and using them in a particular sequence. Most surprising of all, the chorus returns to line 14, "Und trotzdem bete ich. . . ," in the first and only repeat after an interlude of a textual passage that has already been sung. In short, Schoenberg seems to have been without a clear sense of how to move forward. Rather than moving ahead to the final summing up of his text and asserting the bliss of union with God, the music ceases in an attitude of unfulfilled prayer, bringing the ending of "Modern Psalm" into congruence with the endings of *Die Jakobsleiter* and *Moses und Aron*. In a final bit of irony, the soprano line in the final measure outlines a clear dominant-tonic cadence in C-minor, hardly what we might expect as a last musical gesture from the composer who had emancipated the dissonance and ended the reign of the tonal harmonic system as the organizing principle of Western musical art.

What, then, are we to conclude from this last passage? In contrast to the earlier sections, we find a completely different, obviously systematic method of setting the text through the use of hexachordal sets in conjunction with a series of text repetitions unlike anything that has come before. The first iteration of line 14 falls where it should, following the pattern of the rest of the piece. In the last five measures, however, we find this line repeated four more times, placing a tremendously heavy emphasis on the words "And yet I pray. . . ." The last page of the autograph manuscript shows clearly that he made more than one attempt at a continuation, and possibly due to his weakened condition, he chose to give himself a rest from the artistic and spiritual conflicts that had troubled him for so long. Aware that his time was growing short, he may have chosen to conclude what he had begun by leaving the line that most clearly voiced his feeling as the last of all. While the structure of the final measures suggests that he was searching for a new means of expression for these crucial lines, the last measure, sung by the soprano, sounds like the deliberate rounding off of a work that Schoenberg knew he would not live long enough to complete in the way he had begun. It seems an unlikely coincidence that the last measure outlines a cadence in a key already heard in mm. 16–18. We are left, then, with a distinction between the final thirteen bars as a whole and the last measure considered in isolation: in the former, Schoenberg is searching for the solution to an open-ended line of text, while in the latter, his tonal closing gesture may represent a conscious choice to cease his activities and leave as his final words in music the thought which had held him for so long: "Und trotzdem bete ich."

NOTES

This essay began as a paper for a seminar on "Schoenberg in America" led by Reinhold Brinkmann at Harvard University. I am greatly indebted to Professor Brinkmann for his guidance and criticism, both on this project and on others undertaken during my graduate career.

1. Hans Keller, "The New in Review: Schoenberg—II: The Last Work," *Music Review* 18 (1957): 221, 224.

2. Arnold Schönberg, *Moderne Psalmen von Arnold Schönberg*, ed. Rudolf Kolisch (Mainz: B. Schott's Söhne, 1957). The facsimile shows that Schoenberg wrote the dates of completion for most of the first fifteen texts at the end of each; he dated the last at the top of the page.

3. Schönberg, *Moderne Psalmen*.

4. Arnold Schönberg, *Briefe*, ed. Erwin Stein (Mainz: B. Schott's Söhne, 1958), 296.

5. The best overview and analysis of the texts are provided in Karl H. Wörner, "'Und trotzdem bete ich': Arnold Schönbergs letztes Werk: *Moderne Psalmen*," *Neue Zeitschrift für Musik* 118 (1957): 147–51. Keller raises ques-

tions about whether some of them (no. 9 in particular) could ever have made sense as pieces of choral music. See Keller, "New in Review," 222.

6. Arnold Schönberg, *Chorwerke II*, Series A, vol. 19 of *Sämtliche Werke*, ed. Josef Rufer and Christian Martin Schmidt (Mainz: B. Schott's Söhne, 1975), 137–38 and 141–48.

7. Schönberg, *Moderne Psalmen*, 10r.

8. Keller, "New in Review," 223.

9. Ps. 130:1, Ps. 130:7 RSV.

10. Schönberg, *Der Erste Psalm*, 9v. Used by permission of Belmont Music Publishers, Pacific Palisades, California 90272.

11. Translation mine.

12. Schönberg, *Chorwerke II*, 151–72.

13. Schönberg, *Briefe*, 30–1. Translated in Dika Newlin, "Self-Revelation and the Law: Arnold Schoenberg and His Religious Works," *Yuval* 1 (1968): 205–6.

14. Transcription in Jean Marie Christensen, "Arnold Schoenberg's Oratorio *Die Jakobsleiter*" (Ph.D. diss., University of California, Los Angeles, 1979), II, 29–30. Used by permission of Belmont Music Publishers, Pacific Palisades California 90272.

15. Translated in Newlin, "Self-Revelation and the Law," 209. The last sentence is a paraphrase of Matt. 7:7.

16. Arnold Schönberg, *Chorwerke I*, Series A, vol. 19 of *Sämtliche Werke*, ed. Tadeusz Okuljar (Mainz: B. Schott's Söhne, 1980), 42–3. Used by permission of Belmont Music Publishers, Pacific Palisades, California 90272.

17. Translation mine.

18. David Schiff, "Jewish and Musical Tradition in the Music of Mahler and Schoenberg," *Journal of the Arnold Schoenberg Institute* 9/2 (1986): 229–30.

19. Facsimile reprinted in Arnold Schönberg, *Chorwerke II: Kritischer Bericht*, Series B, vol. 19 of *Sämtliche Werke*, ed. Christian Martin Schmidt (Mainz: B. Schott's Söhne, 1977), viii. My transcription does not include words that Schoenberg crossed out. Used by permission of Belmont Music Publishers, Pacific Palisades, California 90272.

20. From a 1932 letter to Rudolf Kolisch: "I cannot warn often enough against the over-valuation of these analyses, since they lead only to what I have always fought against—the recognition of how the piece is *made*; whereas I have always helped my students to recognize—what it *is!*" See Schönberg, *Briefe*, 179. Translated in Newlin, "Self-Revelation and the Law," 205.

21. Alexander Ringer, *Arnold Schoenberg: The Composer as Jew* (Oxford: Oxford University Press, 1990), 187.

Contributors

Naomi André is an Assistant Professor of Musicology at the University of Michigan. Her main scholarly interest is issues of character and gender in the operas of Verdi. She has published in the *New Grove Dictionary of Women Composers* and the *International Dictionary of Black Composers*.

William E. Benjamin is a music theorist and Professor of Music at the University of British Columbia. Among his publications are studies of works by Debussy, Stravinsky, and Bruckner, critiques of present-day analytical method, and contributions to the theories of harmony and meter. A major study of the music of Canadian composer Istvan Anhalt is in press. Dr. Benjamin lectures regularly at Canadian and American universities, and has served on boards and committees of numerous journals, professional societies, and community organizations.

Russell A. Berman is the Walter A. Haas Professor in the Humanities at Stanford University, where he teaches in the departments of German Studies and Comparative Literature. He has published widely on German literature and thought, including his most recent book, *Enlightenment or Empire: Colonial Discourse in German Culture* (1998).

Camille Crittenden completed her Ph.D. at Duke University, where she is currently Visiting Assistant Professor of Music (1998–99). She worked as Research Associate and Assistant Archivist at the Arnold Schoenberg Institute in Los Angeles from 1995 to 1998. She has also completed research on the operettas of Johann Strauss, and her book *Strauss's Vienna: Operetta and the Politics of Popular Culture* is forthcoming from Cambridge University Press.

Charlotte M. Cross received her Ph.D. in historical musicology from Columbia University, where she held a Whiting Fellowship in the Humanities. Her articles on Schoenberg's philosophy, aesthetics, and theories have appeared in *Current Musicology, Theoria, Musikleben: Studien zur Musikgeschichte Österreich*, and *The Reader's Guide to Music History, Theory, and Criticism*. Her translation (with Severine Neff) of Schoenberg's treatise *Zusammenhang, Kontrapunkt, Instrumentation, Formenlehre* was published in 1994 by the University of Nebraska Press. Dr. Cross has taught in the music departments of Columbia University, Barnard College, and Mercy College.

Stephen Davison is currently completing a dissertation on Schoenberg's *Von heute auf morgen* at the City University of New York. A native of Australia, he has taught at Baruch College, CUNY, and at the University of Southern California. He was Research Associate at the Arnold Schoenberg Institute during its final two years, where he contributed to the correspondence inventory (*Journal of the Arnold Schoenberg Institute* XVIII/XIX, 1995–96) and other research projects. He is currently Music Librarian for Special Collections and Systems at the University of California, Los Angeles, and serves as the curator of the Ernst Toch and Eric Zeisl archives. He is the author of "The Music of Karl Weigl (1881–1949): A Catalog."

Robert Falck studied musicology at Brandeis University and in Göttingen as a Fulbright fellow. His research interests have been the music of the twelfth, thirteenth, and twentieth centuries. He is the author of *The Notre Dame Conductus: A Study of the Repertory*, and co-editor of *Cross Cultural Perspectives on Music*, as well as articles on Berg and Schoenberg. Published in *The New Grove*, the *Handwörterbuch der musikalischen Terminologie*, and the *Dictionary of the Middle Ages*, he is also Senior Editor for "Music to 1500" in *A Guide to Music in Collected Editions, Historical Sets and Monuments*. He is currently professor of musicology at the University of Toronto, where he has served as Associate Dean and as Acting Dean of the Faculty of Music.

Bluma Goldstein is Professor of German at the University of California, Berkeley; Chair of the Jewish Studies Committee; and Co-Chair of the Joint Doctoral Program in Jewish Studies of the University of California, Berkeley and the Graduate Theological Union. Her work centers largely on German/Austrian literature and philosophy from the late-eighteenth through the mid-twentieth century. She has published articles on Brecht, Kafka, and Heine. Her book *Reinscribing Moses: Heine, Kafka, Freud, and Schoenberg in a European Wilderness* was published in 1992 by Harvard University Press. Currently, she is completing a book entitled *Doubly Exiled in the Diaspora: "Agunahs"/ Deserted Wives. Cultural, Socio-Historical Studies.*

Edward D. Latham is currently a Ph.D. candidate in music theory at Yale University. His dissertation focuses on twentieth-century operatic works by Gershwin, Britten, Debussy, and Schoenberg. Mr. Latham teaches theory and composition at the Educational Center for the Arts in New Haven, Connecticut. His work has been published in *Music Theory Online* and is forthcoming in the *Indiana Theory Review*. He also has an article forthcoming in *Schoenberg and Words: The Modernist Years*, edited by Charlotte M. Cross and Russell A. Berman.

David Isadore Lieberman completed the Master of Arts degree at Indiana University in 1996. He is now pursuing his doctorate in the Department of Musicology at Brandeis University.

Mark P. Risinger is a Lecturer on Music at Harvard University, where he completed his Ph.D. with a dissertation on compositional process in the works of Handel. His primary interests are music and literature of the eighteenth century, though he has taught courses and written articles on German lieder of the nineteenth century as well. His forthcoming publications include a revision of his dissertation, an article on Handel's instrumental music, and an article on the lieder of Robert Schumann.

David Schroeder has written books on Haydn and Mozart and is now writing a new book on cinema and opera. His articles on the influence of literature on Berg have appeared in both music and literary journals, and he has also written articles on Webern and Schubert. He holds a Ph.D. from Cambridge University and is professor of music at Dalhousie University in Halifax, Canada.

Jennifer Shaw received an M.A. in musicology from the State University of New York at Stony Brook and honors degrees in music and law from the University of Sydney. Active in both fields, she has lectured on music in the United States and in Australia and has published articles on the music of Schoenberg, early productions of Richard Wagner's operas, and Australian sociolegal policy. Ms. Shaw currently teaches law at the Flinders University of South Australia, and, through the State University of New York at Stony Brook, is writing her Ph.D. dissertation on Schoenberg's choral symphony and his oratorio *Die Jakobsleiter*. She is a member of the Executive Committee of the Musicological Society of Australia (South Australian Chapter).

BORDER CROSSINGS
DANIEL ALBRIGHT, *Series Editor*